STREETWISE®

ACHIEVING
WEALTH THROUGH
FRANCHISING

JOHN'S FRANCHISE

STREETWISE®

ACHIEVING WEALTH THROUGH FRANCHISING

A Comprehensive
Manual to Finding,
Starting, and
Succeeding in a
Franchise Business

by Robert T. Justis & William Slater Vincent

Adams Media Corporation
Holbrook, Massachusetts

A Streetwise® Publication.
Streetwise® is a registered trademark of Adams Media Corporation.

Published by Adams Media Corporation
260 Center Street, Holbrook, MA 02343
www.adamsmedia.com

ISBN: 1-58062-503-7

Printed in the United States of America.

J I H G F E D C B A

Library of Congress Cataloging-in-Publication Data
Justis, Robert T.
Streetwise achieving wealth through franchising / by Bob Justis and William Slater Vincent.
p.   cm.
ISBN 1-58062-503-7
1. Franchises (Retail trade)–United States. 2. Franchises (Retail trade)–Law and Legislation–United States.
I. Vincent, William Slater II. Title.
HF5429.235.U5 J877   2001
658.8'708–dc21   00-053604

This publication is designed to provide accurate and authoritative information with regard to the subject matter covered. It is sold with the understanding that the publisher is not engaged in rendering legal, accounting, or other professional advice. If legal advice or other expert assistance is required, the services of a competent professional person should be sought.
—From a *Declaration of Principles* jointly adopted by a Committee of the American Bar Association and a Committee of Publishers and Associations

Many of the designations used by manufacturers and sellers to distinguish their products are claimed as trademarks. Where those designations appear in this book and Adams Media was aware of a trademark claim, the designations have been printed in initial capital letters.

This book, the authors, and the publisher do not recommend or endorse any particular franchise. We strongly recommend that you hire an experienced franchise attorney and perform your own independent investigation of any franchise before signing any agreement.

Cover illustration by Eric Mueller.

This book is available at quantity discounts for bulk purchases.
For information, call 1-800-872-5627.

Visit our exciting small business Web site: www.businesstown.com

CONTENTS

Acknowledgments viii

SECTION ONE: BECOMING A PLAYER: RULES, REGULATIONS, AND CONTRACTS

CHAPTER 1:
Almost Anyone Can Be a Franchisee 3

CHAPTER 2:
The Rules of the Game 17

CHAPTER 3:
The Uniform Franchise Offering Circular
(UFOC) 31

CHAPTER 4:
The UFOC–The Rest of the Story 45

CHAPTER 5:
Fear Not—The Contract Is Here 61

CHAPTER 6:
You Can Negotiate
the Rules of the Game! 77

SECTION TWO: COSTS, PROFITS, OBLIGATIONS, AND LOCATION

CHAPTER 7:
The Fees
(Franchise Fee, Royalties, Advertising) 87

CHAPTER 8:
Earning Claims:
How Much Money Can I Make? 97

CHAPTER 9:
Products and Services 109

CHAPTER 10:
Obligations 119

CHAPTER 11:
Location and Site Selection 131

SECTION THREE: TRAINING CAMP AND PREPARATION

CHAPTER 12:
Training Camp 151

CHAPTER 13:
Preparing for the Grand Opening 159

SECTION FOUR: MARKETING AND ADVERTISING THE FRANCHISE

CHAPTER 14:
Marketing the Business 169

CHAPTER 15:
Playing the Selling Game 177

CHAPTER 16:
Advertising and Public Relations 185

SECTION FIVE: MANAGING FOR SUCCESS

CHAPTER 17:
Managing the Business 197

CHAPTER 18:
Motivation and Leadership 205

CHAPTER 19:
Recruitment 213

CHAPTER 20:
Hiring and Selection 223

CHAPTER 21:
Orientation and Personnel Policies 239

CHAPTER 22:
Performance Evaluations 249

CHAPTER 23:
Discipline and Termination 255

CHAPTER 24:
Special Employment Issues 267

SECTION SIX: INFORMATION, MONEY, AND ACCOUNTING RECORDS

CHAPTER 25
Money 275

CHAPTER 26:
Account, Record Keeping, and
Financial Statements 289

CHAPTER 27:
Red Flags: Purchasing, Inventory Levels,
Labor Costs, Credit, Taxes 297

SECTION SEVEN: WORKING WITH THE FRANCHISOR—BLESSING OR CURSE?

CHAPTER 28:
The Franchisor/Franchisee Relationship . . 307

CHAPTER 29:
Renewal, Termination, or Transfer 325

CHAPTER 30:
Resolving Disputes 343

Contents

Section Eight: Multiunit Franchising, Growing (or Closing)

CHAPTER 31:
Opening the New Store
(Multiunit Franchising) 359

CHAPTER 32:
Building a Franchisee Empire 367

CHAPTER 33:
The Final Decision:
Sell or Go Out of Business? 377

APPENDIX A:
Investigating Franchising Opportunities . . 389

APPENDIX B:
Top 50 Web Sites for
Franchising Information 393

APPENDIX C:
Top 200 Franchises 396

Glossary 399
Index 402
About the Author 406

Acknowledgments of Robert T. Justis

I would like to thank all of the franchisors and franchisees who have contributed to the book, including Steve Hammerstein, Kwik Kapp; Burt Cohen, McDonald's; Tom Murphy, Continental Franchise Review; Charlie Valluzzo, McDonald's; Mark George, Wendy's; and Kim Herzer, International House of Pancakes.

Special thanks are also given to those who assisted in writing and developing the chapters including: Ye-Sho Chen, Tony Martinez, Lori Marjerison, Brian Osborne, Susan Sartwell, Miles Farr, Erin Hebert, Erin Meradith, and Aparra Mathur.

Finally—I would like to thank Sue Justis, Jill Justis, and Jen Justis for all their encouragement and support.

Acknowledgments of William Slater Vincent

There are several people I would like to acknowledge for their hard work and assistance. First, I would like to thank my students from my Franchise Law Class at Kennesaw State University who helped me with the research. They are Linn 'Sas Frailing, Jill Bowen, Guy Jackson, Amber Bostler, Laura DeRiemer, Keely Boyer, Seana Benoit, Katherine Watkins, Toya Seay, Steven Cady, Ryan Robinson, Beth Wells, Gerald Foster, and Mark Richardson.

I would like to particularly thank the following people for the valuable insights they provided me with. They are Nathan Talbot, Val Kilmer, Brenda Pauley, Robert Rechsteiner, Darryl Cohen, Don DeBolt, Bruce Bloom, Raymond Margiano, Michael Leven, Leone Ackerly, Frank Belatti, Gregg Kaplan, Dick Holbrook, Tim Mescon, dean of the Coles College of Business at Kennesaw State University, the Honorable Joe Frank Harris, retired Governor of the state of Georgia, and the Honorable Newt Gingrich, former Speaker of the U.S. House of Representatives.

Finally, I would like to thank the following people for their assistance in writing the book. They are Debbie Massey, Janet Payne, Natalie Jill Vincent, Amanda Slater Vincent, William "Billy" Slater Vincent Jr., and Sandra Morgan Vincent.

Becoming a Player: Rules, Regulations, and Contracts

In this section, you'll learn:

- **Types of franchises available**

- **Why franchising can be so successful**

- **Rules you need to know**

- **Rules your franchisor must follow**

- **Everything you need to know about the Uniform Franchise Offering Circular—the most important document in franchising**

- **How to read, understand, and negotiate a contract that is satisfactory to you and your franchisor**

CHAPTER 1 ALMOST ANYONE CAN BE A FRANCHISEE **CHAPTER 2** THE RULES OF THE GAME
CHAPTER 3 THE UNIFORM FRANCHISE OFFERING CIRCULAR (UFOC) **CHAPTER 4** THE UFOC—THE REST OF THE STORY
CHAPTER 5 FEAR NOT—THE CONTRACT IS HERE **CHAPTER 6** YOU CAN NEGOTIATE THE RULES OF THE GAME!

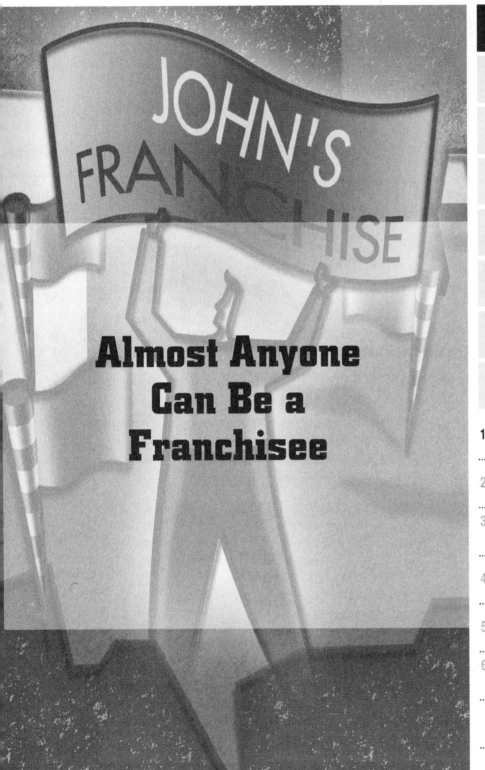

Almost Anyone Can Be a Franchisee

1: ALMOST ANYONE CAN BE A FRANCHISEE

2: THE RULES OF THE GAME

3: THE UNIFORM FRANCHISE
OFFERING CIRCULAR (UFOC)

4: THE UFOC—THE REST OF THE STORY

5: FEAR NOT—THE CONTRACT IS HERE

6: YOU CAN NEGOTIATE THE RULES
OF THE GAME!

There are approximately five minutes remaining in the Superbowl XXXIII first half and the Denver Broncos are leading 10–3. John Elway takes the snap from center, moves back to his right, fakes a handoff to Terrell Davis, continues back to the 11-yard line, sees his right side wideout, Rod Smith, running down the middle of the field. Elway arches a 50-yard pass that Rod Smith takes in on the 40-yard line and races to the end zone to score what many believe is the major play in Superbowl XXXIII when the Denver Broncos beat the Atlanta Falcons for the world championship. John Elway is a franchisee.

Almost anyone can start a business, but franchising is more fun. Franchising is the greatest game played. Franchising provides an individual the opportunity to use a tried and successful business system at his or her own chosen location. Franchising is simply the right granted (by the franchisor) to someone (the franchisee) to sell a company's goods or services in a specific area.

Franchising is a huge and rapidly growing method of doing business both in the United States and throughout the world. In the United States alone, franchising accounts for more than $1 trillion in sales annually and employs more than 8 million people, or 1 in every 7 adults. These numbers continue to grow rapidly. A new franchised outlet is opened every 8 minutes of each business day, totaling more than 180 franchised outlets a day. This tremendous growth, coupled with its businesses' complexity, makes it extremely difficult for an independent businessperson to compete and succeed. Franchising provides an opportunity for success. It provides the opportunity for you to be in business for yourself but not *by* yourself.

> Franchising provides an opportunity for success. It provides the opportunity for you to be in business for yourself but not *by* yourself.

Why Franchising?

The reason for franchising is simple. Today most independent business people have their hands full just relating to the numerous challenges they face on a daily basis. There is little time for the entrepreneur to develop strategies and to analyze the business situations they confront. Markets continue to change. The demands and needs of the consumers are constant. There is a tremendous need for help.

Franchisees, on the other hand, have the staff and support of a multifaceted organization behind them. They have the ability to draw upon the franchisor, their training and systems, and many other franchisees whom they can call upon and collaborate with. Most franchisors have dedicated personnel focused specifically on addressing not only the future trends of their business but also research and development relating to equipment, products, services, training, and marketing strategies.

What Types of Franchises Are Available?

Generally, individual and multiunit franchise opportunities are available in many retail and service businesses. The initial sale of a franchise is often a single store. However, several franchise organizations provide the opportunity for purchasing small areas (area development agreements) and multiunit programs.

Franchisee Satisfaction

Franchise Times 1999 Survey indicates that 90% of their respondents recommend franchise ownership. In addition, a full 87% are satisfied with their franchising experience with 46% being very satisfied, while 41% are somewhat satisfied. A mere 4% expressed that they were "not at all satisfied."

Franchising Level of Satisfaction

The vast majority of franchisees would recommend the industry to others.		Most franchisees are glad to be where they are.	
Years as Franchisee Mean = 10.3 years		Very Satisfied	45.7%
Own 1–10 locations	97%	Somewhat Satisfied	41.3%
Satisfied with Franchising	87%	Not Too Satisfied	8.65%
Recommend Franchising	89.9%	Not At All Satisfied	4.35%

Franchise Times, September 1999, page 20.

After an initial store has been opened and proven to be successful, then the franchisee may be allowed to expand and build a second or third store. The development of a second or third store often requires the franchisee to rank in the top half of stores in that region or system.

An area development agreement provides a time period as well as a requisite number of stores that must be built within a designated area. For example, no one will generally offer an area development agreement for the entire state of Texas. However, they will provide one for the city of Houston or Dallas. It is often the case that a premium payment is required for obtaining an area development agreement. This ensures the franchisee of a five-year time period wherein no other franchisees will be granted the right to build in their territory. The cost often is around $5,000 to $10,000 per store, depending upon the size of the system.

What Can I Expect when I Franchise?

There are at least 20 important items that a franchisee will be able to obtain when starting and developing their franchise business. These include the following:

1. A business
2. A product or products
3. Services
4. Methods of doing business
5. Accounting and finance systems
6. Forecasting methods
7. Strategic planning
8. Analyzing market trends
9. Marketing, advertising, and promotion
10. Sales techniques
11. Product research and development
12. Quality control methods
13. Training
14. Customer relations

Auntie Anne's Hand-Rolled Soft Pretzels

In 1988 Auntie Anne opened her first hand-rolled soft pretzels stand in the Amish farmers' market of Downingtown, Pennsylvania. Today they have over 500 locations worldwide. At Auntie Anne's they believe the pretzel can be that good. To become a franchisee they request that you meet the following requirements:

1. The initial investment to open an Auntie Anne's store is $156,000–$252,000.
2. They require that interested candidates have a minimum net worth of $300,000.
3. Franchisees must live within 60 miles or one hour's drive of their first store location.

15. Pricing strategies
16. Real estate criteria
17. Hiring and firing
18. Construction and design
19. Equipment specifications
20. Legal aspects of business

A Business

A franchise is really a business. A franchise may be a fast-food restaurant, it may be an accounting service, it may be a domestic cleaning business. The franchise provides the opportunity for the franchisee to take a successful business practice and develop it in a new location. Today McDonald's has over 24,500 different store locations. They train their people successfully in all phases of the operation.

A franchise contract is a legal document between the franchisor (parent company) and the franchisee (you) where the franchisor agrees to allow the franchisee to utilize the name, logo, products, services, and the methodologies of the franchisor's business. In return, the franchisee agrees to pay the franchisor certain fees, generally including an initial franchise fee, royalty fees, and advertising fees, while adhering to the operations and methodologies described by the franchisor for operating the business. Simply stated, the franchisee is going to be trained by the franchisor to run what will probably be a very successful business.

A Product/Products

Most businesses provide some type of a product to the consumer whether this be a hamburger, tax form, or a transmission. The product should be of high quality, in demand by the consumer, and readily available for the franchisee to sell.

An advantage in most franchising systems is that they have the ability and history to develop high quality and useful products. Ray Kroc found a hamburger stand that the McDonald brothers were using in California and developed this into the largest franchising business in the world today. Their franchisees have been able to

Mutual Benefits

Franchisors have learned that their success is dependent upon the success of the franchisee. They want the franchisee to be successful.

develop several new products, including the Big Mac and their breakfast sandwiches.

Services

One of the main reasons why people go into a business in the first place is because of the advertising, but the reason they come back is because of the high-quality service and products that they receive. Franchising systems have generally been able to refine and develop their services so that they provide the best possible service for the customer. Service is their number one concern.

Many people now traveling the interstates stop in at a fast food restaurant, not primarily for the food, but for the extremely clean restrooms. Fast-food restaurants have discovered that these travelers, while they stop for a clean restroom, will also purchase a product, such as a soft drink, french fries, ice cream, or sandwiches.

Methods of Doing Business

The franchisor knows they are only as strong as their franchisees. They also realize that the franchisee will help develop the brand image and the brand name of their company. Because of this, they are very serious about developing the very best possible operating systems for their franchisees.

The franchisor will want the franchisee to understand all the various aspects of franchising including how to open, operate, and close the business on a daily basis. In addition, the franchisor will train the franchisee in all aspects of the operation and help them with location analysis, the store design, the construction, securing the lease, training, and providing extensive, ongoing support. The franchisor will provide the support and training concerning all marketing, advertising, promotion, forecasting, accounting, record keeping, equipment handling, and customer relations. The franchisor wants the franchisee to succeed.

Franchisees will be kept informed of the latest developments in the company through newsletters, Internet and Intranet programs, video updates, and national and area-wide meetings.

Accounting and Finance Systems

Because of the rapid growth and widespread use of the computer, most franchisors provide accounting and software packages for their franchisees to help them with their accounting and record keeping systems. The franchisor often provides point of sale (POS) systems, which allow the franchisee to keep track of items being sold, inventory, and revenues being received.

It is common for a franchisor to obtain information on a daily or weekly basis concerning the sales, cost of goods sold, and labor costs that a franchisee incurs. The costs of goods sold and labor costs are often controllable expenses that the franchisee needs to keep track of and stay within the guidelines of the franchising system. An accurate record keeping system will allow the franchisee to watch over the revenues and expenses occurring on a daily and weekly basis.

Pizza Store Finances

For many pizza stores, the cost of goods sold is approximately 30–32%. The combined cost of goods sold and labor costs for most hamburger fast-food restaurants is between 53–57%. It is often common that these restaurants will also have paper costs of up to 3 or 4%.

Forecasting Methods

One of the great strengths of any business is the ability to forecast sales revenues and inventory requirements. A good franchising system will be able to place the franchisee in the proper ballpark relative to the sales and expenses that they should incur in their operations. Most printing businesses, such as Kwik Kopy, have extensive forecasting techniques which allow their franchisees to properly price and bill their customers for their costs of doing business.

The Merry Maids, Molly Maids, or The Maids domestic cleaning systems provide very accurate forecasting techniques for the costs of cleaning different sized homes and residences.

Strategic Planning

A great advantage that a franchise system provides is the opportunity to develop a good business plan and to lay out a strategic program for the coming two or three years. The franchisor can provide a tremendous amount of information that the franchisee can use to develop the plan including information about marketing, advertising, location, pricing, promotion, management, organization, accounting, finance, and even handling the legal matters of the business. The strategic plan allows the franchisee to develop a vision for the future.

Analyzing Market Trends

One of the great advantages of franchising is having somebody to help the franchisee understand the markets and the movements of the markets in the future. Franchisors spend considerable time and energy in understanding the demands of the market and customer needs. Many organizations will change their operations to include the advancing market demands.

Mail Boxes Etc., which was originally based on providing a mailbox location for businesses, has now expanded into providing a complete series of small business services including packaging, mailing, faxing, printing, copying, and computer services.

Marketing, Advertising, and Promotion

A tremendous expense of any business is the establishment of good advertising copy. The franchisee has the advantage of using the advertising slicks and prepared advertisements of the franchisor. The franchisor can provide a wide variety of gifts and knick-knacks for the consumer markets.

It is amazing to watch the Christmas gifts, dolls, and toys that many franchise systems provide their customers through their franchisees during the Christmas season. It is also interesting to note that McDonald's has a major contract with Walt Disney for providing the distribution and sale of toys, dolls, and images related to new major movies.

Sales Techniques

Periodically, franchisors provide sales programs for their franchisees. These allow the franchisees to offer special sales to their customers. These are generally focused around special holidays or special events during the calendar year. In addition, some programs may provide a two-for-one sale or a reduced price on a specific product or service.

McDonald's

McDonald's is regarded as the largest and best-known global food service retailer with more than 28,000 restaurants in 120 countries. However, on any day, even as the market leader, McDonald's serves less than one percent of the world's population. Approximately 80% of McDonald's restaurant businesses worldwide are owned and operated by franchisees. Their efforts to increase market share, profitability, and customer satisfaction have produced high return to shareholders-a compound annual total return of 21% during the decade of the nineties.

Product Research and Development

It is difficult for a franchisee to develop his or her own research and development program. The franchisor will spend a considerable amount of time and money in performing research for its franchisees and customers. The franchisor wants to provide the franchisee with the latest knowledge and information concerning all products and services available. Because of the rapid growth of technology and information, it is important that a businessperson be aware of emerging markets. This can generally be done only through appropriate research and development programs.

Quality Control Methods

Although difficult at times for the franchisee to follow, the quality control methods installed by the franchisor is one of the main advantages to purchasing a franchise. People want consistency and quality. Franchisors demand adherence to the quality standards established in their operations manual and by their franchise agreement.

Why does the Subway sandwich taste the same in New York, Louisiana, and Oregon? Why do the homes cleaned by Merry Maids employees meet the same high-quality standards whether done in Seattle, Atlanta, or Boston? The answer is found in the quality control systems established by the franchisor and followed by the franchisee.

Training

Most franchising systems today divide their training into three different categories.

1. *Initial headquarters training.* At this time the franchisee will be taught all the basic operating systems and procedures of the business. This often lasts from three days to three weeks at the organization's headquarters.
2. *In-store training.* The initial headquarters training is often followed by an in-store training experience at another successful franchisee operation. This allows the new franchisee to meet an existing successful franchisee and gain experience at their

Mail Boxes Etc. (MBE)

Mail Boxes Etc. is the world's largest franchisor of independently owned and operated postal service centers. There are more than 3,700 MBE Centers worldwide in 61 countries. They generate more than 58 million customer transactions per year. The MBE network generates more than 300,000 mailbox holders in the United States. Their services include: 24-hour mailbox service with street address, USPS products and services, packing, domestic and international shipping, self-service/full-service copies (black and white/color), global fax transmittal and receipt, document and presentation preparation services, binding and laminating services, office supplies, business cards, passport photos, and notary services. Services may vary by location.

store. This also helps franchisees bond to each other and helps them work together later on during their careers.

3. *Ongoing training.* The third phase of training is the ongoing training that the franchisee will receive from the grand opening throughout the remainder of their career. In some cases it may be necessary for a franchisor to provide two or three weeks of support training for the franchisee as they open their initial store. In addition the annual franchisee conference is generally devoted to training franchisees in new developments, products, and services available to the franchise system.

Customer Relations

There may be nothing more important than for a franchisee to learn how to develop proper and good customer relationships. One of the major reasons for the increase of sales in a store is the strong acknowledgment by a business staff of the importance of their customers. Customers are the life-blood of any business. The relationship that exists between a staff member and the customer will either solidify that relationship or cause it to break down. Many stores continue to grow because of unique staff members and their ability to work with and have a positive influence on customers.

Pricing Strategies

Franchising is unique in that a franchisor may suggest pricing strategies to the franchisee, but the franchisee gets to make the final price determination. A franchisor may help a franchisee by suggesting different pricing structures and even explaining the reasons for the price determination; however, the franchisee gets to choose the final price the customer will be charged. It is true that a Big Mac may have different prices within the city of Miami, or even have a different price in Orlando or St. Petersburg, Florida.

Real Estate Criteria

Franchisors generally provide suggestions to the franchisee about choosing the proper location. Most franchisors request the franchisee to choose their favorite two or three locations and then the franchisor makes a recommendation. The franchisor then approves the final site selection. This review by the franchisor will help the franchisee to make sure they have covered all the different factors in choosing the proper location. The demographic population, the age of the consumers, the accessibility to the store, and the related costs of the location all need to be examined. The three most important decisions a business owner makes are (1) location, (2) location, and (3) location. The franchisor will generally provide a checklist detailing the various components of the proper retail site. Papa John's Pizza restaurant, for example, has required a six-plus page analysis for each location.

Hiring and Firing

Another advantage that a franchise system provides to a franchisee is the proper information about hiring and firing their staff members. One of the great advantages of any franchising system is to learn from different franchisees their success stories in hiring their best employees. It is also important to be aware of the legal requirements that limit the questions that are asked in a hiring situation. These are often taught by the franchisor to the new franchisee and provide greater knowledge and ability for the franchisee in choosing the correct employees.

Construction and Design

Franchisors also provide the proper layout, design, and architectural drawings for laying out the store or business. Simple franchising service groups surprisingly also provide good information about laying out desks, cabinets, and spaces required to set up the proper store or unit. Many businesspeople will save $10,000 to 20,000 by utilizing a franchisor's architectural designs rather than having to create and develop their own.

Equipment Specifications

What equipment should you place in a fast-food restaurant? What ovens do you need to use? What equipment is needed to run a domestic cleaning business? The answers to these questions are easily provided by the franchisor. The ovens of a Ruth's Chris

Initial Investments

Volume III of *The Profile of Franchising*: A Statistical Abstract of 1998 UFOC Data (research conducted by Washington, DC-based FRAN-DATA Corp.) states that 53% of all franchise systems studied had 50 or fewer total units—both company-owned and franchisee-owned. The profile revealed that a majority of franchise companies (75%) had initial investment levels below $250,000, excluding real estate. Almost three-fourths (70%) charged an initial franchise fee of $30,000 or less. Fast-food concepts, comprising the largest segment of the overall franchise population, levied an average $20,000 initial fee.

Steakhouse, for instance, have to be able to provide a steak cooked at 1700–1800 degrees. The steak needs to be cooked on both sides at the same time to retain its best flavor and juices. This is a very important and peculiar specification of one of the finest steakhouses in the world. These kinds of specifications are developed throughout the years and are provided to the franchisees to help ensure the success and prosperity of their business.

Legal Aspects of Business

Franchisors want their franchisees to operate within the rules and laws of where they live. Franchisors spend a considerable amount of money in making sure that the franchisees understand the appropriate rules and laws. There are zoning, tax, and building codes that must be adhered to and followed. The franchisor will help the franchisee to properly understand the rules and regulations under which they need to operate.

Steps to Becoming a Franchisee

Most franchisors take similar steps in awarding franchisees a franchise. The initial steps are generally exploratory (each side finds out what the other offers), followed by qualifying (enough motivation, money, and desire). Next comes the franchise offer and contract (both agree to work with each other), finishing with the training and grand opening.

Smoothie King employs the following 12 steps for an individual to become a franchisee:

Step 1: Obtain Franchisee Information Packet. You may request a franchise information package by submitting an inquiry.

Step 2: Submit Information Forms, Financial Statements, and Resume. Complete and submit the forms in the packet to Smoothie King. The information will be reviewed by their executive staff. Upon preliminary

> Franchisors spend a considerable amount of money in making sure that the franchisees understand the appropriate rules and laws.

approval, you will be notified of their interest. This information will be kept confidential.

Step 3: Interview/Presentation. A Franchise Development Representative schedules an interview with you at their headquarters in Kenner, Louisiana. During this visit, you will get an in-depth introduction to the Smoothie King operation, receive your Uniform Franchise Offering Circular (UFOC), meet the executive staff, and have an opportunity to visit several existing franchise locations.

Step 4: UFOC Reviewed by Prospect. The UFOC contains valuable information to help you analyze Smoothie King's franchise system.

Step 5: Meet with Existing Franchisees. After careful review of the UFOC and your visit to headquarters, you may wish to interview some existing Smoothie King franchisees.

Step 6: Information Review. Smoothie King will evaluate your information forms, financial statements, credit forms, and background information. Upon a mutual decision to proceed, if necessary you are scheduled for a second interview.

Step 7: Second Interview. At this meeting, you will meet corporate franchise support staff and visit the training center in Metairie, Louisiana.

Step 8: Enter Into a Franchise Agreement. By this point, you should have enough information about Smoothie King to make a prudent decision. If you are approved, you may sign a franchise agreement.

Step 9: Orientation. As soon as possible you will attend a one-day orientation class. At this class you will be oriented on all of the steps involved in opening your store. This will include budgeting, financing, planning, site selection, ordering, construction, and much more. After orientation, the real estate department will work with you to find the perfect site.

After orientation, the real estate department will work with you to find the perfect site.

Step 10: Training. You and your management staff attend training at the training center.

Step 11: Complete Construction. Upon completion of construction, store setup and on-site training begin.

Step 12: Open For Business!

Conclusion

As a franchisee you will have a chance to run your own business without being alone. You will be supported by the franchisor that you have chosen. You will also have the advantages of local and national support in the areas of operations, management, promotion, planning, training, advertising, marketing, real estate development, construction, accounting, sales techniques, purchasing, and equipment. You can achieve personal satisfaction both as an owner/operator and as a member of your franchising family. You will experience personal growth and business knowledge from the franchisor's extensive training and support systems.

> As a franchisee you will have a chance to run your own business without being alone.

For more information on this topic, visit our Web site at www.businesstown.com

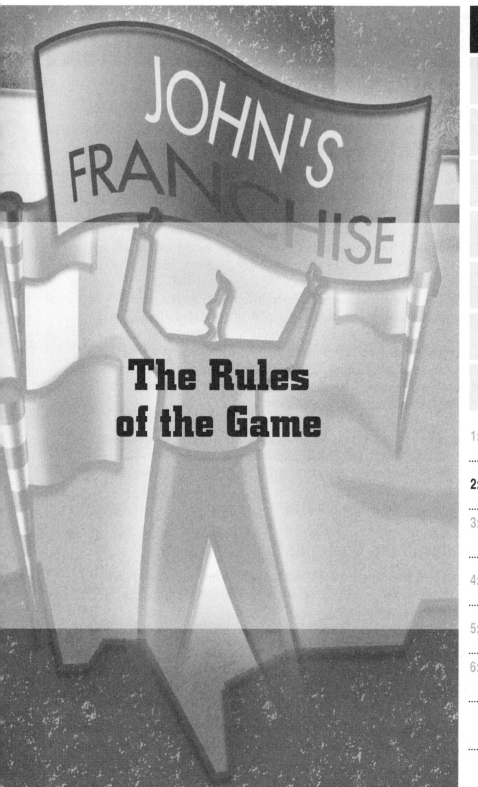

The Rules
of the Game

Chapter 2

1: ALMOST ANYONE CAN BE A FRANCHISEE

2: THE RULES OF THE GAME

3: THE UNIFORM FRANCHISE
   OFFERING CIRCULAR (UFOC)

4: THE UFOC—THE REST OF THE STORY

5: FEAR NOT—THE CONTRACT IS HERE

6: YOU CAN NEGOTIATE THE RULES
   OF THE GAME!

To win in franchising, you need to know the rules of the game. If you are looking for a franchise, give yourself a pat on the back. You are in the process of taking one of the most important steps in your life. Today there are over 3,000 franchisors doing business in the United States and the choices can be scary.

There are some basic rules of the game that you should be aware of. Most games have rules—franchising does also. For instance, did you know that it is illegal under antitrust laws for the franchisor to forcibly set the price of your products that you will sell to the end consumer? The franchisor may suggest a pricing structure, but the franchisee makes the final determination. Did you also know that most franchisors (approximately 80%) do not provide earnings claims or statements of profits to prospective franchisees? If a franchisor does provide any form of an earnings claim, then it must stipulate such claims in Section 19 of its UFOC (Uniform Franchise Offering Circular). However, there is a way to determine earnings claims of most publicly held companies even though not stipulated in the UFOC.

Franchisors play by certain rules. What are they? What are the rules of the game called franchising? Some people claim that they are as complicated as Monopoly and almost as risky while others claim that the rules are fairly simple and straightforward. Let's investigate.

> Did you know that it is illegal under antitrust laws for the franchisor to forcibly set the price of your products that you will sell to the end consumer?

Rules of the Game for the Franchisee

Let's look at the list of items that you as a franchisee should and can do to enhance your possibility of becoming the best franchisee in the business.

Research

The franchisee may do whatever research they would like to do. They need to. The franchisee can ask the franchisor almost any question they want. The problem is that the franchisor cannot always respond.

The franchisee needs to gather up as much information about the business, its management, its training, its marketing programs, and any information about what the franchisor does.

Talk to Other Franchisees

If you think you can find out everything you need to know about franchising simply by talking to the franchisor, then you have missed the boat. You need to go out and talk to other franchisees, talk to those who are very successful and those who are less successful. You should try to talk to at least 5 to 10 franchisees of the company that you wish to join. When questioning existing or previous franchisees, you should include the following questions:

1. Their average profitability?
2. Their investment start-up?
3. Their relationships with the franchisor: favorable or unfavorable?
4. Strength of operations?
5. Does the franchisor keep promises?
6. Strength of training?
7. Exclusive territory—do you have one?
8. Strength of marketing programs?
9. Strength of advertising programs?
10. Strength of staff support?

Talk to the Franchisor

It is important that you ask any and all questions that you would like of the franchisor. Included in your questions should be the following:

1. All fee payments
    A. Initial franchisee fee?
    B. Royalty fees?
    C. Advertising fees?
    D. Other fees?
2. Total investment?

Mail Boxes Etc.

Mail Boxes Etc. has been franchising since 1980 and today consists of over 3,700 stores worldwide. To insure profits for their franchisees, Mail Boxes Etc. has positioned their locations in upscale neighborhoods where many small business and home-based entrepreneurs often live. These centers will offer everything from mail services, copying, faxing to e-mail services.

At Mail Boxes Etc. they will treat you right. You will learn how you can develop public relations or advertising materials and how to properly place those materials in the media. You will learn how to write your own press releases, to develop the correct physical appearance of a press release as well as to develop the proper the proper content and content length.

3. Training programs? (How long? Where?)
4. Exclusive territory? (Probably no?)
5. Renewal/Termination rights? (In the legal profession, this is the litmus test for the strength of the contract. The franchisee needs to be careful of this because many legal claims come later on if a franchise turns bad or if there is a need to terminate the franchisee.)
6. Contract length? (5, 10, 20 years?)
7. Franchisor restrictions? (Am I restricted to the food products being offered, the services being provided, or may I provide some of my own food or services?
8. Marketing programs?
9. Advertising programs? (Monthly, yearly; domestic, regional, national?)
10. Strength of franchisor's staff? (Do they provide a lot of support?)
11. Determine the values of the product or service?
12. Determine the value of the trademark (McDonald's and Coke probably have the two greatest trademarks in the world. Their value is inestimable.)
13. Determine the value of training?
14. What continuous value do you provide the franchisee after they have been in existence for a period of three to four years?

Determine How Much Cash and Money You Can Afford to Invest in the Franchise

It is important that you realize that you are probably going to have to put up the total initial franchise fee with cash on hand. Most franchisors require that you have at least sufficient cash to pay the initial franchise fee and anywhere from 25 to 50% of the total franchise investment. The rest of the investment may be borrowed either from friends, banks, or possible finance companies specializing in loans to franchisees.

Obtain a UFOC
(Uniform Franchise Offering Circular)

The franchise disclosure rule was established by Congress in 1979 and requires all franchisors to provide a disclosure document to potential franchisees at least 10 business days prior to the time that the franchisee executes any contractual documents associated with the franchise or pays any consideration in connection with it (either sign up or pay your franchise fee). The disclosure rule does not attempt to regulate the nature of the relationship between a franchisor and its franchisees. It controls the franchisors conduct by requiring the franchisor to make specific disclosures in a specific fashion. There are now 23 sections of a UFOC. Every franchisor is required to give detailed and extensive disclosure of information that the FTC has deemed important or helpful to a prospective franchisee.

UFOC Table of Contents

1. The Franchisor, its Predecessors, and Affiliates
2. Business Experience
3. Litigation
4. Bankruptcy
5. Initial Franchise Fee
6. Other Fees
7. Initial Investment
8. Restrictions on Sources of Products and Services
9. Franchisee's Obligations
10. Financing
11. Franchisor's Obligations
12. Territory
13. Trademarks
14. Patents, Copyrights, and Proprietary Information
15. Obligations to Participate in the Actual Operation of the Franchise Business
16. Restrictions on What the Franchisee May Sell
17. Renewal, Termination, Transfer and Dispute Resolution
18. Public Figures
19. Earnings Claims
20. List of Outlets
21. Financial Statements
22. Contracts
23. Receipt

Exhibits
A. Franchise Agreement
B. Equipment Lease
C. Lease for premises
D. Loan Agreement

Money Requirements

Many franchisors are looking for you to have a certain cash investment. This is generally around 20 to 35%. Precision Tune Auto Care has an initial fee of $25,000 plus start-up costs up to $200,000. They look for approximately $50,000 in cash or liquid assets from the franchisee. They then look to the franchisee for the ability to finance between $125,000 to $200,000 to start up the franchise business.

Their Precision Auto Wash is looking for approximately $70,000 in cash availability plus the franchisee's ability to finance between $275,000 to $300,000 to start the franchise business.

Smoothie King simply indicates that the cash investment will generally be one-third of the total investment cost.

Be careful and do not assume that the UFOC provides all information. It doesn't. Most franchisors do not disclose earnings claims. Most franchisors do not explain all of their training programs, their length, or duration. Most franchisors do not disclose an in-depth detail explanation of their accounting or financial packages that you will be required to use. Most franchisors do not disclose their marketing programs or their advertising programs. Much of this information is not disclosed because of its proprietary nature and because they do not wish the competition to know EVERYTHING that the franchisor is doing. Much of this information you can acquire by asking the franchisor specific questions about these operations.

Continuous Value—What Will the Franchisor Continue to Provide?

One of the main reasons for franchising success is that franchisors realize that they must provide continuous value to their franchisees. By this we mean that the franchisor will continuously strive to improve their products and services; to improve their marketing, advertising, and promotional programs; to enhance and ensure the continuous growth and success of the franchisee. Nowhere in any disclosure document, UFOC, or franchise contract will the franchisor explain this in depth. You need to find out what form of continuous value the franchisor will provide. ASK!!! The franchisor generally provides continuous value through their marketing, product development, and research programs.

Training—How Much?

One of the great thrills of starting your own business is to be trained in that business. Surprisingly the average franchisor trains the new franchisee for only two to three weeks before it sends them out to start the business. Many old well-established franchise systems, however, will require a much longer time commitment in their training programs. One important training session that all new franchisees will experience is the initial training program conducted by the franchisor before the grand opening. This is generally a two-week training program that is focused on the operations and the daily activities of the business. Be prepared to take a test, in fact several tests, throughout the duration of this program. For example, Dunkin' Donuts has historically required all new franchisees to make a doughnut during the first day or two of training and be able to eat that doughnut. Surprisingly, these tests are not only to ensure that you have learned but may also be used later on to show that you are actually trained in these skills and areas.

Train With Other Franchisees Before Opening

A program that started up several years ago was the idea of going out and spending a week with another franchisee before opening your own store. This training is separate from the training that you receive at the organization's headquarters. If your franchisor is not presently offering this training, you may ask it for the opportunity to train with another franchisee before opening your own store. This will also allow you to meet other franchisees in the system and get you on a first-name basis with these individuals.

Fees

Make sure that you understand all fees associated with franchising. There are at least three standard fees found in almost all franchise systems. These include the up-front, one time only, initial franchise fee, which may range from $5,000 to $50,000 or much higher if you are buying a hotel. A second standard fee is the royalty fee, which generally ranges from 3 to 8% of total sales and is generally paid on a biweekly or monthly basis to the franchisor. A third fee common among most franchisors today is the advertising fee. This fee generally ranges from .5% to 4% of total sales. The advertising fees are generally collected by the franchisor in a separate account because they can only be expended for marketing and advertising of the franchising system.

Exclusive Territory—a Myth of Giant Proportions

Most franchisors today do not provide an exclusive territory. They provide an address and your exclusive territory is that address or that block on which your business is located. Some franchisors will provide you with an exclusive territory and often these are bound within zip codes, towns, cities, counties, or states. Because

Success Traits

Fastframe has over 200 stores worldwide and another 40 new stores expected to open in the year 2000. Fastframe's success comes from the company's insistence that prospective franchisees have the right attitude. They require a certain amount of loyalty and enthusiasm from their franchisees. It is their attitude, commitment, and business savvy that ensures the continuing success of Fastframe. They offer a Managing Partner program which gives prospective franchisees the opportunity to grow and eventually own a Fastframe without the capital necessary to buy a store outright. For an investment, which can be as low as $5,000, versus the $120,000 it costs to open a new Fastframe store, potential franchisees can partner with either Fastframe USA, Inc. or an existing franchisee.

the demand of the consumer is changing so rapidly, it is very difficult to give exclusive territories unless you wish to build more than one unit to start (you may initially want to build two or three).

Area Development Agreement

If you are interested in building two to five units, you may seek from the franchisor an area development agreement, which will provide you an exclusive territory, such as the city of Austin, Texas, for you to build two to five franchises during the next three to five years. The area development agreement gives you an exclusive territory but you must pay (generally $5,000 to $8,000 per store) for the right to own that exclusive territory.

Gingiss International Inc.

Development Store Number	Development Store Opening by Date	Cumulative Number of Development Stores to be Open and in Operation No Later Than the Developing Store Opening Date
1	No later than 12 months from the date of this Agreement	1
2	No later than 12 months from the opening of Development Store No. 1	2
3	No later than 12 months from the opening of Development Store No. 2	3
4	No later than 12 months from the opening of Development Store No. 3	4
5	No later than 12 months from the opening of Development Store No. 4	5

Note: The above chart reflects development rights for five Development Stores; DEVELOPER may be granted rights for fewer or greater number of Development Stores.

Termination

If you want out of the business, most franchisors are willing to work with their franchisees if they are desirous of leaving the system. However, they do not want to lose the revenue stream from your business. Therefore they are more interested in selling your business to another franchisee rather than simply closing the store. Make sure that you are aware of Section 17 of the UFOC, which explains all termination procedures and rules that both the franchisor and the franchisee must adhere to.

Rules of the Game for the Franchisor

It is advisable that the franchisee also understand the rules of the game that the franchisor is supposed to follow. This allows the franchisee to know what a franchisor is supposed to do and what it is not supposed to do. Occasionally you might even run into a franchisor that does not know what it can or cannot do. Be very, very careful of these franchisors.

Included in the items that a franchisor needs to follow are the following major points:

Earnings Claims

The famous napkin—some unscrupulous franchisors have been found to take a prospective franchisee into a restaurant to discuss with them the possibility of joining their franchising system. While they do not formally disclose earnings claims or sales figures, they may take a napkin and write on it the sales levels of different franchisees in the local area. The strange thing about that napkin is that the franchisor always ends up with it.

Earnings claims, when properly reported, are found in Section 19 of the UFOC. They will generally include a sales level accompanied by the percent of franchisees whose sales have exceeded, or are less than, that stipulated. For example, if the average McDonald's franchisee's sales is $1.52 million, then that would often be accompanied by a statement such as 52% of franchisees exceed this average. You can find earnings and sales claims by discussing them with other franchisees in the system.

> ### Site Selection—Who Finds and Who Approves?
>
> In most cases in franchising, the franchisee will seek two to three ideal locations from which the franchisor will approve the best location. Notice that the franchisee finds and the franchisor approves.

PostalAnnex+

A proven leader in the fast-growing packaging, shipping, and business services industry, with approximately 240 stores nationwide. *Entrepreneur* magazine has ranked PostalAnnex+ #2 in the industry. Franchisees receive assistance with site selection, lease negotiations, store design, construction, and financial assistance is available for start-up. Ongoing support to the franchisee is provided with advertising and public relations materials from the Grand Opening Kit. Additionally, brand building is developed as a result of Home Office initiatives. They are now looking at nontraditional site expansion in major grocery chains and hotels.

Pricing

Surprisingly, franchisors are not allowed to determine the price that a franchisee charges the end consumer. The franchisor may suggest a price that the franchisee should charge, but the final determination is made by the franchisee. The pricing decision is governed by the antitrust laws of the United States.

UFOC (Uniform Franchise Offering Circular)

The UFOC is the disclosure document that is required by the Federal Trade Commission and the U. S. Congress for disclosing specific information to all prospective franchisees. Some of this information includes the background and business experience of the franchisor coupled with any litigation and bankruptcy it has faced. In addition, the UFOC will contain a list of the initial franchise fee and all other fee payments a franchisee will be required to pay for the duration of their contract. The total initial investment is estimated in the UFOC and the obligations of both franchisees and franchisors are listed accompanied by territory, trademarks, and copyright restrictions. The UFOC also contains any earnings claims, renewal, and termination information. Finally, a list of franchising outlets, the franchise contract, and three years of financial statements of the franchisor are also included in the UFOC.

Registration States

There are approximately 14 "registration states" found in the United States. These states, generally found on the west and east coasts as well as certain northern states, require in addition to the UFOC a one- or two-page statement listing the names of people selling franchises in their particular state. If you live in one of these registration states and you make a request from a franchisor for a UFOC or information about its franchising system, you may be told that they are not yet registered in your state and are therefore not allowed to send you information about the franchise system.

Offers on the Internet

Because of the recent rapid growth of the Internet, many franchisors have been and will continue to use the Internet to communicate information about their franchise systems to prospective franchisees. These are not to be considered as offers to purchase or buy a franchise. Most franchisors are now including words to the effect that their franchises are not being offered to the residents of certain states. However, you should know that the Internet is a great place to get information about a franchising system.

Training Programs

One of the greatest strengths (or weaknesses) of any franchising system is the training programs that they provide. Some of the best training programs have been developed and prepared by franchisors. McDonald's, Mail Boxes Etc., Kwik Kopy, and Wendy's training programs are considered to be among the best training programs offered throughout the world. However, many of these training programs are short in duration. Some may last less than one week. Most franchise programs provide two to three weeks of training. Some franchisors, such as Kwik Kopy Corporation, have established expansive training campuses that looks more like an exclusive Minnesota campground than a common training facility. Because of the shortness of duration, most franchise training programs focus around the day to day operations of the business. If you are seeking additional business training, you may be wise to use other available programs such as your local university or Internet sites.

> One of the greatest strengths (or weaknesses) of any franchising system is the training programs that they provide.

Accounting Records

Many franchisors require that you utilize its accounting systems. The franchisor will often seek at least three specific items depending upon the business–(1) Total sales for the day or week; (2) Cost of labor for the day or week; and (3) Cost of goods sold for the day or the week. In many pizza establishments it has long been held that the cost of goods sold around 28 to 32% of the total sales price. When the cost of goods sold is higher or lower than this, many franchisors may become extremely anxious about the quality of the product being served.

Using the Computer

Because of the rapid growth of PCs in our culture, many franchisors are now requiring their franchisees to have a personal computer. These computers are often used to maintain accurate accounting records as well as payroll records and business records associated with the franchise system. In addition these computers now link up to the Internet and may be part of the Intranet (an exclusive Internet messenger service from the franchisor only, received by those franchisees with the proper log-on and password). This excludes nonfranchisees from the Intranet system and allows the franchisor to communicate directly with all franchisees in the system.

Site Selection—Encroachment

Generally the franchisee will select the site and the franchisor will approve the site. However, it is important for the franchisor to make sure that the addition of a new franchise business does not encroach upon the market of an already existing franchise business (encroachment).

Involuntary Termination

In very rare circumstances, franchisors will be forced to involuntarily terminate existing franchisees for lack of performance or failure to pay fees. These are not nice experiences; however, the rules and conditions established for termination have to be disclosed in the UFOC in Section 17. This allows all franchisees to properly understand under what conditions and situations a franchisor may terminate a franchisee. Surprisingly, this is an extremely rare occurrence in franchising but there are cases when it is done.

Operations Manual—Property of the Franchisor

The operations manual is intellectual property of the franchisor. Therefore, all operations manuals remain the property of the franchisor and are only on lease to the franchisee for the duration of the franchise contract. The copying or reproduction of any parts of the operations manual is against the law. Franchisees must return the operations manual to the franchisor at the end of the franchise agreement unless the contract is renewed.

It is important for the franchisor to make sure that the addition of a new franchise business does not encroach upon the market of an already existing franchise business (encroachment).

Renewal

Except for illegal activity, failure to pay fees, and inappropriate behavior on the part of the franchisee, almost all franchise contracts are renewed. Unless you as a franchisee do not wish to renew the franchise agreement, most franchisors provide an automatic renewal process for franchisees to renew their contracts. You must know, though, that when you do renew, you will sign the then-existing (new) franchise agreement. Often, this is different than the original one signed 10 or 20 years before. There may be a small renewal fee charged, but the major point is that the fee structures for royalties or advertising may have been raised since the original franchise agreement.

Exclusive Territory

Generally the franchisor no longer provides exclusive territories. However, you may obtain an area development agreement for the establishment of two or more franchises which does give you an exclusive right to a city, county, or multiple counties for a certain period of time—generally three to five years.

Conclusion

Franchising is a fascinating game. It is one of the greatest games currently being played throughout the world. There are certain rules to the game that one must adhere to. These rules should be learned and followed. The UFOC provides certain disclosure information that all franchisees may receive from their franchisor. However, additional information needs to be obtained from existing franchisees and the franchisor before you, as a prospective franchisee, will know all the rules of the game for that specific franchise system.

Generally the franchisor no longer provides exclusive territories.

For more information on this topic, visit our Web site at www.businesstown.com

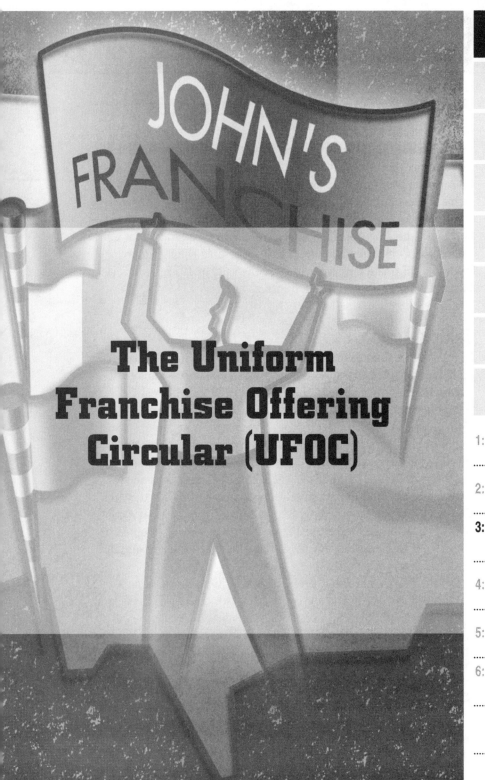

The Uniform Franchise Offering Circular (UFOC)

Chapter 3

1: ALMOST ANYONE CAN BE A FRANCHISEE

2: THE RULES OF THE GAME

3: THE UNIFORM FRANCHISE OFFERING CIRCULAR (UFOC)

4: THE UFOC—THE REST OF THE STORY

5: FEAR NOT—THE CONTRACT IS HERE

6: YOU CAN NEGOTIATE THE RULES OF THE GAME!

The Beginning of Franchising

Franchising in this country is believed to have been started in the 1850s by the Singer Sewing Machine Company through a system they set up to sell their sewing machines. However, franchising did not undergo its tremendous growth until the 1950s when it appeared to explode on the scene with companies such as McDonald's, Holiday Inn, and others. Prior to the 1950s, the growth of franchising in this country had mostly been in the areas of automobile dealerships and gasoline stations. During the early 1900s, restaurant chains started to appear; however, it was not until the 1950s that franchising started to spread like wildfire. This attracted the attention of many people looking to invest and become the owners of their own businesses.

Franchising Starts to Play by the Rules

Many abuses in the sale of franchises occurred in the 1950s and 1960s. This led to the enactment of state and federal franchise laws. The franchise laws provided for a disclosure document containing information about the franchisor, its management, and the material terms and conditions of the franchise agreement. By law, this document must be provided to the prospective franchisee prior to the execution of a binding franchise agreement between the franchisor and franchisee. Consequently, some franchisors would simply supply incorrect information in order to close the sale. In 1971, California became the first state to pass a franchise law.

Taking Action

The disclosure laws passed by several states were a step in the right direction; however, there was a need for a national uniform format for disclosure. In response to this need, in 1975 the Midwest Securities Commissioners Association adopted the *Uniform Franchise Offering Circular* (UFOC). This group is a national association of the securities law regulators of all of the states. Currently, this association is known as the North American Securities Administrators Association (NASAA). The UFOC, as it became known, was the first uniform disclosure format in the United States. This format would later be rewritten and updated in 1993. The current UFOC is based on the 1993 comprehensive revision adopted by NASAA. In 1995, this document was adopted by all the appropriate state and federal authorities.

At the same time that the Midwest Securities Commissioners Association was developing a uniform format for disclosure, the federal government, through its Federal Trade Commission (FTC), was also working on adopting a national disclosure format. Finally, in 1978, the FTC adopted what has become known as the FTC Rule.

FTC Rule vs. the UFOC

The FTC rule is formally titled *Federal Trade Commission Rule Regarding Franchising and Business Opportunity Ventures*

Disclosure Requirements and Prohibitions. The FTC Rule can be found at 16 C.F.R. part 436. In laymen's terms, it can be found in Volume 16 of the Code of Federal Regulations in Part 436.

Throughout the years, franchisors have used either the FTC format or the UFOC for their disclosure documents. However, as a practical matter, the vast majority of franchisors utilize the UFOC. Even though the FTC format disclosure document can be used in most states, those states that have adopted their own franchise registration or disclosure statutes will not accept a disclosure document written according to the FTC Rule. These 15 states, which include California, New York, and Illinois, will only accept a disclosure document written along the requirements of the UFOC format. The reason for this is that the UFOC format, though substantially similar to the FTC Rule format, requires more information to be disclosed on the part of the franchisor. The benefit to the franchisee is obvious. The more information on which a franchisee can base his decision, the better off a prospective franchisee is in making the decision to purchase the franchise. The FTC has acknowledged that the information required to be disclosed under the UFOC format provides the same as, or greater protection to, a prospective franchisee than does the required disclosures under the FTC Rule. Therefore, the FTC allows for the UFOC format to be used in lieu of the FTC Rule format. Since the vast majority of franchisors utilize the UFOC format, which is acceptable in all 50 states, the UFOC-required disclosures will be discussed in this chapter as opposed to the FTC Rule disclosure items. With only a few exceptions, the two formats essentially require the same information to be disclosed.

The information that must be disclosed in the UFOC is found in 23 items. In addition to the 23 items and exhibits, the UFOC requires two cover pages, which are the initial pages seen by a prospective franchisee. In the UFOC, one of the cover pages is proscribed by the FTC Rule and the second cover page is proscribed by the UFOC. The cover page required by the FTC Rule displays required language stressing the importance to the prospective franchisee of investigating the franchise offering carefully and to contact federal and state authorities if anything is missing from the disclosure document that is required to be there. The cover page required by the UFOC follows the FTC cover page and contains a brief

> Since the vast majority of franchisors utilize the UFOC format, which is acceptable in all 50 states, the UFOC-required disclosures will be discussed in this chapter as opposed to the FTC Rule disclosure items.

summary of the range of fees and expenses in the franchise offering along with a one line description of the franchise. Also, on the UFOC cover page, there is set forth a list of risk factors that a prospective franchisee should be aware of that could have a serious effect on their ability to purchase a successful franchise. After the two required cover pages, there is a table of contents. It lists in order the 23 items that are required to be disclosed within the UFOC.

On the UFOC cover page, there is set forth a list of risk factors that a prospective franchisee should be aware of that could have a serious effect on their ability to purchase a successful franchise.

Item 1: The Franchisor, Its Predecessors, and Affiliates

The Franchisor Must Disclose in Summary Form:

A. The name of the Franchisor, its predecessors, and affiliates
B. The name under which the Franchisor does or intends to do Business
C. The principal business address of the Franchisor, its predecessors and affiliates, and the Franchisor's agent for service of process
D. The Business form of the Franchisor (i.e., limited liability company, corporation, etc.)
E. The Franchisor's Business and the franchises to be offered in this state

The UFOC Must Contain the Following under E:

1. Whether or not the franchisor sells or grants franchises
2. Whether the franchisor operates businesses of the type being franchised
3. The franchisor's other business activities
4. The business to be conducted by the franchisees
5. The general market for the product or service to be offered by the franchisee (For example, is the market developed or developing? Will the goods be sold primarily to a certain group? Are sales seasonal?)
6. In general terms, any regulations specific to the industry in which the franchise business operates (It is not necessary to include laws or regulations that apply to business generally.)
7. A general description of the competition

F. The prior business experience of the Franchisor, its predecessors, and affiliates including
   1. The length of time the franchisor has conducted a business of the type to be operated by the franchisee
   2. The length of time each predecessor and affiliate has conducted a business of the type to be operated by the franchisee
   3. The length of time the franchisor has offered franchises for the same type of business as that to be operated by the franchisee
   4. The length of time each predecessor and affiliate offered franchises for the same type of business as that to be operated by the franchisee
   5. Whether the franchisor has offered franchises in other lines of business, including:
      (a) A description of each other line of business
      (b) The number of franchises sold in each other line of business
      (c) The length of time the franchisor has offered each other franchise
   6. Whether each predecessor and affiliate offered franchises in other lines of business, including:
      (a) A description of each other line of business
      (b) The number of franchises sold in each other line of business
      (c) The length of time each predecessor and affiliate offered each other franchise

Item 1 requires the franchisor to set forth its name, its predecessors, and affiliates. This section gives a prospective franchisee a general background on the franchisor and any predecessors and affiliates. Further disclosure requires the name under which the franchisor does business, or intends to do business, along with the principal business address of the franchisor, its predecessors and affiliates, and the franchisor's agent for service. Also required is the business form which the franchisor operates under, including which state the business is incorporated in, along with the type of business organization. Of most importance in this section is that the franchisor must disclose what the business is and the franchise it plans to offer.

Questions to Ask About Item 1

- How experienced is the franchisor in the business it is franchising?

- How many years has the franchisor been franchising?

- How long was the franchisor in business perfecting and developing its system prior to franchising?

- Does the franchisor own and operate company units it uses to further refine its concepts and to introduce new products, concepts, and systems in order to perfect them prior to introduction to the franchisees?

- Is the general market for the product or service to be offered by the franchisee a large market? A niche market?

- It is a growing market? A promising market, etc?

A common question that often arises: When is this disclosure document required to be delivered to a prospective franchisee? At the minimum, the prospective franchisee must have this document in his or her hands at least 10 business days prior to execution of any legal documents, or payment of any financial consideration. A business day does not include Saturdays, Sundays, federal holidays, or the date on which one receives the disclosure document. Further, when a prospective franchisee is ready to purchase a franchise, the franchisor must provide him or her with the agreements, completely filled out and in final form, at least five business days before execution of the agreements (such as the franchise agreement or any other related documents). This way, the prospective franchisee has five business days to review the documents and decide if they meet his or her approval.

Item 2: Business Experience

Franchisor must list by name and position the directors, trustees and/or general partners, the principal officers and other executives or subfranchisors who will have management responsibility relating to the franchises offered by the offering circular. All franchise brokers must be listed. Each person's principal occupations and employers during the past five years must be listed.

Item 3: Litigation

Franchisor, its predecessors, any person identified in Item 2, or an affiliate offering franchises under the Franchisor's principal trademark, must disclose the following:

A. Any administrative, criminal, or material civil action pending against that person alleging a violation of a franchise, antitrust or securities law; fraud; unfair or deceptive practices; or comparable allegations. In addition, actions must be included, other than routine litigation incidental to the business, that are significant in the context of the number of franchisees and the size, nature, or financial condition of the franchise system or

---

Questions to Ask About Item 2

- How much experience in years and types of jobs does the franchisor's personnel have in this industry?

- Does the number of people disclosed appear to be proportional to the size of the franchise and hence sufficient to support the franchisor's operation?

Questions to Ask About Item 3

- Is the number of lawsuits, injunctions, and restrictive orders out of proportion (too many) for the size of the franchise system?

- If so, this is a red flag. Who were the parties to the lawsuits?

- If most of them were franchisees alleging misrepresentation or lack of fulfillment by the franchisor of the terms of their agreements then these lawsuits need to be looked at further.

its business operations. If any of the above apply, the names of the parties, the forum, nature, and current status of the pending action must be disclosed. The Franchisor may include a summary opinion of counsel concerning the action if a consent to use of the summary opinion is included as part of the offering circular.

B. Has during the 10-year period immediately before the date of the offering circular been convicted of a felony or pleaded nolo contender to a felony; has been held liable in a civil action by final judgment; or has been the subject of a material action involving violation of a franchise, antitrust, or securities law, fraud, unfair or deceptive practices, or comparable allegations. If there are any such convictions or judgments, the names of the parties, the forum and date of conviction or date judgment was entered, penalty or damages assessed and/or settlements, must be disclosed.

C. Is subject to a currently effective injunctive or restrictive order or decree relating to the franchise or under a federal, state, or Canadian franchise, securities, antitrust, trade regulation or trade practice law resulting from a concluded or pending action or proceeding brought by a public agency. If so, the name of the person, the public agency and court, a summary of the allegations or facts found by the agency or court, and the date, nature, terms and conditions of the order or decree, must be disclosed.

> ## Questions to Ask About Item 4
>
> - What were the reasons for the bankruptcy?
> - Was the bankruptcy relevant to the operation of the franchise system?
> - If so, in what ways was it relevant and have these issues been adequately addressed by the franchisor?

Item 4: Bankruptcy

The Franchisor must disclose whether the Franchisor, its affiliate, its predecessor, officers or general partner during the 10-year period immediately before the date of the offering circular

A. Filed as Debtor (or had filed against it) a petition to start an action under the U.S. Bankruptcy Code;

B. Obtained a discharge of its debts under the Bankruptcy Code; or

C. Was a principal officer of a company or a general partner in a partnership that either filed as a debtor (or had filed against it) a petition to start an action under the U.S. Bankruptcy Code or that obtained a discharge of its debts under the

Questions to Ask About Item 5

- Is the initial franchise fee similar to the franchisor's competitors?
- If substantially higher, what does this franchisor offer to the prospective franchisee that the other franchisors don't offer to warrant the higher fee?
- Is the fee refundable if something happens prior to the opening of the franchise (such as the franchisee changing his or her mind)?

Questions to Ask About Item 6

- After a review of all the "other" fees, how do the numbers of and types of fees, their dollar amounts, percentages of total gross sales, etc. compare to the competition?
- If the numbers and types of fees and/or their dollar amounts are too high or too low, the prospective franchisee would want to explore these "other" fees in more detail with the franchisor to see what he would be getting in return.
- What is the total financial obligation for all forms of advertising–local, cooperative, regional, or national, etc? In return for the advertising fees, what benefits can the franchisee expect?

Bankruptcy Code during or within one year after the officer or general partner of the franchisor held this position in the company or partnership.

If any of the above has occurred the name of the person or company that was the debtor under the Bankruptcy Code, the date of the action, and the material facts must be disclosed.

Item 5: Initial Franchise Fee

The initial franchise fee must be disclosed and the Franchisor must state the conditions under which this fee is refundable.

A. The "initial fee" includes all fees and payments for services or goods received from the Franchisor before the franchisee's business opens. The initial fee includes all fees and payments whether payable in a lump sum or in installments.

B. If the initial fee is not uniform, the formula or the range of initial fees paid in the fiscal year before the application date and the factors that determined the amount must be disclosed.

Item 6: Other Fees

The Franchisor must disclose other recurring or isolated fees or payments that the Franchisee must pay to the Franchisor or its affiliates or that the franchisor or its affiliates impose or collect in whole or in part on behalf of a third party. Included must be the formula used to compute these other fees and payments. If any fee is refundable, any conditions that apply must be stated.

A. The fees must be disclosed in tabular form. Footnotes or a "remarks" column will be used to elaborate on the information in the table or to disclose caveats.

B. The amount of each fee must be disclosed. A dollar amount or a percentage of gross sales is acceptable if the term gross sales is defined. If dollar amounts may increase, the formula that determines the increase or the maximum amount of the increase must be disclosed.

C. The due date for recurring payments must be disclosed.

D. If all fees are payable to only the Franchisor, this must be disclosed.

E. If all fees are imposed and collected by the Franchisor, this must be disclosed in a footnote.

F. If all fees are nonrefundable this will also be stated in a footnote.

G. The voting power of Franchisor-owned outlets on any fees imposed by cooperatives must be disclosed. If Franchisor outlets have controlling voting power, a range for the fee must be disclosed.

H. Examples of fees are as follows: royalty, lease negotiation, construction, remodeling, additional training, advertising, group advertising, additional assistance, audit, accounting/inventory, and transfer and renewal fees.

Item 7: Initial Investment

The following expenditures must be disclosed, stating to whom the payments are made, when the payments are due, whether each payment is refundable, the conditions when each payment is refundable, and, if part of the franchisee's initial investment in the franchise may be financed, an estimate of the loan repayments, including interest:

A. Real property, whether purchased or leased. If neither estimable nor describable by a low-high range, describe requirements, such as property type, location, and building size.

B. Equipment, fixture, other fixed assets, construction, remodeling, leasehold improvements and decorating costs, whether purchased or leased.

C. Inventory required to begin operation.

D. Security deposits, utility deposits, business licenses, other prepaid expenses.

E. Additional funds required by the franchisee before operations begin and during the initial phase of the franchise.

F. Other payments that the franchisee must make to begin operations.

Of particular importance is the following information: Remember that the numbers listed under this Item are estimates only. Your numbers could be higher or lower.

Questions to Ask About Item 7

- Based upon the estimates, do you have available to you enough working capital so that you will not run out of money?

- Will you have enough money to not only open your franchise business but also to cover your living expenses until you become able to pay yourself from the business?

- Based upon the dollar amounts, percentages of total gross sales, and estimates found in items 5, 6, and 7, do you have sufficient financial resources to cover all these expenses, and, if you do, is this opportunity still financially viable for you to proceed and become a franchisee?

Item 8: Restrictions on Sources of Products and Services

Franchisee obligations to purchase or lease from the Franchisor, its designee, or from suppliers approved by the Franchisor or under the Franchisor's specifications must be listed. For each obligation the following must be disclosed:

> Franchisee obligations to purchase or lease from the Franchisor, its designee, or from suppliers approved by the Franchisor or under the Franchisor's specifications must be listed.

A. The goods, services, supplies, fixtures, equipment, inventory, computer hardware and software, or real estate relating to establishing or operating the franchised business in which its source is restricted.

B. The manner in which the Franchisor issues and modifies specifications or grants and revokes approval to suppliers.

C. Whether, and for what categories of goods and services, the Franchisor or its affiliates are approved suppliers or the only approved suppliers.

D. Whether, and if so, the precise basis by which the Franchisor or its affiliates will or may derive revenue or other material consideration as a result of required purchases or leases.

E. The estimated proportion of these required purchases and leases to all purchases and leases by the franchisee of goods and services in establishing and operating the franchised business.

F. The existence of purchasing or distribution cooperatives.

Of particular importance are answers to the following questions. How many (in numbers and as a percentage of all purchases of products and services) products and services must be purchased from the franchisor or one of its affiliates? If more than a few must be purchased from the franchisor, this is a **red flag**. One then must question the franchisor as to why so many products and services must be purchased from the franchisor and/or its affiliates. What is the franchisor's policy in approving new vendors for the purchase of these products and services? Is it reasonable or is it overbearing?

By reviewing this Item you can determine: How much of your goods or services you are obligated to purchase from the franchisor, an affiliate, or an approved supplier; how reasonable the franchisor's policy is for approving new suppliers; and whether the franchisor's product or service specifications are reasonable to ensure uniformity, consistency, and quality control—or just a way to exercise more control over you.

Item 9: Franchisee's Obligations

The principal obligations of the franchisee under the franchise agreement and other agreements after the signing of these agreements must be listed in tabular form. The section of the agreement that contains the obligation and any Item of the UFOC that further describes the obligation is listed here as well. The categories of franchisee obligations to be listed are:

A. Site selection and acquisition/lease
B. Preopening purchases/leases
C. Site development and other pre-opening requirements
D. Initial and ongoing training
E. Opening
F. Fees
G. Compliance with standards and policies/operating manual
H. Trademarks and proprietary information
I. Restrictions on products/services offered
J. Warranty and customer service requirements
K. Territorial development and sales quotas
L. Ongoing product/service purchases
M. Maintenance, appearance, and remodeling requirements
N. Insurance
O. Advertising
P. Indemnification
Q. Owner's participation/management/staffing
R. Records and reports
S. Inspections and audits
T. Transfer
U. Renewal
V. Post-termination obligations
W. Noncompetition covenants
X. Dispute resolution
Y. Other (describe)

> The principal obligations of the franchisee under the franchise agreement and other agreements after the signing of these agreements must be listed in tabular form.

Of particular importance under this Item is to be sure to read the entire franchise agreement and any other agreements you could be required to sign to determine if there are any other franchisee's obligations not listed in the UFOC or if an obligation was listed incorrectly.

Item 10: Financing

The terms and conditions of each financing arrangement that the Franchisor, its agent, or affiliates offers directly or indirectly to the franchisee is listed under this item.

"Financing" includes leases and installment contracts.

A written arrangement between a franchisor or its affiliate and a lender for the lender to offer financing to the franchisee or an arrangement in which a franchisor or its affiliate receives a benefit from a lender for franchisee financing is an "indirect offering of financing" and must be disclosed under this item. The franchisor may either list the terms or summarize the terms of each financing arrangement in tabular form, using footnotes to entries in the chart to provide additional information. Specimen copies of the financing documents must be included as an exhibit to Item 22. Additionally, the franchisor must disclose the following:

A. A waiver of defenses or similar provisions by the franchisee in a document.
B. The Franchisor's practice or its intent to sell, assign, or discount to a third party all or part of the financing arrangement.
C. Payments to the franchisor or an affiliate(s) for the placement of financing with the lender.

A prospective franchisee should compare the terms of franchisor financing with what is available from other sources, along with asking existing franchisees where they received their financing and what it cost them.

> Be sure to read the entire franchise agreement and any other agreements you could be required to sign to determine if there are any other franchisee's obligations not listed in the UFOC or if an obligation was listed incorrectly.

Conclusion

The UFOC is the main disclosure document of franchising. The first part of the UFOC is primarily concerned with the franchisor, its predecessors, affiliates, legal background, franchisee fees, franchisee obligations, and financing. The first half of the UFOC requires that the franchisor disclose the minimum and maximum franchisee cost. The UFOC is a wealth of knowledge and provides the prospective franchisee with valuable information needed to make the right business decision.

> The UFOC is a wealth of knowledge and provides the prospective franchisee with valuable information needed to make the right business decision.

For more information on this topic, visit our Web site at www.businesstown.com

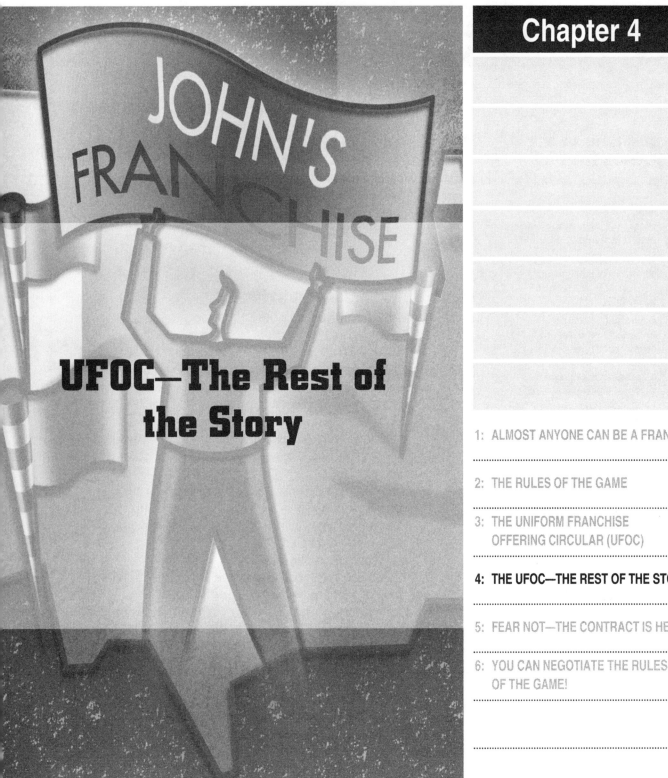

UFOC—The Rest of the Story

Chapter 4

1: ALMOST ANYONE CAN BE A FRANCHISEE

2: THE RULES OF THE GAME

3: THE UNIFORM FRANCHISE
   OFFERING CIRCULAR (UFOC)

4: THE UFOC—THE REST OF THE STORY

5: FEAR NOT—THE CONTRACT IS HERE

6: YOU CAN NEGOTIATE THE RULES
   OF THE GAME!

P rospective franchisees need to have sufficient information to understand economic commitments and to develop a personal business plan. Territory, trademarks, patents, copyrights, proprietary information, and the franchisee's obligation to participate in the actual operation of the franchise business are now explained in the UFOC. This is vital information that you need to make the right business decision.

Let's start with the franchisor's responsibilities to you, the franchisee. Look for what the UFOC does contain as well as what it does not contain (the franchisor is not going to run the store for you).

Item 11: Franchisor's Obligations

The following must be disclosed by the Franchisor:

A. The obligations that the Franchisor will perform before the franchise business opens, citing by section the provisions of the agreement requiring performance including assistance to:
   i. Locate a site for the franchised business and negotiate the purchase or lease of this site, conform the premises to local ordinances and building codes, and obtain the required permits (i.e. health, sanitation, building, driveway, utility, and sign permits).
   ii. construct, remodel, or decorate the premises for the franchised business.
   iii. Purchase or lease equipment, signs, fixtures, opening inventory, and supplies.
   iv. Hire and train employees.
B. The obligations to be performed by the Franchisor during the operation of the franchise business are listed here.
   i. The following assistance by the Franchisor must be listed if provided:
      a. products or services to be offered by the franchisee to its customers
      b. hiring and training of employees
      c. improvements and developments in the business
      d. pricing
      e. administrative, bookkeeping, accounting and inventory control procedures

Questions to Ask About Item 11

- Is the franchisor's training program ongoing so you receive training, not just prior to opening your business, but while it is open?

- How comprehensive and complete is each part of the franchisor's training program?

- Does the franchisor undertake research and development projects on a regular basis to continually improve its products, services, operations, etc?

- Is the advertising program set up so that the location of your franchise will benefit?

- What type of communication occurs on a regular basis from the franchisor to the franchisee (e-mail, newsletters, magazines, etc.)?

f.   assisting in solving operating problems encountered by the franchisee

ii. In the Franchisor's advertising program for the product or service offered by the franchisee the Franchisor must:

a.   Disclose the media in which the advertising may be disseminated (for example, print, radio, or television).

b.   Disclose whether the coverage of the media is local, regional, or national in scope.

c.   Disclose the source of the advertising. (For example, in-house advertising department, a national or regional advertising agency).

d.   Disclose the conditions when the Franchisor permits franchisees to use their own advertising material.

e.   If there is an advertising council composed of franchisees that advises the Franchisor on advertising policies, disclose:

1.   how many members of the council are selected.

2.   whether the council serves in an advisory capacity only or has operational or decision-making power.

3.   whether the Franchisor has the power to form, change, or dissolve the advertising council.

f.   If the franchisee must participate in a local or regional advertising cooperative, the Franchisor must disclose:

1.   how the area or membership of the cooperative is defined.

2.   how the franchisee's contribution to the cooperative is calculated.

3.   who is responsible for administration.

4.   whether the Franchisor has the power to require cooperatives to be formed, changed, dissolved or merged.

g.   If applicable, for each advertising fund not described in above subpart (f) the Franchisor must disclose:

1.   who contributes to each fund.

2.   whether the franchisor-owned units must contribute. to the fund and, if so, whether it is on the same basis as franchisees.

3.   how much the franchisee must contribute to the advertising fund(s).

> In the Franchisor's advertising program for the product or service offered by the franchisee the Franchisor must disclose whether the coverage of the media is local, regional, or national in scope.

> The Franchisor must state whether the Franchisor must spend any amount on advertising in the area or territory where the franchisee is located.

4. who administers the fund(s) whether the fund is audited and when, and whether financial statements of the fund are available for review by the franchisee.

5. for use of the fund(s) in the most recently concluded fiscal year, the percentages spent on production, media placement, administrative expenses, and other (with a description of what constitutes "other"). Totals should equal 100%.

6. whether the Franchisor or an affiliate receives payment for providing goods or services to an advertising fund.

h. The Franchisor must state whether the Franchisor must spend any amount on advertising in the area or territory where the franchisee is located.

iii. The franchisor must disclose if it requires that franchisees buy or use cash registers or computer systems, providing a general description of the systems in nontechnical language and disclose the following information:

a. Identify each hardware component and software program by brand, type, and principal functions.

b. State whether the franchisee has any contractual obligation to upgrade or update any hardware component or software program during the term of the franchise, and if so, whether there are any contractual limitations on the frequency and cost of the obligation.

c. For each electronic cash register system or software program, describe how it will be used in the franchisee's business and the types of business information or data that will be collected and generated.

iv. After describing its obligation, the Franchisor must cite the section number of the agreement imposing the obligation.

v. The Franchisor must disclose if it is not obligated to provide or to assist the franchisee in obtaining the above items or services.

vi. The Franchisor must disclose the table of contents of the operating manual(s) provided to the franchisee as of the Franchisor's last fiscal year end or a more recent date. Stated must be the number of pages devoted to each subject and the total number of pages in the manual as of this date.

C. The methods used by the Franchisor to select the location of the franchisee's business is stated here.

　i. Disclosed here is whether the Franchisor selects the site or approves an area selected by the franchisee. How and if the Franchisor must approve a franchisee-selected site is also listed.

　ii. The Franchisor must disclose the factors that the Franchisor considers in selecting or approving sites (for example general location and neighborhood, traffic patterns, parking, size, physical characteristics of existing buildings, and lease terms.)

　iii. The Franchisor must disclose the time limit for the Franchisor to locate or to approve or disapprove the site and the consequences if the Franchisor and franchisee cannot agree on a site.

D. The typical length of time between the signing of the franchise agreement or the first payment of consideration for the franchise and the opening of the franchisee's business must also be disclosed.

E. The training program of the Franchisor as of the Franchisor's last fiscal year end or a more recent date must be disclosed including:

　i. the location, duration, and general outline of the training program;

　ii. how often the training program will be conducted;

　iii. the experience that the instructors have with the Franchisor;

　iv. charges to be made to the franchisee and who must pay travel and living expenses of the enrollees in the training program;

　v. if the training program is not mandatory, the percentage of new franchisees that enrolled in the training program during the preceding 12 months; and

　vi. whether any additional training programs and/or refresher courses are required.

> The training program of the Franchisor must be disclosed including the location, duration, and general outline of the training program.

This Item is typically one of the longest in the UFOC. Also, you will want to review the operations manual in its entirety for completeness. And finally, you want to make sure the franchisor performs its stated obligations, which it must if it uses the word "will" or its equivalent. The word "may" does not a promise make.

> You want to make sure the franchisor performs its stated obligations, which it must if it uses the word "will" or its equivalent.

Item 12: Territory

Under this section the Franchisor must describe any exclusive territory granted the franchisee. Concerning the franchisee's location (with or without exclusive territory), the Franchisor must state whether:

A. The Franchisor has established or may establish another franchisee close by who may also use the Franchisor's trademark.

B. The Franchisor has established or may establish a company-owned outlet or other channels of distribution using the Franchisor's trademark within the vicinity of the franchisee's location.

   i. As used in Item 12, trademark includes names, trademarks, logos, and other commercial symbols.

   ii. If appropriate, the minimum area granted to the franchisee is described. The Franchisor may use an area encompassed within a specific radius, such as a distance sufficient to encompass a specified population or another specific designation.

   iii. Stated here is whether the franchise is granted for a specific location or one to be approved by the franchisor.

   iv. The conditions under which the Franchisor will approve the relocation of the franchised business or the establishment of additional franchised outlets is stated here.

   v. Restrictions on the Franchisor regarding operating company-owned stores or on granting franchised outlets for a similar or competitive business within the defined area are listed under this Item.

   vi. Restrictions on franchisees from soliciting or accepting orders outside of their defined territories are described.

   vii. Restrictions on the Franchisor from soliciting or accepting orders inside the franchisee's defined territory along with compensation that the franchisor must pay for soliciting or accepting orders inside the franchisee's defined territories are listed.

    viii. Franchisee options, rights of first refusal, or similar rights to acquire additional franchises within the territory or contiguous territories are described here as well.

C. The Franchisor or its affiliate must disclose if it has established or may establish other franchises or company-owned outlets or another channel of distribution, selling, or leasing similar products or services under a different trademark within the vicinity of the franchisee's location.

D. If continuation of the franchisee's territorial exclusivity, if one is granted, depends on achievement of a certain sales volume, market penetration, or other contingency and under what circumstances a franchisee's territory may be altered.

Item 12 is one of the more controversial disclosure requirements. This topic has led to quite a few lawsuits and much unrest among franchisees within the franchise community. You must be sure that you are given an exclusive territory within which to operate and you must know how big it is. Franchisees do not have problems with competition; however, a franchisee does not expect to compete against his or her own system. This could happen if the franchisor locates another franchise or company unit too close to you or establishes alternative channels by which it distributes its goods or services, consequently taking away your customers and hurting your profitability. Therefore, being given an exclusive territory in which another franchise or a company-owned unit cannot be located and in which an alternative channel of distribution for its goods or services cannot be used without adequate compensation to you can make the difference in whether you purchase one particular franchise over another.

> Item 12 is one of the more controversial disclosure requirements. This topic has led to quite a few lawsuits and much unrest among franchisees within the franchise community.

Item 13: Trademarks

The franchisor must disclose the principal trademarks to be licensed to the franchisee including:

A. Whether the principal trademarks are registered with the United States Patent and Trademark Office. For each registration the

Franchisor must state the registration date and number and whether the registration is on the principal or supplemental register.

B. The Franchisor must disclose currently effective material determinations of the Patent and Trademark Office, Trademark Trial and Appeal Board, the trademark administrator of any state or any court; pending infringement, opposition, or cancellation; and pending material litigation involving the principal trademarks.

C. Disclose agreements currently in effect that significantly limit the rights of the Franchisor to use or license the use of trademarks listed in this item in a manner material to the franchise.

D. Whether the Franchisor must protect the franchisee's right to use the principal trademarks listed in this Item, and whether the franchisor must protect the franchisee against claims of infringement or unfair competition arising out of the franchisee's use of them.

E. Whether the Franchisor actually knows of either superior prior rights or infringing uses that could materially affect the franchisee's use of the principal trademarks in any state or the state in which the franchised business is to be located.

> A well-recognized trademark that is federally registered with the U.S. Patent and Trademark Office is vital to the financial well-being of its franchisees.

If a franchisor does not have exclusive use of a well-recognized and incontestable trademark, a prospective franchisee could find his or her franchise's financial well-being seriously compromised because of the ability of others to use the same trademark. If anyone could use the name "McDonald's," what value would it be to a prospective franchisee to have the right to use the name, since it couldn't differentiate its products from others using the name? Therefore, a well-recognized trademark that is federally registered with the U.S. Patent and Trademark Office is vital to the financial well-being of its franchisees.

Item 14: Patents, Copyrights, and Proprietary Information

If the Franchisor owns rights in patents or copyrights that are material to the franchise, these patents and copyrights and their relationship to the franchise are described here. Information pertaining to their duration and whether the franchisor can and intends to renew the copyrights is included. To the extent relevant, the Franchisor must disclose information required by Item 13 concerning these patents and copyrights. If the Franchisor claims proprietary rights in confidential information or trade secrets, their general subject matter and the terms and conditions for use by the franchisee are listed.

The prospective franchisee needs to determine whether the products and/or services critical to the success of the franchise have been patented or copyrighted by the franchisor, and if not, if they can be provided by the franchisor. If so, this allows the franchisee and other members of the franchisor's system the exclusive use of such products and services giving you a competitive advantage over the competition.

Item 15: Obligation to Participate in the Actual Operation of the Franchise Business

The Franchisor, in this Item, discloses the franchisee's obligation to personally participate in the direct operation of the franchise business and whether the Franchisor recommends participation. Included are obligations arising from written agreement (including personal guaranty, confidentiality agreement, or noncompetition agreement) or from the Franchisor's practice. If personal "on-premises" supervision is not required, the Franchisor must state limitations on whom the franchisee can hire as an on-premises supervisor, and whether this on-premises supervisor must successfully complete the Franchisor's training program. The restrictions that the franchisee must place on its manager (for example, maintain trade secrets, noncompetition) are also stated.

Most franchises require either hands-on, day-to-day participation in the operation of the franchise or at least some substantial investment. If you plan to be a passive franchise owner with little direct involvement in the franchise's operation you might not want to purchase it. After all, no one is more concerned with the success of the franchise and willing to work as hard toward that end than the owner of the franchise. Most managers are nothing more than just paid employees.

> The Franchisor, in this Item, discloses the franchisee's obligation to personally participate in the direct operation of the franchise business and whether the Franchisor recommends participation.

Item 16: Restrictions on What the Franchisee May Sell

Disclosed are restrictions or conditions imposed by the Franchisor on the goods or services that the franchisee may sell or that limit the customers to whom the franchisee may sell goods or services.

Under this Item, important issues to address include: Whether the restrictions on what the franchisee may sell are reasonable. Also, one needs to determine if local market conditions where one plans to locate a franchise would necessitate selling products or services in addition to those provided by the franchisor to ensure success.

> Disclosed are restrictions or conditions imposed by the Franchisor on the goods or services that the franchisee may sell or that limit the customers to whom the franchisee may sell goods or services.

Item 17: Renewal, Termination, Transfer, and Dispute Resolution

The provisions of the franchise and other agreements dealing with termination, renewal, transfer, dispute resolution, and other important aspects of the franchise relationship are summarized under this Item in tabular form. The categories that must be included in the table are:

- A. Length of the term of the franchise
- B. Renewal or extension of the term
- C. Requirements for the franchisee
- D. Under what conditions the Franchisor can terminate your franchise
- E. Under what conditions the Franchisor can terminate your franchise without cause
- F. Under what conditions the Franchisor can terminate your franchise with "cause"
- G. "Cause" defined—curable defaults
- H. "Cause" defined—defaults that cannot be cured
- I. Franchisee's obligations on termination/nonrenewal
- J. Assignment of contract by Franchisor
- K. "Transfer" by franchisee—defined
- L. Franchisor approval of transfer by franchisee
- M. Conditions for Franchisor approval of transfer
- N. Franchisor's right of first refusal to acquire franchisee's business

O. Franchisor's option to purchase franchisee's business
P. What happens upon the death or disability of the franchisee
Q. Noncompetition covenants during the term of the franchise
R. Noncompetition covenants after the franchise is terminated or expires
S. Modification of the agreement
T. Integration/merger clause
U. Dispute resolution by arbitration or mediation
V. Choice of forum
W. Choice of law

There is a lot of critical information provided in this Item and it must be carefully reviewed. Of particular importance is the length of the term of the franchise and under what conditions the franchise can be renewed or extended. Depending on the size of the investment required, it could take several years before you would be able to receive a return on your investment sufficient for you to invest in the franchise. Therefore, the term of the franchise must be for enough years to make your investment worthwhile. Also, of major importance: Under what conditions, listed by the franchisor, would the franchisor be able to terminate your franchise agreement without cause? More than just a few ways listed here is a huge red flag. All of these categories are important and need to be studied in detail.

> Of particular importance is the length of the term of the franchise and under what conditions the franchise can be renewed or extended.

Item 18: Public Figures

The following is disclosed concerning public figures (celebrities):

A. Compensation or other benefit given or promised to a public figure arising from:
   1. the use of the public figure in the franchise name or symbol; or
   2. the endorsement or recommendation of the franchise to prospective franchisees.
B. The extent to which the public figure is involved in the actual management or under the control of the Franchisor.
C. The total investment of the public figure.

Of particular importance under this Item is whether the celebrity being used by the franchisor actually uses the products and services of the franchisor. Endorsement by a celebrity is no guarantee of your success, especially if the celebrity doesn't use the franchisor's products or services. In this case, there is little value to such endorsements. How can the public figure convince people to purchase a product or service if he doesn't have enough faith in that product or service to use them himself? How can you sell someone on something if you don't have enough faith in the products and services to use them yourself?

> Endorsement by a celebrity is no guarantee of your success.

Item 19: Earnings Claims

A. An earnings claim or claims made in connection with an offer of a franchise must be included in full in the offering circular and must have a reasonable basis at the time it is made. If no earnings claim is made under this item of the offering circular, then this item must contain a prescribed negative disclosure.

B. An earnings claim, if made, shall include a description of its factual basis and the material assumptions underlying its preparation and presentation.

An earnings claim is one in which a prospective franchisee can ascertain what his range of actual or potential sales, costs, income or profit from franchised or nonfranchised units may be. Also, the franchisor is allowed to present claims regarding future performance. Most franchisors do not include an earnings claim in their UFOC. If a franchisor does not make an earnings claim in their UFOC, yet verbally or "on a napkin" gives you information from which to determine how much money you can make, you need to be very careful. Not only does this violate federal law, but you must ask yourself why the franchisor didn't put this in print in the UFOC. If a franchisor does publish an earnings claim, you need to carefully study it, along with your accountant, to determine if the numbers are representative of the entire system or just its best units, and how representative such claims would be concerning your proposed location.

Item 20: List of Outlets

The Franchisor must disclose the following:

A. The number of franchises of a type substantially similar to those offered and the number of Franchisor-owned or -operated outlets as of the close of each of the Franchisor's last three fiscal years. Franchises that are operational are segregated from franchises not yet operational. Disclosure is also segregated by state. Each category is then totaled.

B. The names of all franchisees and the addresses and telephone numbers of all of their outlets must be listed.

C. The estimated number of franchises to be sold during the one-year period after the close of the Franchisor's most recent fiscal year.

D. The number of franchisee outlets in the following categories that, for the three-year period immediately before the close of Franchisor's most recent fiscal year have:
   1. transferred controlling ownership
   2. been canceled or terminated by the Franchisor
   3. not been renewed by the Franchisor
   4. been reacquired by the Franchisor
   5. been reasonably known by the Franchisor to have otherwise ceased to do business in the system

E. The name and last known home address and telephone number of every franchisee who has had an outlet terminated, cancelled, not renewed, or otherwise voluntarily or involuntarily ceased to do business under the franchise agreement during the most recently completed fiscal year or who has not communicated with the Franchisor within 10 weeks of the application date.

> The names of all franchisees and the addresses and telephone numbers of all of their outlets must be listed.

The information gathered here not only tells you how large the franchise system is and in what states franchises are located, but also the names and addresses of current franchisees. It is important to contact several current franchisees and ask questions. Who best to answer your questions than those in the field. Who can really tell you whether the franchise is profitable or not? This way you are able to substantiate the information provided by the franchisor. Furthermore, you can call those franchisees who were canceled, terminated, and/or not renewed to find out why.

Item 21: Financial Statements

Financial statements in accordance with generally accepted accounting principles must be disclosed. These financial statements must be audited by an independent certified public accountant. Unaudited statements may be used for interim periods. The following financial statements are to be included.

> Financial statements in accordance with generally accepted accounting principles must be disclosed.

A. The Franchisor's balance sheets for the last two fiscal year ends before the application date. Included are statements of operations, of stockholders equity, and of cash flows for each of the Franchisor's last three fiscal years. If the most recent balance sheet and statement of operations are as of a date more than 90 days before the application date, then an unaudited balance sheet and statement of operations as of a date within 90 days of the application date is also included.

B. Affiliated company statements. Instead of the disclosure required by Item 21(A), the franchisor may include financial statements of its affiliated company if the affiliated company's financial statements satisfy Item 21(A) and the affiliated company absolutely and unconditionally guarantees to assume the duties and obligations of the Franchisor under the franchise agreement.

It is very important to have the financial statements reviewed by your accountant, so that he or she can, as an expert, advise you on the financial soundness of the franchisor and whether the franchisor has the financial strength to operationally service its current franchisees and projected system growth. If any of the financial statements are unaudited, except for those for the interim periods, it is a violation of the federal disclosure laws and may raise serious questions as to why they were not audited.

Item 22: Contracts

A copy of all agreements proposed for use or in use regarding the offering of a franchise, including the franchise agreement, leases, options, and purchase agreements, must be attached as exhibits to the UFOC.

You need to carefully review all agreements attached as exhibits to the UFOC required by this Item. Since you will be required to sign at least some, and possibly all, of these agreements (contracts) you need to be aware of what you are agreeing to, so that you don't sign off on something you later find you can't uphold, or wouldn't have agreed to if you were aware of all the provisions. It is important to have an experienced franchise attorney (not a business attorney) review these contracts and advise you accordingly.

> You need to carefully review all agreements attached as exhibits to the UFOC.

Item 23: Receipt

The last page of the offering circular is a detachable document acknowledging its receipt by the prospective franchisee. It must contain the following statement in boldface type:

This offering circular summarizes certain provisions of the franchise agreement and other information in plain language. Read this offering circular and all agreements carefully.

If (Franchisor's name) offers you a franchise, (Franchisor's name) must provide this offering circular to you by the earliest of:

1. the first personal meeting to discuss the franchise; or
2. ten business days before the signing of a binding agreement; or
3. ten business days before a payment to (Franchisor's name).

You must also receive a franchise agreement (completely filled out) containing all material terms at least five business days before you sign a franchise agreement.

If (Franchisor's name) does not deliver this offering circular on time or if it contains a false or misleading statement, or a material omission, a violation of federal and state law may have occurred and should be reported to the Federal Trade Commission, Washington, D.C. 20580 and (State agency).

Conclusion

The required disclosure document is critical for several reasons. First, it can be an effective sales tool for the franchisor in setting forth positive information about his franchise. Additionally, a full disclosure helps to prevent any misunderstandings or false assumptions made by a prospective franchisee. Finally, a franchisee is able to make a fully informed and well-thought-out decision on whether or not to purchase the franchise. It is important that both the franchisor and prospective franchisee make a fully informed decision as concerns the other. It is almost always a disaster when someone who is qualified financially but not qualified and capable to operate within the franchise system becomes a franchisee. The lack of a fully informed decision by either party often leads to failure, which helps no one. Now that you know what is required to be disclosed, don't let the UFOC ambush you.

> It is important that both the franchisor and prospective franchisee make a fully informed decision as concerns the other.

For more information on this topic, visit our Web site at www.businesstown.com

Fear Not—The Contract Is Here

1: ALMOST ANYONE CAN BE A FRANCHISEE

2: THE RULES OF THE GAME

3: THE UNIFORM FRANCHISE
   OFFERING CIRCULAR (UFOC)

4: THE UFOC—THE REST OF THE STORY

5: FEAR NOT—THE CONTRACT IS HERE

6: YOU CAN NEGOTIATE THE RULES
   OF THE GAME!

Introduction

No two franchise agreements are the same, although all franchise agreements have similar provisions. Each franchise system has terms and conditions in its franchise agreement that are unique because of the differences in operation among franchise businesses.

It will become evident in your review of the franchise agreement, that it was written to afford the maximum protection and benefit possible to the franchisor and not to you, the franchisee. After all, it was the franchisor and his attorneys that drafted the contract.

Once you have been presented with the franchise agreement, the franchisor will encourage you to sign the contract "as is" and to make no changes. However, you must take your time and carefully review the contract. It is to your benefit to have a qualified franchise attorney review the agreement, since after all, you are probably not a lawyer, or at least not up to date on franchise law.

Also, it is important to have an accountant review the agreement as well. He or she could better explain your obligations as they pertain to financial items, accounting items, and bookkeeping items. Everything in a contract, including a franchise agreement, is negotiable and can be changed if both parties agree to it.

Clauses Most Franchise Agreements Have in Common: What to Expect

There are many types of businesses that franchise. Each industry has items that are peculiar to that industry and, therefore, will only be found within the agreements that pertain to the franchised businesses within that industry. However, there are certain key elements of a franchise agreement that are basic to all franchise systems. The basic key items common to all franchise agreements are as follows:

1. **Recitals:** Also referred to as introductory preliminaries, recitals appear at the beginning of the franchise agreement. This portion of the franchise agreement names the parties entering into the agreement, the date of the agreement and lists the basic mutual benefits of entering into the contract, and the distinctive components of the relationship. Additionally, the recitals often include a definition of

the franchise system and identify the trademarks that will be licensed to the franchisee. Importantly, there will probably be language to the effect that you have read the UFOC and the franchise agreement in their entirety, and that you accept and agree to abide by all of the terms, provisions, and covenants found in them, and that they are reasonable and necessary to the viability of the system. Sometimes this clause is included at the end of the franchise agreement under an item marked miscellaneous.

2. **Grant, Term, and Renewal:** After the initial recitals, the franchise agreement will state a specified period of time in which you are granted rights to operate a franchise. Included will be language stating that in accepting the right to operate a franchise, you will operate the business only in conformity with the company's standards of operation, which are for the most part, found in its operations manual.

In addition to granting you a franchise for a specific term, there will also be language concerning renewal rights. This allows you to renew your franchise for a specified period of time after the expiration of the initial term. This section will state the conditions to be met before the franchisor will allow the renewal of the relationship. Also addressed are items such as renewal fees, obligations to execute the then current form of the franchise agreement, and obligations of the franchisee to renovate and upgrade its facilities to the latest standards and designs.

3. **Territory:** Most franchises, in this section, will grant you the right to operate a franchise only at a specific location. The franchisor then, normally, will reserve the right to place other franchised units and/or company units anywhere it wants around your specified location without restriction. Occasionally, a franchisor will grant you a specified territory, which is usually a defined geographical area. If you are granted an exclusive territory, it will be specified in this section, and the size of the territory (as well as what the size is based on, such as a radius or a population count) will be indicated. An exclusive territory means that the franchisor cannot locate another unit, whether franchise or company, within your territory.

> The franchise agreement will state a specified period of time in which you are granted rights to operate a franchise.

4. **Site Selection:** The responsibility for finding a specific site where the franchise business will operate is generally that of the franchisee, with the franchisor's approval. However, it could also be the responsibility of the franchisor. This section indicates who is responsible for site selection and what assistance the franchisor will provide the franchisee in finding a location. Almost always, if the franchisor does not approve the site, the franchisee is not allowed to locate there. Also included could be items dealing with leasing arrangements and obtaining lease approval from a landlord.

5. **Development and Improvement:** Most franchise agreements dictate that within x number of days or months after the execution of the franchise agreement, the franchise business must be open and operating. The period of time in which you have to find your site and open and operate your business could be as short as 90 days. Often, there are provisions that dictate that if you fail to open the franchise business within the allotted period of time, you will either be penalized in the form of an additional fee you must pay, or the franchisor might reserve the right to terminate the franchise agreement. You must be careful with the language here to make sure you have adequate time in which to open your franchise business.

6. **Services to be Provided by the Franchisor:** The products and services to be provided to the franchisee by the franchisor or its affiliates are stated here. Included will be those products and services to be provided during the preopening of the business and continuing assistance or support to be provided from the date of opening to the end of the term of the franchise agreement.

The responsibilities taken on by the franchisor within this section often include extensive training programs both before and after opening; on-site assistance and troubleshooting; location preparation; use of confidential operations manuals; accounting and bookkeeping systems; inventory and equipment specifications; standard construction, building, and interior design plans; grand opening promotion and advertising assistance, along with regional and/or national advertising and promotional campaigns. This section delineates the responsibilities of the franchisor

> Most franchise agreements dictate that within x number of days or months after the execution of the franchise agreement, the franchise business must be open and operating.

to the franchisee and what products and services it is required to provide to the franchisee.

7. **Fees Payable to the Franchisor:** The nature and amount of fees payable to the franchisor by the franchisee, both initially and on an ongoing basis, are listed here. Found here will be the size and payment terms of the initial franchise fee and whether it is refundable. Normally, the franchise agreement dictates that this fee is payable upon execution of the franchise agreement. This fee is for the granting of the franchise and the franchisee's use of the franchisor's trademarks, trade secrets, training and assistance, etc.

Also included here is the royalty fee, its amount, and payment terms. This is an ongoing fee that is normally fixed as a percentage of gross sales payable weekly or monthly. Another category of recurring fees is an advertisement fee or a contribution to a national cooperative advertising and promotion fund. This is also normally a percentage of gross sales payable weekly or monthly. Any other fees payable to the franchisor either initially, or which will be ongoing, will also be included. These could be fees for the sale of goods and services to the franchisee by the franchisor; consulting fees; audit and inspection fees; renewal fees; transfer fees; and so on.

> Also included is the royalty fee, its amount, and payment terms. This is an ongoing fee that is normally fixed as a percentage of gross sales payable weekly or monthly.

8. **Reporting Requirements:** This provision provides that the franchisee must prepare and give to the franchisor, either weekly or monthly, detailed reports of its sales activity. If the franchisee must maintain its records in electronic or computerized form in a format set forth by the franchisor, it is also stated. The franchisor reserves the right to physically inspect the premises of the franchise business and review the franchisee's financial books and records. If, after an inspection and audit of the records, it is found that the franchisee has under-reported its sales and hence payment of royalties to the franchisor, the franchisor will charge a fee to compensate for its expenses in performing the audit.

9. **Advertising and other Promotional Activity:** Franchise systems, usually over 100 units in size, often have requirements as to the advertising and promotional activity of the franchise business. This section will regulate the content and appearance of advertising, through what means the franchisee can promote its business, and what type of regional and/or national advertising will be provided by the franchisor.

10. **Quality Control (Image and Operating Standards):** In this section there are a variety of provisions designed to ensure quality control and consistency throughout the franchise system. This section includes what products and services, if any, must be purchased from the franchisor. Those items and services not required to be purchased from the franchisor can be purchased from other sources. Normally the franchisor places restrictions on the franchisee's sources of products and services to maintain quality control and consistency. Therefore, most franchisors have an approved list of suppliers you must buy from and will state under what conditions they will approve a new supplier. Other operating procedures that could be found here include, hours of operation, insurance requirements, operating standards, and so on.

11. **Insurance Requirements:** The franchisor will require the franchisee to carry various kinds of insurance in varying amounts for not only the franchisee's protection, but the franchisor's protection as well. Typically, the franchisor will be named as an additional insured under these insurance policies. Also, the franchisee will be required to indemnify the franchisor for any damages or judgments against the franchisor that result from the franchisee's negligence in its operation of the franchise business.

12. **The Obligations of the Franchisee:** This section dictates the responsibilities and obligations of the franchisee. For example, the franchisee will be obligated to follow every detail of the prescribed business operation as found in the confidential operations manuals and other materials provided by the franchisor. The franchisee will be obligated to maintain and enforce quality control standards, not only as they pertain to the franchise business, but also to its employees and suppliers as well. Generally, the franchisee

This section includes what products and services, if any, must be purchased from the franchisor. Those items and services not required to be purchased from the franchisor can be purchased from other sources.

will be required to comply with all applicable federal, state, and local laws that pertain to the operation of the franchise business.

Additionally, the franchisee will have a duty to upgrade, renovate, and maintain the facilities and equipment along with the obligation not to sell goods and services that are not approved by the franchisor. Often in this section there will be a requirement that the franchisee must personally participate in the day-to-day operations of the franchise business.

13. **Transfer and Assignment of the Franchise Agreement:** This section normally contains a strict obligation on the part of the franchisee not to transfer the franchise agreement without the prior written approval of the franchisor. Additionally, the franchisee cannot assign the franchise agreement.

Further, if the franchisee wants to sell its business, then normally the franchisor will reserve the first right of refusal. It is very common for the franchisor to include several restrictions and covenants in this section in order to ensure that the franchise business is not transferred to a person or persons whom the franchisor would not have otherwise approved as being competent to operate one of its franchises.

14. **Condemnation and Causality:** The franchisor will state under what terms and conditions you can cease operating your franchise business without penalty, such as if your location is condemned by a government entity through its rights of eminent domain, or your facility is destroyed due to a natural disaster.

15. **Default and Termination:** All franchise agreements include a section dictating under what conditions you will be found to be in default of the franchise agreement and under what circumstances you can be terminated. The vast majority of grounds for termination will include the right of the franchisee to cure the default within a set period of time, thereby avoiding termination.

However, there will be certain conditions included under which, if they occur, your franchise agreement will be automatically terminated with no right to cure the default. For example, some franchise agreements

> If the franchisee wants to sell its business, then normally the franchisor will reserve the first right of refusal.

contain a clause to the effect that if the franchisee should die or become permanently disabled, the franchisee's family cannot inherit the business, and that the franchise business will revert back to the franchisor. Also listed will be the administrative provisions that pertain to the implementation and determination of defaults and their cures, and when termination occurs.

16. **Obligations of the Franchisee on Termination or Expiration:** Once the relationship comes to an end and the franchise agreement has either been terminated or has expired, the franchisee will be required to immediately cease using the trademarks and any other identifying features of the franchise business.

   For example, the ex-franchisee will be required to take down any signs, remove all forms of decor, color scheme, and other designs that would identify the franchise. Often there will be a provision that the franchisee must turn over to the franchisor the telephone numbers it had been using for its business.

17. **Intellectual Property Protection and Noncompetition Covenants:** The franchise agreement will dictate when and how you can utilize the franchisor's trade secrets, trademarks, copyrights, and patents. This section will dictate that these items can only be used in conjunction with the business. If you see that someone unauthorized is using the franchisor's intellectual property, then you must notify the franchisor immediately.

   Also the franchisor will set forth various forms of noncompetes. For example, once you leave the franchise system, the noncompete might state that you will be unable to enter into a like business for a one- to two-year period. There can be other types of noncompetition covenants in which you are not allowed to utilize any of the trade secrets or proprietary information learned or acquired from the franchisor. You may not be allowed to actively solicit employees or customers away from the franchise business.

18. **Relationship of the Parties:** You, as a franchisee, are not in an employment relationship with the franchisor, nor are you an agent

> The franchise agreement will dictate when and how you can utilize the franchisor's trade secrets, trademarks, copyrights, and patents.

of the franchisor. The franchise agreement will make it very clear that you are nothing more than an independent contractor allowed to operate under the franchise system.

Often, the franchise agreement will dictate that you prominently display a plaque or sign in your business, in plain view of your customers, that tells them you are an independent contractor of the franchisor and not an agent or employee.

19. **Miscellaneous:** This is the last section in the franchise agreement prior to the execution page. This section includes a large number of boilerplate provisions that can be very comprehensive.

For example, this section states that it is the final agreement and supersedes all previous agreements between the parties. It might contain a covenant "not to sue." This means you have given up your right to sue the franchisor upon termination or expiration of your franchise agreement. Often, this section specifies which state law will govern the interpretation of the contract and in what court a lawsuit must be filed if one is filed by the franchisee against the franchisor.

> **General Questions to Ask Yourself**
>
> 1. Have you read the franchise agreement in its entirety and do you understand all of its provisions and covenants?
> 2. If you understand all of the provisions and covenants in the franchise agreement, can you live with them if you sign the franchise agreement?

What Issues to Address Once the Franchise Agreement Is in Your Hands

You know you must sign a franchise agreement to purchase the franchise. You know what clauses to expect. Now you have been given a franchise agreement to sign. But you still have questions you need to ask and issues you need to address. Once the franchise agreement is in your hands you know that you are almost to the point of no return in your purchase of this particular franchise. Therefore, not only must you review this agreement in its entirety, but you need to know what questions to be asking.

The following is a list of questions that you should ask prior to signing the franchise agreement. If these questions are not answered within the franchise agreement, then they need to be directed to and answered by the franchisor. This list of questions is by no means complete.

Therefore it is imperative that you have a qualified franchise attorney review the agreement, since he or she will likely come up with additional questions to ask.

Grant, Term, and Renewal:

1. What is the length of your initial term?
2. Are there renewal terms, and if so, how many and what is the term of each renewal?
3. What are the requirements you must meet to be able to renew?
4. Is the initial term long enough for you to recoup your investment and make a reasonable profit?

> Does the franchisor reserve the right to place company-owned and/or franchise units anywhere around you it deems advisable?

Territory:

1. Are you given a specified territory in which to operate?
2. Are you given the right to operate a unit only at a specified location?
3. Does the franchisor reserve the right to place company-owned and/or franchise units anywhere around you it deems advisable?
4. Do you have an exclusive territory in which the franchisor cannot place any other franchise units or company-owned units within?
5. If you are given an exclusive territory, is your ability to maintain the exclusivity of the territory dependent upon you achieving a certain level of sales or other requirements?

Site Selection:

1. Who is responsible for finding the site?
2. Who negotiates the purchase and/or the lease for the site?
3. Who does the build-out at the site?
4. Does the franchise agreement require you to lease back the site from the franchisor?
5. Exactly what services does the franchisor provide in selecting a suitable site, and what are your responsibilities in locating and developing such a site?

Development and Improvement:

1. Is there a requirement that you must open the business within a certain number of days or months of the signing of the franchise agreement?
2. Is this period of time reasonable?
3. What will happen if you miss the deadline in opening?

Services to Be Provided by the Franchisor:

1. What training does the franchisor provide?
2. Does the franchisor provide initial training, on-site training, and ongoing training?
3. What on-site assistance does the franchisor provide?
4. What expenses or costs are you expected to pay for any of the training provided by the franchisor?
5. Does the franchisor provide you with operating manuals?
6. What responsibilities does the franchisor have for researching and developing new products and services?
7. What are all of the services that the franchisor is responsible for providing to you?

> What expenses or costs are you expected to pay for any of the training provided by the franchisor?

Fees Payable to the Franchisor:

1. Is an initial franchise fee required to be paid, and if so, is it refundable?
2. What is the amount of the royalty fee that is required to be paid?
3. In what time frame must the royalties be paid, weekly or monthly?
4. What is the percentage amount or dollar amount of the advertising fee?
5. Is the advertising fee payable weekly or monthly?
6. How are the royalty fees and advertising fees determined?
7. What other fees are required to be paid by the franchisee?

Reporting Requirements:

1. What records are you required to keep?
2. What is the franchisor's rights as concerns the inspection of your premises and records and the auditing of your records?
3. Is there an audit fee if it is found that you underreported your sales?
4. If such an audit fee is required, how is it determined? How much of a variance is allowed between what you reported and what the sales actually were before the payment is triggered?

Advertising and Other Promotional Activities:

1. How much of the advertising fee is spent for regional ads?
2. How much of the fee is spent for national advertising?
3. How much of the fee is spent for local advertising?
4. On what mode of advertising, such as print media, radio, or television will the monies on the local, regional, and national levels be spent?
5. Is any portion of the advertising fee used for administrative purposes? How much?
6. Do the franchisees have any input on how the money is spent for advertising?
7. What, if any, advertising materials, such as direct mail pieces, circulars, and so forth, are provided to the franchisees?
8. And if any are provided, is there a cost?
9. Are the franchisees entitled to a yearly audit on how the advertising dollars are spent?
10. What kind of advertising, and in what dollar amount, are you required to do on the local level?

How much of the advertising fee is spent for regional ads?
How much of the fee is spent for national advertising?
How much of the fee is spent for local advertising?

Quality Control:

1. Are the mandatory operating standards reasonable and necessary?
2. What, if anything, must be purchased from the franchisor?

3. Is there an approved list of suppliers, and if so, under what conditions can you get a new supplier approved?
4. Have you seen and reviewed the operations manual and how it interacts with quality control?

Insurance Required of the Franchisee:

1. What types of insurance are you required to maintain?
2. What are the dollar amounts required on the different types of insurance?
3. Are you required to have the franchisor as an additional named insured?
4. Are you required to indemnify the franchisor?

The Obligations of the Franchisee:

1. Have you made a comprehensive list of all of the obligations and responsibilities you are required to perform?
2. Once you have made such a list, are the items reasonable and necessary?
3. Are you required to upgrade and renovate your equipment, premises, and so forth, at set times, such as every five years, or upon renewal of the franchise agreement?
4. What is the extent of your obligation to maintain and enforce quality control standards within the franchise business, your employees, and vendors?
5. What is your obligation to promote the products and services of the franchisor?
6. Are you required to sell only those goods and services that the franchisor dictates?
7. Are you obligated to participate personally in the day-to-day operation of the franchise business?
8. Are you allowed to participate in a similar business as an owner, officer, manager, or employee?

> Have you made a comprehensive list of all of the obligations and responsibilities you are required to perform?

Transfer and Assignment of the Agreement:

1. Does the franchisor have a right of first refusal to purchase your franchise business if you decide to sell it?
2. What are the restrictions contained in the franchise agreement if you want to transfer or assign the franchise agreement to another?
3. If you should become disabled or die, will your heirs or successors lose all ownership rights to the business?
4. If you have a business entity that runs the franchise, must any transfers of stock within the corporation, or of membership interests within the limited liability company, or of partnership interests within the limited partnership, be approved by the franchisor?

Condemnation and Causality:

1. What happens if part or all of your location is condemned by the government?
2. What happens if part or all of your business is destroyed due to a natural disaster such as a fire, earthquake, tornado, or flooding?

Default and Termination:

1. Under what conditions can you be terminated?
2. Under what conditions can you be terminated automatically without notice and a right to cure?
3. Under what conditions are you given notice and the right to cure the default?
4. Are the default and termination provisions reasonable and necessary?
5. Does your state have laws preventing a franchisor from unilaterally terminating your franchise agreement without good cause?
6. Depending upon the default, is the amount of time given to remedy the default reasonable?
7. Do you fully understand all the reasons for which the franchisor can terminate you, and those reasons that require a

> If you should become disabled or die, will your heirs or successors lose all ownership rights to the business?

notice with a right to cure period and those that require no notice?

Obligations of the Franchisee upon Termination or Expiration of the Franchise Agreement:

1. What are your obligations upon termination or expiration of the franchise agreement?
2. What are the franchisor's obligations?
3. Will you have to vacate the premises?
4. Will you have to turn over your franchise phone numbers to the franchisor?
5. Does the franchise agreement prohibit you from operating a similar business?
6. If so, is it reasonable?

Intellectual Property and Noncompete Covenants:

1. Are the trademarks associated with the franchise business registered with the U.S. Trademark and Patent Office?
2. Does the franchisor have exclusive use of the trademarks or logos that are registered with the U.S. Patent and Trademark Office?
3. Are the trademarks and logos actually registered or has the franchisor merely applied for them to be registered?
4. Are there any other businesses, institutions, or people using the trademarks and logos that are associated with the franchise business?
5. Once your franchise agreement is terminated or expires, are there any noncompete covenants that you must abide by?
6. If so, what do they apply to and what is the period of time over which they can be enforced?
7. Do the noncompete covenants disallow you from entering into a similar business for a set period of time within a set geographical area?
8. Are there any restrictions on you actively soliciting employees and/or customers from your franchise business after the franchise relationship ends?

> Does the franchise agreement prohibit you from operating a similar business? If so, is it reasonable?

Relationship of Parties:

1. Does the franchise agreement make it clear that you are an independent contractor and not an agent or an employee of the franchisor?
2. Does the franchise agreement state that you are liable for any and all debts, liabilities, and taxes that you incur?

Miscellaneous:

1. Have you carefully reviewed the boilerplate provisions under this section to make sure that each of them is reasonable and necessary?
2. Is there a provision dictating which state laws apply to interpret the franchise agreement and in which court a lawsuit must be filed?
3. Is there a clause that says you have read and understood the franchise agreement prior to signing?
4. Is there an integrations clause that states that any and all previous conversations and/or agreements have been incorporated into this franchise agreement and that nothing not found in this franchise agreement is legally binding on the parties?

> Is there a provision dictating which state laws apply to interpret the franchise agreement and in which court a lawsuit must be filed?

Conclusion

This is only a partial list of questions for which you need complete answers. Depending on which industry the franchise business is in, there may be additional questions and/or different questions that should be asked. Therefore, you should be sure to seek the assistance of a qualified franchise attorney to review this list and formulate his or her own set of questions.

For more information on this topic, visit our Web site at www.businesstown.com

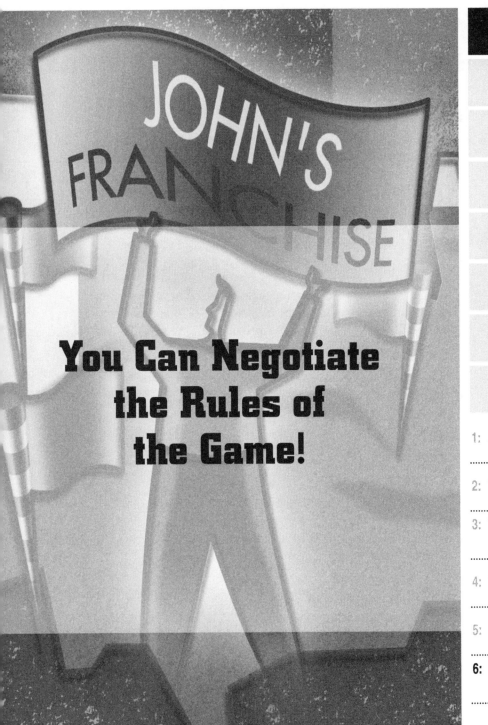

You Can Negotiate the Rules of the Game!

1: ALMOST ANYONE CAN BE A FRANCHISEE

2: THE RULES OF THE GAME

3: THE UNIFORM FRANCHISE
OFFERING CIRCULAR (UFOC)

4: THE UFOC—THE REST OF THE STORY

5: FEAR NOT—THE CONTRACT IS HERE

6: **YOU CAN NEGOTIATE THE RULES
OF THE GAME!**

Choose Your Battles

It might sound empowering to decide to attempt to renegotiate every single item in the franchise agreement, but this is self-defeating. If you decide to take this approach, the franchisor will likely feel that you are not serious about pursuing this opportunity and that you are requesting too many changes that will affect the uniformity and consistency of the system. Therefore, it is imperative that you decide what your priorities are in your negotiations with the franchisor. The only way to do this is to determine what your goals are for yourself and for your business.

Introduction

Naturally, the franchisor would like for you to accept the franchise agreement as written. After all, it is much easier for the franchisor to have franchisees sign off on the franchise agreement without any changes. This helps to maintain the consistency of the provisions throughout the system. However, it is to your benefit to negotiate at least those points that would make or break the deal for you.

Often, you will be told that the franchise agreement is non-negotiable because of federal and state laws and regulations. This is simply not true. However, there are practical restraints on the franchisor's ability to negotiate. Based upon franchise registration in some states, a franchisor is required to update its UFOC if a franchisee negotiates terms not disclosed within the current UFOC. Everything is subject to negotiation and nothing should be accepted as sacred.

Negotiation

There is a wide discrepancy among professionals as to how much one is able to negotiate. For example, if you are an individual franchisee purchasing the rights to establish one unit and you are dealing with an older and well-established franchisor, then chances are you will be able to negotiate very little. However, if you are purchasing multiple units and are dealing with a small franchisor wanting to expand, then your chances to negotiate are much better. But, there is a limit as to how far a franchisor will bend in its negotiations. Most major points of the franchise agreement will not be negotiable.

Know What Your Goals Are

Before you decide to negotiate, you need to take some time and determine what your goals are. What are you looking to achieve for yourself and for your business? In reviewing the franchise agreement, what provisions need to be renegotiated because they will determine whether you will execute the franchise agreement?

For example, do you want to have the ability to acquire additional units since you want to become a multi-unit franchisee? Or since you have other business interests, do you want to be an absentee owner and want to have the right to hire a general manager to operate your unit? Or is it important to you that upon renewal of your franchise the terms and conditions remain the same, as opposed to having to sign a new franchise agreement with different clauses and provisions? Is it important that you be able to pass your business to your family and/or heirs in the event of your death or disability?

Therefore, prior to your review of the franchise agreement, you need to take the time to determine what is important to you. Once you determine what is important to you and what your goals are, you know what to look for in your review of the franchise agreement. Then, if the terms and provisions of the franchise agreement are not in line with what you must have, you know what items you will need to negotiate.

How to Negotiate

In negotiations there are certain steps you need to take to be effective. A successful negotiation begins before you start bargaining with the franchisor. Prior to presenting your requests as to what you want negotiated, you must have your goals set, as explained previously. Once you have determined your goals and those items that you want to renegotiate, you need to decide what you will accept if your first position is unattainable and what you will settle for in negotiating each issue. Often, a franchisor will not want to negotiate. Therefore, it is critical that you are able to provide evidence and reasons why you need to change a provision. In other words, you need to have something to back up your position. If you have no evidence or lack a list of good reasons why a particular provision needs to be renegotiated, the franchisor will probably not budge.

The party that has the most leverage is the one who can most easily walk away from a negotiation if an agreement is not reached. Therefore, you need to identify several alternatives that will allow you to achieve at least some of your goals. Once it has been determined what the franchisor will negotiate, you need to know if it is enough to make the deal work for you or if you need to walk away. You need to clearly know under what circumstances you would be willing to call off the negotiations and leave.

> Prior to your review of the franchise agreement, you need to take the time to determine what is important to you.

Clauses Most Commonly the Subject of Negotiations

Everything in the franchise agreement is subject to negotiation. Some prospective franchisees will use a scattered approach by trying to renegotiate every provision. This is not good or appropriate. However, the vast majority of prospective franchisees have certain clauses that they want to try to negotiate and have changed, either completely or at least partially. The most common provisions the prospective franchisee tries to negotiate over are as follows:

1. The amount of the initial franchise fee and whether it can be financed. Many times the franchisee wants to reduce the amount of the initial fee or at least make provisions for payment in installments. Some want the franchisor to finance it.
2. The amount of royalties and advertising fees. Many times the franchisee wants to have the ongoing royalties, advertising fees, and similar fees reduced. However, the chances of success in this endeavor are very slim.
3. The renegotiating or elimination of other financial obligations of the franchisee to the franchisor.
4. Franchisor's right to purchase or lease the franchised premises. A franchisee might not want the franchisor to have the right to purchase or lease the franchise premises since the franchisee might want to retain the premises upon termination or expiration of the franchise agreement.
5. Term of the franchise. A prospective franchisee may want to lengthen the initial term of the franchise to allow more time to recover his or her investment along with a sufficient rate of return.
6. Renewal rights. You may want to have the right to renew the franchise agreement for additional periods of time. You may want to lessen the conditions under which you must abide in order to renew. Additionally, you may try to reduce the amount of any renewal fee required, and at the same time, request a longer period for the renewal term or increase the number of times the franchise agreement can be renewed. Also, you may try to negotiate it whereby you would not have to sign a new franchise agreement and abide by its new terms and conditions. On this point, the franchisor usually will not budge because the franchisor

needs to change the franchise agreement to correspond with changes within the system and with the competition.

7. Franchisee's right to acquire equipment, signage, products, services, or leasehold improvements from nonapproved sources. Usually the franchisor will require you to obtain products and services from it or from a list of approved suppliers. However, most franchisees want to have the ability to acquire these items from nonapproved sources provided that the nonapproved sources meet the reasonable requirements of the franchisor.

8. The right to sell nonapproved products and services. Many times there will be regional differences in consumer tastes and expectations. As a result, a prospective franchisee might want to negotiate the ability to sell nonapproved services and products. However, unless you have verifiable evidence confirming this, the franchisor most likely will not allow you to do this.

9. Territorial protection. Normally, the franchise agreement will give you the right to operate a unit only at a specified location. Therefore, most franchisees will try to negotiate some sort of territorial exclusivity. This can be based on having the exclusive right to operate within a certain distance from the unit such as a radius or some other geographical designation or based upon population. Usually, the franchisor will negotiate on this issue.

10. Covenants not to compete. Most franchise agreements contain covenants not to compete with the franchisor, not only while you are operating the franchise, but also for a period of time after termination or expiration of the franchise agreement. This is because the franchisor does not want you to use its trade secrets and other proprietary materials in operating a similar business. Consequently, usually all a prospective franchisee can do in this area is try to reduce the terms and conditions of the noncompete.

11. Transfer, assignability, right of first refusal. Normally the franchise agreement is very restrictive as to the terms and conditions that must be met before you are allowed to transfer or assign your franchise agreement. The reasoning behind this is that the franchisor does not want to have someone in the system who does not meet its qualifications. In this case, the franchisor will want to have a right of first refusal to purchase your unit in such an event. Even

A prospective franchisee might want to negotiate the ability to sell nonapproved services and products.

though the franchisor will want to keep most of its terms and conditions, you can negotiate certain terms. One such term is having the ability to transfer the unit upon your disability or death to a family member if the family member meets the current qualifications of the franchisor.

12. Options to acquire additional locations. Even though the franchise agreement will cover a specific location, often prospective franchisees want to have the option to acquire additional locations if the franchised business performs to expectations.

13. Default, rights to cure, termination provisions. This is an area in which you want to ensure that, with only rare exceptions, you have the right to cure any defaults under the franchise agreement or other agreements prior to being terminated. Also, you will want the time period in which you have the right to cure to be of reasonable length to correspond with the type of default.

14. Personal participation. Some prospective franchisees have other business interests. They want the right to hire a general manager to be involved in the day-to-day operations. Therefore, if the franchise agreement does not allow for an absentee owner, this provision will need to be changed.

15. Personal liability limitations. Most franchisors require that the individual franchisees be personally liable for any and all debt to the franchisor. However, if you will have a substantial investment in the franchise business, often you can renegotiate this provision to confine your personal liability to the assets of the franchise.

16. Training. If the amount of training is excessive or the expense of training is too great, then you will want to negotiate to lower your costs of training and to eliminate any unnecessary training.

17. Operational assistance. Occasionally, one will want to negotiate for greater operational assistance from the franchisor than what it has listed in the franchise agreement.

18. Build-out requirement. Most franchise agreements have a clause that dictates that you open the franchise location within a specified period of time. Often a franchisee will want to negotiate an extension to this period. Also, prospective franchisees want to build safeguards into this time frame by which they must be up

> Even though the franchise agreement will cover a specific location, often prospective franchisees want to have the option to acquire additional locations if the franchised business performs to expectations.

and running. After all, there could be delays beyond your control that you should not be penalized for.

19. Performance quotas. Occasionally, a franchise agreement will have certain specifications that obligate the franchisee to achieve a minimum market penetration within a specified time period. However, the prospective franchisee, due to his or her considerable investment in money and time, will often decide to renegotiate, feeling that the performance quota may be unrealistic for the franchise's particular market.

These are the most common clauses and provisions in franchise agreements in which the franchisee opts to renegotiate. However, what provisions you will try to renegotiate is determined by your goals and objectives and by what your franchise agreement actually contains.

Supplemental Agreements

Even though the franchise agreement is the heart and soul of your relationship with the franchisor, there will most likely be several other agreements you will be required to sign. Even though these other agreements are not as comprehensive as the franchise agreement, you still need to review these agreements with the same kind of completeness as you have the franchise agreement. It is very important that you have your qualified franchise attorney review these agreements as well.

The types of agreements that might require the signature of a prospective franchisee are too numerous to list here. Further, these agreements vary widely from one franchise system to another and from one industry to another. However, there are some supplemental agreements that a significant number of franchisors will have you sign. These supplemental agreements are as follows:

1. *Personal guaranty.* Most franchisors will have you sign a separate document in which each individual involved in the franchise agrees to be held personally responsible for the franchisee's obligations under the franchise agreement and any other agreements signed with the franchisor. This way the franchisor will hold you

> What provisions you will try to renegotiate is determined by your goals and objectives and by what your franchise agreement actually contains.

personally liable, as opposed to only being able to go after a corporation, limited liability company, or some other entity you have set up for tax and legal purposes to own the franchise.

2. *Assignment of lease option.* This agreement provides the franchisor with the right to be substituted as the tenant under the franchisee's lease (for the premises on which the franchise business is located). This agreement is exercisable upon the termination of the franchisee's franchise agreement.

3. *Employer-employee agreements dealing with nondisclosure and noncompete clauses.* These agreements are signed by the franchisee's employees. These agreements state that each employee that comes into contact with information that is of a proprietorial nature will keep it confidential. Often these agreements impose on the employees covenants not to compete so that they cannot take the proprietary materials and jump ship to a similar business.

4. *General release.* In this agreement the franchisee agrees to release the franchisor from all existing and potential claims the franchisee may have against the franchisor.

These four agreements are only a few of the agreements that you could be required to sign at the same time that you execute your franchise agreement. These agreements require the same degree of careful review as the franchise agreement.

Conclusion

The vast majority of franchisors will not present you a one-sided agreement because this is often a barrier to the sale of franchises. Most franchisors will start out with an agreement that reflects a balanced approach and tries to be mutually fair. Therefore most franchisors will not negotiate much because they do not want your contract to adversely affect those they have entered into with its other franchisees.

However, you should always try to negotiate the best deal possible based on your goals and objectives before making your final decision on whether or not to sign the franchise agreement. Often, the best deal is one in which both parties, you and the franchisor, have made compromises and concessions to come to a mutually beneficial agreement.

> Most franchisors will start out with an agreement that reflects a balanced approach and tries to be mutually fair.

Costs, Profits, Obligations, and Location

In this section, you'll learn:

- **The different fees required of franchisees**
- **How to compare and analyze the fees**
- **How to determine your profit margin**
- **Where and how to obtain the materials you'll need to run you business**
- **How to select the perfect site for your franchise**

CHAPTER 7 THE FEES (FRANCHISE FEE, ROYALTIES, ADVERTISING) **CHAPTER 8** EARNINGS CLAIMS: HOW MUCH MONEY CAN I MAKE? **CHAPTER 9** PRODUCTS AND SERVICES **CHAPTER 10** OBLIGATIONS **CHAPTER 11** LOCATION AND SITE SELECTION

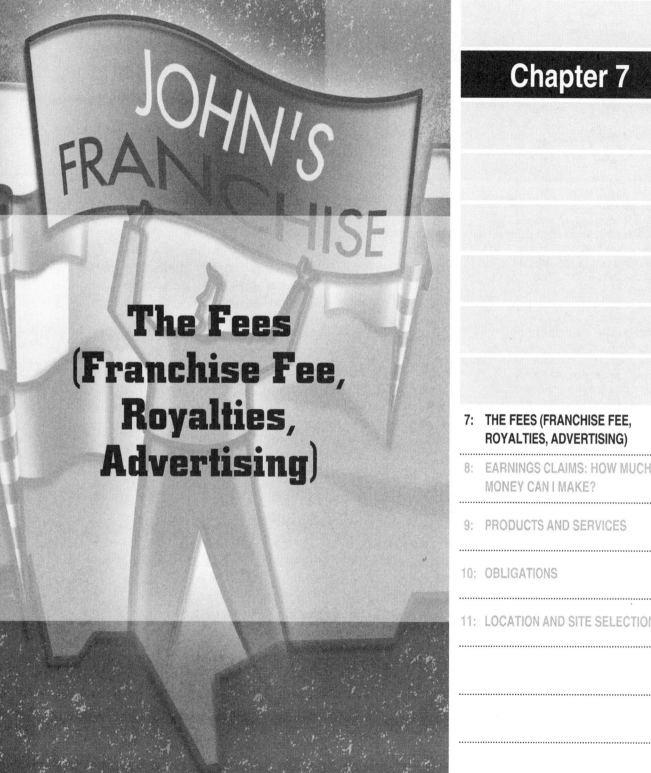

The Fees (Franchise Fee, Royalties, Advertising)

7: THE FEES (FRANCHISE FEE, ROYALTIES, ADVERTISING)

8: EARNINGS CLAIMS: HOW MUCH MONEY CAN I MAKE?

9: PRODUCTS AND SERVICES

10: OBLIGATIONS

11: LOCATION AND SITE SELECTION

Chapter 7

Get What's Right for You

It is important to determine if the fees charged by the franchisor you are investigating are comparable to those in other franchise systems. If they are significantly higher then you need to investigate further and ask the franchisor why. For example, your franchise system might charge more fees and a higher dollar amount per fee because it provides more goods and services, a higher quality of services and goods, and more comprehensive goods and services than its competitors. If you find such is the case in the investigation of your franchise system, then you will need to look at your own unique situation to determine if you need and will use these additional goods and services If you do not need these added extras, look into another franchise system within the industry that requires payment of lower or fewer fees because it provides fewer and less comprehensive goods and services.

Introduction

The prospective franchisee must investigate all costs associated with the franchise. Included in these start-up costs and operating costs are fees paid directly to the franchisor, or an affiliate of the franchisor, for services or goods received from the franchisor. Even though fees are a part of your initial investment, they are different from other start-up and operational costs, which are normally paid to third parties.

Costs for land, buildings, equipment, inventory, supplies, and so on are common to a business whether or not it is a franchise. Upon reviewing the UFOC, the franchisee will be able to determine those fees that are required by the franchisor and understand when and how these fees are to be paid to the franchisor. When reviewing these fees you need to compare them to other franchise systems within the same industry in order to determine how comparable these fees are to those required by other franchise systems. For example, is the initial franchise fee of the franchise system you are investigating significantly higher than those required by other franchise systems in the same industry? Are the royalties significantly higher in comparison to other franchise systems?

What Fees the UFOC Requires to Be Disclosed

To begin your investigation of the required fees, you must start by reviewing the franchisor's UFOC. The franchisor is required in the UFOC to discuss all fees, whether frequent or isolated, that are required to be paid to the franchisor and whether such payment is required prior to the opening of your unit or after your unit is opened and in business. To determine what fees are charged, review Items 5 and 6 of the UFOC.

Item 5 requires that the initial franchise fee be disclosed and list under what conditions this fee is refundable. The initial franchise fee is defined to include all fees and payments paid to the franchisor for services or goods received from the franchisor before the franchisee's business opens. This fee includes all fees and payments whether paid in a lump sum or in installments.

Item 6 sets forth all other recurring or isolated fees or payments that the franchisee must pay to the franchisor, its affiliates, or that the franchisor or its affiliates imposes or collects in whole or on behalf of a third party. These fees may require payment either before or after the franchised business is open. Examples of such fees are royalty fees, lease negotiation fees, construction fees, remodeling fees, advertising fees, group advertising payments, additional assistance fees, audit fees, accounting and inventory fees, and transfer and renewal fees. Some prospective franchisees feel that the fees charged by a franchisor are only limited by the franchisor's imagination.

Finally, Item 7 must be reviewed as well. Item 7 contains a list of all costs in the opening of the franchised business. Item 7 contains a comprehensive list of the initial investment. Contained in Item 7 may be some fees paid to the franchisor that are not covered in Items 5 and 6. Therefore, it is imperative that you review Item 7, as well, to determine if there are any hidden fees to be paid to the franchisor not previously disclosed in Items 5 and 6.

> **How the Initial Fees are Assessed**
>
> In determining the initial fee, the franchisor will take into consideration factors such as: its cost of recruiting a potential franchisee; the cost of training the franchisee; the cost of signs, advertisements, plans, or other services used in opening the franchise; the cost of assisting the franchisee with his or her business plan and other initial start-up items; the perceived value of the franchisee's market; and the perceived value of the franchised business.

Types of Fees to Be on the Lookout for

There are many types of fees. Some of these fees are listed in almost all UFOCs because most franchise systems charge these fees. However, there are other fees that are less common, but that you need to be on the look out for.

Fees Charged by Almost All Franchise Systems

The following fees are those most commonly found in almost all franchise disclosure documents.

1. **Initial franchise fee:** The initial franchise fee is paid by the franchisee upon signing the franchise agreement. This payment gives the franchisee the right to open a single franchised unit at a particular location and to use the franchisor's trade name, operating manuals, other particulars

Questions to Ask About the Initial Franchise Fee

1. How much is the initial franchise fee?
2. What do you receive in exchange for the initial franchise fee?
3. Does the initial franchise fee include items such as the right to use the franchisor's trademarks, patents, and copyrights; training; site selection assistance; start-up advertising; promotional expenses; grand opening expenses; and so on?
4. Does the initial franchise fee vary from one location to another, and if so, why?
5. How does the initial franchise fee for this system compare to the initial franchise fee paid by franchisees in other systems in the same industry?

of the franchise system, and so on. Sometimes this fee gives the franchisee the right to open multiple units within an exclusive territory in which the franchisor is not allowed to place other franchised units or company units. The initial franchise fee normally covers the initial training of the franchisee and other services provided by the franchisor, which enables the franchisee to get up and running.

Often, the initial franchise fee is viewed as giving that franchisee the right to open a franchised business at a particular location utilizing the system that the franchisor has developed. The initial franchise fee can vary from $500 to $75,000 or more. Most initial franchise fees are in the range of $10,000 to $30,000. It is rare for a franchise system not to have some type of initial fee. The amount of the initial franchise fee is set by the franchisor to cover the costs it incurs in putting the franchisee in business.

The franchisor's determination of the amount of its initial franchise fee depends on the franchise system and what is required to open a unit. For example, some franchisors require you to construct a building for your unit and will include in the initial franchise fee the cost of the architectural plans and blueprints it provides. Also, if a franchisor assists you with site selection and with your grand opening, then, included in the initial franchise fee, will be a cost component for this as well. Therefore, it is important to ask the franchisor what services and benefits you will receive in return for payment of the initial franchise fee.

2. **Royalty Fees:** The royalty fee is the fee that becomes payable on an ongoing basis once the business is opened. The royalty fee is paid either weekly or monthly by the franchisee to the franchisor. It is usually a percentage of gross sales; however, sometimes it is a fixed amount. For example, if your royalty fee is 5% then for every dollar of sales that you have in your franchise business, you will send five cents (or 5% of each dollar) as an ongoing royalty payment to the franchisor. In most cases, the royalty fee is charged on either the gross sales or net revenues of the franchised unit.

Even though the average franchisee's royalty fee is 5% of gross sales, royalty fees can range anywhere from ½ of 1%, all the way up to 15% of gross sales. The royalty fee should reflect the worth of your franchise and the maturity of the franchisor. Therefore, it is quite common for a fairly new franchisor to charge a relatively low royalty fee as opposed to a substantially higher royalty fee charged by a franchisor who has been in existence for years and is extremely well known. There are a number of questions the franchisee should ask the franchisor concerning the royalty fee, including the following:

- How much is the royalty fee?
- How often is the royalty fee to be paid—weekly, monthly, other?
- Is the royalty fee a percentage or is it a fixed amount?
- If the royalty fee is a percentage, what is the percentage based on—sales? net revenues? other?
- If the royalty fee is to be paid on gross sales, how are gross sales defined?
- Are royalty fees due even on the tax dollars you must pay to various governmental authorities?
- How does the royalty fee for your franchise compare to the royalty fee paid by franchisees of other franchise systems in the industry?

> The royalty fee should reflect the worth of your franchise and the maturity of the franchisor.

3. **Advertising Fees:** Advertising fees are the third major fee required by the franchisor to be paid by its franchisees. Normally an advertising fee is based upon a percentage of gross sales or net sales; yet sometimes it is a stated amount. Advertising fees are used to advertise the franchise system. Often these fees are deposited into a regional or national account on behalf of all franchisees in that region or nationally. Sometimes a franchisor has an advertising cooperative to which the fee is paid. An advertising cooperative is comprised of a group of franchise units (and company units) of a franchise system who contribute money to the cooperative for it to engage in advertising on behalf of the group.

Item 11 of the UFOC requires extensive disclosure regarding advertising fees and advertising funds. You must carefully read Item 11 to determine what you will receive in exchange for the advertising fees. If you have

Where to Put Ad Fees in the Budget

Typically, advertising fees are paid into a special cooperative fund set up to segregate advertising fees from other monies the franchisor receives. However, in some cases, the money ends up in the franchisor's general operating fund.

any questions, you must ask the franchisor so there won't be any misunderstandings. Advertising fees vary from one franchise system to another, but typically range from 1% to 5% of gross sales. Sometimes the advertising fee is a flat fee paid on a monthly basis. However there is a substantial number of franchisors that do not require payment of an advertising fee. Most of these franchisors are in their start-up phase and have very few units, and as a result would not achieve any real increase in sales or awareness through a regional or national advertising program. However, even those franchisors require the franchisee to spend a certain amount of money for local advertising. There are several questions one should ask a franchisor concerning advertising fees. Some of the questions that need to be asked are:

- Does the franchise agreement allow the franchisor to spend the franchisee's advertising royalties anyway it sees fit?
- How much is the advertising fee required by the franchisor and how does it compare to other franchise systems within the industry?
- Do all franchisees pay the same advertising fees, or does it vary among the existing franchisees?
- Is the advertising fee a set dollar amount paid monthly or is it a percentage fee based upon gross sales or some other measurement to be paid weekly or monthly.
- Is the franchisor large enough so that your advertising fee will result in a benefit to your franchise business?
- How much of the advertising fee is spent on advertising?
- How much of the fee is spent on regional advertising? National advertising?
- Will the advertising fees spent on regional and/or national advertising benefit your location?
- How much are you required to set aside for local advertising?
- Is any of the advertising fee used for administrative purposes, and if so, how much?
- Are audited figures on how the advertising fees collected for the franchise system were spent available upon reasonable request?
- Are any advertising materials such as circulars, direct mail pieces, camera ready art, and other types of advertising materials provided to the franchisees?

- If advertising materials are provided to the franchisees, is there an additional cost other than the advertising fee for these materials?
- Are the franchisees allowed any input to determine how to use the advertising dollars?

Through the years there have been a large number of complaints from disgruntled franchisees about the franchisor's use of advertising funds. Additionally, there has been a ground swell of litigation on this issue resulting in some fairly significant decisions against the franchisor. Therefore, it is best to determine up front, prior to signing the franchise agreement, exactly what you will be receiving for your advertising fees.

Other Fees You Might Be Charged

Following are some of the fees that you may be charged depending upon the franchise system you purchased. Some of these fees are fairly common, but some are less common because they result from a unique service provided by a particular type of franchise system.

1. **Training fees:** Training fees are the fees that a franchisor charges to train you in the franchise business so that you will have the knowledge necessary to operate a unit successfully. This training occurs prior to your opening and operating the unit. Even though some franchisors charge an additional fee for training, most include this as a part of the initial franchise fee.
2. **Training of additional employees fees:** Some franchise systems will charge an additional fee per employee for training them. Most franchise systems will include in the initial franchise fee the training for the franchisee. However, some systems, even though they do not charge an additional fee for the franchisee, will charge for training they provide to the franchisee's employees.
3. **Ongoing training program fees:** Once your franchise business is open, there will be a need for periodic ongoing training.

> Through the years there have been a large number of complaints from disgruntled franchisees about the franchisor's use of advertising funds.

Comparison Shopping

The franchisee must make sure he or she does not pay too much for fees by comparing the fees charged by other franchise systems within the same industry. The franchisee's best defense against paying unreasonable fees is good research and comparison shopping. Therefore, one must perform a comprehensive investigation of all fees payable to the franchisor, to insure that the fees are reasonable.

This training could be in the form of video tapes sent to each franchisee, to requiring annual training of the franchisee at the franchisor's training facility.

4. **Consulting fees:** If a franchisor provides consulting services in connection with the operation of your franchise unit, then there will be an additional fee. Consulting can be in the area of managing your business, marketing, operational matters, on-site training, and so on.

5. **Site selection assistance fees:** If the franchisor provides assistance in locating a site, it will sometimes charge a fee. The size of the fee is in direct relation to the amount of assistance the franchisor gives you in selecting the site. Sometimes this fee is a special value location fee.

6. **Leasing fees:** If the franchisor leases directly to you, or provides for such leasing indirectly through a third party, for equipment, signage, buildings, and/or land, then often it will charge a fee for this service. Additionally, if the franchisor directly leases any of these items to you then you can expect your monthly lease payment to be increased by an amount sufficient for the franchisor to make a profit.

7. **Auditing fees:** Almost all franchisors will charge an audit fee. In the franchise agreement the franchisor reserves the right to audit your financial records in order to determine if you have been properly reporting your sales. If the franchisor determines, after such an audit, that you have underreported your sales, then it will charge an audit fee in an amount equal to its cost of the audit.

8. **Up-front security deposits:** This is sometimes referred to as a hidden cost or hidden fee to be paid to the franchisor. If you lease your equipment, signage, buildings, or land from the franchisor, frequently you are required to pay an up-front security deposit to the franchisor. Normally, the security deposit is payable back to you if you have met the terms and conditions of your lease agreement.

9. **Fees for plans and specifications:** Some franchise systems require the building or leasing of a facility in which to open your franchise business. In these cases, the franchisor will

provide you with plans and blueprints if you build a facility or specifications for leasehold improvements if you are improving an existing space.

10. **Grand opening fees:** Often franchisees will be charged additional fees for grand openings. Usually the franchisor will supply staff and promotional materials for the grand opening. For these services the franchisor charges a fee, which is based upon how much it provides for the grand opening in the form of staff and services.

11. **Accounting, data processing, and bookkeeping fees:** If the franchisor provides you with any services in the areas of accounting, data processing, or bookkeeping, then it will charge you a fee based upon the amount of service provided.

12. **On-site management assistance fees:** Most franchisors make provisions for providing on-site management assistance if a franchisee so requires. For this, the franchisor charges a fee, which is based upon the amount of staff and time needed for such assistance.

13. **Application fees:** Some franchisors charge a set fee that must be paid just to fill out an application, upon which the franchisor will base its decision on whether or not to approve you as a franchisee. This fee is nothing more than paying money to the franchisor to see if you are qualified to be a franchisee.

14. **Guarantee fees:** This is a fee charged by the franchisor to insure the execution of the franchise agreement. Though such a fee is rare in this country, it does occur with some frequency in franchises based in other countries.

15. **Exclusive territory fee:** Most franchisors will not give you an exclusive territory within which they will not open another unit, whether it be a company unit or another franchise. Those franchisors that do provide an exclusive territory will probably charge you a fee. This fee can either be a set dollar amount or it can be based on a formula such as the size of the territory or the number of residents within the territory. For example, one such franchise that awards exclusive territories charges a fee that is equal to four cents, multiplied by the number of residents in the specified territory.

> Most franchisors make provisions for providing on-site management assistance if a franchisee so requires.

16. **Renewal fees:** Almost all franchisors charge a renewal fee to renew your franchise agreement for an additional period of time.
17. **Other fees:** You need to carefully review the UFOC of a franchisor, because there could be other fees listed that have not been covered within this chapter.

Conclusion

A franchisor must charge reasonable fees to cover all of its costs in the operation of its franchise system. Also, it must add enough to the fees it charges to make a reasonable profit. It is imperative that the franchisor charge fees not only in the appropriate amounts, but also the appropriate number of fees based on the services provided in order to cover all its costs and to stay financially healthy.

A franchisor must charge reasonable fees to cover all of its costs in the operation of its franchise system.

For more information on this topic, visit our Web site at www.businesstown.com

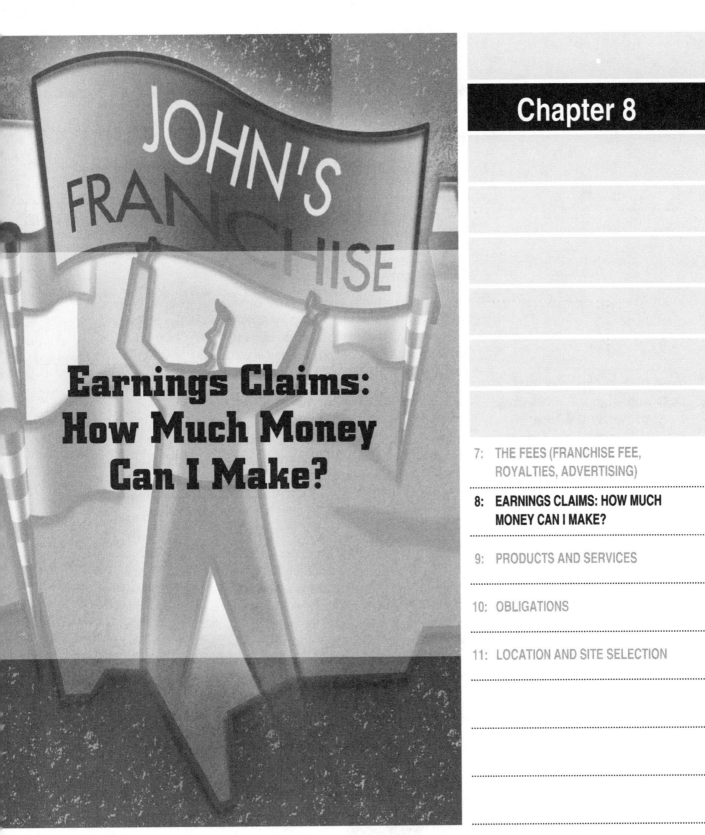

Chapter 8

Earnings Claims:
How Much Money
Can I Make?

7: THE FEES (FRANCHISE FEE, ROYALTIES, ADVERTISING)

8: EARNINGS CLAIMS: HOW MUCH MONEY CAN I MAKE?

9: PRODUCTS AND SERVICES

10: OBLIGATIONS

11: LOCATION AND SITE SELECTION

Introduction

What level of sales can I expect? How much income will I earn? How much will I make in profits? Just how much money can I make? These are very important questions, because after all, since you are buying a career and not a job, you want to know how much money you will earn.

Franchisors

Most franchisors recognize that earnings information is probably the most desired information sought by prospective franchisees before making their investment decision. However, despite considerable ongoing regulatory and legislative debate, the UFOC's disclosure requirements do not require that the franchisor make earnings claims though he may make detailed disclosures under Item 19. It has been estimated that only approximately 20% of all franchisors make earnings claims under Item 19. There are many reasons given by franchisors for their failure to make earnings claims.

First, let's discuss the disclosure requirements of Item 19 when a franchisor does make an earnings claim, followed by why most franchisors do not disclose earnings claims, and finally, how you can independently determine how much money you can make.

> Most franchisors recognize that earnings information is probably the most desired information sought by prospective franchisees before making their investment decision.

Earnings Claims Disclosure Requirements

The franchisor may choose whether or not to make a claim regarding actual or projected sales, costs, income, or profits of their franchise. Any earnings claims made in connection with an offer of a franchise must be included under Item 19 of the UFOC. Whatever is disclosed under Item 19 must have a reasonable basis at the time it was made and must include a description of its factual basis and the material assumptions underlying its preparation and presentation.

Required Disclosures

If a franchisor does make earnings claims under Item 19, it must also make the following required minimum disclosures:

1. The material assumptions underlying the preparation and presentation of the earnings claim, other than matters of common knowledge, must be disclosed. A material assumption is one that a reasonable prospective franchisee would consider important in making his or her decision regarding the franchise.

2. A concise summary of the basis for the claim, including a statement as to whether or not the claim is based on the actual performance of existing franchised units and, if so, the percentage of franchised units in operation for the period covered by the earnings claim that have actually obtained the stated results or have surpassed the stated results.

3. A conspicuous statement that a new franchisee's individual financial results are likely to differ from the results stated in the earnings claim in Item 19.

4. The franchisor must state that he will provide substantiation of the data used in preparing the earnings claims upon a reasonable request by a prospective franchisee.

Your BIG Question

In a survey by the *Wall Street Journal* of franchisors' primary prospects, the number one and most important question asked by prospective franchisees and the most important factor in their evaluating a franchise offering was what their return on investment would be. More than 72% of the respondents ranked potential return on investment as the most important factor in evaluating a franchise offering. Prospective franchisees want to know how much they can expect to earn.

No Earnings Claims

If no earnings claim is made by the franchisor under Item 19, the franchisor is still required to list what is referred to as a negative disclosure. This states that the franchisor does not furnish, nor does it authorize its salespersons to furnish, any oral or written information concerning the actual or potential sales, costs, income, or profits of a franchised unit. Also, the franchisor must state that the actual results would vary from unit to unit and therefore it cannot estimate the results of any particular franchise.

Finally, there are two last points to be considered. First, earnings claim means any information given to a prospective franchisee by the franchisor from which a specific level or range of actual or potential sales, costs, income, or profit from a franchise unit or a nonfranchise unit may be ascertained. In effect, if the franchisor does not disclose earnings information under Item 19, then for all practical purposes it cannot disclose any earnings information to a prospective franchisee. Second, a franchisor is allowed to make earnings claims limited solely to the actual operating results of a specific unit being offered for sale, without needing to comply with the disclosure requirements of Item 19, as long as such information is given only to the prospective franchisee who is thinking of purchasing that unit and it is accompanied by the name and last known address of each owner of that unit during the prior three years. Therefore, if you are considering purchasing an existing franchise that has been operational for a period of time, then the franchisor will be allowed to give you the actual operating results of that specific unit without running afoul of the disclosure requirements.

Why Franchisors Do Not Make Earnings Claims

There are several reasons franchisors cite as to why they do not make earnings claims, such as:

> Franchisors feel that there is great difficulty in making earnings-claim projections based upon actual past earnings due to the many variables that may affect such a projection.

1. The difficulty and cost of preparing earnings claims in accordance with the disclosure requirements
2. The difficulty and costs of satisfying varying and ambiguous standards of substantiation
3. Liability for possible misrepresentations or admissions

For Franchisors

There are risks in making even earnings-claim projections. You want to know not only how much money franchisees have made in the past, but you are also very interested in how much money you will be able to make in the future. However, by their very nature, projections are speculative. Franchisors feel that there is great difficulty in making earnings-claim projections based upon actual past earnings due to the many variables that may affect such a projection. Variables that could affect such a projection include the business location itself, the demographics and socioeconomic data for the area surrounding the business, and the experience, motivation, determination, and competency of the management of that particular franchise. Therefore, even if projections are made, if the franchisee fails to achieve the projected sales and profit levels, the franchisor is unwilling to take the risk of the franchisee filing a lawsuit for misrepresentation.

Franchisors often state that not only will they not make projections, but also they will not present historical earnings data from existing franchises under Item 19. The reason being that even though such historical earnings data is verifiable, such data may be felt by the prospective franchisee to contain an implicit representation of future sales and earnings based on the assumption that the variables accounting for the historical results will remain constant.

In summation, franchisors feel that earnings claims, whether actual or projected, are too costly to develop, the formula for determining them is too unreliable, and that they can result in a substantial increase in litigation against the franchisor by franchisees who did not do as well as they felt they were led to believe, due to misrepresentation by the franchisor.

How Do You Determine How Much Money You Can Make?

Even if the franchisor makes earnings claims under Item 19 of the UFOC, you must still be very careful. If you have gotten lucky and have decided to purchase a franchise from a franchisor who makes earnings claim disclosures, you are still not home free. You must still analyze the numbers that have been provided in the UFOC. You cannot blindly assume that you will achieve the same numbers since these numbers are generally just averages or estimates. Therefore, you must prepare your own financial projection for your business. However, if the franchisor has made earnings claims, there are several items you need to explore to determine the validity of the numbers as concerns you. The items you need to consider are as follows:

1. If an earnings claim is made you must look at the basis of the claim. Did the franchisor use historical figures or did he

The "Cocktail Napkin" Mistake

As a caveat, there are problems for a franchisor if it does not disclose earnings claims. A person employed by the franchisor who is trying to sell a franchise without being able to use earnings claims will be under pressure to make oral or other informal claims to a prospective franchisee with or without the knowledge or authorization of the franchisor. This has oftentimes resulted in the representative of the franchisor informally writing down certain numbers to indicate how much money the person could make if they purchase the franchise. Such "cocktail napkin" disclosures and other unauthorized earnings claim disclosures are very dangerous and have inspired significant litigation by franchisees claiming fraud and a violation of federal and state laws.

make projections that are essentially unsubstantiated? Were all units included in the calculations? Are the assumptions on which the franchisor based his earnings claims reasonable? What disclaimers have been set forth by the franchisor in relation to the earnings claim? Did an independent certified public accountant prepare the earnings claim? If so, was the earnings claim prepared in accordance with the American Institute of Certified Public Accountants' (AICPA) standards for projections? Also, do the earnings claim figures include all units lumped together so that you cannot determine how much money can be earned by a unit open for a year or two, as opposed to a unit that has been open for several years? It is very important to realize that a unit that has been open for five or more years will normally have a much higher level of sales and profits than a unit that has been open for only six months to two years.

2. You need to look at the sample size that a franchisor utilized in determining his earnings claims. A franchisor may claim that franchisees in its system earned, for example, $100,000 last year. This claim, however, may be deceptive if only a few franchisees earned that income and if the number does not represent the typical earnings of franchisees. Therefore, you should ask how many franchisees were included in the sample.

3. A franchisor may claim that the franchisees in its system earned an average income of, for example, $150,000 a year. The trouble with an average income figure is that it tells you very little about how each individual franchisee performed. It is very possible that a few very successful franchisees can inflate this average and, therefore, make it unrepresentative of the system in general. Therefore, an average figure may make the overall franchise system look more successful than it actually is.

4. Some franchisors may provide figures for the gross sales revenues of their franchisees. Even though gross sales revenues are an important indication of the success of the franchisees this number does not tell you anything about the fran-

> It is very important to realize that a unit that has been open for five or more years will normally have a much higher level of sales and profits than a unit that has been open for only six months to two years.

chisees' actual costs or profits. An outlet, for example, with a very high gross sales revenue may actually be losing money because of high overhead, high rent, and other expenses. After all, a unit in downtown New York City might have a gross sales revenue 5 to 10 times that of a franchisor's more typical unit, but due to the high costs of doing business in downtown New York City the franchisee could actually be losing money.

5. Occasionally a franchisor will provide you with net profit numbers on their franchisees. Usually the franchisor does not have such data, but if such appears under Item 19, ask whether the net profit numbers included company-owned outlets as well. Company-owned outlets might have lower costs because they can buy equipment, inventory, and other items in larger quantities or may own, rather than lease their property and equipment. If such is the case, this could artificially inflate the net profit that could be earned by the typical franchisee.

6. Earnings may vary in different parts of the country depending on the franchise. For example, an ice cream franchise in a southern state, such as Florida, may expect to earn much more income than a similar franchise in a northern state, such as Minnesota. Therefore, if you hear that a franchisee earned a particular income, you need to ask where that franchisee is located since the geographical location of a franchise can be a critical factor depending on the franchise and its products and services.

Last, but not least, even if the franchisor made an earnings claim presentation, it is still imperative that you speak to other franchisees in the system in order to obtain an estimate of the earnings potential of the franchise. You will want to speak with franchisees who are located in the same geographical region of the country you are in, particularly, if possible, within your same state. Also, you will want to talk to franchisees who are located in the same type of city environment you are going to be in, whether you are in an urban or rural area, and if they have the same size unit you have. Finally, you

Popeye's Chicken & Biscuits

Popeye's Chicken & Biscuits' UFOC states the following:

"These sales figures are for specific franchise and company restaurants and should not be considered as the actual or potential sales that will be achieved by any other franchise restaurant. We do not represent that any franchisee can expect to attain these sales results. Actual results vary from restaurant to restaurant and we cannot estimate the results of any specific restaurant. A new franchisee's results are likely to be lower than the results shown. We recommend that you make your own independent investigation to determine whether or not the franchise may be profitable, and consult with an attorney or other advisors before signing any franchise agreement."

Heel Quik!

Heel Quik! has a reputation for being the number one provider of shoe repair. However, it makes no earnings claims. But it is still possible to determine how much money you can earn, because of the availability of statistics that give a good idea of what percentage of each sales dollar goes towards operating costs. For example, it has been determined that, on average, the following costs are normally certain percentages of each sales dollar.

Material	20%
Labor	25%
Social Security and Unemployment	4%
	(17% of Labor)
Rent	10%
Utilities and Insurance	2%
Advertising	4%
Miscellaneous	2%
Franchise Royalty	4%
Total Operating Cost	71% of each sales dollar
Gross Sales	100%
Net Profit	29%
(before debt	of each sales dollar
service and taxes)	(based on actual sales
	and cost averages)

Now all you have to do is to determine a reasonable annual sales estimate and make allowances for cost adjustments due to items peculiar to where you plan to open your store. You have developed your own estimates upon which to base your decision.

will be most interested in talking to those franchisees who have been in business for only one to three years, since the earnings potential in the initial years is always lower than the earnings potential in later years when you are an established business.

How Do I Determine How Much I Can Make Without Information from the Franchisor?

Ask Others

The most important step in determining how much money you can make if there are no earnings claims made by the franchisor is to contact current franchisees. As stated previously, the best information you can obtain on how much money you can make will come from those franchisees who already own and are operating their own franchise business in the system you are considering. As noted earlier, you need to contact several franchisees to get this information so that your numbers come from several different sources, but at the same time you must make sure that each of these franchisees are substantially similar to you in the type and location of the franchise you will be operating.

Business Plan

There are ways to calculate the potential sales, cash flow, and profit of a franchise business, other than the earnings claim disclosure from the franchisor or by talking to other franchisees. One of the most important things you can do before making a franchise decision is to construct a business plan to forecast your potential earnings. A good business plan will predict your revenue from sales, types and amounts of expenses, and gross profit, along with predicting the cost of goods, including the cost of ongoing franchise warranties, setting budgets for your expenses, and forecasting your cash flow. Therefore, a properly drafted and conceived business plan can give you reasonable estimates of how much money you can make. In any good business plan you will have to use realistic estimates for most items.

> The most important step in determining how much money you can make if there are no earnings claims made by the franchisor is to contact current franchisees.

Cinnabon—World Famous Cinnamon Rolls

It is difficult to accurately predict how much money one can make. Therefore, the vast majority of franchisors make no earnings claims. The following disclosure taken from the UFOC of Cinnabon—World Famous Cinnamon Rolls points out these difficulties.

We do not make any representations or statements of actual, average, projected, or forecasted sales, profits, or earnings to franchisees with respect to our franchises. We do not furnish or authorize our salespersons to give you any oral or written information concerning the actual, average, projected, forecasted, or potential sales, costs, income, or profits of a franchise.

Actual results vary from franchise to franchise, and we cannot estimate the results of a particular franchise. We recommend that you make your own independent investigation to determine whether or not the franchise may be profitable, and consult an attorney and other advisors of your choosing before signing any agreement.

A good place to start is by using statistics from other businesses in the same field. You can estimate most of your future expenses simply by doing a little research. However, it would be to your advantage to hire a certified public accountant, business broker, or an investment counselor to formulate this business plan for you. Certain members of these three groups of people specialize in developing comprehensive business plans upon which people base their decisions in determining whether or not they want to invest in such a venture. Also, they are able to provide information such as average gross monthly sales of a store already established in your city, information about seasonal fluctuations, and other factors that would affect the sales of a business.

Additionally, a comprehensive business plan will provide you with the basis for obtaining financial assistance if you should require it as further discussed in the chapter on financing. You can go to your local small business development center that is supported by the Small Business Administration (SBA) to acquire information on how to construct your business plan and where you can attend seminars on this topic. However, depending upon your business background, more than likely it would be extremely beneficial for you to hire a professional who has a lot of experience in creating business plans. Why? Because you want the most accurate picture possible of just how profitable this venture will be and how much money you can earn since you are making one of the biggest decisions in your life—one that will have profound ramifications for your future.

Average Sales Figure per Unit

You, or the professional you hire, can begin collecting information from the UFOC even if no earnings claims are made. It is relatively easy to determine an average sales figure per unit in the franchise system by reviewing the franchisor's audited financial statements. Franchisees are highly unlikely to inflate their gross sales, especially since the royalties they pay are typically based on gross sales. As a result, the franchisor will have a strong incentive to prevent underreporting. Therefore, you can review the audited financial statements to determine the royalty income received by the franchisor. This will give you the combined gross sales of all the franchisees. First, you will divide the royalty income as stated in the audited financial statements by the percentage that is charged as a royalty rate.

This number will give you the combined gross sales of all the franchisees. Then all you need to do is divide this gross sales number by the number of franchised units in the company to get the approximate average sales per unit. Once you have average gross sales per unit, you can use this as a starting point for not only the gross sales you can expect from a unit in your location, but also for your business plan. Once you estimate what the gross sales will be for a particular location, often the professional you have hired will be able to consult research material that will indicate what your percentage costs will be for certain items like labor, equipment, food costs, and so on to determine what your estimated profit would be.

Finally, there are a couple of other points to consider in trying to determine how much money you can make. First, find out if the franchisor has any company-owned units. If it does, ask for their financial statements. If the franchisor is willing to make them available to you, these statements will give you important insights and information concerning significant financial issues. Also, the importance of the location of your franchise business cannot be underestimated. No matter how comprehensive and well done your business plan might be, it is meaningless if your franchise site is poorly selected. In essence, if a franchise business is located at a poorly selected site, you will fail regardless of what profits your business plan projects.

Once You Estimate Cash Flow

After you have developed your proposed franchise's future profits and cash flows, you will be in possession of very important information. Now you will have a realistic snapshot of how well this type of business can do in your own market, and you will have a clear view of how much you can expect to earn. You will also know how much working capital you will need to keep the business going until the business becomes profitable.

Conclusion

It is very important to determine how much money you can expect to make before you purchase your franchise. After all, you will be making one of the biggest financial decisions of your entire life. Such

Church's Chicken

Church's Chicken determines annual sales for its franchised restaurants based on the royalty reports submitted by franchisees. Church's Chicken does not audit the royalty reports submitted by franchisees because it has no information to indicate the reports are unreliable. There are 976 free-standing Church's Chicken restaurants in the United States and Puerto Rico, which includes both franchised and company locations. Of this number, 494 locations are franchises. By dividing the royalty income by the percentage royalty rate and then dividing this number by 494 it was determined that the average sales per free-standing restaurant was $649,934 for 1998.

a decision should not be made without adequate research and information. If you are fortunate, the franchisor from whom you are looking to purchase a franchise has disclosed earnings claim information, which you can use in determining the profitability of the franchise. However, even if the franchisor makes earnings claims, whether actual or projected, you must still do a comprehensive business plan. After all, the earnings claims provided by the franchisor are only estimates. Even though they may be carefully calculated so as not to be misrepresented, they may or may not be comparable to what you can expect, due to the unique factors affecting your location. There are intangibles such as differing costs of living and operating expenses in various parts of the country that also contribute to the difficulty of calculating earnings claims. Therefore, regardless of the information provided by the franchisor or by other franchisees, it is still imperative that you consult a professional in developing your own comprehensive business plan to make sure that your franchise will be a financial success.

For more information on this topic, visit our Web site at www.businesstown.com

Chapter 9

Products and Services

7: THE FEES (FRANCHISE FEE, ROYALTIES, ADVERTISING)

8: EARNINGS CLAIMS: HOW MUCH MONEY CAN I MAKE?

9: PRODUCTS AND SERVICES

10: OBLIGATIONS

11: LOCATION AND SITE SELECTION

Can It Last?

Before you accept point blank the franchisor's representations you must ascertain that its products and services are such that if you purchase one of its franchises you are bound to be successful. You must determine through your own research whether the franchisor's products or services are not only successful now, but will be successful throughout the term of your franchise agreement.

Introduction

The foundation of a successful franchise system is its ability to provide a product or service that the public needs, or feels it needs, and that is better than the competition's. One of the advantages of owning a franchise is that you will be offering the public established products or services. These products and services have already been proven and have name recognition, along with a reputation of being uniform, consistent, and of a high quality no matter where they are purchased. The marketability of the products or services has already been confirmed through the franchisor's efforts.

Therefore, before you commit to a particular franchise system, you must ask the following questions and receive appropriate answers:

1. What products and services must I offer to the public?
2. Can I develop my own products and services to offer to the public?
3. Can I offer other products and services of my own choosing?
4. What restrictions do I have, if any, on what products and services I can offer to my customers?
5. Where can I purchase the products and services I will be offering?
6. Can I purchase the products and services from a supplier of my own choosing or must I purchase the products and services from the franchisor or a supplier who has been approved by the franchisor?

It is important to receive complete answers to these questions. However, where do you start? Where do you go to find the answers? To search for the answers, you need to start at the beginning—the UFOC.

The Place to Start: The UFOC

The franchisor is required under the Federal Trade Commission Rule and UFOC guidelines to disclose restrictions it has placed on a franchisee as to what products or services it may sell and from what sources it is required to purchase such products and services. This information is disclosed under Items 8 and 16.

A. *Item 16—Restrictions on what the franchisee may sell.*
Under this item, the franchisor must disclose any restrictions or conditions it imposes on the goods or services that the franchisee may sell or that limits the customers to whom the franchisee may sell its goods or services. The franchisor must describe the franchisee's obligations to sell only its goods and services. Disclosed are franchisee obligations to sell all goods and services authorized by the franchisor, whether the franchisor has the right to change the types of authorized goods and services, and whether there are any limits on the franchisor's right to make changes.

From what is disclosed under Item 16, you will know what flexibility you will have to offer other goods or services at your franchised business. This is important if you need to sell goods or services that compliment the franchisor's goods and services or reflect local market conditions. You will find that some franchise systems impose no restrictions on the goods and services you can offer to the public. However, most franchise systems impose restrictions on the type of goods or services that the franchisee may offer. You must determine if the restrictions are reasonable and if they can have a negative impact on your bottom line.

B. *Item 8—Restrictions on sources of products and services.*
Under Item 8 the franchisor must disclose all restrictions on the sources from which you can purchase your products and services. More specifically, the franchisor must disclose obligations to purchase or lease from the franchisor, its designee, or approved supplier. The franchisor's specifications for its products and services are also listed. All goods, services, supplies, fixtures, equipment, inventory, computer hardware and software, and real estate relating to establishing or operating the franchise business on which restrictions are placed as to who you can purchase or lease these items from must be disclosed.

> From what is disclosed under Item 16, you will know what flexibility you will have to offer other goods or services at your franchised business.

Sample Franchising Agreement

The franchisee understands and acknowledges that every detail of the franchise system is important to franchisor, franchisee, and to other franchisees to develop and maintain high and uniform standards of quality, cleanliness, appearance, services, products, and techniques, and to protect and enhance the reputation and good will of the franchise system. Franchisee accordingly agrees:

1. To use all materials, supplies, goods, uniforms, fixtures, furnishings, signs, equipment, methods of exterior and interior design and construction, and methods of production and preparation prescribed by, and which conform to, the franchisor's standards and specifications.
2. To refrain from using or selling any products, materials, supplies, goods, uniforms, fixtures, furnishings, signs, equipment, and methods of production which do not meet with franchisor's standards and specifications.

(Continued on next page.)

The franchisor must state the manner in which it issues or modifies its product or service specifications and grants or revokes supplier approval. The categories of goods or services under which the franchisor or its affiliates are the only approved suppliers is also listed. Further, the franchisor must disclose under Item 8:

i. whether, and if so, the precise basis by which the franchisor or its affiliates will or may derive revenues or other material considerations as a result of required purchases or leases;
ii. the estimated proportion of required purchases and leases to all purchases and leases in establishing and operating the franchised business; and
iii. the existence of purchasing or distribution cooperatives.

Other information listed includes how the franchisor formulates and modifies the specifications and standards for its goods and services. Also described is the process by which suppliers are evaluated, and approved or disapproved, and whether the criteria set forth by the franchisor for supplier approval is available to its franchisees. Finally, the franchisor must state the procedure for a franchisee to follow in securing approval of a supplier, under what conditions such approval could be revoked, and the time period in which the franchisee will receive notification of approval or disapproval.

By reviewing Item 8, you can determine the following:

1. How much of the goods and services you are obligated to purchase from the franchisor, or affiliate of the franchisor, or approved supplier
2. How reasonable the franchisor's policy is for approving new suppliers
3. Whether the franchisor's product or service specifications are reasonable to ensure uniformity, consistency, and quality, or just a way to exercise more control over you and your operation

Why Does the Franchisor Have Such Requirements?

The franchisor has established its own products and services whose marketability has been confirmed by existing franchisees. Therefore, a franchisor will want you to concentrate your efforts on the sale and promotion of the products and services it has invested its time and efforts in developing. The public is already aware of the name and reputation of the product or service the franchise system offers. This can be a significant advantage to the prospective franchisee.

The franchisor can exert quality control standards over the products and services it has created. The franchisor also doesn't want the franchisee to spread himself too thinly by offering other products and services to the public. A franchisee has only so much time to learn everything necessary about the products and services it offers in order to effectively promote them and maximize their sales.

In order to maintain the consistency, uniformity, and high quality of the products and services that the franchisor has established, it will implement product and service specifications and product/service standardization. These specifications are precise and detailed descriptions of materials, goods, ingredients, and other items used in the operation of the franchise business. These specifications must be followed by the franchisee. Product standardization is the franchisor's effort to make sure its products and services are uniform and consistent as to quality, appearance, and character.

To protect the uniformity and high quality of its products and services, a franchisor often mandates purchase requirements. The franchisor may set forth product specifications, designate a supplier, or have an approved supplier list. If a product or service holds significant importance to the franchise system, the franchisor normally designates a specific supplier from which the franchisee must buy. The designated supplier could be the franchisor himself or an affiliate. When a franchisor sets such specifications often these products and services may be purchased from any supplier so long as the specifications are adhered to.

On a legal note, the franchisor must be careful if it requires that certain products and services only be purchased from the

3. To offer for sale any such products that shall be expressly approved for sale in writing by franchisor and to offer for sale all products that have been designated as approved by franchisor.
4. To maintain at all times a sufficient supply of approved products.
5. To purchase all products, supplies, equipment, and materials required for conduct of the franchise operation from suppliers who demonstrate, to the reasonable satisfaction of franchisor, the ability to meet all of franchisor's standards and specifications for such items; who possess adequate capacity and facilities to supply franchisee's needs in the quantities, at the times, and with the reliability requisite to an efficient operation; and who have been approved in writing by the franchisor. Franchisee may submit a written request for approval of a supplier not previously approved by the franchisor.

This selection came from a sample franchise agreement contained in The Complete Franchise Book *by Dennis L. Foster.*

Buy from Your Franchisor

Even though the franchisor may require you to purchase products and services from an approved supplier or from itself, there are positive benefits from this arrangement for the franchisee. If the purchasing program is set up correctly then this will enable the franchisee to obtain the goods and services at a lower price than it otherwise could. The reason for this is simple. If you have a limited number of approved suppliers, then each supplier will have a higher probability of major purchases being made from it, thereby resulting in quantity discounts for the franchisee. In addition to quantity discounts, the franchisee should be able to count on better customer service, timely delivery, and an overall better working relationship with the supplier. Therefore, if the franchisor sets up approved suppliers in the right way, the franchisees will have what amounts to group purchasing power, which will allow them to obtain not only lower prices but better service and overall higher quality.

franchisor because then it could be in violation of antitrust laws, which encourage competition and discourage tying arrangements. Tying arrangements are illegal. An illegal tying arrangement exists when the franchisor requires you to purchase not only the desired product or service from it but a second product as well. To require a franchisee to purchase one or more secondary items in order to get a required primary item is illegal unless the products so tied together are an integral component of the business method being franchised.

What kind of language can you expect to find in the franchise agreement concerning the franchisor's requirements? A franchisor's requirements concerning what you may sell and from whom you can purchase your goods and services would look like the following taken from a franchise agreement:

IF YOU MUST SELL ONLY THE FRANCHISOR'S PRODUCTS AND SERVICES AND/OR PURCHASE THEM ONLY FROM THE FRANCHISOR AND/OR AN APPROVED SUPPLIER, THEN YOU MUST INVESTIGATE, INVESTIGATE, INVESTIGATE.

As a franchisee you might want to offer goods and services besides those offered by the franchisor. Some of these goods and services will complement the franchisor's or be totally different. You might even want to develop your own goods and services to sell along with the franchisor's goods and services. Yet, your franchise agreement clearly states that you are restricted to selling only the products and services provided by the franchisor.

How do you know these products and services can generate enough sales to make your investment in the franchise a profitable one? You want to invest in a new career with a bright future. You do not want to buy yourself a job! Therefore, you must study and evaluate the franchisor's products and services to determine if there is a market for them that will give you an adequate long-term return on your investment.

Your success as a franchisee will depend upon your ability to sell the franchisor's products and services to the public. If you can't sell the products and services in your area, then it would be impossible to operate a profitable business. Therefore, you must conduct your own market research to make sure that there is not only adequate demand for the products and services currently, but also for the next 5, 10, or more years. You want to be selling a product or service that has a proven demand and has the upside potential for an even greater demand in the future.

In order to conduct your own market research, there are several sources of information you need to explore. In determining the current and future marketability of the goods and services the franchisor will require you to sell, you must gather information from the following sources:

1. Review sales data of similar or related businesses in your area by seeking such information from the local chamber of commerce, local banks, and trade associations.
2. Gather information from the U. S. Small Business Administration and the U. S. Department of Commerce.
3. Review regional and national trade publications and business magazines to determine whether the type of business you are planning to go into has performed well in the past.
4. Review available information from industry analysts and government experts on what they are predicting about the future, such as industry trends, economic forecasts, and projections of future demand for the products and services you will sell to the public.

It would be appropriate to hire a business consultant to explore all the available sources of information to independently determine the demand for the products and services, current and future, offered by the franchise system you are investigating. If the information you acquire doesn't show that the products or services you are required to offer have an adequate demand then you best look elsewhere for the opportunity to purchase a franchise.

As you investigate the franchisor's products and services, you need to find answers to the following questions to determine whether there is adequate demand for these products and services now and 10 to 20 years from now:

> It would be appropriate to hire a business consultant to explore all the available sources of information to independently determine the demand for the products and services, current and future, offered by the franchise system you are investigating.

1. How long has the franchisor's products and services been offered to the public?
2. Are these products and services proven sellers or are they new offerings?
3. Within the next 10 to 30 years could the market for the products and services disappear or the products and services become obsolete?
4. Is the product or service one of those that will be here today and gone tomorrow? A fad? For example, the Pet Rock.
5. What will the market be for these products and services 1 year from now? 5 years from now? 10 years from now? 20 years from now?
6. Are the products a necessity fulfilling a need, or a luxury item fulfilling a want?
7. Is the market for the products seasonal or year round?
8. Do the products and services appeal to all people or only to specifically defined markets?
9. Are the materials, products, services, and techniques to be used and sold by the franchisee of high quality?
10. Are there any federal, state, or local government standards or regulations that would impact the product or service? What are they?
11. If there are any government standards or regulations, do they restrict in any way how the franchisor's products and services can be offered or used?
12. Is the product or service protected by federal or state intellectual property laws, such as by a patent, trademark, or copyright?
13. Is the product or service exclusive to the franchisor? Or is it generic with a special spin put on it by the franchisor?
14. Where must you purchase your products, services, materials, and supplies? From the franchisor? From an affiliate of the franchisor? Or from a supplier on an approved supplier list?
15. Will you pay a competitive price if you must buy from one of the sources?

What will the market be for these products and services 1 year from now? 5 years from now? 10 years from now? 20 years from now?

16. Will you receive reliable delivery, ready availability, and customer satisfaction if you have to purchase goods and services from the sources listed in question 14?

17. Will the supplier produce and sell to you a consistently high quality product or service?

18. As a franchisee, will you be able to offer the product or service at a competitive price?

19. Do you, or does someone else, set the price of the products and services that you offer to your customers?

20. Who will buy the products or services within the area in which you plan to locate?

21. Will the demand be strong enough for the products and services to support your business and allow you to make a reasonable profit? Next year? Ten years from now? Twenty years from now?

22. What kinds of competition will you find in the area in which you will locate?

23. What other companies compete for the same business in the area in which you will locate? What products, services, and pricing do they offer?

24. Is the franchisor aware of any major new competition planning to enter the marketplace?

25. How will the franchisor deal with competition? By improving existing products? By developing new products, services, and systems?

26. What is the level of the franchisor's name recognition? Well known? Barely known? Will the franchisor's name recognition result in the attraction of customers to your business?

27. What products and services does the franchisor offer nationwide? Are you required to offer all of the franchisor's products and services or only some of them?

28. Are there any warranties or guaranties given to the public upon purchase of a product or service?

29. If a warranty or guarantee is given, who backs it up and absorbs the cost—the franchisor or the franchisee?

30. Which products or services must a franchisee buy from the franchisor and in what quantities?

> What kinds of competition will you find in the area in which you will locate?

31. Among the public, what is the reputation of the products and services? What is the reputation of the franchisor's system as a whole ?
32. What objective measurements prove that the product and services you must purchase from an approved source meets or exceeds the franchisor's stated specifications and quality requirements?

Once you have received your answers you will have a clear picture of the quality and strength in the marketplace of the franchisor's products and services. Obtaining answers to these questions can be time consuming, but doing so is important because you will be making a substantial monetary investment along with a substantial time investment in a new career if you purchase the franchise.

> You will be making a substantial monetary investment along with a substantial time investment in a new career if you purchase the franchise.

Conclusion

If the franchisor has a strong product or service with strong name recognition then you have hit a home run. And you have a very good reason to purchase the franchise. However, if the product or service appears to be weak in the marketplace and you are unable to confirm there will be a market for the products or services in the future, then you are best served by walking away from this franchise opportunity and focusing your attention on evaluating other franchise systems. To do otherwise will likely result in you striking out in your new business and new career.

For more information on this topic, visit our Web site at www.businesstown.com

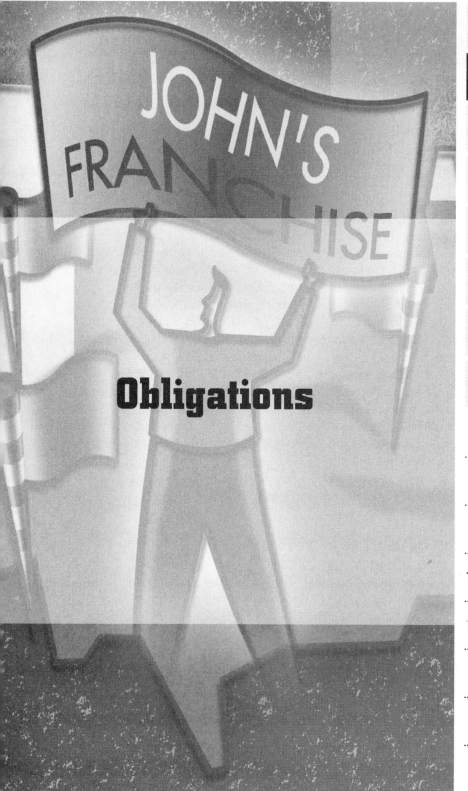

Obligations

7: THE FEES (FRANCHISE FEE, ROYALTIES, ADVERTISING)

8: EARNINGS CLAIMS: HOW MUCH MONEY CAN I MAKE?

9: PRODUCTS AND SERVICES

10: OBLIGATIONS

11: LOCATION AND SITE SELECTION

Introduction

In order to have a successful working relationship both the franchisor and the franchisee must perform certain duties, responsibilities, assistance, or services for each other. Therefore, both sides have what can be summed up as obligations toward each other to ensure the successful operation of not only your franchise, but that of the franchise system as well. The types of such services and assistance required of each side will vary widely from one franchise system to another. As a result, a prospective franchisee, in choosing a franchise system, must carefully consider the types of services and assistance that the franchisor will provide along with the obligations that will be required of the franchisee.

Prior to the execution of a franchise agreement, where can a prospective franchisee find the obligations that will be required of him and of the franchisor in their relationship? This is very important since some franchisees in some franchise systems will require much more assistance than those in other franchise systems. It is critical for a prospective franchisee to determine, prior to the execution of any legal documents, whether the franchisor will be obligated to provide enough assistance to the franchisee to ensure its success and whether the obligations required of the franchisee are reasonable and not too onerous or overbearing. Accordingly, prior to the execution of any agreement, a prospective franchisee must first look to the UFOC provided by the franchisor to determine what obligations will be required of both sides.

The UFOC: The First Place to Look

Within the UFOC are listed the obligations required of the franchisee and the franchisor. These obligations are spelled out in Items 9 and 11. All principal obligations of both sides must be listed under these items.

The principal obligations of the franchisee under the franchise agreement and all other agreements must be listed under Item 9, which is very comprehensive. Once a prospective franchisee reviews his obligations under Item 9, he will be able to determine if they are too onerous or overbearing.

The franchisor's obligations are found under Item 11. First, the obligations that the franchisor will perform before the franchise business

> It is critical for a prospective franchisee to determine, prior to the execution of any legal documents, whether the franchisor will be obligated to provide enough assistance to the franchisee to ensure its success.

opens are listed. The preopening obligations specify whether the franchisor is obligated to:

A. Locate a site for the franchise business and negotiate a lease or purchase of the site
B. Conform the premises to local ordinances and building codes and obtain the required permits
C. Construct, remodel, or decorate the premises for the franchised business
D. Purchase or lease equipment, signs, fixtures, opening inventory and supplies
E. Hire and train employees for the franchised business

Listed next are the obligations required of the franchisor during the operation of the franchised business. Disclosed here are any obligations on the part of the franchisor to assist you in:

A. Products or services to be offered by you to your customers
B. Hiring and training of employees
C. Improvements and developments in the franchised business
D. Pricing of your products and services
E. Administrative, bookkeeping, accounting, and inventory control procedures
F. Operating problems encountered by you in the operation of the franchised business

Also listed are the particulars of the franchisor's advertising program, if any, for the products or services offered by the franchisee. Then listed are any requirements by the franchisor concerning the franchisee's purchase or use of electronic cash registers or computer systems.

The table of contents of the operating manual or manuals is then listed. Even though the table of contents will give you some indication of what is contained in the operating manual, it would be preferable for you to actually obtain a copy of the manual. Only by reviewing it will you know exactly what the franchisor's obligations are, which is difficult to ascertain from the table of contents alone.

Next listed are the methods used by the franchisor to select the location of the franchisee's business. Information disclosed here includes

> Even though the table of contents will give you some indication of what is contained in the operating manual, it would be preferable for you to actually obtain a copy of the manual.

whether the franchisor selects the site or just approves the site, and what factors the franchisor considers in selecting or approving the site. Last, but not least, the training program of the franchisor is listed. The particulars concerning preopening training programs and ongoing training programs are listed.

Item 11 is normally the longest disclosure item in the UFOC. Because of its length, it is very important that a prospective franchisee study this item to get a clear picture of exactly what the franchisor is obligated to do. You need to know exactly what assistance and services the franchisor is required to provide. After all, if a particular item that you have determined that you need assistance with is not listed in Item 11, then the franchisor is under no obligation to provide you with such service or assistance. Therefore, after a careful review, you need to decide for yourself if the franchisor will provide you with enough assistance to ensure your success.

> You need to know exactly what assistance and services the franchisor is required to provide.

Realistically, What Services Should the Franchisee Expect from the Franchisor?

The types of services and assistance expected is based on the type of franchise. It is well settled that a franchisor has an obligation not to engage in unfair business practices. Also, a franchisor cannot break any federal, state, or local laws nor violate the franchise agreement and other agreements both sides have executed. Additionally, the franchisor has a duty of competence, which is an obligation to provide know-how and support to franchisees so that a franchisee can achieve success. The franchisor must provide all reasonable assistance. The following obligations are reasonably expected to be provided by the franchisor as part of its duty.

1. **Site selection:** The site chosen to locate your business will be critical to your success. However, depending on the type of franchise, this is not always true. If you have a franchise that you operate out of your house or you go to your customers instead of them coming to you, then site selection is of relatively minor importance. However, where site selection is important, you want maximum input from the franchisor. You need to be provided

with specific site selection criteria that the franchisor has developed. Also, you want the franchisor to be actively involved in the selection of your site. After all, the franchisor above anyone else, should know what locations are the best ones for success.

2. **Site development:** Franchisors want each unit to have the design characteristics that identify it as part of a franchise system. If your franchise business is such that you provide your goods and services on-site to your customers, you want maximum effort provided by your franchisor in the development of your site. The franchisor should provide, at a minimum, standard plans and specifications for your facility along with extensive assistance during its construction and preparation of the business for opening.

3. **Equipment:** The franchisor is uniquely qualified to provide guidance in the selection of equipment to be used for the business. This is due to the franchisor's experience and its determination as to what equipment is necessary. Also, the franchisor should provide options in the purchasing or leasing of the required equipment. You may purchase the equipment from the franchisor or be provided with a list of approved suppliers. If possible, the franchisor should have negotiated discounts for its franchisees, and provide assistance in helping a franchisee obtain financing. The franchisor will, based on his experience, develop a package of equipment that is standardized for uniformity and consistency. Equipment includes items such as cash registers, computer hardware, computer software, signs, furniture, and kitchen appliances.

> The franchisor is uniquely qualified to provide guidance in the selection of equipment to be used for the business.

4. **Inventory and supplies:** Based on its experience through trial and error, the franchisor is qualified to determine the proper types and levels of inventory and supplies needed to be kept on hand for the operation of the business. The franchisor should be the one to develop the list of items necessary for your inventory and supplies that should be maintained including such specifications as type, quantity, and quality. Further, you should expect the franchisor to get you the best prices on products, goods, and supplies and to provide you with various suppliers from which to purchase your inventory and supplies. For example, you should be able to purchase your inventory and supplies at a competitive price from the franchisor or have him provide you with a list of

approved suppliers, or assist you and the other franchisees in establishing a group purchasing program.

5. **Training:** One of the primary benefits that the franchisor should be providing is access to comprehensive training. The training provided should teach you everything you need to know, A through Z, to operate the franchise business. The franchisor should provide initial training prior to the opening of the franchise business. Then the franchisor should provide on-site training to prepare you for your grand opening and to assist you during your grand opening. Ongoing training should also be provided over the term of the franchise agreement to allow you to stay ahead of the competition. This ongoing training, instead of being conducted at the franchisor's headquarters, could be accomplished through meetings, videos, newsletters, e-mails, manuals provided, and so forth. The best franchisors provide extensive comprehensive training from the time you execute your franchise agreement through the entire term of your relationship.

6. **Operational assistance:** Extensive operational assistance should be provided by the franchisor through all stages of the franchise relationship.

   A. *Preopening assistance:* Assistance at this point pertains to helping you with those items that will allow you to successfully open your business. Preopening assistance could include the following: stock and inventory, decorating the unit, screening and hiring applicants, helping set up your initial record-keeping system, and having headquarters' employees present at the grand opening. Preopening assistance varies from one franchise system to another.

   B. *Grand-opening assistance:* A franchisee needs to make the right impression the first time around. After all, first impressions are the most lasting impressions. A customer's initial experience with the products and services you offer must be positive and as flawless as possible. A franchisor must assist you to make sure that everything has been done that needs to be done to ensure a smooth, successful grand opening. The franchisor needs to spell out to the last detail everything that needs to be done in order to ensure this success. Finally,

One of the primary benefits that the franchisor should be providing is access to comprehensive training. The training provided should teach you everything you need to know, A through Z, to operate the franchise business.

the franchisor should have a public relations and advertising plan in place for the grand opening so as to attract people and allow you to get good press.

C. *Ongoing operational assistance:* The best franchisors provide extensive ongoing operational assistance. Ongoing operational assistance can take many forms. The most common forms are the following:

- Assistance in helping solve problems—such problem solving could be on matters that concern quality control, personnel matters, customer relations, proper use and maintenance of equipment, etc.
- Assistance in obtaining inventory and supplies
- Assistance with training for you and your employees
- Assistance with sales and marketing efforts
- Assistance with public relations programs
- The performance of inspections of your premises and evaluations by field personnel to check for quality control, cleanliness, service, etc.
- The performance of profitability reviews, financial evaluations, industry updates, and competitive reviews
- Providing you with an extensive operations manual (this will be discussed later)
- Last, but not least, there should be regular communication by the franchisor through various media such as newsletters, e-mails, videos, cassettes, etc.

There are many other ways in which a franchisor can provide ongoing operational assistance. Such assistance is dependent upon the franchise system and the services and products it provides. However, all franchisors should provide you with ongoing attention, care, advice, guidance, marketing, advertising, and product promotional development.

7. **Use of the franchisor's trademarks, service marks, copyrights, and proprietary information:** One of the primary benefits that you are purchasing is the use of the franchisor's system of doing business. You are purchasing the right to use his established method of operation. Also, you are purchasing the right to use his

> The best franchisors provide extensive ongoing operational assistance.

identifying trademarks and service marks. Therefore at a minimum the franchisor should provide you with its comprehensive system and method of operation along with the use of its identifying trademarks and service marks.

8. **Operations manual:** It is imperative that all franchisors provide franchisees with a comprehensive operations manual. The operations manual contains the franchisor's trade secrets and sets forth in chronological order the step by step operation of the business from the preparation and selling of its goods and services to the cleaning up of the bathrooms. It is a reference tool to assist you in the day-to-day management of the business. The operations manual will also cover such daily operational issues as days and hours of operation, inventory control, sales reports preparation, quality control, customer relations, personnel policies, employee responsibilities, opening and closing procedures, how to promote, develop and advertise the business, the proper use of trademarks and copyrights, repair and maintenance of the equipment, and whatever else is necessary for the successful operation of the business. The operations manual should be a blueprint on how to operate all aspects of the business. It should discuss in precise detail every practice, policy, and procedure you should follow in order to make your business a success. The best franchisors will provide you with a comprehensive operations manual that covers virtually every aspect of operating your franchise business.

9. **National, regional, and local advertising programs:** The franchisor should coordinate and concentrate the advertising efforts for the franchise system. The franchisor should perform several services in connection with the national, regional, and local advertising programs. For local advertising efforts, the franchisor should provide you with certain advertisement materials such as radio commercials, ads for use in local newspapers, yellow page ads, advertising flyers or brochures and even door hangers. Some franchisors will even provide, as a service, lead generation programs.

10. **Research and development activity:** In this day and age change is constant. As a result, a franchisee must change constantly in

> It is imperative that all franchisors provide franchisees with a comprehensive operations manual.

order to meet new customer demands and expectations. The only party with the requisite experience, knowledge, and ability to perform the necessary research and development to meet these new demands and expectations is the franchisor. One should expect the franchisor not only to improve existing products, services, and systems, but also to develop new products, services, and systems. The franchisor should continually upgrade the services, products, and promotions that the franchisee will present to the public.

It is difficult to determine for a prospective franchisee exactly what services a franchisor should be obligated to perform to ensure the franchisee's success. However, the previously listed services should be required of the franchisor before you sign on the dotted line. If you do not have sufficient support provided to you throughout the term of your relationship with the franchisor, then your chances of being a success are lessened.

Obligations Required of the Franchisee

Realistically, what obligations should the franchisee be required to perform for the franchisor? Franchisees, in exchange for the use of a franchisor's trademarks, service marks, and comprehensive system of doing business, will be required to perform certain obligations. These obligations vary from one franchise system to another.

Your obligations will be set forth in the franchise agreement, other agreements, and in the operations manual. Franchisees cannot violate their franchise agreement nor deviate from the obligations set forth in the franchise agreement, other executed agreements, or the operations manual. You should carefully review the obligations required of you so that you don't feel overburdened and therefore resentful of the control being exercised over you. If you cannot tolerate the "control," then franchising is not for you.

The following obligations are frequently required of the franchisee:

1. **Fees:** There are several types of fees that are required to be paid to the franchisor, as previously discussed (see Chapter 7).

> If you do not have sufficient support provided to you throughout the term of your relationship with the franchisor, then your chances of being a success are lessened.

> You will be required to operate your business according to the specifications that the franchisor has set forth in your franchise agreement, other agreements you both executed, and in the operations manual.

2. **Follow the system:** You will be required to operate your business according to the specifications that the franchisor has set forth in your franchise agreement, other agreements you both executed, and in the operations manual. These specifications can dictate, for example, the name of your business, the color of cars and trucks used in the business, facilities you must use, signage you have to use, company uniforms, accounting system, opening and closing procedures, inventory control systems, sales reports to file with the franchisor, quality control systems, preparation and presentation of products and services to the public, how to clean the facility, and quality control standards. Basically, an awful lot can be required of you. Franchisees are also usually required to maintain the condition and appearance of their franchise facility according to exact quality standards and to pay for all routine and normal maintenance and repairs. Further, a franchisee is normally required to replace any worn out or obsolete accessories, fixtures, equipment, signs, inventory, and so on.

3. **Confidentiality and nondisclosure:** You will be obligated to maintain the confidentiality of the materials that you are provided. You are required not to disclose them to anybody other than necessary personnel. Further, you might not have the ability to compete with the franchisor for a minimum period of time after the end of your relationship.

4. **Transfer and resale:** Franchisees must meet the franchisor's requirements concerning the transfer or the resale of their franchise business in order to obtain the franchisor's approval. Often, the franchisor reserves the right of first refusal to purchase your business.

5. **Training:** All training must be attended that is required of you, your personnel, and management, not only prior to the opening of your franchise business, but also on an ongoing basis.

6. **Required advertising:** You must carefully review your documents to see what your obligation is as concerns national, regional, and local advertising.

7. **Insurance requirements:** Usually you will be required to maintain specific types and amounts of insurance coverage. These

coverages are required to be in full force and effect throughout the term of the franchise agreement. Types of insurance required by franchisors include all-risk property coverage, comprehensive broad form public and premises general liability insurance, personal injury liability, workers' compensation, employer's liability, company automobiles and trucks liability coverage, business interruption insurance, and umbrella liability coverage.

8. **Building and improvements:** You will be responsible to have your premises built and/or prepared according to the franchisor's plans and specifications within a certain period of time. Then you will be required to maintain the building and all improvements according to strict standards.

9. **Equipment, inventory, and supplies:** You must purchase all required items in the quantities dictated from the sources approved by the franchisor. The franchisor will dictate what fixtures, signs, equipment, furnishings, inventory, and supplies are required to be purchased along with their brands, quality, quantity, and the names of the approved sources to purchase them from.

10. **Franchisee reports**: As a franchisee, you will be required to file reports with the franchisor on a periodic basis. The reports will be required to be filed either weekly, monthly, quarterly, semi-annually, or annually. Types of reports required to be filed include: financial statements, purchasing and sales reports, marketing plans and reports, and so on. These reports allow the franchisor to determine whether you are in compliance with your agreements. Types of noncompliance include underreporting of sales, purchase and use of unauthorized products, and inattention to local advertising and promotions. In other words, you are not adhering to what is required of you in your relationship with your franchisor.

11. **Periodic inspections:** The franchisor will conduct periodic inspections of your facility and of your business. This is to ensure compliance with franchise system standards for preparation and presentation of products and services to the public, customer service, cleanliness and sanitation, and to ensure that the system is being followed as set forth in the operations manual.

Keep the Lines of Communication Open

There should be ongoing communication from the franchisor. Such communication could take the form of any or all of the following: telephone calls, field visits, newsletters, letters, e-mails, seminars, workshops, and annual conventions.

12. **Auditing the franchisee's books:** The franchisee is obligated to allow the franchisor to examine and audit its books, accounts, records, and other data. This is to ensure that the franchisee is compliant with the terms of the franchise agreement and the operations manual in the payment of fees.

Conclusion

Both the franchisor and the franchisee have certain obligations to perform in their relationship. These obligations are dictated and set forth in the franchise agreement, in other agreements that have been executed, and the operations manual. Obligations are important in order to maintain the integrity of the franchise system. Both sides need to be comfortable with the obligations that they will be required to perform. You, as a prospective franchisee, need to carefully review your required obligations to determine whether or not you would suffocate if you felt you had to perform all of them. But, even if the obligations required of you are not overbearing and onerous, you still must determine whether these obligations are evenly enforced among all the franchisees over the franchise system. This is necessary to maintain the consistency, uniformity, and quality of the franchise system, not only in the eyes of the franchisees, but the customers as well. There is nothing worse than to be part of a franchise system in which some franchisees are favored over others.

For more information on this topic, visit our Web site at www.businesstown.com

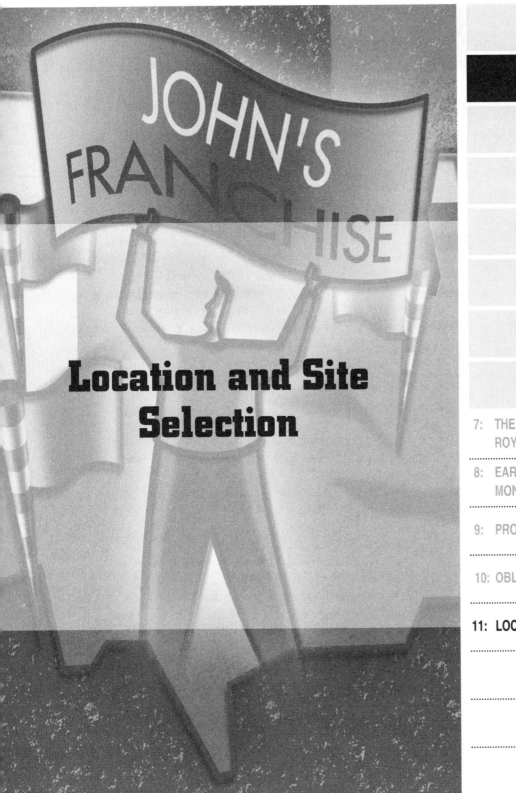

Location and Site Selection

7: THE FEES (FRANCHISE FEE, ROYALTIES, ADVERTISING)

8: EARNINGS CLAIMS: HOW MUCH MONEY CAN I MAKE?

9: PRODUCTS AND SERVICES

10: OBLIGATIONS

11: **LOCATION AND SITE SELECTION**

Introduction

When you purchase a home, the real estate agent always stresses location, location, location. After all, you want to buy a home in a neighborhood that is desirable, has no problems, has good schools, and is convenient to important shopping places such as grocery stores, gas stations, and shopping centers. Therefore, when a person purchases a home they spend a lot of time looking for the right location.

It is no different in selecting a site for your franchise business. You want a desirable location with a low crime rate that will give your franchise maximum exposure, vehicular traffic, and foot traffic. So, just as you would spend a lot of time in selecting a home to purchase, likewise you will need to spend a large amount of time locating the best site upon which to locate your franchise. However, the importance of site selection for your franchise is dependent upon the type of business or service that your franchise will provide.

Location Types

There are three types of franchises when it comes to site selection. They are home-based franchises; retail location franchises, type A (where you, the franchisee, go to your customers); and last, but most commonly thought of, retail location franchises, type B in which the customer comes to you. Site selection is of varying importance to each of these three types of franchises.

A home-based franchise, such as cleaning or decorating services, must be located within easy reach of its clientele. There are certain advantages to a home-based franchise. For example, the cost savings. You have no travel expenses to your office, and there is no additional rental expense. Also, utility expenses are kept to a minimum, since most likely the only additional utility expense will be from the phone system your franchise uses.

However, there are some disadvantages to a home-based franchise. It can be difficult to treat a business that is in your home as a *business* and therefore devote the time to it that is necessary. Also, you might have to put up with distractions, such as dogs barking, people working in their yards, and kids playing in the surrounding

> You want a desirable location with a low crime rate that will give your franchise maximum exposure, vehicular traffic, and foot traffic.

neighborhood. Also, if you live in an unimpressive neighborhood and customers need to visit you, you could suffer from lack of a positive image. However, the most important aspect of locating your home-based franchise is whether you have the appropriate zoning. Therefore, it is imperative that you check with the local zoning commission where you live to see if zoning regulations will keep you from obtaining a home-based business.

The second type of franchise, retail location franchises type A, for purposes of site selection, is a base retail location from which you, the franchisee, normally travel to your customers. Customers seldom visit your establishment. Franchises of this type include employee agencies and home repair services. For this type of franchise, the location that you pick does not need to be in a prime area. Therefore, site selection is important, but only as to whether the location selected is acceptable and inviting to you and your employees and those few customers that do visit your location.

The third type of franchise site selection is that of a retail location where the customers come to you. Examples of this type of franchise include fast-food and sit-down restaurants, the lodging industry, the automotive industry, retail store franchises, and service businesses where the customers come to you to have the services performed. With franchises of this nature, site selection takes on extreme importance. The site that you have selected can determine whether or not you are a failure or success, and if you are a success, how much of a success. Therefore, with these types of franchises, if you do not spend a great deal of time selecting the site, then you might as well pack your bags and go home and forget it.

> The third type of franchise site selection is that of a retail location where the customers come to you.

UFOC Disclosure Requirements

Under Item 11 of the UFOC, entitled Franchisor's Obligations, is listed what assistance is provided to the franchisee in selecting a site. Under Item 11, there is no requirement that the franchisor must offer you any assistance. However, any assistance the franchisor provides must be listed.

The franchisor will list the assistance it provides, or does not provide, to the franchisee such as:

A. Locating a site for the franchise business and helping the franchisee to negotiate the purchase or lease of this site
B. Conforming the site to local ordinance and building codes and helping the franchisee to obtain the required permits
C. Construction, remodeling, and decorating the premises of the franchise business
D. Leasing the equipment, signs, fixtures, opening inventory, and supplies

Item 11 will set forth the criteria that you will use to locate your franchise business. Stated here is whether the franchisor selects the location or merely approves an area in which you, the franchisee, may select a site. How and whether the franchisor must approve the selected site is also set forth. On a last note, the franchisor must state whether or not there is a time limit placed on you to locate a site, for the franchisor to approve or disapprove the site, along with any consequences if you and the franchisor cannot agree.

Degrees of Franchisor Assistance

The first classification includes those franchisors that are older and more established. These franchisors normally maintain sole responsibility for the selection of your site and its development. The franchisors in this group, such as Burger King and McDonald's, will select and develop the site, and then lease the site back to you. Due to their experience, these franchisors have very specific site selection criteria and therefore assume total responsibility. Some of their site selection criteria include items such as the amount of vehicular traffic that passes the site, accessibility of the site to vehicles and pedestrians, availability of utilities, and demographic information regarding the population surrounding the site including income, age, and educational levels.

Universal Information

Most of this chapter is targeted to those franchisees who will need to find a suitable retail location to which customers will come. However, this same material can be used for those franchisees who will still need to find a base retail location from which to operate, even though its customers will not normally visit that location.

The second classification includes those franchisors that are actively involved in the site selection process; however, the franchisee selects the site. Usually, these franchisors have a structured approach under which they have determined the criteria necessary to the success of the franchise, yet allow you to pick the site using such criteria. However, even though the franchisee in this situation is responsible for locating a site, the franchisor almost always stipulates in the franchise agreement and in the UFOC that it must give you final approval.

The third classification includes those franchisors that provide little, if any, assistance in the site selection process. These franchisors are normally those who are fairly small or fairly new to franchising and therefore have not developed comprehensive criteria in determining which sites will be successful. Also, this classification includes those franchisors to which the location of your franchise is of relatively little importance. However, even under this classification, the franchise agreement will normally require that the franchisee receive the franchisor's approval of the site prior to locating the franchise at the site.

> The third classification includes those franchisors that provide little, if any, assistance in the site selection process.

Questions to Ask Yourself

At this point, a prospective franchisee must ask himself just how important the franchisor's assistance will be in locating a site. Some prospective franchisees may have a lot of knowledge about real estate and criteria required for a location's success. However, most prospective franchisees have very little, if any, knowledge of what needs to be looked at in order to pick a location that will ensure the franchise's success. Therefore, there are many questions that you should ask a franchisor concerning its assistance in helping you find the right location. Such questions include the following:

1. Who will locate the site? The franchisor, or me?
2. What criteria does the franchisor look at in determining whether or not a site will be acceptable?

Will the Franchisor Help You?

Most franchisees will expect to receive considerable assistance when selecting a site, or will expect the franchisor to select the site for them. After all, it is reasonable to expect the franchisor to have considerable knowledge in what to look for in the selection of a site that will ensure a franchisee's success. However, how much assistance one can actually expect to receive from the franchisor varies widely from one system to another. The amount of assistance received from a franchisor can range from no or little assistance to complete assumption of responsibility for the selection of your site. Factors that determine the amount of assistance you receive include how large the initial franchise fee is, the experience of the franchisor, and the sophistication of the franchisor. Tentatively speaking, the amount of assistance to be expected from a franchisor will fall into one of three broad classifications.

3. How much assistance does the franchisor provide me in finding a location?
4. Does the franchisor take complete responsibility for site location or do they leave me completely on my own, or do they provide me with assistance somewhere in between?
5. Once the proper site has been located, will it be leased or purchased? If it is leased or purchased, who leases or purchases it? Do I, as the franchisee, lease or purchase the space or does the franchisor sublease it to me?
6. If it is my responsibility to lease or purchase the site, how much assistance does the franchisor provide? How much assistance regarding lease agreements or purchase agreements does the franchisor provide me?
7. Once the site has been selected, the lease or purchase signed, who is responsible for the site development? Does the franchisor develop the site? Or does the franchisor provide me with a blueprint and plan by which I develop the site?

There are many questions that need to be answered by the franchisor so that you know exactly how much assistance, or lack of, you will receive in locating your site and in negotiations to lease or purchase the site.

Territorial Protection

A discussion of site selection would not be complete without reviewing whether or not the franchisor offers the franchisee any type of territorial protection, and if so, how much. A significant number of franchisors now assign territories to franchisees within whose boundaries they will not compete. Territorial protection means that within a certain assigned territory and its boundaries, a franchisor cannot locate another franchisee unit or a company-owned unit, or use some other channel of distribution in which to market its goods or services within the franchisee's protective territory.

A franchisee's assigned territory can be defined and measured in several different ways. Some franchisors will assign an exclusive territory that does not allow the franchisor to compete with the franchisee for a distance of up to 3 miles from the franchisee's location. This is referred to as a radius measurement. Other franchisors will assign protected territories based upon population distribution and count. For example, the franchisor might assign a protected territory that includes 50,000 people. Still other franchisors will measure the exclusivity of the territory by geographical boundaries or zip codes. If a franchisee is awarded an exclusive territory based on a zip code, that means the boundaries of its territory are equal to the boundaries of the zip code, and its protected territory is all the territory within the boundaries of that zip code.

These are only some of the most common ways in which a franchisor defines an assigned territory. However, if a franchisor assigns you a protected territory, you must ascertain whether or not you have a quota that you must meet in order to maintain your exclusivity for the protected territory. For example, you must review the UFOC and your franchise agreement to determine if you must generate a minimum level of gross sales within a certain period of time of opening in order to maintain your exclusive territory. Other franchisors will require you to open a certain number of franchise units within your exclusive territory within a specific time frame in order to maintain your exclusive territory.

The following are some of the questions you should ask (it is wise to get the answers in writing):

1. Are you given a protected territory? If not, why not?
2. Are you given an exclusive territory? If not, why not?
3. How does the franchisor define *exclusive* or *protected?*
4. Does the exclusive or protected territory include an adequate base of customers?
5. Are you required to maintain a minimum sales figure to maintain the exclusive or protected territory?
6. If the franchisor reserves the rights to use an alternate channel of distribution to market its goods and services to customers within my territory, will I be adequately compensated for lost profits?
7. If the answer to number 6 is yes, then what is the formula?

Should I Hire a Real Estate Broker?

Of course, the answer depends on you. If you have little working knowledge of the area where your franchise is to be located, you will need assistance. One advantage to hiring a real estate broker is that the broker will not disclose to the owners of the site who her client is or what franchise it is. If the owner of a site were told that you were going to put a McDonald's at his location, he most likely would increase his asking price. A good broker can save you time and frustration because he should know the market thoroughly and should be able to recognize whether a site meets your criteria for success. A real estate broker will also have much better success than you will in conducting the face-to-face negotiations with the person you will purchase or lease the site from.

Nevertheless, as with all professionals, you need to interview real estate brokers before you select one to make sure you choose someone who you are comfortable with. Your broker should be working for you in finding the right location, as opposed to only wanting to collect a fee for his services.

8. If the franchisor reserves the right to locate another unit anywhere it wants to, what protections do I have that it will not locate a unit so close to me that my profits slip?

Types of Locations

There are a wide variety of types of sites where a franchise business can be located. Normally, the franchisor will include in its site selection materials a profile of the ideal location for one of its units. The ideal site could be a freestanding location, such as for a typical McDonald's, or a site in a particular type of strip mall, such as for a typical Blimpie's.

The following are the most likely locations for retail franchises:

> There are a wide variety of types of sites where a franchise business can be located. Normally, the franchisor will include in its site selection materials a profile of the ideal location for one of its units.

1. **Downtown business districts and shopping areas.**
   Downtown business districts are punctuated with office buildings, hotels, restaurants, and department stores. During the week, there is daytime foot traffic in these areas. However, the nighttime and weekend crowds will vary widely from one city to another. Therefore, in some cities it would not be beneficial to locate a franchise in a downtown business district.

2. **Large enclosed shopping malls.** Enclosed shopping malls vary in size from approximately 50 different stores to over 250 different stores. A mall that is enclosed will attract customers anywhere from a few miles away to over one hundred miles away. There are several benefits of being located in an enclosed mall. The mall is climactically controlled, therefore giving its customers year-round comfortable temperatures without having to worry about getting wet if it rains. These malls are open seven days a week for 12 or more hours a day. Because of the many stores found in such a mall, they tend to draw very large crowds resulting in enormous vehicular traffic to the mall and enormous foot traffic within the mall. Also, due to the large number of stores, you will find a wide diversity of products and services that can be purchased.

However, one drawback is that the cost to lease space in such malls is usually very steep.

3. **Strip shopping centers.** A strip shopping center normally contains anywhere from 10 to 30 stores and is normally located along a busy highway or busy secondary road. Most centers of this type attract and cater to surrounding businesses and surrounding neighborhoods. This usually results in substantial foot and vehicle traffic within the strip center. As compared to the enclosed shopping malls, the cost to lease space is much more affordable.

4. **Freestanding locations.** Frequently, the best location for a franchise is in its own freestanding building. This freestanding building is often located at or near a large enclosed shopping mall or along a busy road or highway. Most sit-down and fast-food restaurants utilize freestanding locations.

5. **Public facilities.** With it becoming increasingly difficult in today's marketplace to locate a franchise business at a typical location, more experienced franchisors have sought out nontraditional locations. A major percentage of these nontraditional locations are within public facilities. It is common to find franchises located within hospital complexes, military bases, airports, sports stadiums, and universities. Benefits of these locations are that you have a captive customer to service. However, at some public facilities, such as a university or sports stadium, there can be substantial periods of time when there is little or no business, such as when no events are being held or when the university is out of session.

> Frequently, the best location for a franchise is in its own freestanding building.

Selection Criteria—Finding a Great Location

According to studies conducted by the Small Business Administration, one of the chief reasons for a business to fail is due to a poor location. The evaluation of a successful site is based on specific factors that address the site's characteristics along with the nature of the franchise business to be located there. Determining whether a particular location will be successful is dependent on two types of information. The first type of information to be gathered is the demographics of the area in which you want to locate. Once you have a demographic profile, then the second item you will want to review is the site characteristics.

The franchisor should provide you with a customer profile so that you can determine if it matches with your local demographics. Demographic information can be obtained from the United States Census Bureau or from the local chamber of commerce. When demographic information is gathered, it should include the following:

1. Total population of the area broken down by age groups
2. Family status of the population—married, with or without children, single, retirees, etc.
3. Number of children in the population
4. Average family income of the population
5. Educational level of the population
6. Types of employment of the population
7. The population's mobility—how many own cars, bicycles, use mass transit, or walk to locations
8. The types of homes of the population—how many live in single-family homes, condominiums, etc.

Besides the local chamber of commerce, there are several companies that specialize in providing demographic information. CACI Marketing Systems (*www.caci.com*) is one of them. CACI provides you with a demographic profile of the area you are looking at that includes the following information:

1. Population density by ethnic group, marital status, age and income
2. Household per capita and family income
3. Number of owner and rental occupied units
4. Property values within the area
5. Education levels of the population
6. Occupations of the population
7. Vehicle registration within the area
8. Retail sales within the area broken down by several product categories

> The franchisor should provide you with a customer profile so that you can determine if it matches with your local demographics.

If there is no match between the demographic information you have obtained and the franchisor's customer profile then there is no reason to go to the second step and find a suitable site within which to locate your franchised business. However, if the customer profile and the demographic information for that area match up, you need to go to step number two, which is to find the appropriate site to locate within that area.

Evaluating Possible Sites

Once you have obtained the necessary demographic information, it is necessary to look at individual location site characteristics. In order to determine whether a particular site has the necessary characteristics to ensure the success of your franchise, there are many factors that must be studied. These factors are as follows:

1. Does the site have the space your business will require in order to operate?
2. What is the visibility of the site? Can this location be easily seen from a distance, or is its visibility obstructed by buildings or commercial signs, etc.?
3. Does the image presented by this site make it appear attractive and welcoming to a perspective customer? After all, first impressions are the most important impressions. Therefore, both the exterior and interior of the premises must make a good impression.
4. What is the accessibility to the site? Can vehicles easily access the location?
5. Is there adequate, convenient, and sufficient parking for the number of customers you are expecting?
6. Is the site in a residential area or a commercial area? Is it on a highway or is a major highway close by?
7. What is the estimated number of cars that will pass by the site? Will there be pedestrians passing by the site every day? Are these numbers sufficient to support your business?
8. What is your competition? How many businesses of the same type as yours are in close vicinity of your site? How many

If the customer profile and the demographic information for that area match up, you need to go to step number two, which is to find the appropriate site to locate within that area.

businesses that might compete indirectly with you are in the vicinity of the site?

9. What other shopping is in the surrounding areas that could generate sales for you?
10. Will the zoning for this site support your business? Is it appropriate for you?
11. What is the commercial history of this site? Has the site had a high turnover of tenants and therefore appears to be a bad site, or has there been only one or two tenants at this particular site?
12. Is the area growing, stagnant, or declining? Is the population around the site growing or declining? Is the make-up of the neighborhood changing? For example, from a middle-class population to a poorer class of people?
13 Are there restrictive ordinances that cover this site that could potentially hurt your business?
14. Which side of the road is the site on? Is it on the breakfast side or on the going home side? Is this important to your particular site?

This is just a sampling of some of the questions that you need answers to in determining whether your site will be sufficient to support your franchise business. If you do a thorough job and obtain the necessary demographics and site data, and they coincide with what is necessary for your business to be a success, then you have located a good site at which to locate your business. After all, where you locate your franchise business will more than likely be the single most important factor in your success.

Negotiating the Lease

Once you have chosen the site for your franchise, you will need to either purchase the site or lease it. If you purchase your site, make sure you have a professional negotiate the best purchase agreement possible. Unless you are experienced in the buying and selling of real estate, it would be best to leave the negotiations to a professional such

> What other shopping is in the surrounding areas that could generate sales for you?

as a real estate broker or real estate attorney. However, most franchisees will ultimately be leasing the site as opposed to purchasing it. Therefore, this section will focus on basic definitions concerning lease agreements and tips on how to negotiate your lease.

Terminology

In preparation for negotiating your lease agreement, there are some basic definitions you need to know. Under a *lease agreement*, you, as the tenant, are granted the right by the owner of the property, the landlord, to occupy and use the site covered by the lease agreement for your business. The lease agreement sets forth the rights and obligations of the landlord and the tenant. A lease agreement may be referred to as a *gross lease, net lease,* or a *triple net lease*. It is very important to understand which type of lease agreement you are being offered so that you will know how to negotiate. A gross lease means that you are responsible, as the tenant, for the monthly rental amount only. Under a gross lease, the landlord assumes all ancillary obligations. Therefore, under a gross lease, the landlord will pay your share of the real property taxes, assessments, and insurance, and make repairs and maintain your space, along with restoring the property in case of destruction.

If some of these ancillary expenses are passed on to the tenant, then the lease is considered a net lease. However, most leases you will be presented with are referred to as triple net leases. In a triple net lease you are responsible for paying not only your monthly rental amount but also your fair share of the real property taxes, assessments, and insurance that covers your leased space. Also, you are responsible for making all repairs and performing all maintenance that is needed to the interior of your space, along with being responsible for maintaining your heating and cooling systems and plumbing and electrical systems. Often, you will be asked to sign a lease that is not only a triple net lease, but also a *percentage lease*. With this type of lease you are responsible for all the items found under a triple net lease, but in addition, your monthly rental amount will increase based on a percentage of your sales. You will pay a base

> Most leases you will be presented with are referred to as triple net leases.

rental amount plus a percentage of any sales above a set dollar amount each month.

You need to make sure that you understand these different types of leases before you try to negotiate. Otherwise, you may end up paying more than you bargained for and the lease may impose a serious economic hardship on your business. As a final note, you need to understand that a lease agreement can be for space located in a building or a strip mall or a freestanding building.

> You need to understand that a lease agreement can be for space located in a building or a strip mall or a freestanding building.

Provisions of the Lease

Once you receive the landlord's standard lease, there will be certain provisions you will need to have changed to reflect your business conditions. These conditions and provisions normally include items such as a description of the premises, lease terms, renewal terms, monthly rent, other expenses, security deposits, build-out, and so on. Which conditions and provisions you will find it necessary to negotiate over will vary from situation to situation and from one type of franchise to another. However, there are certain conditions and provisions that are common to all lease agreements that you will want to review and negotiate. These include the following:

1. **Monthly rent.** Since your monthly rent will most likely be your largest fixed expense, you need to negotiate it down as much as possible. Further, to the greatest extent possible, you need to try to negotiate a fixed rent as opposed to a percentage rent where your monthly sales dictate the size of your monthly rental payment.
2. **Initial term and renewal term.** Franchise agreements normally have initial terms from 5 to 15 years with one or more renewal terms thereafter. Therefore, it is best to negotiate an initial term for your lease that coincides with the initial term of your franchise agreement. Also, you need to have your lease agreement contain renewal terms that coincide with the renewal terms of your franchise agreement. There is nothing worse than to have your lease agreement expire while your

franchise agreement is still in effect. The landlord will then have you over a barrel.

3. **Build-out.** Negotiate with the landlord to have him pay for your build-out in return for you signing a lease for an initial term of five years or longer. Normally a landlord will not consider this issue if the initial term of your lease is for three years or less, but they become very agreeable if you sign a lease that is for a substantial length of time.

4. **Escape clause.** It would not hurt to negotiate an escape clause, so that at least after a certain amount of time, if your business isn't making a profit and you need to cut your losses, you can terminate your lease agreement for an automatic, predetermined payment.

5. **Free rent.** Frequently you can get a landlord to agree to give you free rent for up to six months for signing a lease agreement for five years or longer. If the landlord is not agreeable to this, at the very least make sure your payment of rent does not start until you either open your business to the public, or get a certificate of occupancy so that you can occupy the premises.

6. **Assignment.** It is imperative that you negotiate a clause that allows you to assign or sublet the site you are leasing. The possibility always exists that you may sell your franchise or, for some reason, need to shut down your business.

7. **Noncompetition clause.** Ask your landlord for an exclusivity clause that prevents competing businesses from operating in the surrounding areas that he controls.

8. **Caps.** It is always best to prevail upon the landlord to agree to cap expenses, including rental expenses. How much your monthly rental expenses and other expenses are allowed to increase each year during the initial lease term and any renewal term can have a profound effect on your financial health. Negotiate for a clause that stipulates that if the landlord does not live up to his obligations under the lease, you will not be required to pay rent. At the minimum, any money you spend to cover an expense that the landlord is responsible for should be deducted from your monthly rent.

Lease Know-How

Many franchisees hurriedly sign a lease agreement to their detriment and that of their business. You must carefully review the entire lease agreement to see if you can live with its terms. Then you need to decide what terms you need to negotiate with the landlord. Remember, lease agreements are written with the landlord's interest in mind, not yours. Therefore, you will need to be prepared to negotiate the terms you want. Despite what most landlords will try to lead you to believe, all leases are negotiable.

These are just a sampling of the most common provisions in lease agreements that you will want to negotiate with the landlord. However, dependent upon your unique circumstances and franchise, there could be others. Due to the complexity of modern day lease agreements, it would be wise to hire an experienced real estate broker or attorney to negotiate your lease agreement.

Site Development

Now that you have a signed lease agreement, you are under a time constraint to renovate your space, build it out, or construct a new building. Who will be responsible for your site development? Generally speaking, the larger established franchisor will play a fairly substantial role in developing your site. However, those franchisors with fewer units and less experience will leave more of the responsibility to you.

With a franchisor such as McDonald's, they will often not only lease the site, but develop it completely so that all you have to do is move in. However, in most franchise systems, the franchisee will have the primary responsibility to develop the site, although the franchisor will be actively involved. In many situations, the franchisor will provide you with standard plans and specifications for the architect you hire to adapt to your site. Usually, you, the franchisee, are responsible for building the facility or renovating the leased space in accordance with the plans and specifications supplied by the franchisor. Usually, the franchisor will provide ongoing assistance during such preparation and construction of the site.

Regardless of the assistance the franchisor supplies you, the franchise agreement will most likely dictate that renovated space or new buildings be built in accordance with local zoning laws and building codes. Also you will be required to obtain all building and other permits required to perform such activity so that your business will conform to the local legal requirements. One thing that you need to be careful of is your franchise agreement will probably contain a provision requiring you to complete development of the site and commence operation within a set period of time.

Depending on your background and areas of expertise, you might be uncomfortable in performing more than a cursory role in the development of the site for your franchise. Therefore, it is important that you determine the amount of assistance, or lack thereof, the franchisor will provide you in the development of your site. You might have picked the perfect location and successfully negotiated a lease agreement with the landlord; however, if the site development is left up to you and you are incapable of handling it, then your success will be compromised.

Conclusion

Location, site selection, and site development considerations are usually critical to the successful expansion of a franchise system. They can make the difference between success and failure, not only for a particular franchisee's business, but also for the franchise system. One of the major complaints in litigation between franchisors and franchisees is that the location where the franchise is located is inadequate, therefore causing the business to fail. It is of critical importance to take the time to locate the right site and compare it to the appropriate customer profiles. By doing this, you minimize the possibility of locating your business at an inappropriate site.

> Depending on your background and areas of expertise, you might be uncomfortable in performing more than a cursory role in the development of the site for your franchise.

For more information on this topic, visit our Web site at www.businesstown.com

Training Camp and Preparation

In this section, you'll learn:

- Why training is so important
- Different types of franchisee orientations
- Why ongoing training is essential
- Exciting ways to open the business
- How much help, financial or otherwise, you can expect from the franchisor

CHAPTER 12 TRAINING CAMP **CHAPTER 13** PREPARING FOR THE GRAND OPENING

Training Camp

12: TRAINING CAMP

13: PREPARING FOR THE GRAND OPENING

Each year at the beginning of the football season, all players must report to training camp three to four weeks prior to their first collegiate game or six weeks prior to their first professional game. These camps are designed to develop the basics, to go over the game plan, and to be able to learn and study the game book. A tremendous number of hours have gone into these game books and plans by the coaches as they prepare for their season in hope and anticipation of not just a winning season but also the championship.

Franchising, in many ways, is similar to most sports. There is a need to begin with the basic training. Training is the core, the backbone, of the franchising program.

The reason for the great success in many franchising programs such as McDonald's, Subway, Holiday Inn, Kwik Kopy printing, and Merry Maids is based on their tremendous training programs and their dedication to standards. McDonald's training and adherence to their standards of QSCV—quality, service, cleanliness, and value—have driven them to be the largest franchising system in the world. Their training program is also renowned throughout the world as one of the very best.

What Kind of Training Programs Will I Encounter as a Franchisee?

Some of the training programs you should expect and run into as a member of a franchising system include the following:

1. Headquarters' training
2. Opening training
3. Post-opening training
4. Training from other franchisees
5. Employee training materials
6. Field training
7. Ongoing support training
8. Convention/seminars training

> The reason for the great success in many franchising programs such as McDonald's, Subway, Holiday Inn, Kwik Kopy printing, and Merry Maids is based on their tremendous training programs and their dedication to standards.

Most franchisors will provide these basic training programs. You should inquire of all franchisors what kinds of training they will provide for the duration of your franchise experience.

What To Expect at Training Camp

The first day that you arrive you are going to have to check into your room. At that time you will generally be given your playbook (operations manual), which you must bring to every meeting. There is often an open book policy at all training programs—that is, you are expected to open your book and keep it open, to study it throughout the training period.

After checking in to your room, there is often a welcoming meeting—generally that night, coupled with a get-acquainted dinner. Most training programs at the franchisor's headquarters will last from one to two weeks.

Kwik Kopy Corporation trains their franchisees for three to five weeks, depending on whether the trainee is a domestic or international printer and based on the franchisee's the prior experience in the printing industry. Their training schedule starts with breakfast from 6:30 to 7:30 A.M., and the classroom training generally begins at 7:30 A.M. There is usually an afternoon break from 5:00 to 6:30 P.M. for dinner, after which training programs resume. Training classes are intense. Just like in any sport, the franchisee or player will have tests to see if they have studied and learned the materials.

WARNING!! Failure to satisfactorily complete the examinations generally results in the termination of the training program for that franchisee. The franchisee may be invited back to the next training program, or they may be invited to leave the franchising system. It is important that all franchisees take all training programs seriously. You should take every opportunity to learn what is being taught.

Contents of a Franchisee Training Program

The goal of the initial training program is to teach you how to run and operate a highly successful business. The desire of the franchisor

Gingiss Formalwear

New franchisees will learn about the formalwear business in Gingiss' "Tuxedo U," two weeks of training in Addison, Illinois, with additional training at the franchise owner's actual store location at opening. Gingiss also provides an operations manual to all franchisees on their very first day, and continues its support with audio and video training tapes.

Coverall's Training Covers All

Coverall North America, Inc. has grown to over 4,600 franchisees. Their training is focused around teaching their franchisees to become specialists in specific niche markets. For example, some franchisees clean medical sites and are thereby given complete training about blood-borne pathogens. The medical center or hospital then receives a cleaning service with experienced people certified to work on their sites. The training department develops the franchise owners so that they can provide service with high quality control standards. They have comprehensive training programs, regular workshops, corporate newsletters, video training, and special project seminars. Their training is designed to cultivate their staff members to be experts in their field.

and their staff is to make you the most successful franchisee in their system. They want you to know every detail, every plan, every move that you need to make to be a highly successful business person. Just as the quarterback must learn how to operate the football team, they desire that you learn how to operate the business. The programs range in length from two to five days, to four to six weeks.

Franchisee training is generally broken down into several major areas, including:

1. *Welcome to the business*–The franchisor wants you to learn about its history, its successes and failures, and the standards that allow it to be the best in the business. The franchisor wants you to become intimately familiar with all the experiences of franchising and why their franchise is the very best.

2. *Operations*–Most of the day-to-day operations are explained in the operations manuals. This manual will be discussed extensively at this time in the training program. Areas covered in this training will include opening and closing the store, store operations, housekeeping, maintenance, sales operations, inventory control, unit operations, personnel, and any housekeeping or maintenance programs not previously discussed. If you want to learn how to fry a hamburger or make a bed, this is the time.

3. *Finance*–The financial section will show you how to keep track of all your finances and explain any and all record keeping procedures you should follow. This might also include the cash flow statement (or cash budget), cash register procedures, credit sales procedures, check sales procedures, petty cash, bank reconciliations, night deposits, payroll, social security withholding taxes, leases, insurance, and finally the development of an income statement and balance sheet. Generally as a franchisee you will be required to report to the franchisor on a weekly, biweekly, or monthly basis your total sales, costs of labor, and costs of goods sold. These are financial areas that both the franchisee and franchisor must be intimately familiar with.

4. *Marketing*—One of the great thrills of any business is the marketing side. This is exciting, frustrating, wonderful, and terrible all at the same time. You need to discuss who is the target market. Are there peculiar customer groups? What method of advertising, promotion, grand opening, and merchandising will you use? What form of customer relations programs will you be developing? What are your unique product/service descriptions and features?

5. *Service/production*—Some franchisees are going to require the need for excellent records. You will need to know how to schedule clients and provide services for a specific period of time. In addition, this area is concerned with inventory control, ordering, warehouse control, kitchen operations, portion control, equipment ordering, and even sanitary or waste control systems.

6. *Management/personnel*—Management is both an art and a science. It is important to be involved in both sides. The manager is going to need to know how to hire, train, and fire employees. In addition, the franchisee will need to know the job specifications, and the recruitment and selection processes that are best for their business. How do you develop and maintain work logs or schedules? Also, there may be specific labor laws and regulations that the franchisee needs to be aware of. What kind of personnel development programs should you use? What are some different ways to motivate employees?

7. *Miscellaneous*—whatever is left over—occupation safety, health administration, legal issues, family and medical leave, and even hazardous materials.

Who Attends the Training Camp?

Just a point of interest—when you attend your corporate headquarters training program, you will probably find corporate staff members taking the training along with the franchisees. Many franchisors have learned that not only new franchisees need training, but it is

---

Dunkin' Donuts

Dunkin' Donuts is the largest coffee and doughnut shop organization in the world, providing loyal customers with the finest coffee, doughnuts, bagels, muffins, and other related bakery products since 1950. All together they have nearly 5,000 locations in the United States and in over 37 countries around the world. Each Dunkin' Donuts franchisee must pass an intensive four-week program at Dunkin' Donuts University, established in 1966 in Braintree, Massachusetts.

This university operates just like an actual Dunkin' Donuts with franchisees learning the exact methods used to create the fresh, delicious products for which Dunkin' Donuts shops are known. During the first day of training, the franchisee is required to make, cook, and eat a doughnut. If unsuccessful, the franchisee is generally asked to repeat the training at a later time.

also important that new franchise executives and staff members learn more about the franchise operations. The strange thing is that they also have to take the tests. So one of the things you may want to do occasionally is study with some staff members, as well as other franchisees, because the staff might have some added insights.

Training from Other Franchisees

During the last 10 to 15 years, major changes have occurred in several franchising systems. One such change is allowing and encouraging new franchisees to be taught by existing franchisees. Generally this is done after the headquarters' training program. The new franchisee may then go to one or possibly two very good franchisees and work with them for a week—generally from Monday through Saturday. This allows the new franchisee to learn how things actually operate and why and how different franchisees perform various duties, possibly even in distinctive ways.

An additional reason for this training is an afterthought for the franchisor. The new franchisee generally has made a new friend and instead of just calling the franchisor for support or help solving a problem, the new franchisee may call the franchisee who trained them. This allows new franchisees to work with successful franchisees, even after opening their stores. This also develops team camaraderie and builds team spirit among the franchisees.

Special Types of Training

Grand Opening Training

Don't be surprised if the franchisor brings two or three key staff members along to help you with your grand opening. Just as the football coach is there on the sideline helping to call plays, so the franchisor is there to help you become a winning team.

In many restaurant businesses, the franchisor will send staff to the new franchisee two weeks prior to their grand opening. This allows the franchisor staff to help the franchisee recruit, hire, and train new employees. This helps the new franchisee develop a winning attitude and spirit with the new employees.

You will also probably run into a grand opening checklist. This checklist generally covers tasks that need to be performed from about three months prior to the grand opening to the week following the grand opening. Use the checklist. Follow the details. Work this out with your franchisor and develop a winning team.

Post-opening Training

In some franchising organizations, the franchisor will send a staff member to help you after your have been open for one or two months. In addition, this person may return after three or four months and, yet again, after six or seven months. The first year of operation is most crucial, and the franchisor field staff is there to help make sure that you are a success. If you have any questions during this initial year's time period, you should call your franchisor or seek other franchisees for advice, help, and suggestions.

Employee Training Materials

Part of the operations manual will be materials that you can use as a franchisee to train your new employees. These manuals will explain the services that you offer and how they should be provided. They also explain the operations of your restaurant and the recipes for your food, if that is your business.

Staff/Field Training

Generally the franchisor has a field-training crew. This may consist of 1 to 3 members, or all the way up to 30 to 100 members, depending on the size of the franchise system. These staff people are there to help. They also may come out to evaluate your site and performance, but their primary concern is to help you become the very best that you can possibly become. These people have been trained and have experience in field operations. You may call upon them for help and support at any time during your franchising

Mail Boxes Etc. Training

Mail Boxes Etc., which is now the world's largest franchisor of postal, business, and communication service centers with over 3,500 stores worldwide, provides extensive training programs for their franchisees. They presently provide a four-week training program consisting of two weeks of training at their headquarters in San Diego, California, and two weeks of hands-on in-center training. In addition, they provide grand opening assistance to make sure that your Mail Boxes Etc. center gets off to a tremendous start. They also provide additional field training, franchisee newsletters, an 800 telephone hotline, and regional and national meetings for their franchisees.

sojourn. The quarterback may always go in and ask the coach for advice and suggestions.

Conventions/Seminar Training

Usually, each year the franchisor holds an annual conference for all franchisees. This annual conference generally lasts three to four days and is ordinarily established around training programs to enhance the skills and abilities of franchisees. This training program is for franchisees and helps them meet with other franchisees and develop their knowledge of operations. You should always strive to go to the annual convention. This is designed to help you as well as to allow you to meet other franchisees and expose you to the latest knowledge and activities going on in the field of operations.

Conclusion

Training provides the franchisee the opportunity to learn the franchisor's operations system. Training is the core, the backbone of the franchising experience. Training occurs in a wide variety of forms: headquarters' training, grand-opening training, post-opening training, training from other franchisees, employee training materials, field training, ongoing support training, and convention/seminars training. Both the franchisee and franchisor benefit from training—the franchisee becomes familiar and knowledgeable about the franchisor's operating systems, and the franchisor reaps the payoff of a successful franchisee.

Baskin-Robbins Training

Baskin-Robbins was established in 1948 and currently has over 3,500 units selling some of the finest ice cream in the world. They have a three-week business management education program in Burbank, California, which is mandatory for all new franchisees. For those who think that ice cream is all fun and games, you will be surprised by late night cram sessions on occupational safety, health administration, the family and medical leave act, and many other legal issues, in addition to finding out just how many ounces of frosting are needed to coat ice cream cakes of various sizes and shapes. The franchisees learn that the important act of scooping ice cream is not easy. Various methods and motions, including straight drags, zigzags, semicircles, and deep dives are required depending upon the texture, height, and temperature of the ice cream surface. Yes, for you ice cream lovers, they do have "all the ice cream you can eat" policy for trainees, a very good reason to pass the exams.

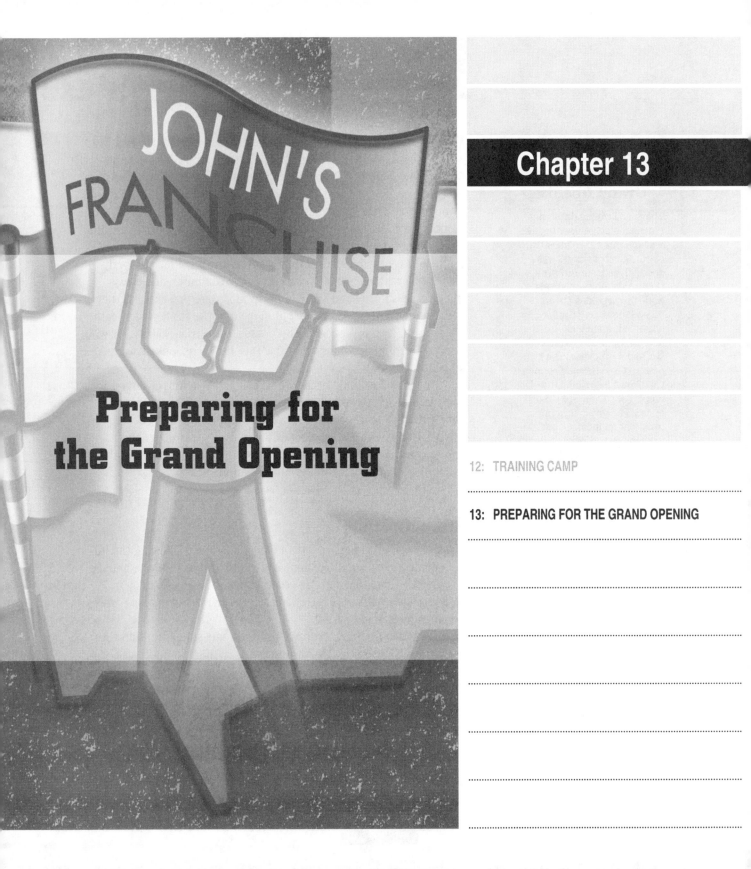

Preparing for the Grand Opening

Chapter 13

12: TRAINING CAMP

13: **PREPARING FOR THE GRAND OPENING**

Recently, a new franchisee was extremely excited. He was about ready to cut the ribbon on the grand opening of his new retail outlet downtown, across the street from a five-star hotel. He had spent the last four months in preparation. He had been through two weeks of headquarter training. He had spent three months watching the construction and development of his store, and he had learned a lot from purchasing his inventory. He was excited to finally have all the shelves fully stocked, the price tags properly placed, the cash registers hooked up to the computer, and everything set. His family and a few of his friends were present, and they had a ribbon-cutting ceremony out in front of the store, underneath the "Grand Opening" banner. There was a pedestrian walking by who noticed the grand opening and came into the store, looked around, and left.

The grand opening occurred at 8:00 A.M. The first customer to come in and actually purchase a product was at 3:42 P.M. What had gone wrong? The franchisee had simply forgotten to advertise, to market, to promote the opening of his store. He was under the impression that simply by opening the store in a wonderful location with a good brand name title, would be an instant success.

Grand Opening

A grand opening generally occurs two to six weeks following the initial opening of the store. In some cases, the opening and the grand opening are done together. However, in many cases, especially in food establishments, it is preferable to have the grand opening after the opening training period.

Generally the franchisor will provide some suggestions and guidelines to the franchisee for a grand opening. The franchisee should look at these plans and then develop their own personal grand opening program. It is important that the franchisee discuss the plan with his or her franchisor. This will allow the franchisor to provide any needed materials, banners, or gifts that are appropriate for the grand opening. A written grand-opening plan should also be forwarded to the franchisor by the franchisee.

Contractual Grand Opening Monies

Many franchisors require by franchise contract that you invest a minimum amount of money, often from $1,000 to $5,000 for the grand-opening event. This grand-opening experience should generally be for a full week, consisting of special activities and offers every day. The big events should take place on Friday, Saturday, and Sunday, which are often the largest shopping days for the franchisee. Downtown locations may prefer Wednesday, Thursday, and Friday as their special customer preference days. The franchisee will do best to develop a theme for the grand opening and plan all events surrounding that theme.

If there are several similar businesses opening in the market around the same time, the franchisee could consider a "group" grand opening. This would help increase the use of the budget, which should subsequently increase awareness for all those involved and provide a more powerful media program.

First Year's Marketing Plan

You should also plan the entire first year's local marketing plan at the time you develop the grand-opening event. Many franchise agreements will also require a franchisee to spend a specific amount of money, or a percent (anywhere from 1 to 4%), of total sales on the first year marketing activities. This money is in addition to the money spent on the grand-opening event.

Publicizing the Grand Opening

When looking at the media needed to publicize the opening, you should consider:

1. *Newspapers*—You should consider using the local daily, weekly, or "shopper" for a grand-opening advertisement (often with coupons). "Buy one get one free" offers are best for grand openings. In association with the advertisement, it

Grand Openings in Asia

In many Asian countries (Japan, Korea, Singapore, and Malaysia) the merchants take one of their products or a gift around to the neighboring stores and offer it as a token of friendship. This allows the new franchisees to get acquainted with other business owners and explain to them what they are planning and when they are going to open. Some of the other merchants will also take the opportunity to come to the grand opening and to participate in the activities of the new store. Many will bring gifts of good will and for good luck.

"Partnering"

You might also consider "partnering" with another local event or establishment: festival, parade, sporting event, food distributor, etc. The partnering idea allows the franchisee to have other events promote and advertise the grand opening. If the business is located in a shopping center, shopping mall, or major building, then the business owners' association in that building may also be involved in the grand opening and promoting the various businesses.

is a good opportunity to provide the business editor of the newspaper a short story about how and why you are opening a business. If you write a press release that is close to publishable—clear, grammatically correct, and newsworthy—a journalist will be more likely to look into your story.

Some of the best materials you will ever see in print are those provided to the local area news media. You have to write it. If you are having a grand opening, then you provide an interesting human interest story that explains why you, as a local businessperson, are starting this particular business, here in this town at this time.

2. *Direct Mail*—This is a great vehicle to promote grand openings and invite people to come in and try your products. There are now a large variety of direct-mail companies that can mail specifically to the zip codes or blocks to which you wish to advertise. It is advisable that you shop around for quality, price, and distribution rates. Many large franchisors have negotiated national rates with some direct-mail vendors—you want to contact your franchisor about this.

3. *Radio*—You may want to negotiate a radio remote or sampling program at your grand opening. If you choose radio advertisements, then your radio spots should begin the week before the grand-opening event. Many radio stations are willing to come out to your business site and do a direct broadcast from there. You may think of inviting them to do so.

4. *Television*—Television is a rather expensive method of disseminating information. However, it is still one of the great advertising tools of our economic system. Most large franchisors use national television advertising to promote their products and keep top-of-the-mind awareness among consumers. However, if you are a small franchisee, then television is a rather difficult method to use unless you have some spectacular event associated with your grand opening.

5. *Billboards*—The billboard can be a tremendous tool in informing people about your grand opening as well as a continuous reminder to them of your store, products, and

location. When going out to eat, most of us do not make the choice of location until approximately one half-hour before we actually leave to go to the restaurant. If on the drive home somebody sees a billboard sign for a particular restaurant, then top-of-the-mind awareness indicates that they might choose that restaurant if they decide to go out to eat.

Signage

One very important item that is often overlooked is signage. One local franchisor was very proud of the signage that had been used on her first five stores. The only problem was that all these stores were very close to the street traffic and could easily be seen from the street. The new store was located in a strip shopping center, at least 100 yards from the street. The sign on the store could not even be read from the street. No one knew that the business was there. The owner was confused as to why the store was not receiving more traffic. The answer: poor signage.

In reviewing signage, you should look at the following:

1. *In store*—It is important that you place the name of your store not only externally, but within the store as well. People need to be reminded at times where they are while in the store. If your business is a restaurant, your menu should contain your name as well as the fare. In addition, you might wish to place signs of the name of the business 7 to 10 days prior to the grand opening. Place these signs outside so that everyone can see them.
2. *Exterior*—The grand-opening banner should be placed high so that everybody can see it and recognize that this is a special event for that particular store. There may need to be signs placed closer to the street so that people will know that a grand opening is occurring.
3. *Decor/ambiance*—The decor of the store is going to set the spirit and feel of the business. If you wish to have a western motif or the highly stylish ambiance of a very expensive

Blimpie Subs and Salads

Blimpie recommends and uses a grand-opening advertisement for local newspapers—daily, weekly, or shoppers. Their message is simply "now open—announcing the grand opening of a new Blimpie's Subs and Salads Restaurant—There goes the neighborhood. Now people will be spending all their free time at Blimpie, enjoying our delicious subs—because once you have tasted the sub made with choice meats, real dairy cheese and crisp vegetables, there is no turning back. We make hot subs, cold subs and fresh garden salads, so come by and savor the Blimpie difference. The world will never be the same." Attached to this announcement are two coupons—one for $1 off any regular 6-inch or 12-inch sub sandwich, and the second is a buy-one-get-one-free.

Smoothie King

Smoothie King provides its stores with a marketing manual and the promotions for the grand opening one month before and within the first three months of the store opening.

jewelry store, then your decor must reflect such. If you are having a grand opening for a restaurant, you may wish to include helium balloons, streamers, and other decorations throughout the interior and even the exterior of the store.

4. *Extraordinary signs*—Some people now use cold air balloons or hot air balloons to draw customers into their grand opening. These generally contain the name of the store and the dates of the grand opening.

Special Events

There are several things you may wish to consider when doing a grand opening. Special events should coincide with the spirit of your store. You need to be careful then and reflect upon both the good and bad of the special events that may occur. Following are some special events you might consider.

Sweepstakes

A sweepstake is simply an advertising or promotional device in which prizes are awarded to participating consumers by chance. There is no purchase or "fee" required in order to win. Sweepstakes can be very valuable to drawing people to your grand opening. Many franchise companies are now beginning to use sweepstakes to draw attention their products and services. However, you should know the legalities of what you can and cannot offer.

Lottery

The lottery, as contrasted to a sweepstakes, is a promotional device wherein items (prizes) are awarded to people by chance but this requires some form of payment in order to participate. Lotteries are illegal in several states. You probably need to stay away from these when you are involved with your grand opening.

Skill Contests

These can be very exciting and wonderful. In a skill contest no entry fee or purchase is required. Several legitimate skill contests include writing a winning jingle, solving puzzles, making up names for mascots, or answering questions correctly. Here knowledge or skill wins the prize, not chance. Children can be invited to participate in drawing contests and winning drawings may be shown during the grand opening.

Premium Offer

Premiums are simply items or gifts that you make available to all recipients who respond according to the company's instructions. A travel bag could be given out to anyone who attends the grand opening, for example. It is important to realize that everyone who responds to this offer receives the same gift item. There is no element of chance—the offer is not a sweepstakes.

A "Moving" Experience

Walk into a major convenience food store during the summer and it is almost guaranteed that you will see a point-of-sale sign for some drink product "waving" at you. Surprisingly, motion works. The waving of an ad or a flag attracts the eye, although for most marketers this is still a secret. A display with motion will outpull the same display without motion. In other words, if you own a business, get moving.

Grand Opening Checklist

1. Display with motion
2. Business card drawing
3. Building awareness with premiums
4. Tying in with another community event
5. Providing gifts for grand opening customers
6. Distribute flyers
7. Eating contests
8. Product sampling
9. Entertainment—such as:
   a. High school pep band
   b. Glee clubs
   c. Clowns

Manchu Wok Grand Opening

"We will prepare and coordinate, if appropriate, a grand opening promotional advertising campaign for your Manchu Wok outlet. The grand opening program is funded by us pursuant to the advertising fund. In connection with the grand opening program, we furnish merchandising material including 'Now Open and/or Under New Management' signs, 'directional' signs and a grand opening banner, the use of our store mascot, the Manchu dragon, and various coupons and marketing fortune cookies which contain a promotional offer in lieu of the traditional fortune. The discount attributable to any coupons used by your customers or free food and beverages that you provide your customers is your responsibility. These promotional items are available for your grand opening. All materials are shipped by ground shipment. Accordingly, we require three weeks notice for shipping and handling the orders." (UFOC—page 21, March 1, 1998)

d.   Jugglers
e.   Local librarian for story hour
f.   Local police departments (McGruff the dog, or Say No To Drugs programs)
10.   Special mascots such as Ronald McDonald or the Blimpie Bear

Grand-Opening Training

Most franchisors are desirous to have part of their staff at your grand opening. They want you to succeed in your business. Therefore, they will usually send one, two, or three members of their staff to help you with your grand opening. You should use these people to help in any and all aspects that you possibly can with the grand opening.

Conclusion

You can open the store before the grand opening, when all guests are invited and special advertising, gifts, and promotions are given. The media should be invited and special news releases should be written for the press. Special events will enhance the grand opening. The franchisor will generally send representatives and materials from its headquarters to help with the grand opening.

This is a once-in-a-lifetime experience—ENJOY IT!!!

For more information on this topic, visit our Web site at www.businesstown.com

Marketing and Advertising the Franchise

In this section, you'll learn:

- **Effective marketing techniques using brand names and customer profiles**

- **How to listen to your customers' needs so you can sell them the appropriate product**

- **The differences between advertising and public relations**

- **How to appropriate advertising funds**

- **How to generate positive publicity**

CHAPTER 14 MARKETING THE BUSINESS **CHAPTER 15** PLAYING THE SELLING GAME **CHAPTER 16** ADVERTISING AND PUBLIC RELATIONS

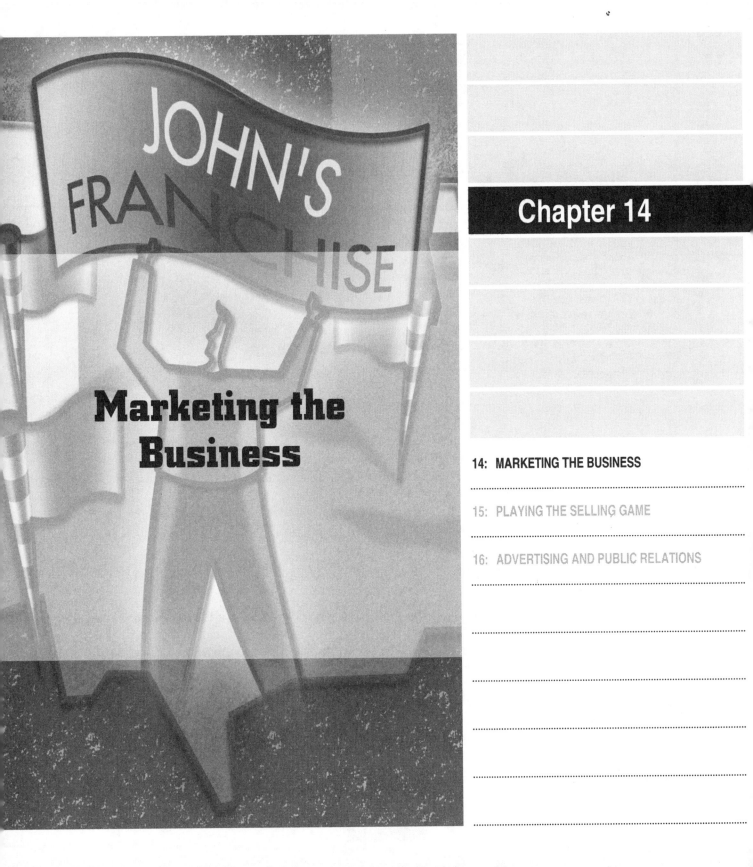

Chapter 14

Marketing the Business

14: MARKETING THE BUSINESS

15: PLAYING THE SELLING GAME

16: ADVERTISING AND PUBLIC RELATIONS

Philip H. Knight was a member of the track team. Bill Bowerman was the coach. Bowerman created a lighter shoe to make his runner faster. He took out the waffle iron and created the sole for a new track shoe. Both Phil Knight and Bill Bowerman invested $500 and a handshake sealed the foundation of a remarkable partnership formed in 1964. Today, that company is known as Nike. They are credited with introducing "jogging" to America, and Bowerman will forever be remembered as the man who poured rubber into his wife's waffle iron in a relentless pursuit to build a better running shoe for his athletes.

Brand Name Identification

A franchise system is only as strong as the franchisees. That is why, even from the start, every step taken by the franchisor is to help and support the franchisee. One of the great opportunities and rights which you have is to use the franchisor's trademark (McDonald's, Wendy's, Marriott), trade secrets, business systems, architectural, and interior designs, which enhance the recognition of the stores throughout the world. As the franchisor's brand name identification grows, the value of your franchise increases.

As you open your store, you should be aware of the three great values that your brand name has:

1. Identification
2. Repeat sales
3. New product sales

Of these three, the brand identification is the most important. The use of a brand allows you to distinguish your business from all others. Brand names become familiar to consumers and many consumers develop loyalty to that brand and business.

The two most widely recognized brand names throughout the world belong to McDonald's and Coca-Cola. The value of such brand names is inestimable. Your brand name can also grow in value and importance. You need to make sure that you do everything you can to enhance the attractiveness and value of that brand name.

Marketing Functions

You are going to need to market your business to your end consumers. Marketing is simply the process of developing, planning, and executing the conception, pricing, promotion, and distribution of products or services to create exchanges that satisfy individual needs and goals. Marketing should be kept simple. The main goal of the marketing process is to capture and keep profitable customers. It is generally more important to capture the customers than to capture market share.

When looking at marketing, the basic target market needs to be analyzed. This target market primarily consists of individuals who are or will be (1) heavy users, (2) moderate users, (3) light users, (4) nonusers, or (5) unprofitable users. Most of the heavy users may use the products or services three or four times a week while the moderate users may use the products or services once or twice a week. The light users may use the products or services once a month or twice a year. The nonusers are those who generally never use the products or services and basically they are not a concern. The unprofitable users are those who require extensive care, devotion, and provide little income to the business. These are the individuals who insist upon private service and require specific goods or services with little chance for profit.

The effective marketing plan is generally neither complex nor expensive. The main idea behind effective marketing is to capture and keep customers. It is important to reward these valued customers so that they will keep coming back and become loyal to the business.

Profiling Customers

Just as the franchisor has developed a profile for the best franchisees, a profile should also be developed for the best customers. The total number of possible customers in the immediate vicinity of the business should be determined. Most businesses have customers coming from a 1-to 3-mile radius of the store. Demographics need to be determined of a 1-, 3-, and 5-mile radius from the business.

Customer Loyalty

Think about the following business cases: Business A and business B each spend $30 to capture one new customer. Business A has 100 customers and each customer spends $15 weekly. At the end of the year, this business has to replace 20 of the 100 customers.

Business B has 75 customers and each customer spends $20 weekly. At the end of the year, business B has to replace 5 of the 75 customers. Which business would you rather own? Why? Which of these two businesses makes more money? Business B makes more money, has more profits, even though they have fewer customers, and their customer loyalty allows them to increase their profits.

Therefore, the focus does not need to be on market share, which is "old school," but rather the focus should be on customer share.

The profile should consist of demographic information, purchase frequency of the best customers, favorite products of the best customers, brand usage, brand loyalty, amount spent, and profit potential.

The value of each customer needs to be recognized. For example, if a heavy user frequents a fast-food restaurant three times a week and spends on average $8, then it might be concluded that she is a 3 × $8 = $24 per week customer. However, looking at the value of this customer over a year, instead of as a $24 customer, she is an $18 × 52 = $1248 customer. Over a six-year period, this would equal roughly $7,500. Now this customer has tremendous worth.

Market Development

When starting an exciting new concept in franchising, product/service awareness and market strength needs to be developed. But before developing the market, the current status of the market must be determined. Users of the products/services can be classified as opinion leaders, early majority, mass majority, or laggards.

The *opinion leaders* are those who purchase a product first. These are those individuals who purchase every new product that comes out, and they are the first ones on the block to have that product.

The *early majority* are those who hear about the product from others and then decide that they want to try to it. An analogy can be made to the personal organizer market. Some individuals now are using hand held "computers." This allows an individual to take their planner/calculator/computer together in one very nice nifty hand-carried unit. The early majority are those people who want to be in the forefront and who desire those things that will enhance life and provide satisfaction to one's lifestyle.

The *mass majority* are those who want the product after hearing that everyone else has used it and after it is perfected. For example, most people today use a microwave oven to heat or prepare our food. It seems almost impossible to live without one. That's an example of mass majority.

The *laggards* are those who may never buy this product and who simply do not need such products for their personal satisfaction or enjoyment. The laggards are individuals who may never be influenced or brought to your way of thinking.

The average franchise business will lose 10 to 30% of its customer base annually. The goal is not to have a customer visit just once but to motivate the customer to return often and to enjoy the visits.

Developing a Business's Competitive Edge

Think of Wendy's, Domino's, Kentucky Fried Chicken, or Marriott. What comes to mind? Is there really a difference between Coca-Cola and Pepsi Cola? Are there differences between a McDonald's Big Mac and Burger King's Whopper? What are the advantages of each product or brand name? What disadvantages or baggage might these products or brand names carry? What is the first thing or image that comes to mind when it is your store or business or brand image?

Unique, or even unusual, attributes need to be developed for each product or service you sell. Your business needs to be distinguishable from your competition's. This differentiation will help your business attract customers and it will create customer loyalty.

The main goal is to create a positive image of your products or services in the minds of the customers. When the customers think highly of the product or service, then a loyal relationship is created. The "competitive edge" consists of those unique attributes and practices that are developed and promoted to the customers. Your customer service should be more than just outstanding—it should be fantastic. Don't just smile at the customers, but also greet them in a friendly manner and even use their names if they are return customers. Show pride in the products and in the service and try to lift the customers through positive and honest conversation.

If a competitive edge can successfully be developed, it will always lead to success. The United States women's soccer teams have won several world championships because they have developed a edge. They continuously strive to maintain and expand on that edge. If a significant competitive edge is not developed by a business, then

Fast Fact

It is 7 to 10 times more costly to obtain a new customer than it is to keep an existing customer.

most likely its products or services will not be differentiated from those of the competition, making success less likely.

Marketing and Sales

Many confuse the terms marketing and sales. While they are both needed and designed to increase profits, their directions are very different.

	Marketing Orientation	Sales Orientation
Focus	Outward—satisfying wants and needs of customers	Inward—satisfying organization's needs
Business	Satisfying customer wants and needs	Selling products, and/or services
Individuals involved	Hopefully everybody	Those contacting consumers
Primary goals	Profit through customer satisfaction	Profit through maximizing sales
How goals are achieved	Coordinated marketing activities	Intensive promotion
Target market	Specific groups of people	Everybody

Marketing Implementation

The implementation of the marketing program is going to be harder than you think. It is wrong to assume that customer service can just be "turned on." The franchisee needs to set a standard and then constantly push, push, and push. You are going to have to enthusiastically develop, embrace, and perform the concepts of marketing and encourage these concepts throughout your staff and organization.

McDonald's developed a new target market that they had no idea about until they finally realized that many travelers were stopping in at McDonald's to use their clean restrooms. The concept of cleanliness is so important to McDonald's that traditionally their restrooms are perceived to be the cleanest in the world. Therefore, travelers will stop at McDonald's. While there, they often purchase something to take on their trip. What a fantastic market they have developed. This is the result of implementing the marketing strategies and concepts of the franchisor.

Conclusion

Marketing is one of the most exciting aspects of any business. The potential target market must be identified and the heavy users need to be determined. The best, better, and good customers must also be identified for your business. At all costs, try to avoid the wrong customers or the unprofitable customers. The marketing functions—pricing, promotion, product, and distribution—of the goods or services must be built around capturing the desired customers. Those customers must be kept by rewarding them and always encouraging them to return.

The Pricing (Exchange) Phenomenon

Surprisingly, in your business, you are going to ask people to give up something so that they can receive something they would rather have. In other words, if you are a Smoothie King franchisee, you are going to ask people to give up money so that they can receive a nutritious, delicious Smoothie. Money is normally the medium of exchange. Money is "given up" so that your customers can "get" the products and services they desire.

In your business, you will also need to recognize that this exchange does not always require money. You may barter or trade your products or services for something else. Many franchisees exchange their food service products for printed materials from printing companies.

For more information on this topic, visit our Web site at www.businesstown.com

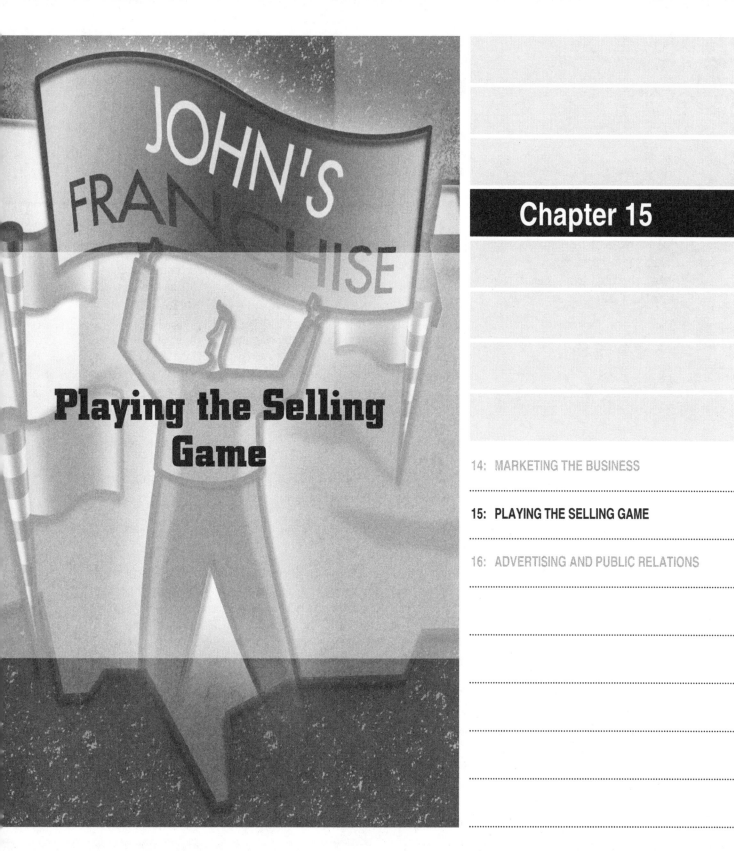

Chapter 15

Playing the Selling Game

14: MARKETING THE BUSINESS

15: **PLAYING THE SELLING GAME**

16: ADVERTISING AND PUBLIC RELATIONS

If you are going to be able to sell your product or service correctly, you are going to need to know about sales promotion and personal selling. These activities will increase your effectiveness and profits.

Sales Promotion

Sales promotions are exciting activities where an incentive is offered to induce the customer to purchase particular goods or services. Sales promotions offer products with an incentive to buy while advertising products with a reason to buy. Sales promotion incentives often include coupons, contests, premiums, sweepstakes, and even free samples. Sales promotions are generally aimed at either the ultimate consumer or the business trade market.

Sales promotions can be fun. They are usually cheaper than advertising and also easier to measure. A national TV advertising campaign may easily cost over $1 million to create, produce, and place on television. It is also difficult to measure how many people buy a product as a result of seeing a TV ad while, with most sales promotions, you can measure their effectiveness by the coupons, premiums, or free samples used.

> Sales promotions can be fun. They are usually cheaper than advertising and also easier to measure.

Selling

Selling is both an art and a science—an art because it takes continuous practice to stay within the lines and a science because there are certain steps or requirements necessary to close the sale. Selling is the ability to get the customer to make a buying decision. You should remember that everybody in your organization at some time or other is involved in selling. Therefore, you might want to teach your staff some of the proper procedures and steps in selling.

Selling is a game. Most people don't understand this. Those who do learn how to play the game, when to play it, where to play it, and with whom they should play it. One of the easiest and most fun experiences that you will have as a franchisee is taking the time to teach your staff how to sell.

As in any activity, you need to understand that certain plays and certain moves have to be mastered so that you can be effective. You will often see a dog chasing a car, but what happens if the dog catches the car? Let's take a look at what to do when the customer has actually decided to buy.

There are basically five steps in the selling process. These include the following:

1. Mission Statement
2. Probing
3. Listening
4. Supporting Benefit Statements
5. Closing

Mission Statement

Your mission statement will introduce you and your business to the customer. Everybody is rushed, attention time is short, but with a mission statement you can make a person feel welcome, wanted, and explain how you can benefit them personally. A mission statement should basically cover: your name and/or company name, business objectives, and benefits of your products or services.

An example of a mission statement:

"My name is Lynn Richard from Merry Maids. We help you save precious time by providing home or apartment cleaning for you."

Probing

Probes are simply designed to ask questions of the individual to discover their desires and wants. The easiest way to ask a question in a nonconfrontational manner involves using the words: who, what, when, where, how, or why.

For instance, if you are a Foot Locker franchisee, you may ask your customer the following question: "Mrs. Tracy, what kind of running shoe are you looking for today?" This allows the customer to express what she wants and needs.

Try to have your staff stay away from such questions as: Can I help you? Is this what you want? These are very basic frontal, tactless,

Suggestive Selling

A practice commonly used among most retailers is suggestive selling, in which the sales person tries to broaden the customer's purchasing decision with related items. Suggestive selling works. For example, Burger King cashiers will often ask customers if they would like french fries with their hamburgers and drinks. The idea behind suggestive selling is simply to help shoppers recognize values as well as enhance their purchasing decision.

even accusatory questions. It is best to simply find out from the customer what their desires are.

Listening

It is estimated that 50% of all successful selling is listening. A skill that is almost never developed is listening. Courses in marketing, management, accounting, and finance might be taken, but how many businesspeople take courses in listening? Your staff members need to be able to listen for accuracy as well to find out what the customer wants and why. The best sellers are generally the best listeners.

Supporting Benefit Statements

A person will buy a product or service because it is of personal benefit to them. People generally never buy anything that they don't want. One week after it is bought it might not be wanted or ever used again, but when it was bought, it was wanted.

The idea behind a benefit statement is to explain to a person how buying the product or service will benefit them. By purchasing the Smoothie King fruit sensations drink, you will be obtaining the nutritional elements and energy level you need this afternoon.

One easy way to remember to sell benefits rather than just features is that a benefit will generally satisfy one of the five "Ps": Pride, Power, Pleasure, Prestige, and Profit.

You can explain the features of a Nike running shoe, which will provide the customer with information, but only when you explain that it is one of the best shoes made (pride), or that it will give the customer great pleasure or even prestige, are you providing the benefits that will make a person want to buy.

Closing

You want to get the customer to commit to a purchase. The easy way is to close. Closing is when you move toward allowing the customer to buy. Closing is not manipulating—it is an opportunity to allow the person to make a positive decision.

The Successful Salesperson

- Follows the 80/20 rule—top 20% of the salespeople get 80% of the business

- Doesn't fear rejection—the greatest single obstacle to closing a sale is the fear of rejection

- Has high levels of self-confidence

- Has high levels of self-esteem

- Sincerely cares about the customers

- Accepts 100% of the responsibility for success (or lack thereof)

- Is willing to develop friendships

- Is low key, easy going, empathetic

There are basically two parts in each close:

1. Assume the sale is made—the customer's problem has been resolved.
2. Ask for the order—once again use the indirect words who, what, when, where, how, and why. For example, when would you like us to come and clean your home? Would you like me to wrap your running shoes? When would you like us to deliver your six-foot-long sub sandwich?

Your successful staff member should realize that the customer has a problem that she can solve. If the person is coming in for a Whopper with cheese, he is hungry. Now you can ask him if he would like that in a Value Meal or even if he would like to super-size it. You need to try to solve the problem today and get the customer's commitment today. If the problem is not solved today, it will generally remain a problem and the order will not be taken. You need to continue to provide benefits for the consumer until they realize that they need their car properly lubricated or their home professionally cleaned or that their six-foot-long sub sandwich will be the talk of the office for the rest of the year.

> ### Questions Help Identify Needs
>
> - Use open-ended questions with the following words: who, what, when, where, how, and why—these identify needs.
> - Use closed-ended questions (answers are yes or no) to obtain specific information.
> - Use negative-answer questions to get customers to qualify themselves—Are you happy with the products you currently buy?

Sales Playbook

In addition to all the other materials that you provide your employees, you might also want to give them a separate sales playbook or make this part of their employee handbook. The sales playbook should simply consist of the five important items previously outlined (the mission statement, probes, listening, supporting benefit statements of each, and closing) plus some written samples of each. This allows all members of the organization to review the sales ideas periodically. In addition, you may want to keep a brief one-page outline by each cash register that the employees can refer to periodically.

Knowledge Is Power

The problem that many franchisees do not even know exists is that their employees do not know the products or services that they can sell. For example, how many fast-food restaurant employees know that you can mix a drink with half Coke and half orange drink, formulating what in many locations is called "swamp water"? A proactive approach should be taken to learn what the products and services are and their combinations. Some of the specifications and features of specific products need to be learned. In some cases, such as a Molly Maid franchisee, you need to learn how to price your services—how much does it cost to clean a 2-bedroom apartment or a 10-room house? If you can offer your customers information and insights that they might not know about, then you have given added value to your customer's decision to purchase.

If you want to try something, go to a Wendy's hamburger restaurant and ask for a large Frosty in the same container size as a large drink. Many employees will say that they do not and cannot do that, while others will, even creating a price for a product that they do not sell. If you are a customer who desperately wants a giant Frosty and you can only get the size of a medium drink container, then you would become very disgusted with that particular location. Remember you can empower your employees to make both products and profits for your organization while satisfying customers needs and wants.

Consultant Selling

Many times members of your staff will be called upon for their advice and opinions. Your staff members then become consultants to your customers. The good consultants will try to find solutions and provide answers to your customers' questions. The Merry Maids franchisee will be able to help the customers understand if they should clean their homes on a weekly, biweekly or monthly basis and at what particular cost. This practice also helps develop trust between the business and its customers. When the customers come to rely on your business for help and suggestions, you move ahead of your competition by getting not only the initial sales but the repeat business as well.

Average Sale Facts

1. The average sale is closed after the fifth closing attempt.
2. The average salesperson does not even try to close once.

Selling with a Smile

Probably the most important feature of your body is your face. And above all, the most important part of your face is your smile. It is amazing how a smile offers more comfort and support to customers.

The rule of telephone sales, whether taking an order for a pizza or a request for a business service, is that the smile is the greatest attraction. Smile, smile, smile. A smile can be felt over the telephone lines. When a person smiles while on the telephone, their voice becomes elevated and the listener perceives someone's genuine attention and warmth. It is a good rule, regardless of your telephone manner, to always–sometime during the conversation–smile while on the telephone. The listener will appreciate it and will feel better about the conversation.

> **McDonald's Value Meals**
>
> A good McDonald's employee has been trained to ask a customer if he or she would like a Value Meal today. The reason: many McDonald's franchisees sell 65% of all sandwiches as Value Meals. Suggestive selling increases profits.

Honesty Pays

Honesty and integrity are probably the greatest attributes that successful sales people have. Customers have a tendency to sense when they are being dealt with honestly. Satisfying the customer's wants and desires is crucial, but at the same time, you need to be honest about what you can and cannot provide. Most people understand that there are limits in the business world, and if you simply explain what is available, most people are reasonable and accepting. Honesty encourages trust and repeat business.

Be Positive

People love positive people. Positive words build bridges and negative words may destroy those bridges. People often affiliate with others with whom they have positive interactions. People shy away from others after negative interactions.

Customers are always right. They desire a certain amount of respect and trust. They expect that what they order will be properly prepared and delivered.You need to commit yourself to being positive and enthusiastic every day. You need to always strive to be honest with your customers and live with the highest level of integrity. Respect yourself. Respect others. Respect your business and always, always, be positive.

Conclusion

Selling is a game. It is the best game you will ever play. Almost all businesses use sales promotions to induce the customer to purchase a particular product or service. Develop a sales playbook to keep track of how you are doing with the sales game. Your playbook should include: mission statements, probes, listening methods, supporting benefit statements, and closures. Remember that 20% of the salespeople get 80% of the sales. Know your products, be honest, be positive, and smile—and you will have great success in selling.

> Selling is a game. It is the best game you will ever play. Almost all businesses use sales promotions to induce the customer to purchase a particular product or service.

For more information on this topic, visit our Web site at www.businesstown.com

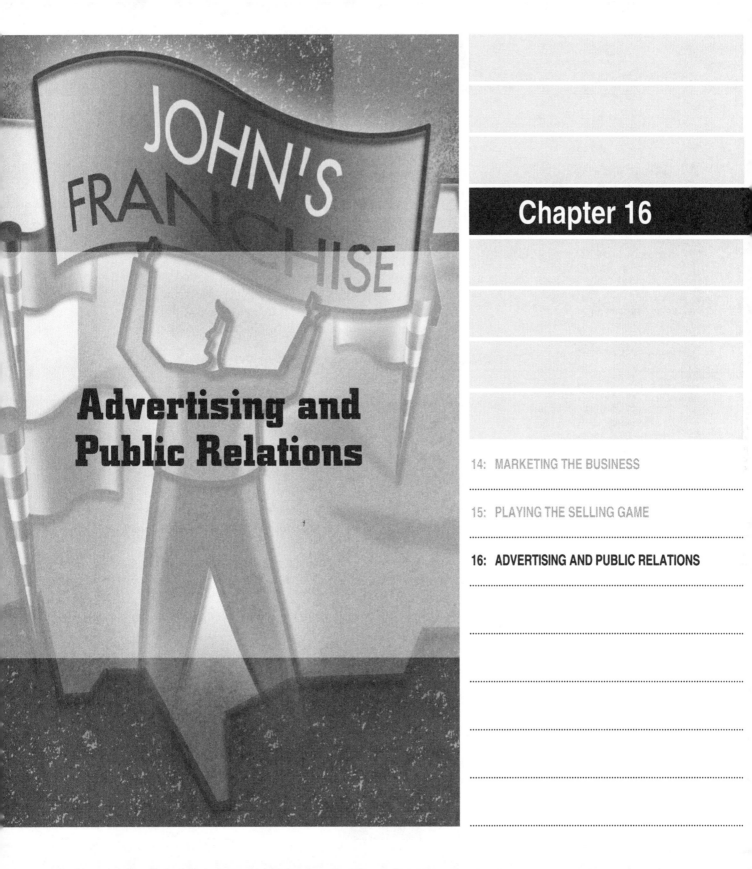

Advertising and Public Relations

Chapter 16

14: MARKETING THE BUSINESS

15: PLAYING THE SELLING GAME

16: ADVERTISING AND PUBLIC RELATIONS

Advertising brings the customer in the first time—operations brings the customer back.

Advertising

Advertising is generally viewed as any form of paid communication where the sponsor or company is identified. Advertising is initially used to help develop brand awareness and build successful brands and consumer products. Coca-Cola and McDonald's continue to spend millions of dollars each year to build heavy advertising programs and increase top-of-the-mind awareness for their products. After the brand has been developed, advertising needs to be continuously used to maintain the brand awareness and the market share.

Advertising to the Consumer

Advertising affects all of our daily lives. Advertising influences many of our purchases and helps us to make informed decisions. Consumers turn to advertising for both its information value as well as its entertainment value. As consumers we are exposed to hundreds of advertisements each day, from a wide variety of advertising media such as TV, radio, billboards, newspapers, and magazines.

Advertising is a very powerful tool. It does have the ability to develop and change attitudes. However, it generally cannot change strongly held values. Advertising, therefore, will generally fail if you are trying to change an attitude based on a person's value system or moral code.

Advertising does, though, have the advantage of providing information from which attitudes are formed. Advertising has a tendency to help develop high degrees of brand loyalty. Advertising will also help an individual understand a product or brand attribute.

Goals of Advertising

Advertising, while providing information about the business, is primarily designed to achieve one or more of three specific goals: provide information to the target audience, persuade the target audience to like or purchase your product, or remind the target audience about the products and their benefits.

Probably the greatest advantage that advertising has is informing people about your products and or services. Behaviors are based upon attitudes formulated from information, knowledge, or previous experiences. By providing the proper information, companies increase people's desire to learn more about the products and services and then to purchase the goods. Children are highly attracted to McDonald's because of their tremendous advertising to their primary target audience of children ages 3 to 11 years old.

Persuasion is designed to help motivate a person to purchase or use a particular product such as Coca-Cola or a Wendy's sandwich. Persuasion is heavily used while a product is going through the growth and early maturation stage in the product life cycle. The important thing to remember, though, is that the promotional side switches from informing customers about the product to persuading them to buy your particular product rather than that of the competition. The focus of persuasion is emphasizing the product's benefits and competitive advantage.

Reminder advertising is also very important, especially for products that are bought on the spur of the moment. Because most decisions as to the location of where to eat are made within a half-hour prior to eating, it is a good idea to use billboards as well as signs around the restaurant so that people will know and remember where you are located.

Signs

One of the best ways of attracting attention to your business is a highly noticed sign. Signs send messages to more people per dollar invested than through almost any other advertising medium that is known. For example, if you actually have a sign that you display for $100 for one year at a location where 10,000 cars happen to pass by every day, then more than 3.5 million impressions have been made, and you should end up gaining approximately 15 customers for every penny that you spend.

> Persuasion is designed to help motivate a person to purchase or use a particular product such as Coca-Cola or a Wendy's sandwich. Persuasion is heavily used while a product is going through the growth and early maturation stage in the product life cycle.

Signs need to be noticeable. They must identify, direct, and inform the public. It is estimated that adding a border to a sign helps the viewer read it more than 26% faster. Using a second color generally increases the reader's retention by 78%.

Sign Suggestions

A sign's lettering is best seen with light colored letters on a dark background—the contrast allows the lettering to appear larger and makes it easier to be read. Black letters on a yellow background or yellow letters on a black background have been proven as the color combinations most effective and easiest to read. Other power mixes are black on white, white on black, and white on blue. If your logo is noticeable on the sign, this is distinctive for your business. The forward slant of the type style is also important and can communicate action and positive feelings, while backward slants generally create negativity and coldness with the reader. Thin letters often provide the message with elegance, while thick letters provide a sense of stability and strength. If using a billboard or outdoor sign, you need to remember that the reader will generally only have sufficient time to read 15 words.

Franchisor Requirements

Most franchisors greatly appreciate the value of advertising and publicity. Therefore most franchisors will require the franchisee to pay anywhere from .5% to 4% of gross sales as the franchisor's "advertising fee." You should know where these funds go. Generally, these funds will be deposited in a separate banking or checking account of the franchisor. They are to be used at the franchisor's sole discretion; however, they are earmarked specifically for advertising. It is from these funds that the franchisor will develop their local, regional, and national advertising. Your advertising payments are then spent to advertise the franchising system as well as to influence the end consumer to purchase your products or services.

Additional Advertising Commitments

You need to investigate all the requirements of a franchisor concerning advertising and marketing expenses. Many franchisors require you to develop and implement an initial local marketing plan that includes coupon and monthly events.

Use of Advertising Funds

Advertising funds are generally used for payment of media time, production of media materials (generally for radio, television, newspaper, or store level materials). In addition these funds may be used for flyers, posters, or any other type of advertising or marketing need.

Advertising expenses may also include costs for personnel, operating expenses, advertising agencies, management fees, research and development, matching fund programs, administrative expenses, production expenses, education and training materials, production of commercials, focus groups, marketing research, purchase of television or radio or other media time, print advertising, and other marketing and advertising uses as authorized by the majority of the elected members of the advertising committee or local co-op.

Advertising Groups

There are generally at least two advertising groups that are formulated in the franchising system. One is a voluntary advertising committee, which is formulated primarily from volunteer franchisees who provide advice and counsel to the franchisor for advertising expenditures. This advertising committee is often a subcommittee of the franchisee association, which is comprised of all franchisees of your franchise system. As a franchisee, you are automatically a member of the franchisee association and therefore, if you wish, you can volunteer to serve on the advertising subcommittee.

Secondly, many franchisors encourage the formation and operation of voluntary franchisee cooperative advertising associations or franchisee co-op. This co-op is organized for the purpose of creating a specific team in a specific area to help coordinate advertising, marketing efforts and programs to help maximize the effective use of local advertising media. When a co-op is formed in your region, you will generally be required to participate in the co-op or lose the right to vote in the decisions regarding advertising and marketing efforts and programs in your area.

The *Los Angeles Times*

The *Los Angeles Times* has published a pamphlet, entitled, "How to get your press release into the right hands at the *Los Angeles Times*." The 22-page booklet explains that a good press release will provide the reader with information about (1) an upcoming event, (2) an event that has just occurred, or (3) notification of important personnel or procedural changes within an organization.

It is important that you include the who, what, where, when, why, and how in the first two paragraphs of your release. Remember to keep your piece short, but if its length exceeds one page, type "more" at the bottom of each continuing page and "end" on the last page.

Franchisor Rights

Most franchisors reserve the right to establish the general standards and guidelines for the operation of all committees and co-ops. They (the franchisor) have the final say in the use of any advertising or in the hiring of any advertising agencies and paying for any advertising programs sponsored by the committee or co-op. No final decisions are generally made about the spending of advertising funds without the franchisors written approval.

Public Relations

Somebody on the team needs to put together the game plan. In sports, this is when the coaches get together after reviewing films about the competition and then decide how they can do better than the competition. Public relations is putting together a game plan. It is involved in evaluating the attitudes of customers and identifying those areas that the public may be interested in and then the plan is executed to earn public understanding and awareness.

Public relations is designed to help an organization communicate with the customers, suppliers, government officials, employees, and the community in which the business is located. Public relations should be used in the business to help develop and maintain a positive image. The public needs to be educated about the products, services, offerings, and especially the competitive edge.

Publicity

Publicity is generally the free public information about the company that is printed in mass media as a news item. Many times the franchisee does best when they write their own news articles (of human interest) and submit these to the local newspapers or business magazines to be printed locally. This may be involved with a special sale or the appearance of a public figure. Additionally if a game day is going to be held and special events will take place either in the parking lot or close to the business, then publicity would make this known throughout the community.

There is a tremendous opportunity here for the business owner to take advantage of free publicity. Think about it—if you were the business editor of the local newspaper and knew that it was going to take two to three days to go out and write a human interest story about a local business, or you were given the opportunity to rewrite a story that was submitted by a local businessperson, and this rewrite would take you only two hours, which would you select? Many business editors are very pleased to get well-written human interest stories that they can rewrite, put their byline on, and publish in their newspaper.

Another thing that can be done with the publicity is to get copies from the newspaper and frame them to place on the walls in the business. Restaurants do this when they get favorable news copy printed in the local newspaper.

Merry Maids

Merry Maids, during their first 10 years of franchising, used to keep track of all their press releases published and found that the value of the business they attracted exceeded $1 million per year.

Conclusion

Advertising and public relations are mainstays in the business. The advertising will bring the customer in the first time, while operations must bring the customer back. The franchisor is generally going to require an advertising fee from .5% to 4% of gross sales to be paid to the franchisor. These advertising funds will be used to promote the business. Advertising is designed to inform, persuade, and remind people about the products or services that are being used. Publicity may be easily written and developed by the franchisee to insure greater exposure of the business in the community. Advertising and public relations help insure the success and growth of the business.

For more information on this topic, visit our Web site at www.businesstown.com

AmeriSpec

Name of Fee	Amount	Due Date	Remarks
Earned Service Fee	7% of Gross Receipts, with a minimum of $250 per month	By Friday of each week, based on gross receipts for the prior week, and on the last day of each calendar month for the balance of the amount due that month.	
Advertising Contribution	3% of Gross Receipts, with a minimum of $125 per month	Same as Earned Service Fee	We will separately account for these amounts in an advertising fund managed by us.

Applebee's Neighborhood Grill & Bar

Name of Fee	Amount	Due Date	Remarks
Royalty	4% of total gross sales. But can be increased to 5% by us after 1/1/2000	Payable monthly on the 12th day of the next month	Gross sales includes all revenues from the restaurant. Gross sales does not include sales or use tax
Advertising (National Fund)	1.5% of total gross sales. But can be increased by us at any time to 4%	Same as Royalty	
Advertising (Local Market)	1.5% of total gross sales. But can be increased by us at any time		

Applebee's Neighborhood Grill & Bar (continued)

Name of Fee	Amount	Due Date	Remarks
Coopertive Advertising	Maximum 1.5% of total gross sales		We can require you to form, or you and another franchisee(s) in the same market can form, an advertising coopertive to spend the local advertising fee noted above. We have no vote in these cooperatives unless we have restaurants in the market. If so, our vote is determined in the same way yours is

Comfort Inns, Suites

Name of Fee	Amount	Due Date
Continuing Franchise Fee	5.25% of the preceding month's Gross Room Revenues (GRR) for Comfort Inn, Comfort Inn & Suites, and Comfort Hotel. 5% of the preceding months GRR for Comfort Suites	Reports on the previous month's GRRs are due monthly by the 10th day of the month. We will bill you on the 15th of the month and your payment is due by the 1st of the next month
Marketing Fees	2.1% of the preceding month's GRR	Same as Continuing Franchise Fee
Reservation Fees	1.75% of the preceding months GRR	Same as Continuing Franchise Fee
Satellite Communication Fee	$130 per month	Payable monthly on the 1st day of the month

Managing for Success

In this section, you'll learn:

- **How to motivate your employees so they're productive and loyal**

- **Laws pertaining to hiring and firing**

- **How and why to write an employee handbook**

- **Different employee evaluation methods**

- **The proper way to terminate an employee— and how to protect yourself legally**

CHAPTER 17 MANAGING THE BUSINESS **CHAPTER 18** MOTIVATION AND LEADERSHIP **CHAPTER 19** RECRUITMENT **CHAPTER 20** HIRING AND SELECTION **CHAPTER 21** ORIENTATION AND PERSONNEL POLICIES **CHAPTER 22** PERFORMANCE EVALUATIONS **CHAPTER 23** DISCIPLINE AND TERMINATION **CHAPTER 24** SPECIAL EMPLOYMENT ISSUES

Managing the
Business

Chapter 17

17: MANAGING THE BUSINESS

18: MOTIVATION AND LEADERSHIP

19: RECRUITMENT

20: HIRING AND SELECTION

21: ORIENTATION AND PERSONNEL POLICIES

22: PERFORMANCE EVALUATIONS

23: DISCIPLINE AND TERMINATION

24: SPECIAL EMPLOYMENT ISSUES

Many businesspeople entering the franchising field prefer the following analogy: If two companies, one a small business just starting and the other one very successful, merge and create a new unit, what happens to the abilities, skills, and opportunities of the weaker company? The start-up company is taken over by the successful corporation and trained in the various fields and operations of the business. A franchise business is also watched over, looked after, and taught all the skills that are necessary to become successful. Both businesses become profitable and learn not to just depend upon each other but develop an interdependency that strengthens their union. Both businesses are financially justified. Both businesses grow and thrive. This is a successful franchise system.

Franchising requires a tremendous amount of work. However, the potential for reward and success is phenomenal. The opportunities are truly present. The success is generally dependent upon the desire and attitudes of the new franchisee.

Take the time to learn those skills, techniques, and procedures that will allow you to become the best possible owner and manager. If you own the business, you are going to have to manage the business. You are going to have to be a manager. Successful managers are individuals who get things done through other people.

Managing Priorities

How do you decide what to do first on your "to do" list? Most of us take the easy jobs first. You need to change. You need to know what your top priorities are. You need to know what results you are seeking before you can know what jobs to do first. You need to control your time and not let others control your time for you.

You can manage your priorities and your business by:

1. Defining the results you are seeking
2. Establishing the tasks (steps) that will accomplish the results
3. Doing those tasks that are most important
4. Not letting others control your time

Management Functions

Successful management is simply successfully working with people. It involves a proper balance between head and heart. When the proper balance between head and heart is achieved, the results are fantastic. Management is the process of teaching, motivating, directing, delegating, changing and even prioritizing the tasks, goals, and direction of yourself and your staff.

As a franchisee, you are going to have to make decisions, direct activities of others, allocate resources, and help everyone obtain their goals. You are going to need to develop an organization. You are going to need to be able to plan, organize, direct, and control members of your organization. These are the four basic management functions.

Planning

A planning function is going to require that you establish goals, develop a strategy for accomplishing those goals, and develop the plans that allow you to integrate and accomplish activities. Planning is an essential function of all organizations, whether with family, friends, or business. The planning process might be overlooked—when this occurs the old adage is true:

WHEN YOU FAIL TO PLAN, YOU PLAN TO FAIL.

Organizing

This is it. You need to take the responsibility to develop your organizational structure. You need to determine who is going to be doing what, when, where, how, and why. You need to look at all the tasks that need to be done, how to group those tasks, and how those tasks will be performed. You also need to figure out who reports to whom and who is going to be making what decisions.

Can you imagine Brett Favre, quarterback of the Green Bay Packers, going to the line of scrimmage without organization—everyone standing around wondering what to do? You need to take the time to organize and make sure that everyone knows what he or she should be doing.

First Things First

You should always remember: first, plan your work; second, work your plan.

Directing

All teams or organizations contain people. As the coach, franchisee, or manager, you need to take the responsibility to direct and lead these people. When you take the time to motivate your players, develop communication links, direct activities, and resolve player conflicts, you are in the process of directing or leading.

Controlling

You need to take the time to monitor your players' performance. You need to compare their actual performance with established standards. You need to see if each player performed his proper activities. Just as the coach of the soccer team reviews films of each play, you should review the activities of your employees to ensure that what they are doing is in accordance with what they should be doing.

Management Skills

You should always remember that you are trying to not just improve yourself and others, but also optimize your profits. To do this you need to make sure that you have developed proper skills and have established procedures for others to achieve their necessary skill levels. There are essentially four different management skills with which you need to be familiar: business skills, operations skills, human skills, and conceptual skills

Business skills

Business skills refer to the ability to provide business knowledge and application to your business. You should be able to understand how to market, promote, advertise, manage, and comprehend the legal, accounting, and financial operations of your business. You should take the time to acquire the knowledge that helps you understand franchising, opening a new store, managing your store, and the financial aspects of your new store.

Operations Skills

Operations skills refer to the ability to run and perform the different tasks and operations of the business. A civil engineer needs to know how to build a road, building, or bridge, while tax accountants need to understand tax law and accounting principles. You are going to need to know how to perform the different tasks and functions of your business. You need to be trained in all the tasks about your business so that you can also help train others. All tasks, or jobs, require specialized expertise.

Human Skills

All of us need to continue to develop our human skills or our abilities to work with, understand, motivate, and help other people. You need to be able to work with individuals as well as in groups. You need to develop your listening skills. You need to be able to understand the needs and wants of others. If you are going to be able to get things done through other people, you must be able to develop your communication, motivation, and delegation skills. These skills will allow us to be better people.

Something that will be mentioned several times in this book is smiling. The smile is a sign of warmth, of friendship, and of understanding. It has a tendency to include people rather than exclude. At times, you need to learn how to smile so that you can draw other people to you.

Conceptual Skills

The mental ability to analyze difficult or complex situations is referred to as a conceptual skill. Your decision-making skills are based primarily on your ability to spot problems, identify alternatives that may solve these problems, evaluate these alternatives, and choose the best one. Even though you may have the business operations and human skills necessary to be a tremendous success, you may yet fail because of your inability to process and interpret information.

The Sports Analogy

Some of us are comfortable with examples or illustrations taken from athletics. Let us compare the franchising relationship between the franchisor and franchisee, franchisee and manager/assistant managers, and employees. Regardless of the team sport, it really doesn't matter which player makes the points. When one individual scores, the whole team scores.

You need to recognize that each and every individual on the team can score. You also need to realize that many times that third string member or the person who is paid the least in the entire organization (such as the cashier/order taker) is the front line contact with the customer. You need to recognize the opportunity and necessity of training everyone on your team and helping them all to become a success, because when they succeed, you succeed.

Strategic Planning

Planning takes time but the results are invaluable. The strategic planning process is simply those decisions and actions that are going to be required for you to achieve competitive advantages and earn the profits you desire. Strategic planning is a combination of:

1. Philosophy
2. Vision
3. Mission
4. Goals
5. Objectives
6. Strategies

The final strategies will answer those questions of how and what to do to satisfy and achieve the objectives you have established.

Philosophy

The philosophy for your business is simply those general principles governing the business and the employees' behavior. Today, this is often grounded in ethical intentions and contact. You need to be able to write down and determine the basic philosophy you want to use to run and operate your business. One franchisee in the travel industry uses a dress code for all female employees concerning the lengths of their skirts. It is simply that, when you kneel down, if the skirt does not touch the floor then the skirt is too short, and you should go home and change your clothes.

Vision

The vision is where you want to be in 20 to 30 years. This is an explanation of your personal desires and what you would like to do relative to your business. The vision is a desire statement. It is very personal and it helps declare the ambitions and expectations of the owners.

Mission

The mission defines your business. It is a statement of your unique purpose, the scope of your operations in both product and marketing terms. It generally looks 10 years into the future. Defining a business mission statement is divided into two sections:

A. Internal
  1. Who are we?
  2. What do we do?
B. External
  1. What is being satisfied?
  2. Who is being satisfied?
  3. How is the need being satisfied?

Many franchisees have found it invaluable to develop mission statements for themselves as well as to have each employee develop his or her own personal mission statement accompanied with goals and objectives.

> The mission defines your business. It is a statement of your unique purpose, the scope of your operations in both product and marketing terms. It generally looks 10 years into the future.

Goals

Goals define the areas that you wish to allocate your time and energies to accomplish something of value. When you establish goals, you are generally thinking about a five to ten year period of time in the future. Goals are general. For example, you may wish to obtain higher revenue growth.

Objectives

Objectives are specific and they also provide measurable activity. An operational objective is defined as an activity containing three parts: 1) definable, 2) measurable, and 3) within a specific time period. For instance, "we are going to increase sales" is a goal and not an objective. An objective would be the following: "We wish to increase sales by 10% this coming year over last year's sales." This objective is definable—you are talking about the sales of the business, measurable—10% increase, and time period—this coming year. The time frame for objectives is generally one to two years.

Strategies

Strategies simply answer the questions of how to fulfill and achieve the objectives. These are the tasks or activities that will be performed to satisfy the objectives. For example, your strategy for increasing sales by 10% might be to hire one additional salesperson or to add a fish sandwich to your menu.

Conclusion

Practically speaking, management is the ability to "Walk the Talk." The basic management functions include planning ("When you fail to plan, you plan to fail" and, "First plan your work; second work your plan"), organizing, directing and leading, and finally controlling. You need to develop your management abilities, including your business skills, operations skills, human skills, and your conceptual skills. Finally, as owners and/or managers, you must develop your strategic plans including your philosophy, vision, mission, goals, objectives, and strategies. You must be able to "Walk the Talk."

> Objectives are specific and they also provide measurable activity. An operational objective is defined as an activity containing three parts: 1) definable, 2) measurable, and 3) within a specific time period.

For more information on this topic, visit our Web site at www.businesstown.com

Motivation and Leadership

Chapter 18

17: MANAGING THE BUSINESS

18: MOTIVATION AND LEADERSHIP

19: RECRUITMENT

20: HIRING AND SELECTION

21: ORIENTATION AND PERSONNEL POLICIES

22: PERFORMANCE EVALUATIONS

23: DISCIPLINE AND TERMINATION

24: SPECIAL EMPLOYMENT ISSUES

Leadership is simply the ability to influence an individual or group toward the achievement of goals. Leaders play a heavy role in understanding and working with groups. The leader generally provides the direction necessary to achieve goals.

The Individual

All individuals have values, beliefs, opinions, and attitudes that help form their personalities. Simply stated, if you can understand the attitudes and motivation of an individual, you will generally understand why they act or behave in a certain manner. The leader's role is to learn to understand how these attitudes and motivations affect their staff.

Because nearly all of our behavior is based on motives and attitudes, you need to understand where these come from. Our attitudes are generally developed from our own knowledge.

KNOWLEDGE → ATTITUDES → MOTIVES → INDIVIDUAL
BEHAVIOR → GROUP BEHAVIOR

Knowledge

The knowledge that you have is simply information or experience that you have acquired about a subject, an object, or a person. Surprisingly, this knowledge does not have to be true or correct. There are three primary sources that are often present, including parents (family), friends, and our working environment. The media provides us a tremendous amount of information about what is happening locally, nationally, and internationally. You need to recognize that if you provide knowledge to people and they retain or accept that knowledge, then you have, in part, helped develop their attitudes or opinions. Therefore, as franchisees or leaders in your business, you need to continuously provide knowledge, information, and training to your employees so that they will always have reason to perform at their best levels.

Customer Service

Customer service is the most important function in your business. It is the one thing that differentiates you from your competition. It is your job as a franchisee to exercise your company's promise to the customers and to get your employees to make that promise come alive. The research data is clear: Customers are three times as likely to do business with you again if you can solve the problem faster, better, and easier than the competition. Can you do it and are you willing to train your employees to do it?

Attitudes

An attitude is simply a predisposition to behave. The wonderful thing about attitudes is that they are generally formulated based on prior knowledge, information, or experience. Can you think of one attitude that you have that is not based on prior knowledge, information, or experience?

In your business it is advantageous to provide positive and favorable information to your employees. This increases their positive attitude about you and the business.

Motives

Motives are simply those functions that help an individual activate, direct, and channel behavior toward specific goals. When a motive is strong enough (I need a glass of water), then the behavior necessary to fulfill the desire usually follows (the individual gets a glass of water). Most of us work so that we can receive the money that allows us to live the lifestyle that we want.

Most franchisees have a desire to succeed. These desires and motives are excellent. What you need to do is to provide knowledge and information to your employees so that they will have positive attitudes that will allow them to be motivated in the right direction to achieve the goals of the company.

Behavior

Behavior is simply an action or a performance by an individual. This is a result of the knowledge, attitudes, and motives of the individual.

The reason why you advertise and market your business is so that you can provide knowledge or information to potential customers so that they will have a positive attitude and be motivated to purchase the product or service.

Once you have a large number of individuals purchasing your products and services, then they in turn will encourage others. This forms group behaviors.

College Scholarships

Many franchisees, particularly McDonald's and other quick-service restaurants, have found that by offering their college students employee scholarships, they can retain the employees through their college programs. Some franchisees offer $1,000 to high school seniors and college students who work an average of 20 hours a week for at least 12 months while maintaining a C+ grade point average. These incentives help students appreciate their work while attending college and challenge them to study hard while at school.

Home Instead Senior Care

Home Instead Senior Care provides a very unique and motivating incentive program for their franchisees. Each year they have a "qualified" leadership conference. The qualifiers receive roundtrip airfare for two and all inclusive accommodations at a luxurious resort hotel for four days and three nights for achieving service revenues in excess of $150,000 between May 1 and August 31 in one year. In other words, for a four-month period, May, June, July, and August, the franchisees need to have sales of $150,000 for their franchise program. If they do this, then they go to a resort hotel for a "leadership conference" and enjoy the bounties and blessings of Mexico, Hawaii, or a similar resort area. Do people achieve these lofty goals? More than the franchisor ever expected.

Think about it. Estimating royalties of 6%, or $9,000, in franchisor revenue, the $1,000 to $1,200 cost is well worth the incentive for the entire franchising system.

Here is the question: What are you going to do as a franchisee to influence or provide knowledge to your employees on a monthly, weekly, or daily basis so that they will be motivated to achieve goals?

Motivation

People act. People perform all kinds of behaviors. The exciting part is when a person is motivated because, then, the person is exerting a level of effort towards satisfying an organizational goal or achieving individual goals. The exciting part is when the personal need and the organizational goal achieve the same results.

Everyone is different in their basic motivational drives. No two individuals respond the same way to any reward, stimulus, or encouragement. Many people have the capability of reading a book in one day, while others of us find it difficult to read for more than 20 minutes at a time. Motivation is generally the difference between those people who are highly involved and those people who have a much lower level of activity.

How do you motivate? It is generally through the accomplishment or satisfaction of some personal need. The person perceives that they want something. If the desire is strong enough, then the person's behavior will be to obtain that reward.

All of us have been motivated at one time or another, but few of us understand exactly why we were motivated or why we did specific acts. How do we turn it on within ourselves or how do you motivate others? Most of us do not know.

Even staff, colleagues, and family want you to motivate them at times. They want you to have the responsibility to influence them to act or perform the duties they should. This is a task you cannot put aside. It is a simple task that you need to learn more about.

Motivation is not permanent. Like any activity, it stops and starts. But motivation needs to be done on a regular basis. If you take the time, you can even see the two words that make up motivation—the first part is *motive*, which leads to the second part, which is *action* or—motivation. You need to be aware of the actions necessary to accomplish the tasks in your business. Awareness is the first key to successful motivation. You also need to be aware not just of the tasks but of the people with whom you work and their abilities and needs.

As you get to know people, you learn that most of them are motivated by incentives, growth opportunities, and fear. One of the main reasons why people work is the incentives associated with the work such as pay, recognition, and achievement. One of the reasons that people enjoy work is because of the opportunities to expand, learn, and to accomplish new tasks. People also must face the fear of failure or the fear of being rejected and not accomplishing the tasks at hand.

The strongest factor in motivation is growth opportunities. This provides all of us with the chance to develop and to succeed. This offers each of us the possibility of experiencing that "fifteen minutes of fame." But more importantly, it allows us to reach the potential that is within us.

Training becomes a part of successful motivation. Training could include learning about job characteristics, job skills, attitude, goal setting, self-esteem, and even parenting. Training will help your employees improve their skills and abilities and to achieve self-confidence and improve their behavioral skill levels. It is easier to be motivated to do something if you have the ability to do it.

People will stay where there is an opportunity for growth. The benefit of growth motivation is that people will be retained and be able to perform at a higher level of skill. But it also requires a long-term orientation and commitment from you, the franchisee. You must provide those opportunities for growth and allow people to stay and develop your business.

Action

A strange phenomenon of motivation is just getting people to act. When people are actually involved in the action of a business, they feel better. Simply getting up in the morning feels better than staying in bed. Action changes attitudes. Successful actions lead to successful businesses. As an owner/manager, you need to recognize the need to get your people to act. They need to take those actions that will cause your business to be a success. At times you simply

An Example of Motivation

Just as in any sporting activity, the U.S. women's soccer team had tremendous incentives to be in the world championship of soccer. They knew that by doing so they would increase their pay, but also win world recognition for the United States and for their team. There were tremendous growth opportunities associated with their game and the winning of the world championship. Finally they were able to overcome fear of failure and the fear of competing to be the very best that one can be. They succeeded. They were motivated. They achieved.

have to motivate them so that they will go out and perform the action, develop a positive attitude, and repeat the action over and over again.

Leadership Behaviors

Robert House developed a leadership theory that is often referred as the path-goal theory. The idea behind this leadership model is that it is the leader's responsibility to assist his or her followers in attaining the goals to which they have been directed. The efficient leader, therefore, helps the followers get from where they are to accomplishing the work goals along the path that has been made easier by the leader. There are basically four major leadership behaviors that many of us will fall into at one time or another. These include:

Directive Leader

The directive leader, like most of us, lets the office personnel know what is expected of them, then schedules the work, and finally gives specific guidance as to how the tasks should be accomplished. The directive leader develops the structure and the tasks that must be accomplished. Just as the coach of the soccer team will organize the practice and take the players through the different activities, so a leader will also outline the tasks and explain how they are to be accomplished.

Supportive Leader

This is a friendly person who shows concern for the needs and desires of the employees. The supportive leader is considerate of others and tries to help them to better understand how they can accomplish what needs to be done.

Participative Leader

Many people enjoy a participative leader, wherein the leader works with and consults with the subordinates in the business. The suggestions are received from everyone before a decision is made.

Compensation Package?

Jerry Wilkerson of Franchise Recruiters estimates that the average costs of hiring and training a manager for a franchise store is $27,000. This does not include the start-up time it takes for the manager to develop skills and get up to speed. Therefore, they try to keep good managers by giving them a salary hike of $5,000, coupled with a bonus of $10,000—and they are actually saving money by not having to hire a new manager.

The participative leader encourages input from fellow workers and tries to use as many of their suggestions as is efficient and feasible.

Achievement-Oriented Leader

The achievement-oriented leader establishes goals and expectations at a fairly high level. The leader then helps the staff reach those goals and expectations. Many leaders have found that by establishing goals for their staff, the staff generally responds in a positive way and will strive to accomplish those tasks. One businessperson told his sales force that if they increased the total sales for the company by 20% over the next year, he would take each salesperson, including a spouse or friend, to Hawaii for a week (where they would hold their next sales conference). In just 11 months and a few days the salespeople came back to their leader and showed him the sales figures while asking what time the plane left for Hawaii.

> The achievement-oriented leader establishes goals and expectations at a fairly high level. The leader then helps the staff reach those goals and expectations.

Developing Loyalty with your Staff

Loyalty is something that must be earned. Being honest and showing respect for those who surround us creates loyalty. You need to learn how to create and strengthen the loyalty among your own staff and with your coworkers. Loyalty cannot be commanded or demanded. It must be earned.

Building loyalty is very important in your business. It will help build trust and persistence among your workers. It will provide an incentive and drive for your workers. If you show loyalty, role-play loyalty, and expect loyalty, then generally you will be able to develop a loyal relationship with your staff.

You need to recognize that being dishonest or not telling your staff the full story will greatly reduce the chances for developing loyalty in your organization. Your staff will see through any dishonesty or any lack of support. They actually want to be loyal, but loyalty is something that has to be earned and it is only developed through respect and trust. But once it is established, it becomes one of the greatest motivation and growth factors in successful businesses.

Work with your staff and they will respect you for it. Honor your staff and they will return the honor. Trust your staff and they will trust you. Be loyal to your staff and they will be loyal to you.

Conclusion

You as a leader must develop the ability to influence others so that they will achieve the goals of the organization. Individuals are influenced through five levels, including knowledge (experience), attitudes, motives, individual behavior, and finally, group behavior. People are motivated because of their desire to achieve and to accomplish new tasks or goals. Your staff will be loyal to you as you are loyal to them and you build a relationship of trust and respect with them. A good leader can be directive, supportive, participative, achievement-oriented, and help the employees achieve their goals and tasks. By motivating and leading your employees, you will generally reach the highest pinnacles of success.

> You as a leader must develop the ability to influence others so that they will achieve the goals of the organization.

For more information on this topic, visit our Web site at www.businesstown.com

Recruitment

Chapter 19

17: MANAGING THE BUSINESS

18: MOTIVATION AND LEADERSHIP

19: RECRUITMENT

20: HIRING AND SELECTION

21: ORIENTATION AND PERSONNEL POLICIES

22: PERFORMANCE EVALUATIONS

23: DISCIPLINE AND TERMINATION

24: SPECIAL EMPLOYMENT ISSUES

Hiring Costs

Most franchisees are not aware of the time and expense of recruiting and hiring a new employee. There is a significant cost incurred by the franchisee because of the time it takes to identify, hire, and train new employees so that they can become productive and earn their pay. Therefore it is critical once you have identified and hired a good employee that you are able to keep that employee from taking employment elsewhere. Only by doing this can you reduce your turnover and cost.

One of the keys to success, once you are open, is the ability to hire the best employees you can find, manage them effectively, and use appropriate discipline if and when needed. If you are to succeed as a franchisee you must be able to identify and hire good employees that possess honesty, integrity, a good work ethic, and the ability to get along with you, other employees, and with the customers.

Recruitment

First things first. Where do your find quality employees? There are several methods by which one can locate potential employees. Which of these methods would work best for you will depend upon your circumstances and the labor market where your franchise is located.

Following are several sources from which you can recruit quality applicants.

Employee Referrals and Recommendations

Ask employees. One of the best sources for new employees, who will perform effectively on the job, is a recommendation from a current employee. This is because an employee will seldom recommend someone to work for you unless he or she believes that person will do a good job. After all, if an employee makes a recommendation, the quality of his or her friend's performance will reflect on the employee's own reputation. It is quite safe to say that a current employee will not recommend someone who is inappropriate. Further, an employee referral usually reduces the chance that the referral will have unrealistic expectations. Consequently, the likelihood that this employee will stay on the job increases.

Ask Customers

Many franchisees find it very easy to ask their good customers if they would like a job. Many quick-service restaurants find most of their new employees from the customers that walk through the doors. If a business is close to a university or high school then it is easy to locate potential employees. Just ask the most friendly and courteous students if they are interested in employment. Many accounting services hire their clients. Look for good people wherever you go.

Advertisements

These are announcements communicating to the general public that a position in your franchise is open.

Newspapers

This is probably one of the most popular methods used to recruit new employees. However, at the same time, it is probably one of the least effective methods of recruiting employees. Most advertisements are placed in the local newspaper by the franchisee. Even though this advertisement will usually result in a large number of applications, often the applicants are either not qualified or are only looking for a job to fill an immediate need for a short period of time. With newspaper advertising you reach everyone within the distribution area of the newspaper.

Due to the pressures against discriminatory hiring practices, there will be a need on your part to process all of the applications received as a result of the newspaper advertisement so that you can document that you did not practice discrimination. This can be costly and time consuming. However, if there is substantial unemployment within the area of your franchise, an ad in the newspaper will be much more effective in recruiting quality employees.

Signs

A very effective advertisement for hiring employees is to place a Help Wanted sign in the window of your location. The cost to place this advertisement is $0 and you will be amazed at the number of people who see your Help Wanted sign and apply. This is a very effective way to advertise.

Radio

Also, you might consider buying a brief advertisement spot on the local radio station. If you were to use the radio for advertisement

Newspaper Ad Procedures

If you do decide to place advertisements in the local newspapers and other print sources, there are several procedures you must follow. First, your ad must describe the nature and responsibilities of the position and the characteristics you are looking for in a prospective employee. You must stress the positive aspects of your business and the position you are hiring for without including what you plan to pay. Further, due to federal statutes barring discrimination you must write an ad that meets legal requirements so that you will not be sued for discrimination. You must be careful in the verbiage you use in the job ad so that it doesn't appear that you are discriminating against a group of people that is protected by these statutes. Therefore, your job advertisement should stick strictly to the job skills needed and the basic responsibilities required of the position.

purposes, you would want to choose the radio station that is most listened to by the group of people that most of your employees would be coming from. For example, if your hiring needs require you to hire large numbers of young people, you would buy an advertising spot on a radio station that broadcasts top 40 hits and rock 'n roll as opposed to classical music.

Flyers

Another effective means of advertisement is to distribute flyers in the neighborhoods surrounding your franchise. This method puts out notice to those who live closest to your location that (1) You are in the process of opening a new business that they would want to visit, but also, (2) You are looking for employees. After all, since traveling to and from work is a major expense for an employee, it is best to hire employees who live the closest to you. The further away an employee lives from your location the less likely the employee will stay with you for any length of time.

Networking

During the course of your life and career, you have probably met a lot of people. Subsequently, you have been involved in networking situations. In finding qualified employees, your networking can be very valuable. For example, if you are a member of a church, then you can look to other members or their children as prospective quality employees. After all, you know these people and you have already developed a relationship with them. Also, if you have participated with other organizations such as the Boy Scouts and Girl Scouts, these can be valuable sources for prospective qualified employees. The opportunity to find quality employees through the networking you have already done is limitless. And in these cases, there is minimal cost and time needed to locate these prospective employees.

Employment Agencies

There are several types of employment agencies from which you can locate quality employees. All states provide a public employment

> Flyers put out notice to those who live closest to your location that (1) You are in the process of opening a new business that they would want to visit, but also, (2) You are looking for employees.

service. The main function of these agencies is to locate jobs for those individuals who have registered with their state employment agency. These individuals tend to be unemployed, unskilled, and have minimum training. However, there are large numbers of jobs in the franchise setting that require minimal skills.

Second, there are private employment agencies. The major difference between a private employment agency and a public employment service is image. Private agencies have the reputation for offering positions and applicants of a higher caliber and therefore tend to attract more qualified people. Further, a private employment agency normally screens its applicants against the criteria specified by the employer.

Finally, to fill those positions within your franchise that are mid and upper level, you might try a management employment agency or consultant. These employment agencies are referred to as headhunter firms. They specialize in placing people in middle and top level positions. You would use an employment agency of this type to fill only management positions and above.

Outplacement Services

In the current economy, companies are constantly letting go large numbers of employees. Many of these companies will offer their employees outplacement services in assisting them to find new employment. If you become aware of such a situation, you should take advantage of it. Even though these employees will probably need to be retrained, at least you will be able to find out some information concerning their work habits and work ethics.

Professional Organizations, Trade Associations, and Trade Magazines

Many professional organizations operate placement services for the benefit of their members. Also, trade associations and trade magazines will have listings of available people who are already in the trade or business. Usually these applicants are considered to be low risk since they have already been prescreened. Once again, as with headhunters, these types of resources would be better used for the more specialized and executive level positions within your organization.

> To fill those positions within your franchise that are mid and upper level, you might try a management employment agency or consultant. These employment agencies are referred to as headhunter firms.

High Schools, Technical Schools, Colleges, and Universities

Educational institutions at all levels offer many opportunities for you to find quality employees. Students of all educational institutions usually must work in order to make money for their own support, the support of their family, and/or to help defray expenses of their education. These students realize that they might not be able to find their dream job while in school and therefore they are motivated to find and keep a job that supports them while getting their education. Students who are looking for employment while in school can be expected to stay with you until graduation, which can be several years down the road. Also, all educational institutions operate placement services where prospective employers can review the credentials of the graduates. Therefore, educational institutions are an excellent source of quality employees, both from the prospective of those students who must work and earn money while in school and those who are looking for permanent full-time employment upon graduation. The advertisement cost incurred in locating such employees is minimal.

Senior Citizens

People who have worked their entire lives that are now retired comprise a growing group of quality employees. Many retired senior citizens realize that they miss having a job to go to along with the fact that their retirement income may not meet all their needs. Therefore, they are looking for part-time work to have something to do and to accommodate their financial needs. Senior citizens tend to be hard working and reliable. As a result, they are a good source of prospective employees. The first place to look for senior citizens would be by contacting local retirement organizations and local governmental agencies where you live that cater to senior citizens. For example, most counties will have an extensive listing of courses that senior citizens are allowed to take to further their education. This would be an excellent place to find quality employees. After all, senior citizens are taking these courses to enhance their skills for both personal reasons and potentially for new job opportunities. Also, each state has large retirement organizations that people who

> Students who are looking for employment while in school can be expected to stay with you until graduation, which can be several years down the road.

are retired from their profession belong to, and who might be very interested in finding employment. Senior citizens will be a growing source of quality employees in the years to come.

Your Franchisor

Your franchisor has spent many years in the business and knows a lot of people. The field representative for your franchisor is probably aware of potential employees looking for work in your area. Therefore, it is always wise to talk to your franchisor when looking for quality employees.

Family and Friends

A franchisee should convey to members of their family and to their close friends that they are in the process of hiring quality employees for their franchise. Many times this is a successful strategy. However, you must always be careful when looking to these sources because of the potential negative outcome. Even with this in mind, this source is too important to over look.

Other Sources of Potential Quality Employees

Temporary-help organizations and employee-leasing companies are good sources to consider when certain situations arise. These organizations can be a source of employees when they are needed on a temporary basis or for short-term fluctuations. Employee leasing is where you lease employees for a long period of time from an employee-leasing firm that actually employs them. The benefit here is that the employee-leasing firm handles all of the paperwork and pays all the taxes as concerns the leased employees. This is certainly an asset when you have little time to fill a position. Leased employees typically remain with an organization for a longer period of time. However, the down side is that because the leased employees are retained by the leasing firm and then leased to you, further expenses are incurred by you because there is an additional layer of costs for using these services. Temporary-help organizations and employee-leasing firms are

> A franchisee should convey to members of their family and to their close friends that they are in the process of hiring quality employees for their franchise. Many times this is a successful strategy.

mentioned as potential sources of employees. However, the likelihood of these sources being utilized, especially in the early days of your franchise, is usually insignificant. The purpose here is that you need to be informed of these sources should the appropriate occasion arise.

Final Words on Hiring

In the previous sections we have listed several ways in which to find quality employees. Whichever route you choose it is always best to hire experienced people. You may have to pay experienced employees more money, but it is money well spent. After all, if the person already has experience in your industry there are probably several things you can learn from this employee. It is important to remember that when you are hiring management, it is crucial that they have experience in your industry. In reviewing applications for management, you should look for employees that have substantial experience in managing people, dealing with customers, and knowledge of your industry.

Often the question arises of whether to hire just full-time employees or both part-time and full-time employees. This is an important consideration since your employees are a large cost in doing business. Most franchises, in order to minimize employee costs, hire both full-time and part-time employees. Most franchises have periods of time that are slow and during this time will require only a minimal number of employees. However, at other periods when business is brisk, additional employees are required. Therefore you would hire part-time employees to work only during those brisk periods. Another benefit to hiring part-time employees is that you are able to pay them a lower hourly rate without the full benefit package that you offer to your full-time employees. Because of this the cost per hour of your part-time employees is significantly less. However, when there is an opening for a full-time employee and you have a part-time employee who wants to fill the slot, you already have someone who is well trained and is qualified for the position. In this case, you are left with only a part-time position to fill.

It is important to remember that when you are hiring management, it is crucial that they have experience in your industry. In reviewing applications for management, you should look for employees that have substantial experience in managing people, dealing with customers, and knowledge of your industry.

Potential Recruiting Problems

Depending upon several variables, you might encounter difficulties in recruiting and selecting the employees of your choice. These constraints are as follows:

The Image of Your Franchise

If the image of your franchise or industry is low or negative, then the likelihood of you being able to attract large numbers of applicants is reduced. Some industries have a reputation for being in decline or engaging in practices that result in polluting the environment or being indifferent to employee's needs. Such reputations can reduce your effectiveness in attracting quality employees.

The Job Itself

If the job that needs to be filled is unattractive, then the recruiting will be difficult. A job that is viewed as low paying, lacking promotion potential, boring, full of anxiety, or even hazardous will seldom allow you to attract quality applicants.

Internal Organizational Policies

Even though it is important to promote from within whenever possible, this can reduce the number of applicants for the lowest-level entry positions, since such positions tend to be low paying or boring.

> If the job that needs to be filled is unattractive, then the recruiting will be difficult.

Governmental Policies

Due to the laws banning discrimination, one can no longer seek out preferred employees based on nonjob-related factors such as physical appearance, sex, or religious background. You must only hire based on job-related factors.

Recruiting Costs

A constraint on finding quality employees is cost. Recruiting efforts are expensive. Therefore, you might have a difficult time finding quality employees because of the expense involved.

The previously listed items are constraints on a franchisee's recruiting efforts. However, whether these constraints will affect you and limit your freedom to recruit and select a candidate will largely depend on the labor market in which you operate. If there is high unemployment in your franchise area you will have minimal problems in being able to recruit quality employees at a reduced cost. Inasmuch, if unemployment is very low, then the reverse will be true.

Conclusion

Recruiting great employees is at the heart of a successful franchise. You have the ability, and the people are available. Now just do it. Ask employees for suggestions, ask customers/clients if they want employment, advertise, use your network, employment agencies, placement services, schools, senior citizens, even family and friends. Recruitment can be fun when you do it right.

> Recruiting great employees is at the heart of a successful franchise.

For more information on this topic, visit our Web site at www.businesstown.com

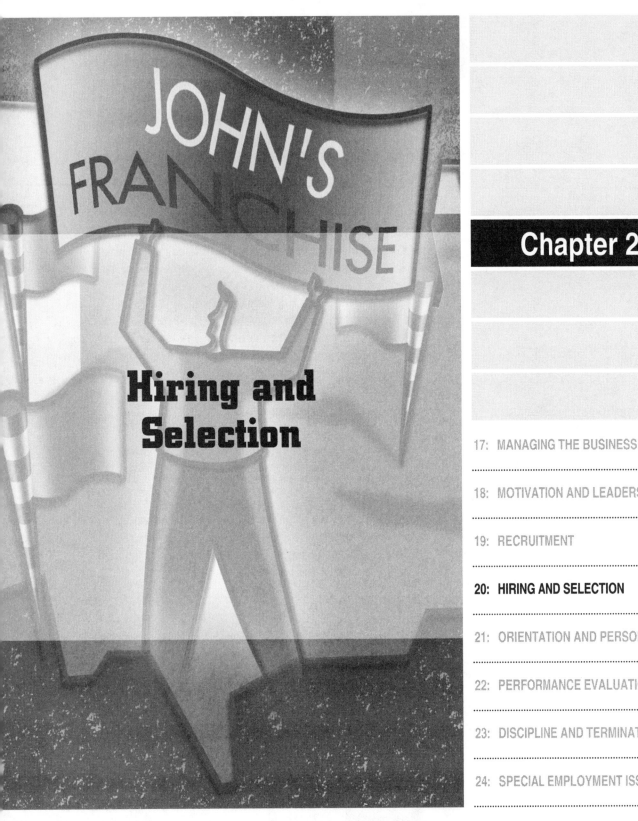

Hiring and Selection

Chapter 20

17: MANAGING THE BUSINESS

18: MOTIVATION AND LEADERSHIP

19: RECRUITMENT

20: HIRING AND SELECTION

21: ORIENTATION AND PERSONNEL POLICIES

22: PERFORMANCE EVALUATIONS

23: DISCIPLINE AND TERMINATION

24: SPECIAL EMPLOYMENT ISSUES

You want to be a success and make a great profit. When you begin the process of selecting and hiring employees there are a few objectives to which you must adhere. These objectives are as follows:

1. You want to find an employee who wants to work for you for the long term.
2. You want to find an employee who is well qualified, who possesses good personality traits, who has a good work ethic, who demonstrates flexibility, and is motivated to do a good job. Keeping all of these qualities in mind, you still must select a candidate who is able to be trained.
3. Due to the large numbers of federal and state statutes dealing with employment matters, you want to reduce and eliminate, if possible, any allegations of discrimination in the hiring of new employees and avoid lawsuits against you for negligent hiring.

These three objectives should be paramount in any search for new employees and the promotion of existing employees.

Legal Matters

Prior to beginning the process of selecting and hiring employees, you must first develop a set of legal guidelines so that you do not find yourself a target of a lawsuit. Following are seven main areas for which you need to develop legal guidelines to minimize or eliminate the potential for lawsuits in the hiring process.

Illegal Discrimination

Federal and state statutes prohibit you from discriminating against an employee or applicant because of race, color, gender, religious beliefs, national origin, physical disability, or age if the person is 40 years old or older. Additionally, in your area, there might be laws prohibiting employment discrimination based on sexual orientation or marital status. These federal, state, and local statutes apply to all stages of the employment process, from the preparation of job descriptions all the way to termination. At the hiring stage, in order

> Due to the large numbers of federal and state statutes dealing with employment matters, you want to reduce and eliminate, if possible, any allegations of discrimination in the hiring of new employees.

to avoid violation of antidiscrimination laws, you should avoid application forms and screening techniques that have an unfair impact on a particular group of applicants. You should advertise for employees in places where the ads come to the attention of a diverse group of people. You should also specify in your job specifications and descriptions only those skills and education necessary to perform the job. It is very easy for an unhappy applicant or employee who thinks they were discriminated against to file a lawsuit against you and your business. Additionally, there may be investigations against you and your business by federal and state agencies. Finally, allegations of discrimination can negatively impact your reputation and, consequently, your ability to draw customers.

Job Security Promises

Generally employees can be let go by the employer at any time for any reason, or for no reason at all. Also the employee is free to leave at any time. Therefore, employees have little job security other than that afforded to them by various federal and state statutes. Even though in most states you are allowed to terminate employees at will, you must be diligent in what you say to the employee during the hiring process and in employee handbooks. When you are trying to select and hire new employees do not make promises that you may not be able to honor or those that may give the prospective employee a false sense of security. You need to make sure that your job application, and your employee handbook, if you have one, specifically states that the job is at will and that the employee can be let go at any time by the employer with or without cause. Further, if you should enter into an employee agreement with the new employee this needs to be stated as well, unless your intention is different. In summation, be very careful what you, as the employer, state verbally or put into writing to an applicant or to a new employee. It would be advisable to have an employment lawyer to advise you in this area.

Negligent Hiring Claims

Unfortunately, you cannot take what a prospective employee tells you completely at face value. Since in all likelihood this is the

Privacy Rights of Applicants

It is important to gather as much information as possible about a prospective employee prior to hiring. However, your attempt to gather such information can violate federal and state statutes. Therefore, be sure that you obtain the prospective employee's written consent before you gather any information about him, such as education transcripts, credit reports, former employer recommendations, or criminal records.

first time you have met this person, you have no idea what kind of jobs they have held in the past and what kind of adverse situations they might have been involved in. Therefore, you must do a comprehensive investigation on a prospective hire. You have a legal duty to protect your employees, customers, clients, visitors, and members of the general public from injury caused by employees you know or should have known pose a risk of harm to others. Therefore, if you do not adequately investigate a new employee's background and they harm or steal from another employee or customer, you will be held liable for damages. You must check an applicant's criminal history, along with checking out their references, and how they performed their previous jobs. If you do not do this you could be sued under the theory of negligent hiring.

> If you do not adequately investigate a new employee's background and they harm or steal from another employee or customer, you will be held liable for damages.

Unfair Competition

There is always a possibility that people you have hired, trained, and shared information with will leave you and go to work for a competitor. Or they may even start their own business. It is always possible that employees will have access to trade secrets and other confidential information that gives your franchise a competitive advantage. Therefore, all new employees should sign agreements that specifically state that they will not disclose or use to their advantage any trade secrets or confidential information they have gained from employment with you. Also, depending on the position that the employee holds with you, you might want her to sign an agreement with a covenant not to compete. A covenant not to compete states that when an employee leaves your employment she cannot work in the same business doing the same things she was doing for you during a certain period of time within the area surrounding your franchise.

The Fair Labor Standards Act

This Act, along with other federal and state statutes, places restrictions upon your ability to hire employees under the age of 18. If you hire any employees under the age of 18, these laws will limit the type of work for which they may be hired and/or the hours that they can work. Therefore, you must pay attention to who you hire with regard to the federal Fair Labor Standards Act.

Undocumented Aliens

Federal law prohibits you from hiring undocumented aliens. You, as the employer, along with each new employee are required to complete a form I-9 from the INS, titled Employment Eligibility Verification. The form I-9 is produced by the Immigration Naturalization Service. If you do not verify the eligibility of your new employee then you can be subject to a fine up to $1,000 per employee. With people from all over the world working in the United States today, you must make sure that each employee is either a citizen of the United States or a lawful, permanent resident alien, or an alien with work authorization. If the person you hire does not satisfy these qualifications, then he or she cannot lawfully work for you.

The 11 Steps for Selection

During the selection and hiring process there are certain steps that should be followed. These steps should be documented and are designed to produce quality employees with a strong work ethic. These steps are:

1. Job descriptions for each job
2. Job specifications for each job
3. Initial screening of potential employees
4. Evaluation of job applications and resumes
5. Pre-employment testing
6. Interviews
7. Immigration issues (I-9)
8. Background investigations of potential new employees
9. Personalities of potential employees
10. Medical examinations
11. Making the final decision, a job offer, or rejecting the applicant

> With people from all over the world working in the United States today, you must make sure that each employee is either a citizen of the United States or a lawful, permanent resident alien, or an alien with work authorization.

These eleven steps are basic to the selection and hiring process and should be followed and documented for each new hire to minimize the possibility of litigation and to ensure that only those people best suited for the position are hired.

Job Descriptions and Specifications

All positions should have both a job description and job specifications. The job description sets forth the actual functions and duties of the position. It lists such items as physical demands and minimum physical requirements along with the working conditions. It also describes the equipment the employee is expected to use, if money will be handled, and the minimum skills needed to perform the work in a satisfactory fashion. Also, contained in the job description are the specific duties and responsibilities that the job requires and the days and hours needed to do that job.

> The job specifications build on the job description. The job specifications define the type of person best suited for the position.

The job specifications build on the job description. The job specifications define the type of person best suited for the position. It states those personal characteristics such as sociability, politeness, personality, character, behavior, assertiveness, and so on, that are necessary to the performance of the job. Additionally, the job specifications lists educational background, experience, and general knowledge required. Also, any specialized training or development required is specified. Without a complete job description and detailed job specifications for each position to be hired, it would make it impossible for you to hire the best person for each job position.

Initial Screening

The next step in the hiring and selection process is that of initial screening. Now that you have started your recruitment efforts, you do not have the time to go through the hiring and selection steps with each applicant. Obviously some applicants are unqualified and cannot perform the functions of the job. Therefore, prior to giving an applicant a job application you first perform an initial screening. During the initial screening you will contact each person who has expressed an interest in the positions you are hiring for and share with them the job's description and job specifications. This alone frequently encourages a potential employee who is unqualified or only marginally qualified to withdraw from the running.

Also, during this step, you will share with the person the salary range. Most people have already determined what salary is acceptable. If prospective applicants are informed, during the initial screening, of the salary you are willing to pay you will be able to eliminate those people who will not work for the pay you are offering.

Job Application

Once the initial screening has been completed, those still in the running should be asked to complete your job application. Often you will receive from the applicant a resume that reveals a lot of information. The care with which the resume is prepared and presented can provide insight into how serious the applicant is about the position. Even though you will retain and study the resume, you need to have the applicant complete your job application. The completed job application will give you information regarding the skills, accomplishments, and prior work history of the applicant.

In order to avoid potential liability you should use a standard application form that is limited to the gathering of job-related information. At a minimum your job application form should request the following of each applicant:

1. What position are you applying for?
2. What other positions would you like to be considered for?
3. Name, address, and phone number.
4. Are you a citizen or permanent resident of the United States? If not, do you have the proper work permits from the federal Immigration and Naturalization Service?
5. When can you start if you are hired?
6. Are you available to work overtime?
7. What education have you achieved? Include space to allow the applicant to answer which high school, college, or other school they attended, along with names, addresses, number of years attended, degrees obtained, and major.

> If prospective applicants are informed, during the initial screening, of the salary you are willing to pay you will be able to eliminate those people who will not work for the pay you are offering.

Have the applicant list his or her last four jobs, including the name, address, and phone number of each employer listing first his most current employment.

8. Have the applicant list his or her last four jobs, including the name, address, and phone number of each employer, listing first his most current employment. Also have the applicant list his job title, dates of employment, and his supervisor's name. Additionally, under this heading, have the applicant list what his job duties and responsibilities were and the reason for leaving each employer.
9. Any special training or achievements the applicant has received during the last five years.

There are additional questions you may want to ask, but the previously listed questions are the minimum that should appear on the job application form. It is also very important that at the end of the job application there is a place for the applicant to sign his name below language giving you the applicant's consent for you to perform a background investigation, criminal investigation, and reference check. If you do not state this at the end of the job application form above the applicant's signature, then any investigation you do can be construed as an invasion of the applicant's privacy.

Further, it should be stated above the applicant's signature that she will be an employee at will if hired. This language also serves to protect you from any possible claims that she was promised job security. A comprehensive, completed job application can give you protection against future claims by an employee as to what promises were made, what jobs she interviewed for, and whether she authorized a background investigation and acknowledged that she is an employee at will. On a final note, the application should also state above her signature that any false statements made by the applicant will be considered sufficient cause for rejection of her application or, if employed, dismissal.

Pre-Employment Testing

Companies have historically relied to a significant extent on pre-employment tests as a major component of the selection process. The number of franchisors who are in a position to provide pre-employment tests to their franchisees has been steadily increasing. These tests are used to measure a prospective employee's intelligence, aptitude, ability, interests, honesty, and personality. Another type of pre-employment test that has gained considerable momentum is the drug test. It has been estimated that more than 60% of all organizations use some type of employment tests today.

The most common pre-employment test goes by several names. It is referred to as a job skills test, a performance simulation test, work sampling test, or just a skills test. This test creates a miniature replica of the job you are being considered for to see if you demonstrate the necessary talents. This test actually reflects "hands-on" experience. In more general terms this test is also used to measure the amount of knowledge a prospective employee has about specific subjects. This test is used extensively in all types of industries and particularly in the franchise industry.

Another type of test is an aptitude test. This type of test is usually a multiple-choice test to enable the employer to gain additional insights into an applicant's abilities, in certain skill areas, such as sales, administrative, clerical, and mechanical. They have a variety of applications in the franchise industry. A variation on the aptitude test is the so-called personality test. A personality test will measure the degree of certain personality and psychological traits that are considered necessary to a specific job performance.

A third test is the intelligence test. An intelligence test is used to measure a prospective employee's mental ability and capacity and is used where intelligence is crucial to performance. This type of test is more likely to be utilized when hiring managerial employees or mid- to upper-level executives.

Finally, there are the so-called honesty or integrity tests. Historically, the business community has utilized lie detector, or polygraph, tests to determine one's honesty. However, these tests are seldom used today as they have been virtually outlawed by the federal Employee Polygraph Protection Act. In today's employment environment about the only use an employer can make of a lie detector test is when an employee is reasonably suspected of being involved in workplace theft or embezzlement.

> The most common pre-employment test goes by several names. It is referred to as a job skills test, a performance simulation test, work sampling test, or just a skills test.

The Drug Test

Probably the most universally given pre-employment test is the drug test. The legal environment requires that employers provide a drug-free, safe environment for their employees and customers. Many of the major franchisors and retail chains now require that all employees be screened for drug use before being employed. Several of these franchisors also furnish detailed instructions to their franchisees concerning how to conduct drug tests. However, before you perform drug tests on your prospective employees there are a couple of procedures you must follow. First, the Americans with Disabilities Act forbids you from testing a prospective employee for drugs until you have made that person a conditional offer of employment. Further, many states now have laws that deal with drug and alcohol testing. Therefore, you must have a legal professional check with the laws of the state in which you plan to operate to determine what restrictions, if any, there are on you that limit drug testing. However, in the vast majority of states you are allowed to conduct drug testing with either no restrictions or limited restrictions.

Interviews

Once an applicant has passed the initial screening, completely filled out the job application, and satisfactorily passed your pre-employment tests, you will then need to interview the applicant. The interview is only as effective as you are at interviewing potential employees. During the interview you will want to discuss areas that cannot be easily addressed on the job application or through tests. These areas include assessing a person's motivation, ability to work under pressure, and the ability to fit in with the organization. However, this information must be job related in order to avoid potential litigation. Prior to interviewing an applicant you should write down a set of questions focusing on the job duties and the applicant's skills and experience. By having these questions already formulated and in writing before you, and following the same questions for each job opening, you will reduce the risk of a later claim by an applicant of unequal treatment. It's also smart to summarize an applicant's answers and keep them on file.

The Pros and Cons of Tests

Pre-employment tests, if they are job related, have proven to be very valuable in the selection process, but they can be costly and time consuming to administer. Also, on a final note, if you do decide to give one or more pre-employment tests as a condition of employment, be sure that you seek out not only the advice of a competent legal professional, but your franchisor's guidelines as well.

The employment interview is a two-way process that should provide both parties with the opportunity to ask questions of each other. For example, you want to ask questions to confirm the personal and employment history that the applicant wrote on the job application. Further, you will want to explore in greater detail the applicant's employment history, including actual duties and responsibilities. You will need to explain completely all positive and negative information about the job so that you can obtain a better picture of the applicant's interest. Also, at this juncture, you can explain the wage information, benefits of the position, and general work rules of the company. Finally, the interview will give you an opportunity to evaluate the applicant's personality, character, and work ethic.

It is also good to ask questions of the applicant as to why he or she left former positions and what types of relationships he or she had with their former employers. You do not want to hire an applicant who has a list of complaints against former employers and/or employees. If you should hire such a person, then you and your business might very well be the next recipient of this person's rage. Another cautionary note: do not hire an applicant who volunteers trade secrets or confidential information from a previous position. If an applicant will do this to a past employer, just imagine what harm this employee could potentially do to your trade secrets and confidential information.

You should review with a field representative of your franchisor or an employment attorney the legal restrictions on what questions you can and cannot ask. It is beyond the focus of this chapter to delve deeply into this topic and to give you anything more than just a broad overview. Therefore, it is imperative that you undergo adequate training in order to not only hire and select the best employees, but to minimize any potential litigation as well.

Checking Citizen Status

The first item you will have done is to have what is called an INS form I-9 Employment Eligibility Verification form properly filled out by the applicant (see page 227). As a result of the enforcement of this federal statute, all employers are required to verify that the individual about to be hired is either a U.S. citizen, has permanent residence

> The employment interview is a two-way process that should provide both parties with the opportunity to ask questions of each other.

status, or has a valid work or student visa. All individuals about to be hired are required to complete the I-9 form even if they are born and raised in the United States. It is wise for you to make photocopies of the documents that the prospective employee produces to keep in the employee's file in case the INS questions your hiring practices. Also, in that employee's file, you must keep for at least three years the I-9. If the INS requests to see the I-9s on your employees and you are unable to produce them, you can be fined up to $1,000 per employee.

Background Checks

Now you are at the point where you must perform a comprehensive background investigation of the prospective employees that have made it to this point. If a prospective employee has made it this far along in the selection process there is an excellent chance that you will make a job offer to him. Therefore, it is imperative that you do a comprehensive background investigation for several reasons, including protecting yourself from lawsuits alleging negligent hiring practices on your part. However, before you conduct a background investigation, you must have the applicant sign a consent form either as part of the job application or as a separate document. This consent form must make clear that you will be requesting information concerning him from former employers, schools, credit reporting sources, and law enforcement agencies. You must have this consent in writing in order to avoid a claim of invasion of privacy made against you in a lawsuit.

First, in the background investigation you want to verify what was stated in the application form as being true and accurate. When you speak with former employers, you must learn to read between the lines. For example, if the former employer is neutral or offers only faint praise or praises only one aspect of the applicant's previous job performance, then there is a good chance that there is negative information that he will not disclose to you. Consequently, it is always wise to ask a former employer if she would rehire this employee if she could.

Second, you will want to check all references that the applicant gave you. There will be a tendency on the applicant's part to provide

It is wise for you to make photocopies of the documents that the prospective employee produces to keep in the employee's file in case the INS questions your hiring practices.

you only with names of people that will speak well of him. Still you will want to contact these people to see if you can draw out of them any information that might be negative or contradicts what the applicant expressed to you earlier.

Third, you will want to get proof from the schools and universities that the applicant listed to make sure he actually attended those schools for the dates he stated and earned the degrees he listed. Occasionally, as part of the background investigation, you will want to request a credit report from one of the credit bureaus. Normally credit information is not relevant to employment and is usually unnecessary. However, if this person will be handling money or will be required to manage your franchise's finances, then you must obtain his credit report. You would not want to hire a person who cannot keep his or her personal finances in order.

Fourth, it might be appropriate to contact your local department of motor vehicles to obtain a driving record on the applicant. If part of the job description requires the employee to drive, it is important to check on his driving record. You need to determine if he has traffic offenses that could be potentially damaging to you. You would not want to hire an applicant who has a drunk driving conviction or several speeding tickets over the last three years.

However, in today's litigious climate, probably the most important part of the background investigation is to determine the applicant's criminal history. You are allowed to inquire about an applicant's conviction and to reject an applicant because of a conviction that is job related. Most states have laws on the books that place some restrictions on what you are able to discover about that person's criminal history. For example, state laws may specifically prohibit you from asking about arrest records since they did not lead to a conviction. Also, most states have laws that allow individuals to expunge or seal their criminal records. If such a record is sealed, then it is not available to you or anyone else other than criminal justice agencies and the courts. Therefore, if a criminal record has been expunged or sealed, that prospective employee is generally allowed to deny that he or she has a criminal record.

It cannot be stressed or overemphasized enough how important it is to get complete information on each prospective employee's

Verify Data

Since many applicants doctor their employment history to hide potential warning signs of past violent conduct, you must at least verify all dates of employment and all education to determine if there are any discrepancies between this information and what the applicant provided you with earlier. Danger signs include discrepancies that you uncover and long lapses of time between jobs.

Should I Hire a Firm to Check Backgrounds?

It is very important to conduct a comprehensive background investigation of a prospective employee. However, your expertise to conduct the background investigation and the time available is such that you are probably not the best person to conduct this investigation. Even though there is a greater cost associated with this option, you should err on the side of caution and hire a firm that specializes in conducting these background investigations. Not only do such firms have a better track record of gathering pertinent information but they are also better informed as to the privacy rights issues that apply in each state.

criminal history. There have been numerous lawsuits over the last several years against many major franchise companies for negligent hiring practices. The typical scenario is that a franchisee hires an employee who has a criminal history, but the franchisee did not do an adequate background investigation to discover such information. Then the employee commits a crime against another employee or a customer. Subsequently it is discovered that the employee has a previous conviction record and that if the franchisor or franchisee of that unit had performed a diligent background investigation it would have discovered this information. Now you have all the requirements present for a negligent-hiring lawsuit to be filed against the franchisor and the franchisee, and you will definitely lose.

Personalities of Candidates

Last, but not least, you are at the stage of your selection process where you need to concern yourself with the personality of the prospective employee. Your workplace is a unique blend of human temperaments and egos. Therefore you will want employees who are positive, who have a good work ethic, and are easy to get along with. Many professionals in this business will state that they pay as much attention to an applicant's personality as they do to the applicant's professional skills. Your attitude and behavior and that of your employees is important to your success with your customers. Accordingly, you should not hire someone whose personality is not appropriate.

Medical Exams

One last note before you make your final decision. If you have a job to fill that requires certain physical characteristics, then it might be advisable that the applicant have a physical examination. In those instances that require certain physical characteristics you need to make sure that employee has a medical clearance to indicate that he is physically fit for the job.

As a result of the Americans with Disabilities Act, don't ask the applicant about his or her medical history or conduct any medical exam before you make that person a job offer. Once you make the person a job offer, make it conditional on the applicant passing a medical exam. Even though few jobs will necessitate a medical exam, it is imperative that those jobs that do require it have the satisfactory passing of such an exam as a precondition. Otherwise you could hire an employee who is not capable of performing the functions of the job and this could result in various legal claims that could have been avoided.

The Final Decision

Now you are at the last step of your selection process. Should you reject the applicant or should you make that applicant a job offer? If you reject an applicant it is always courteous to let them know that you have hired someone else for the job. Do not give them an explanation about why they were not hired. If they ask, simply tell them that the person you hired is, in your judgment, more appropriate for the job.

For the person that you do hire, you should be careful in what you say orally or in writing. Any verbal or written statements that you make when you make a job offer can come back to haunt you if you later fire the employee. You might even want to extend that person a job offer through a simple and short employment letter that makes it clear exactly what you and your company are promising to this person. Also it should state that their employment is "at will" and that you have the right to terminate their employment at any time. As a final note, for all prospective employees to whom you extend a job offer, you must condition such employment on them passing a drug test.

When it comes to hiring your management personnel and those who will be in charge you need to take a different tack. Of course, you need to perform the selection process as set forth in the previous paragraphs. However, since managerial personnel will have more responsibility and control of your business there are additional matters you need to take into consideration. First, it is very important that your managerial personnel have experience in your type of business. You want someone who has considerable experience managing people and dealing with customers. True, you will have to pay this person more as a result of her experience, but it is money well spent.

> Now you are at the last step of your selection process. Should you reject the applicant or should you make that applicant a job offer?

You must determine whether those you plan to hire as managers have a strong work ethic, the desire to do every task no matter how small, and the motivation to treat those employees under her, customers, and others fairly and with dignity. Further, you must make sure your management personnel knows what has to be done and how to do it. Additionally, he or she needs to have the ability to think ahead. You do not want someone who has a management style that approaches that of a dictator. You do not want a high turnover because the personality of the manager does not fit in with the personality of the other employees.

Whenever possible it is best to promote from within. Obviously, this is a sound approach for many reasons. For example, it builds moral and encourages quality employees who are ambitious because they see that they can be promoted. Also when you promote from within it is less costly than going outside to hire and the probability of this person becoming a good manager is much higher since you are already aware of this person's work ethic and personality. Additionally, those promoted to management from within need little or no additional training since they already know your business and what is required of them.

> You do not want a high turnover because the personality of the manager does not fit in with the personality of the other employees.

Conclusion

The selection and hiring of good people are very important to your business. Follow the legal guidelines to prepare your hiring procedures—be careful to develop the proper forms and ask the correct questions. Always maintain a safe and drug-free work environment—it is your duty and responsibility.

For more information on this topic, visit our Web site at www.businesstown.com

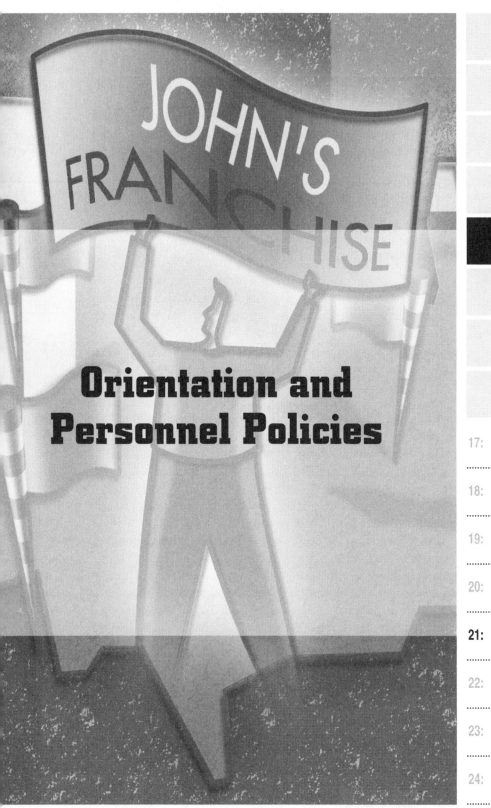

Chapter 21

Orientation and
Personnel Policies

17: MANAGING THE BUSINESS

18: MOTIVATION AND LEADERSHIP

19: RECRUITMENT

20: HIRING AND SELECTION

21: ORIENTATION AND PERSONNEL POLICIES

22: PERFORMANCE EVALUATIONS

23: DISCIPLINE AND TERMINATION

24: SPECIAL EMPLOYMENT ISSUES

Prior to beginning work the new employee needs to go through a new-employee orientation. The new employee is only going to know what to do and how to think based on what you tell him or her and how you orient and train him or her. Accordingly, let's provide your new hire with a lot of good information about your franchise business and how she should perform in your franchise.

Orientation

A comprehensive new-employee orientation allows you to set the proper tone with a new employee so that she begins her job with a positive image of your franchise and not a negative one. You will need to introduce the new employee to your franchise and to her work unit and familiarize her with the objectives, history, philosophy, procedures, and rules of your franchised business. Then you will cover your policies, rules, and regulations, such as work hours, pay procedures, overtime requirements, and company benefits. Also reviewed are the specific duties and responsibilities of the new employee.

It is of particular importance that you stress to the new employee how important customer service is to your business and that she is joining a team and is expected to support and contribute to that team. Also explain the established customs for how employees relate to their managers, other employees, subordinates, and customers. A new employee must learn your company's culture so that she knows how things are done, what matters, and what work-related behaviors are acceptable and which ones are not. Successfully conveying the culture of your business to the new employee will lead to the person successfully fitting in with your business and the other members of your team and increase the likelihood of you gaining a long-term quality employee.

> A comprehensive new-employee orientation allows you to set the proper tone with a new employee so that she begins her job with a positive image of your franchise and not a negative one.

Personnel Policies

In today's society you never know when you might be sued. It makes no difference whether or not the person suing you will win. A lot of people will sue or file complaints with federal or state agencies against you for no other reason than to intimidate you or because they feel like they have been wronged.

So how do you protect yourself from being sued by applicants who never worked for you or by your own employees? The only way to increase your chances of success in case of such a lawsuit is if you maintain complete personnel files on those who applied for a position and on those who work for you. Most legal problems in the workplace can be avoided if you respect the applicants and your employees and treat them well. But no matter how effective you are as a manager and as a leader there will still be situations where an applicant or an employee feels he or she has not been treated fairly. The person will sue you and your business for some perceived abuse of his or her rights. An unhappy applicant or employee may even file a complaint with a government agency, federal or state, alleging that you violated a federal or state statute or administrative rule or regulation. Such complaints could allege that you discriminated against them. Or, they could allege that you violated different standards set forth for sanitation purposes for eating establishments. The list of what a person could sue you or file a complaint against you for is endless. The only way to protect yourself is to make sure that you have in place comprehensive personnel policies including complete files on your employees and previous applicants.

Employee Files

It is imperative that you have a complete file on each employee. Without such a file, how will you protect yourself against a lawsuit or against a complaint filed with a federal or state administrative agency? In order to maintain a solid legal foundation you must establish written rules and procedures in an employee handbook and maintain complete files on each employee to indicate how you implemented your policies and procedures. Later in this chapter we will discuss employee handbooks, but for now we will concentrate on employee files. Even though maintaining a complete file on each employee is time consuming, it is of extreme importance for several reasons. Not only should you maintain such a file on each employee

Small Businesses and Lawsuits

Historically, small businesses and their owners have always been targets of a wide assortment of lawsuits. Small businesses are often the target of lawsuits that are filed in federal or state court. Many of these lawsuits are filed by people who claim they were injured while at your location. Many lawsuits are the result of people claiming they purchased a defective product from you or ate something they purchased from you that made them very sick. However, the fastest growing areas in which small businesses and their owners are being sued are by their own employees or by people who have applied for a job and did not get one.

for your own protection against lawsuits or administrative agency actions but also because federal law requires you to do so.

Legal Requirements

The Fair Labor Standards Act, a federal law, requires that you keep the following in the file of each employee:

1. Personal identifying information including name, home address, social security number, job title or occupation, sex, birth date
2. Hour and day when the work week begins and ends
3. Total number of hours worked each workday and each workweek
4. Total daily or weekly straight time earning
5. Regular hourly rate or salary
6. Total overtime hours and pay for the workweek
7. Deductions from and additions to wages
8. Total wages paid for each pay period
9. Date of payment and pay period covered by that payment
10. Completed I-9 form

Other Files to Keep

As can be seen from the previous paragraphs, there already exists a legal requirement on your part to maintain certain information in individual employee files. However, there are several other items that you will want to keep in these files to protect you from legal actions. At a minimum you should include the following items in each employee's file:

1. Job description and specifications
2. Job application and/or resume
3. Offer of employment
4. IRS form W-4
5. A signed receipt that the employee has received and read the employee's handbook and agrees to abide by it
6. Performance evaluations

> There already exists a legal requirement on your part to maintain certain information in individual employee files. However, there are several other items that you will want to keep in these files to protect you from legal actions.

7. Employee benefit information and the employee's decision on whether to avail himself of the different benefits
8. Any complaints from customers, other employees, or management against the employee
9. Customer letters complimenting the employee on his or her performance
10. Awards or other notations for outstanding performance
11. Complete details of any and all disciplinary actions
12. Any other notes that are appropriate to keep in the file, such as the employee's attendance record

Other items that you would want to maintain in the employee's file would be copies of any insurance or workman compensation claims, compensation history, promotions, transfers, reclassifications, and any other job-related materials.

Once an employee file has been set up there are several procedures you should follow. First, be diligent in correcting any mistakes that are found in an employee's file. Second, you should keep the employees' files locked up and made available only to people in your company who have a legitimate business need to see the files. Third, many states have laws giving employees and former employees access to their own employee files. Currently 20 states have such statutes. Therefore, you need to seek legal advice on this issue to see what the law is in your state. Fourth, the Americans with Disabilities Act imposes very strict limitations on how you must handle information obtained from medical examinations and inquires that occurred after an employment offer was made. You should keep the medical information separate from the nonmedical information in each employee's file to further guarantee the confidentiality of medical records.

Employee Handbooks

No matter how few employees you have, you need to have in writing your personnel policies and procedures. It is a good policy to have a new employee receive the handbook, read the handbook, and state in

Why You Need an Employee Handbook

There are several advantages to having written personnel policies and procedures. Advantages include that by doing so it supports consistency, everyone knows what is expected of them, and if management is replaced continuity is ensured. Additionally, an employee handbook that is clear and reasonable will assist you in having a paper trail if litigation occurs. Further, it will tell your employees who to talk to if they feel they are being discriminated against or otherwise being treated unfairly, or just have a problem. Employees need to know what the rules, procedures, and policies are and where they can turn when they have a problem. A comprehensive employee handbook is critical to your success in minimizing litigation and administrative agency investigations.

writing that such has occurred prior to the first day of work. What should your employee handbook contain?

Obviously, the employee handbook should contain items such as workplace rules and regulations, compensation schedules, work hours, and benefits. The handbook should also state that all government statutes, rules, and regulations must be adhered to and that there can be no disclosure of any trade secrets, confidential information, or other proprietary information. A typical layout of an employee handbook is as follows:

1. *Introduction*—The handbook usually begins with an introduction describing the company's history and the history of the franchisor. The introduction will discuss that particular unit's history. Here, you should state what your philosophy is and how you expect your employees to conduct themselves towards each other and towards your customers. It doesn't hurt to outline the franchise's organizational chart.
2. *Job details*—Next should be listed each of the job descriptions with their specifications.
3. *Hours*—The hours that your location is open should be listed. Also include what a typical employee's normal working hours are such as 8:00 to 3:00, 3:00 to 11:00, and how overtime pay is authorized.
4. *Compensation*—You need to clearly set forth how wages and salaries are set and how they are raised. This is normally broken down by each position and should include what the pay ranges currently are for each position. Also listed is if there is a possibility for bonuses or incentive pay.
5. *Benefits*—Every benefit that your company offers to your employees should be listed here. Such benefits include paid vacation time, paid sick time, medical insurance, dental insurance, paid holidays, etc. Of course you will set your own benefit programs based on your business, your industry, and what you can realistically afford.
6. *Policies and procedures*—Next are listed your policies that pertain to areas such as sexual harassment, drug use, alcohol use, and prescription drug use. Most businesses have policies that

The handbook usually begins with an introduction describing the company's history and the history of the franchisor.

prohibit an employee's use of alcohol or illegal drugs on the job. Also, due to federal laws on this topic, all companies should have in their handbook that sexual harassment is illegal and violates company policy. Finally, a substantial number of companies have started to address prescription drug use. This is because certain prescription drugs interfere with a person's ability to perform their jobs. This section should also include any other policies or procedures that deal with the enforcement of federal, state, and local statutes, rules, and regulations. Also stated is that you expect all employees to adhere to all such statutes, rules, and regulations. Finally, most businesses include a policy concerning smoking cigarettes on the job. Most businesses now either prohibit or restrict smoking in the workplace.

7. *Discipline*–It is imperative that you spell out clearly all your policies and procedures that pertain to disciplinary actions. You must be very clear on what your disciplinary actions are and in what cases an employee will be terminated immediately. Most businesses, for example, follow this chain of disciplinary action: verbal warning, written warning, suspension, and finally, termination.

8. *Dress code*–If your franchise requires all employees to be in uniform on the job, then it should be so stated in the employee handbook. Included here are the personal appearance requirements. However, you must be careful with any specific grooming and clothing requirements since they may be illegal and a violation of the employee's rights.

9. *Complaints*–Listed here are those procedures that are to be followed to resolve customer complaints about products, services, or an employee, complaints from one employee about another, or complaints concerning a manager.

10. *General*–Finally, you should have a catch-all classification that deals with the workplace in general, such as, you expect all employees to abide by the Golden Rule–Do unto others as you would have them do unto you. Also here you would mention that you expect all of your employees to treat each other and customers with respect and dignity. If you have a

> It is imperative that you spell out clearly all your policies and procedures that pertain to disciplinary actions. You must be very clear on what your disciplinary actions are and in what cases an employee will be terminated immediately.

computer at your location that has Internet access and that e-mail capabilities, you need to have a policy stating what an employee may or may not do.

These are only suggestions of what you would definitely want to have in your employee handbook. Depending upon your situation, there may be other items you will want to include. On the last page of each employee handbook, there should be a signature page. This page will serve several purposes, such as:

- First, it will state that the handbook does not give the employee an employment contract, that all employees are employees at will and can be terminated at any time by the employer, and that an employee found to be dishonest or guilty of excessive absenteeism will be fired.
- Second, there should be a statement acknowledging that the employee has received the handbook and that he or she is familiar with the contents.
  Third, to be safe, there should be a statement that the handbook does not contain all of the workplace policies and procedures, and that it is subject to revision on a regular basis. Include here that in the event of a revised handbook, it is expected that the employee will receive and familiarize himself with the new handbook.
- At the bottom of the signature page the employee should sign and enter the date.

It is imperative that you keep in the employee's file the original signature page along with an exact replica of the employee handbook he received. Because employee files and employee handbooks are areas that produce a lot of litigation, you would be wise to obtain competent professional advice.

Compensation

If you are a first time business owner it will be difficult to determine what to pay your employees. On the one hand you want to compensate your employees fairly, but on the other hand you must make a profit.

Most employees will compare the pay you offer with that of like businesses. For example, if they are applying for a position to flip hamburgers and they already know the competition pays $8 an hour, they will expect at least that from you. In the beginning, most of your hired employees are looking for a wage that is comparable in the job market. As you already know, nobody ever believes they are paid what they are worth. This is a problem that you will deal with constantly. This is why, once you set a fair compensation schedule, you must have an effective management style to keep the employee's work ethic high.

Pay Scale

Eventually all companies must set a compensation schedule for each position they fill. Since you are purchasing a franchise you should look to the franchisor for this information. Many times the franchisor will be able to tell you what your compensation schedule should be for each position including those in management. Nevertheless, each geographical area has its own unique characteristics. There is a possibility that you may need to develop your own compensation schedule.

Your first step is to identify each position in terms of its duties, responsibilities, title, educational level required, work experience required, and any other training necessary to perform that job. Once you have gathered this information you will then rank each job in terms of complexity, skills required, difficulty, stress, and the degree of importance to the operation of the franchise. Then, establish the pay range for each position and gather the comparative pay data from your community to see what others are paying for like positions. This is particularly important if the franchisor is unable to provide you with such information that is appropriate to your location.

After this information has been gathered, you will establish a pay range for each category that sets the pay beginning at 80% of the average up to 125% of the average. This wide range will allow you to make adjustments in starting pay to accommodate the employee's experience. Even if you start a new employee at 100% of the average or even 110% of the average, you still have the flexibility to provide him or her with pay raises even if they are not promoted.

Performance Evaluations

If you give performance evaluations, you need to include that information in the employee handbook. Information to include would be how often they are given, what is being measured and how, and if, the evaluation will have an impact on compensation. This subject is discussed in Chapter 22 in detail.

The last step in formulating your compensation schedule is to determine how pay raises are to be calculated and given. For example, are pay raises based upon annual performance reviews or based upon merit increases to recognize an employee's strong work ethic. Only you can determine how your raises will be given.

In summation, you need to first seek as much information from your franchisor as possible. After all, this is the type of information with which your franchisor is most familiar. However, this information will only serve as a starting point. You will need to gather comparative information in your own labor market. This will ensure that your compensation schedule is competitive.

> You will need to gather comparative information in your own labor market. This will ensure that your compensation schedule is competitive.

Conclusion

Our attitudes and opinions are developed from the information and knowledge we have on a subject. Successfully conveying the culture of your business to the new employee will lead to him successfully fitting in with your business and the other members of your team and increase the likelihood of him becoming a long-term quality employee. Therefore a great orientation program would include an explanation and development of the following: personnel policies, employee files, employee handbooks, compensation, and disciplining employees. Be sure to make your handbook comprehensive to cover all your legal bases.

For more information on this topic, visit our Web site at www.businesstown.com

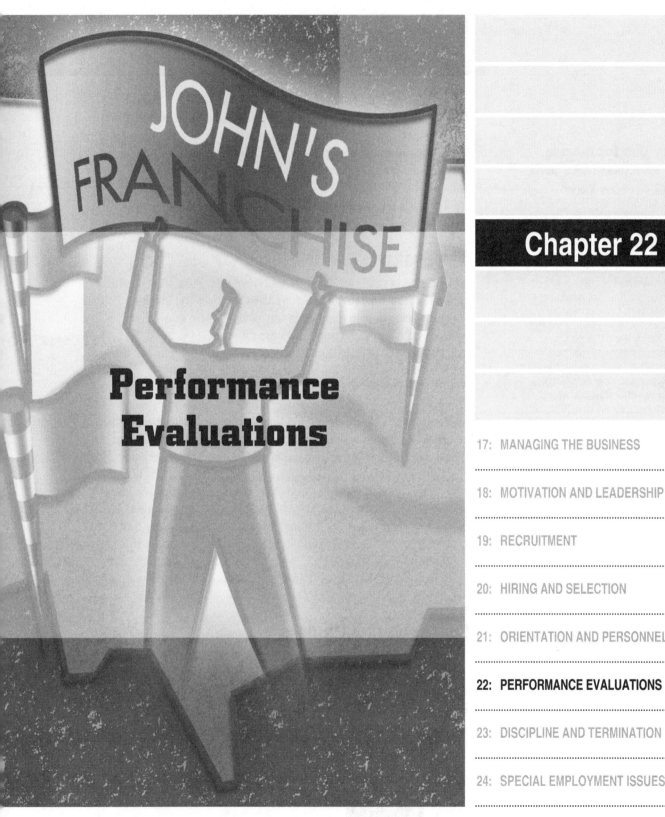

Performance
Evaluations

Chapter 22

17: MANAGING THE BUSINESS

18: MOTIVATION AND LEADERSHIP

19: RECRUITMENT

20: HIRING AND SELECTION

21: ORIENTATION AND PERSONNEL POLICIES

22: PERFORMANCE EVALUATIONS

23: DISCIPLINE AND TERMINATION

24: SPECIAL EMPLOYMENT ISSUES

Performance evaluations are an informative part of the employer/employee relationship. These evaluations are given once or twice a year to let an employee know where he or she stands. It gives the employee a chance to know how great they are doing. Also, if you find it necessary to discipline or terminate an employee, it should not come as a surprise to the employee.

Why Evaluate?

Performance evaluations serve several purposes. First, they let the employee know how they have done their job over the last 6 or 12 months. Their job performance in turn will let them know the amount of any pay raise they could expect.

Performance evaluations must convey to your employees how well they have performed in meeting the company's goals and objectives as they pertain to their job. Without proper feedback about his or her effort you run the risk of decreasing the employee's work ethic and motivation to do a good job. Further, a comprehensive performance evaluation will assist the employee in their development since it will tell him or her in what areas they have a weakness.

By administering written performance evaluations and keeping these evaluations in the employee's file, you will have the documentation you need if situations arise later. For example, you must be able to rebut any possible allegations that you fired an employee for an illegal reason, such as discrimination. The best way to do this is by preserving the employee's written performance evaluations and other documents that support your reasons for firing that employee.

The Evaluation Process

The evaluation process must be consistent and objective. You must treat all employees in the same job classification equally. There are some general guidelines to keep in mind in developing your evaluation process.

The evaluation process must give an accurate picture of the employee's strengths and weaknesses. Next, you need to have in writing specific examples of where the employee has met or exceeded your expectations as well as fallen short of your expectations. At this juncture of the evaluation process you will be in a position to let the employee know objectively in which areas he or she has deficiencies and needs to improve. You will set objective goals for the employee to meet prior to his next evaluation. If an employee's performance is substantially below average then you need to set a date to meet again in the near future to review his or her progress during the interim period. Further, you must state clearly in the evaluation if the employee's lack of progress in improving will lead to disciplinary measures and what these measures could be.

If you do not put everything in writing there is a high degree of likelihood that you will forget to cover a key point with the employee. Whatever approach you take in your evaluation process, you must be consistent and objective. You set yourself up for legal liability if you discharge an employee for poor performance yet give that employee consistently satisfactory or excellent performance evaluations. Also, you cannot give an employee a substantial pay raise if you consistently rate the worker's performance as below average. As a final note, feedback to an employee should be an ongoing process since your goal is to have no surprises about how an employee is doing, especially if that employee is later terminated.

Performance Evaluation Methods

There are several approaches to follow in your performance evaluations. The three main types of performance evaluations are what are referred to as absolute standards, relative standards, and objectives. All three of these types of performance evaluations have their strengths and weaknesses.

The first type of evaluation method is an absolute standard evaluation. When you use an absolute standard you are measuring the employee's performance without comparing that employee to any other employee. You are comparing each employee to an absolute standard. Within the absolute standard evaluation method there are several types.

Two Reasons to Evaluate Employees

Overall, performance evaluations have two main purposes. The first purpose is to let employees know where they stand and what their weaknesses are so that they have the opportunity to improve their performance. The second purpose is to have credible documentation to protect you and your business from false allegations made by former or current employees. To satisfy both of these purposes, it is in your best interest to do comprehensive written performance evaluations twice a year. If you find you are having serious problems with an employee, you will want to conduct more frequent evaluations based on the seriousness of the situation.

First, there is what is referred to as the essay evaluation. A performance evaluation based on an essay is where the person doing the evaluation writes a narrative about the employee. The second type is referred to as a critical incident evaluation. In this situation you will be evaluating the employee by focusing on those critical or key behaviors that make the difference between doing the job effectively or ineffectively. Third is the checklist evaluation. A performance evaluation based on this type allows you to use a list of behavioral descriptions. You check off "yes" or "no" for those behaviors that apply to this employee. The performance evaluation referred to as the graphic rating scale is a method that lists a number of factors that are critical to the adequate performance of the job and then rates the employee along a range from 0 to 10. The forced-choice evaluation method is where you must choose between two specific statements, favorable or unfavorable, about each item of the employee's work behavior. The last type under the absolute standards method is referred to as the behaviorally anchored rating scale. This is a performance evaluation technique that generates critical incidents (discussed previously) and develops behavioral dimensions of performance. Then you evaluate each employee's behaviors rather than the factors of the job. This method is a combination of the critical incident and graphic rating scale and allows you to give the employee a grade along a scale of 0-10.

The second general category of evaluation methods is referred to as relative standards. When you use relative standards you are evaluating an employee's performance by comparing the employee with other employees in the same job classification. Once again, there are several types of evaluation methods that fall under this general category.

The first one is called the group border ranking. This is a relative standard of performance that is characterized as placing employees into a particular classification, such as the top 10% or top 50% or bottom 10%. This way, all the employees within that job classification will rate somewhere along this scale. Because you are rating all employees against each other in each job classification, you will always have those at the top of the scale and at the middle of the scale and those at the bottom of the scale. The second type of relative standard evaluation method is referred to as the individual ranking. Therefore, if you evaluate 10 different employees within the same job classification, only 1 can be the best and only one 1 be the worst. The final type of relative standard is called the paired comparison method. It ranks each employee in relationship to all other employees on a one-on-one basis within the same job classification.

The third approach to performance evaluations makes use of objectives. This category is often referred to as "management by objectives." This method includes mutual objective setting with evaluation based upon the attainment of the specific objectives. The advantage of this method is that each employee knows exactly what is expected of her and how she will be evaluated. Each employee's evaluation will be based on his or her success in achieving the objectives.

This is just a quick overview of the main types of methods used in conducting performance evaluations. You should seek input from the franchisor as to which one of these methods is best.

Factors that Distort Evaluations

Unfortunately, as with most things, there are items that can distort the outcome of an evaluation. As a result, the performance evaluation may not be an accurate portrayal of that employee's performance. What are the factors that can distort evaluations?

- *The leniency error.* This situation arises when the person who is evaluating the employee bases the employee's evaluation on his own value system.
- *The halo error.* This is the tendency on the part of the evaluator to let his assessment of an employee on one trait or factor influence his evaluation of that employee on all the other traits or factors.
- *The similarity error.* This occurs when the evaluator bases her evaluations on the way she perceives herself. Since the evaluator bases her evaluation on the perception she has of herself, she will project these perceptions onto the person being evaluated.
- *The central tendency.* This occurs as a result of the evaluator having a reluctance to make extreme ratings in either direction. Therefore, he has a tendency to evaluate all employees in the midrange or give them all average ratings.
- *Inflationary pressures.* When an evaluator is guilty of inflationary pressures he will have a tendency to evaluate less rigorously.

Unfortunately, as with most things, there are items that can distort the outcome of an evaluation. As a result, the performance evaluation may not be an accurate portrayal of that employee's performance.

The Evaluation Process

1. Establish performance standards for each job classification
2. Manager and employee set measurable goals
3. Measure actual performance on the job
4. Compare actual performance with performance standards
5. Discuss the evaluation with the employee
6. If necessary, initiate corrective action or disciplinary action

The evaluator will give the employee a better evaluation than he or she is entitled to. Hence, the term inflationary. The reason this distortion occurs is because of the fear of legal action being taken against an employer by a disgruntled employee who failed to achieve satisfactory or better evaluations.

- *Inappropriate substitutes for performance.* It is not unusual to find companies using criteria such as neatness, positive attitudes, enthusiasm, promptness, and conscientiousness as substitutes for performance. These terms are such that it makes it difficult to rate someone's performance. All of these terms are susceptible to subjective interpretation by each individual evaluator. Consequently, these types of assessments will lead to inaccurate performance evaluations.

There are other factors that lead to distorted performance evaluations. However, they occur with far less frequency than those listed. In conducting your employees' performance evaluations, you should allow as little distortion as possible.

It is very important that you take the time to have each employee undergo performance evaluations at least twice a year. Even though performance evaluations are time consuming, you must do them. You must have in the employee's file an accurate representation of her strengths and weaknesses along with any problems.

Conclusion

Performance evaluations are given once or twice a year to let an employee know how great they are doing. Under the Americans with Disabilities Act, the performance evaluation process must also be able to measure what is referred to as reasonable performance success. To conduct the performance evaluation process correctly, you need to know the following: the actual evaluation process, methods, and factors that distort evaluations. The evaluations are an opportunity to interact with your employees and reinforce good behaviors.

For more information on this topic, visit our Web site at www.businesstown.com

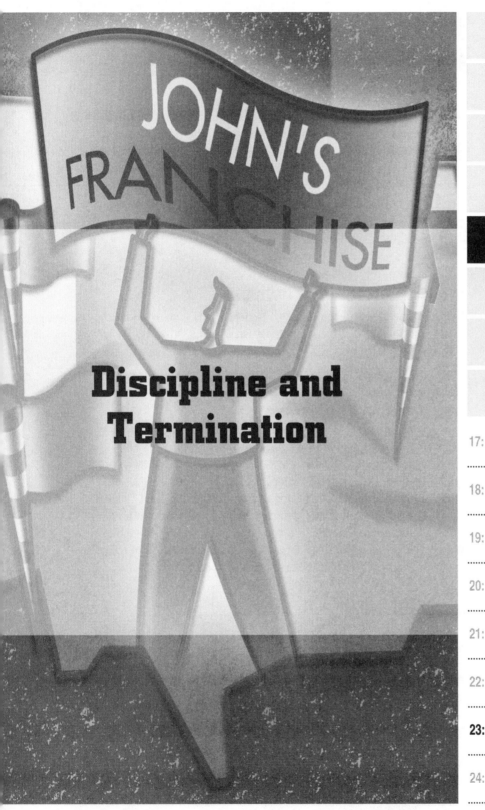

Discipline and Termination

Chapter 23

17: MANAGING THE BUSINESS

18: MOTIVATION AND LEADERSHIP

19: RECRUITMENT

20: HIRING AND SELECTION

21: ORIENTATION AND PERSONNEL POLICIES

22: PERFORMANCE EVALUATIONS

23: **DISCIPLINE AND TERMINATION**

24: SPECIAL EMPLOYMENT ISSUES

Bad-mouthing

Another problem area is when employees bad-mouth your company and thereby tarnish your reputation. This is a situation where you must address the behavior and insist on a change.

isciplining employees is both an art and a science. The art comes from interacting with your staff. The science comes from doing it the right way. When done correctly, this can be a very enjoyable and uplifting experience. Unfortunately there will come a time when an employee must be disciplined for failure to perform his job or for some other reason. So what do you do? What guidelines do you follow? Will you get sued? This chapter addresses these concerns.

Types of Discipline Problems

There are literally dozens of actions performed by employees that require disciplinary actions. Therefore, we will only cover the most frequent violations, which fall into four categories: attendance, on-the-job behaviors, dishonesty, and outside activities.

Attendance

A major problem with employees today is their failure to show up for work. When an employee does not show up for work this places a hardship on the other employees, particularly when it comes to customer service. Another major problem is tardiness. Once again when you have an employee that is tardy on a regular basis, this can upset your workplace. One of the reasons for the increase in tardiness and absenteeism is due to a change in attitude toward employment by people in general. Their values and attitudes toward attendance differ from that of earlier generations.

On-the-job Behaviors

On-the-job behaviors is another category of discipline problems. For example, if an employee is using illegal drugs or alcohol in the workplace you must take immediate action. Unfortunately this problem continues to grow in magnitude. Other on-the-job behaviors that result in disciplinary action include insubordination, fighting, gambling, carelessness, failure to follow procedures, failure to use safety devices, and so on.

Dishonesty

A third category that results in disciplinary actions is employee dishonesty. Dishonest acts reflect directly on that employee's character. The fact is, dishonesty in the form of employee stealing and lying to management is an ever-increasing problem. The biggest problem resulting from an employee's dishonesty is that you may feel that you can no longer trust that employee. If this occurs, it is likely that you will terminate the employee.

Outside Activities

The fourth problem category is outside activities engaged in by the employee. It is common knowledge that in most cases an employer cannot control the activities of their employees outside of the workplace. However, there are many activities that employees may be involved in on their own time that can affect their job performance or reflect negatively on your company. For example, if an employee is arrested for involvement in criminal activity, this will reflect negatively on your company. Some employees are found working for a competitor and as a result misusing confidential information and trade secrets gleaned from your company.

Factors to Consider When Disciplining

There are many types of problems that can result in disciplinary actions. These problems range from minor to quite serious. Before you decide on the type of discipline to take you must analyze the problem first. There are several factors you should consider in determining the severity of the discipline. Some factors to consider are:

> There are many activities that employees may be involved in on their own time that can affect their job performance or reflect negatively on your company.

1. **Seriousness of the problem:** How severe is the problem? Is an employee using illegal drugs at the workplace? Is an employee tardy almost every day? Is an employee tardy only occasionally?
2. **Duration of the problem:** Is the problem an ongoing one that has been occurring over a long time span? Or is this a first

> To what extent have you made an effort to educate your employee about your existing rules and procedures and the consequences of violating them?

occurrence? For example, you would take one type of disciplinary action if an employee had been absent without notification or a legitimate excuse only once or twice. However, you would increase the severity of your disciplinary action if this employee was absent without notification and excuse on a regular basis.

3. **Frequency and nature of the problem:** Is the current problem part of an emerging or a continuing pattern of disciplinary problems? Here we are concerned not just with the duration of the problem but with its pattern as well.

4. **Extenuating factors:** Are there extenuating circumstances related to the problem requiring discipline? Has the person lost his means of transportation? Has there been a death in the family?

5. **Degree of socialization:** To what extent have you made an effort to educate your employee about your existing rules and procedures and the consequences of violating them?

6. **History of the organization's discipline practices:** How have you dealt with similar problems in the past? Have you been consistent and objective in the application of your discipline? You must be consistent and objective when disciplining employees.

7. **Management backing:** If the employee should challenge your disciplinary action, do you have the data in the employee's file to back up your action? Do you feel confident that you have the support of other people in management and above in making your decision?

The items mentioned in the previous list are just a few of the factors to consider in determining what type of disciplinary action to take. It is only fair to the employee to analyze the problem in light of these guidelines to make sure of the appropriateness of any action you take.

Disciplinary Guidelines

Before you decide on the disciplinary action to take there are some other factors to consider. First, you want to make sure that the disciplinary action that you take is to correct the problem as opposed to being punitive. Your objective should be to correct the employee's undesirable behavior as opposed to punishing him.

Although the type of disciplinary action that is appropriate may vary depending upon the situation, it is generally desirable for discipline to be progressive. Only for the most serious violations will you dismiss an employee after the first offense. By being progressive you will have started out with a verbal warning until finally the employee is dismissed for failure to heed prior disciplinary actions.

Types of Disciplinary Actions

There are several steps in the severity of the order of discipline. Customarily, you will start out with a verbal warning. If, however, the employee continues to commit that particular offense or other types of infractions you will then proceed to a written warning. The written warning is often thought of as the first formal step in the disciplinary process. Why? Because a verbal warning is normally not placed in the employee's file whereas the written warning is. As a result, a written warning becomes part of the employee's permanent record.

If, however, the employee persists in continuing with the offenses or infractions, the third step in the disciplinary process is suspension. If you suspend an employee you will be laying him off of work for a period of time, normally without pay. Unless the offense is of a serious nature, you should not suspend an employee until you have previously given verbal and written warnings. The suspension can be for any length of time you choose, but most suspensions without pay are usually for a day or up to a week. There is always the problem that the suspended employee might return to work in a combative mood. For this reason, many companies decide to skip this phase of discipline. However, on the flip side, a suspension can be a wake-up call as to the seriousness of what the employee has done and just might turn that employee around.

Some businesses, if the problem (or problems) continues (continue) to exist, will either demote the employee or cut his pay. These types of disciplinary actions are usually reserved only for members of management. For example, how can you demote an entry-level

Act Immediately

When discipline is appropriate you must immediately administer the discipline, otherwise the impact of the discipline will be lessened. An immediate disciplinary action on your part will have a strong impact on the employee who committed the infraction. He will form an immediate association between the discipline and the infraction. You must always be sure that the employee has been made aware of your company's rules and procedures and what disciplinary action will be taken for a violation. This also requires that your disciplinary action is consistent and impersonal.

Wrongful Discharge Cases

When an employee has been terminated there is always the underlying concern that he or she may bring a legal action against you. Therefore, you must be careful when you terminate an employee. Wrongful discharge cases are those where former employees claim they were either terminated for an improper reason or that the employer bungled the process. There are several legal theories under which a former employee will bring a wrongful discharge lawsuit, such as a violation of a federal or state discrimination statute. Under the law it is illegal to fire anyone based on race, color, religion, national origin, age, gender, alien status, or pregnancy. Also, it is illegal to fire someone based upon a disability, refusal to submit to a lie detector test or sexual harassment, and complaining about safety or health conditions.

You can also be found guilty of a wrongful discharge if you breached an oral or written employment contract with the employee. You must be very careful what promises you make to

(Continued on the next page.)

employee? Or, reduce an employee's pay if all you are paying him is the minimum wage?

Ultimately, you can terminate the employee if nothing else works. Termination of employment is used in two different scenarios. First, termination is an option if you have followed progressive disciplinary actions and the employee has not corrected his inappropriate behavior. Therefore, you have been left with no alternative but to terminate the employee or compromise the integrity of the workplace. Second, there are situations when an employee has had no disciplinary action taken against him but commits an offense so serious that he is immediately terminated. For example, if an employee is caught stealing from the company or a customer, it will lead to his immediate dismissal. Other offenses that are serious enough to result in immediate dismissal include using alcohol or illegal drugs on the job, threatening employees or customers, malicious destruction of company property, attacking an employee with intent to seriously harm, and fighting.

In all situations where an employee is dismissed you must be sure that the employee was not dismissed due to illegal reasons such as his race, color, sex, and so on. If you dismiss an employee for reasons that are protected under federal and state statutes that cover discrimination, sexual harassment, disabled employees, and so forth, you have violated that employee's rights. Therefore, even if you are an employment-at-will company, you still must consider several things when you fire an employee. You need to see if the job was analyzed properly to ensure that the person with the correct mix of skills, knowledge, and abilities was hired. You also need to determine that the employee was trained to do the job and that there were performance standards that he was aware of. Failure to show that these items occurred may lead a court to decide that the discharge was without merit.

Guarding Against Lawsuits

So what are you to do? Clearly you must terminate those employees who commit serious infractions. The safest way to protect yourself from a lawsuit is by ensuring that anytime you fire an employee, you have a legitimate business reason that you have documented in the employee's file. Further, you must have a well-known disciplinary policy that you have applied consistently. Additionally, if you need to let employees go for economic reasons, make sure the layoffs affect all employees and not just one specific group. To do otherwise might make it appear that you have violated some federal statute that makes it illegal to discriminate against certain classes of people. No matter what the reason is for firing an employee you must always be objective, consistent, and have it completely documented in the employee's file.

Another way to guard against lawsuits is to make sure that nothing you have said or put into writing can be construed as an employment contract. You must investigate to see whether you have made a written or oral commitment that may limit your right to fire that employee. At this point it is critical to review your employee handbook to see if in the eyes of the employee, she could reasonably believe you made promises that you did not keep. Your employee handbook and other documents should always preserve your right to terminate employees at your discretion. If you list specific types of conduct that will result in termination, you should also state that these are only some of the actions for which the employee can be terminated. Finally, never make any communication, written or verbal, that can be construed as a long-term job security commitment.

As a final safeguard, you need to completely investigate any complaints against that employee. When a complaint is lodged against an employee you should investigate it quickly, thoroughly, fairly, and confidentially. To begin the investigation process you should have closed-door discussions with each witness and with the accused employee. It is important during each of these discussions to take comprehensive notes or, if you are not a good note taker, have their permission to tape the discussion. Then later you can have someone take the tape and transcribe it into a written report. If you feel that you do not have the ability to adequately investigate a particular complaint, you may want to hire an outside party to conduct the investigation. However, if you do hire an outside investigator you must make sure she is experienced in conducting internal investigations for businesses. Also, you must make sure the investigator follows procedures that respect the rights of the accused employee.

Wrongful Discharge Cases
(continued)

job applicants or employees. Another legal theory that has been effective is violation of public policy or breach of good faith and fair dealing by an employer in his relationship with an employee, which dictates that in every employment relationship there is an automatic commitment by the employer to deal fairly and in good faith with the employees.

Consider an Independent Reviewer

As an additional safety net against wrongful discharge lawsuits, you might want to consider having an independent review done prior to the employee's termination. You would have someone other than the employee's direct supervisor make the final objective decision to terminate. If you do this, there are several matters that the independent reviewer would verify. For example, the independent reviewer would verify that you have followed procedures consistently and objectively and that you have followed your written personnel policies. Also, if the termination is for lack of performance, the reviewer would determine whether the employee has been given adequate and documented warnings that he or she would be terminated if there was no improvement. Finally, this reviewer would need to ascertain that no federal or state statutes or laws would be violated and that there was no verbal or written contract or other statements made that could result in the employee being protected from discharge.

If after a thorough investigation you determine the employee must be terminated then you need to do so immediately. If you do not, this can lead to morale problems with the other employees. However, if you decide the employee does not deserve to be terminated but does deserve to be disciplined, you can pick a type of discipline discussed earlier in this chapter.

The Firing Process

Now that the decision to fire the employee has been made, what do you do next? Even at this point there are several things you can do to lessen the chance of a lawsuit.

For example, you can give the employee a choice to resign. Giving the employee this opportunity, as opposed to firing him, allows him to save face and not be as bitter or angry as he would otherwise be.

Also, you could offer to give him a positive reference to a potential new employer. One of the biggest concerns of someone who is fired is what kind of reference they will get. Most prospective employers want to talk to a person's previous employer to get input on how they might do on the job. Therefore, if the former employee knows he will get a positive reference from you this will alleviate a lot of his stress in finding a new job. *This does not mean that you will tell a lie.* What this means is that you will emphasize his good qualities. Even though this employee was not a good fit for your business, chances are he will be a good fit for someone else's business.

Third, you may even offer to help him in finding a new job that is better suited to his skills and personality. You may allow him to use your phone to contact new employers or lead him to other companies that have positions open. Of course, if you have fired the employee for something very serious, such as stealing or the use of illegal drugs, this would not be advisable. However, the vast majority of employees are dismissed because their skills did not match up with the performance required of them for that particular job.

In some cases, you may wish to offer a severance package and other benefits to help the former employee deal with his dismissal.

Even though you are normally not required to give a severance package, there are certain advantages if you decide to do so. For example, if you agree to provide an additional period of pay and benefits while the former employee is looking for other work this will greatly lessen his ill will toward you and your business. Also, you could use the severance package as an incentive for the former employee to sign a termination letter whereby he agrees to waive all potential legal claims against you. This is what is referred to as a "release of claims." For a release to be enforceable you must give something of value to the employee, called consideration, in exchange for him releasing any claims against you. The severance package satisfies this requirement. If you do offer a severance package and require the employee to release you from any claims he might have against you, you need to give the employee a reasonable period of time to decide whether to accept your severance package and to sign the release of claims form. Chances are, when you offer him a severance package that you are under no legal obligation to offer, he will gladly sign a form releasing all claims against you. This is an easy way to reduce the likelihood of future lawsuits.

Meeting with the Employee

When it comes time to inform the employee that she will be terminated, you need to meet with her in private. You must be honest and straightforward in stating the reasons for the termination. You must make it clear that this is your final decision and that you are not going to change your mind. Then go over any of the items that you have decided to offer the employee to lessen the impact. Next, let the employee speak her peace of mind so that she can get her pent-up feelings out in the open. There have been many stories carried in the press about former employees coming back and hurting and even killing those still in the workplace. Even though this type of violence seldom happens, you still must be aware of the possibility. If you feel that this employee is particularly violent, you must take appropriate measures to make sure that you calm her anger as much as possible. However, if you feel it necessary, you might want to consult first with a psychologist or a local law enforcement officer who specializes in such matters.

What Are Trade Secrets?

Confidential information and trade secrets are formulas, patterns, recipes, compilations, programs, devices, methods, techniques, or processes that aren't generally known to the public and that you have made reasonable efforts to keep secret. These are the items that give you a competitive advantage. The fact that this information is not readily attainable elsewhere and that you have taken precautions to keep it secret will determine whether the information is a trade secret.

As a general rule, terminated employees file for unemployment compensation through their state department of labor. Employees who were terminated for reasons other than serious misconduct are normally eligible for unemployment compensation. Employees who voluntarily leave a job without good cause are not entitled to unemployment compensation. However, most states are very lenient in awarding unemployment compensation. If your employee should file for unemployment compensation you will receive a notice. At this time you can decide whether you want to contest the former employee's unemployment claim. This is a decision you must make for each individual employee. Most of the time you will not want to file a written objection to the former employee receiving unemployment compensation. However, this decision is up to you.

Post-Termination Matters

At the end of the termination meeting it would be appropriate to give the former employee his final paycheck. Most states have laws specifying when you must give a final paycheck to a terminated employee. For example, in some states the terminated employee is not entitled to his final paycheck until the next regularly scheduled payday; in other states, the employee must be paid in full at the time of termination. Contact the wage and hour division of your state's labor department to determine what the laws are in your state.

Cobra

Most small businesses do not offer health insurance to their employees. However, if your business offers health insurance you must be aware of a federal law called the Consolidated Omnibus Budget Reconciliation Act. This federal statute is referred to as COBRA, for short. COBRA requires you to offer former employees the option of continuing their coverage for a period of time after their termination. If you do not abide by this law you can be found in violation and subject to fines.

Protecting Your Confidential Material

If an employee quits or is terminated who has had access to confidential information, trade secrets, or other proprietary information, you need to protect yourself. If the former employee has signed a covenant not to compete or an agreement not to divulge trade secrets, confidential information, and proprietary information, then you are in a strong position. At this time you need to notify the employee that if he divulges or uses to your detriment any of this information you will take the appropriate legal action against him and his current employer. In order to enforce a covenant not to compete and to protect your trade secrets if they are being divulged, you can get a temporary restraining order or preliminary injunction to forbid the former employee from doing either. If you can show that through the former employee's actions you will suffer immediate damage most courts will give you a court order to put a legal stop to the former employee's activities.

Referrals

Finally, you will have to deal with one of the biggest potential problems after an employee has been terminated or quits. That is, you will receive phone calls from prospective employers wanting a referral on your former employee. It is common knowledge that most employers will not give referrals. They are afraid of legal repercussions. Generally, you should avoid making any negative employment references and should only verify employment dates and position.

Conclusion

In order to discipline, it must be done correctly and thoroughly. Your objective should be to correct the employee's undesirable behavior as opposed to punishing him. There are many different types of disciplinary problems: attendance, on the job behaviors, dishonesty, and outside activities. Some factors to consider when disciplining are: seriousness, duration, frequency, and extenuating factors.

Termination of employment is used in two different scenarios. First, if you have followed progressive disciplinary actions to no avail. Second, when an employee commits an offense so serious that he is immediately terminated.

Who to Tell About a Firing

You need to be careful how you deal with employee firings at your business and with other employees. You should never disclose the reasons for firing except strictly on a need-to-know basis. Further you need to avoid discussing employee firings at any employee gatherings or meetings. Even though the employees already have a good idea what happened you cannot be held liable for what they think. Therefore, to minimize your liability you should say nothing nor discuss it with those who do not need to know.

For more information on this topic, visit our Web site at www.businesstown.com

Special
Employment
Issues

Chapter 24

17: MANAGING THE BUSINESS

18: MOTIVATION AND LEADERSHIP

19: RECRUITMENT

20: HIRING AND SELECTION

21: ORIENTATION AND PERSONNEL POLICIES

22: PERFORMANCE EVALUATIONS

23: DISCIPLINE AND TERMINATION

24: **SPECIAL EMPLOYMENT ISSUES**

What Employees Really Want

It is a common perception by management that the number one desire of the employee is good wages. And that the number two item every employee wants is job security. However, such is usually not the case. In a survey done by the School of Business at Indiana University, the number one thing employees want is challenging work. The number two and three things employees want from their workplaces are recognition for good work and being a part of what is going on. It wasn't until they got to the fourth and fifth items that the employees ranked job security and good wages as being important. Employees realize that you cannot pay them as much as they want. Therefore, in order to keep good employees you need to present them with challenging work, make them a part of a team, and recognize them for work that exceeds the standards you have set. Other items that employees ranked in the top 10 that they wanted included promotion and growth opportunities, a

(Continued on the next page.)

Before we leave the topics of recruiting, selection, hiring, and termination, there are certain other issues that need to be covered. What do employees really want? How do you manage employees? Should you hire teenagers?

Motivating the Low-Paid Employee

Probably most of your employees will be making minimum wage or an amount not significantly above it. So how do you motivate these employees? Most of these employees are working just to earn money to pay for whatever they need at that time. This is not a career job for them. Therefore, what can a manager do? There are three possibilities: respect, nonfinancial rewards, and autonomy.

You must treat each employee with respect and dignity. After all, isn't that what you want? If you give these employees the respect and dignity they deserve it increases the likelihood of them doing a better job in spite of the low pay. A little kindness can go a long way. When you walk into most restaurants you will notice that they have a picture of the employee of the month and the employee of the year hanging on the wall. This is a pat on the back, giving public recognition of the employees' hard work. This goes a long way in motivating an employee. Further, you could give the employee a free lunch on her birthday. The types of nonfinancial rewards you can give an employee are only limited by the type of business you are in and by your imagination.

If your employees have the ability to do their jobs without constant supervision, let them operate with some autonomy. No employee enjoys the constant stare of a manager over his shoulder. This is sending the employee the message that he is inferior and that he does not know what he is doing. Therefore, when an employee has learned the job well enough, you need to give that employee some autonomy to show that you trust him and respect his abilities to perform the job without supervision.

Hiring Teenagers

Since many positions you will hire for will be low-paying ones, there is a tendency to fill them with teenagers. Teenagers can become excellent employees. However, there are special considerations that pertain to hiring teenage employees. Normally, teenagers will require more training since this will be their first job. It is difficult to determine how much longer it will take to train a totally inexperienced person because it depends on the complexity of the job. You can assume, however, that it will take you more time to train a teenager than an experienced person.

Since most teenagers are working at their first job, they have not had the time or experience to establish a work ethic. Employees who are at their first job usually have little sense or knowledge of how they contribute to the employer's bottom line. Nor do they realize how their actions affect other employees. Finally, teenagers are strongly influenced by peer pressure. It is a distinct problem with teenage employees giving free food to their friends. Also, there is a problem with young employees talking with their friends as opposed to waiting on your customers. These should not be reasons not to hire teenagers. However, a manager needs to recognize that since most teenagers have not worked before, they need to be handled accordingly. And you need to give them additional training to assist them in establishing a strong work ethic and in order for them to be successful. After all, they have no experience and they need to get it somewhere.

Managing Employees

Running a successful franchise means not only hiring quality employees, but also having a manager or managers that know how to manage people. You, as the franchisee, may or may not be the manager. However, whoever the manager is, you must be sure she is effective and confident, reliable, trustworthy, loyal, and good with people. A good manager also possesses the ability to disagree with you and point out problems as she sees them. After all if you are the owner of the franchise, but she is the manager, she is the one involved in the

What Employees Really Want
(continued)

good work environment, loyalty by management to the employee, appropriate discipline, and employee assistance programs. By doing this you will deal with the most common problems you will have with employees, which are high turnover rates, problems motivating employees, and finding those employees with specialized skills.

Create a Good Work Environment

The quality of the work environment also needs to be highlighted. You need to have a clean workplace that is attractive and that employees enjoy coming to each day. Nothing turns off a customer or an employee more than dirty floors, dirty windows, dirty light fixtures, lack of toilet paper and paper towels in the bathroom, etc. In addition to a clean work environment, you need to provide your employees a friendly place to work. Even though your employees need to know that you are the boss, you should not act like a dictator, and, therefore, make your employees resentful. The best managers seek a happy medium so that their employees enjoy their work and want to do their work well, but fully recognize that you are the boss. It is up to you, the manger, to provide the atmosphere, both physical and psychological, to improve the workplace setting.

day-to-day operations. In other words, she is the one in the trenches with the troops. If a manager is afraid to disagree with you, you have a serious problem.

Second, the manager needs to know how to treat each employee as an individual. Since all employees are different, each of them requires different methods of treatment. You need to remain enthusiastic and positive as you interact with each of the employees since they are looking to you to set the example.

Third, the manager needs to get to know his or her employees. Often a small business takes on the atmosphere of a family. Consequently, each employee's personal life has an impact on their workplace performance. Therefore, you need to know each employee's strengths, weaknesses, and personality. Also, it would help you if you knew what their personal goals and objectives were in working for you.

Next, you need to have the ability to delegate responsibility to those employees who are ready for it. As a manager you cannot handle everything. When you delegate some of the responsibility to various employees not only does this lift a burden off of you, but it increases the worker's morale as well. It makes them feel more important. However, you must make sure that each employee knows what his or her responsibilities are and that you are still the boss.

Employees always like to know how much the other guy is getting paid. Therefore, you need to institute a policy whereby salaries, wages, and bonuses are confidential, emphasizing that compensation matters are not to be discussed among employees. Remind them that each employee's salary, wage, and bonus are based on their experience and the skills they bring to the workplace.

Finally, you need to always be on your toes to make sure that you recognize when your employees' morale is low or turnover is high. Once you recognize that employee morale has gone down, you need to talk to your employees to determine why. Then you need to correct it. High turnover is very expensive. The higher the turnover the more time you have to spend on training, which does not add anything to your bottom line. And, unfortunately, unhappy employees may steal from your business or cause customer dissatisfaction. As a final note, studies show that the main reason employees quit their jobs in a franchise setting is not due to their pay or job security. The main reason employees quit their jobs is poor management.

Leadership

Most franchisees will either be the manager that employees work under or they will be the franchise owner that the manager looks to for direction. Regardless of the role that you play, you must be an effective leader. As a leader, you need to have certain characteristics. You must encourage your management and employees to make suggestions on how to improve on what they are doing. After all, your employee is the one performing the actual job, not you. A good leader provides opportunity for self-expression and gives recognition for work well done. Your behavior as a leader should also be very enthusiastic and positive since the managers and employees will reflect your behavior. However, there is no one best leadership style. The best style is simply the one that is appropriate and meets the needs of those working for you. As the franchise owner, you will be looked upon to lead your team to success. Do not mistakenly assume that since you are highly self-motivated that your managers and employees are as well. Remember, no one is as committed to your success as you are. Therefore, it is up to you as an effective leader to motivate those under you. Hopefully, your employees' performance will lead to a successful business for all.

> There is no one best leadership style. The best style is simply the one that is appropriate and meets the needs of those working for you.

Conclusion

Selecting, hiring, and keeping good employees is often the most difficult and time-consuming task that will face you as a franchise owner. Not only can the finding of enough quality employees be difficult and time consuming, but it can be a constant reoccurring problem as your good employees leave for greener pastures. But by implementing and following the guidelines set forth in Chapters 19 through 24 of this book, you will be well on your way to a successful resolution of one of the most pressing problems of a business owner.

Information, Money, and Accounting Records

In this section, you'll learn:

- Where you can get financing money

- How much money you'll need to get the franchise off the ground

- How to keep track of the money— the basics of bookkeeping

- Problems to watch for, both in your store and in your financial records

CHAPTER 25 MONEY **CHAPTER 26** ACCOUNTING, RECORD KEEPING, AND FINANCIAL STATEMENTS
CHAPTER 27 RED FLAGS: PURCHASING, INVENTORY LEVELS, LABOR COSTS, CREDIT, TAXES

Money

Chapter 25

25: MONEY

26: ACCOUNTING, RECORD KEEPING, AND
FINANCIAL STATEMENTS

27: RED FLAGS: PURCHASING, INVENTORY
LEVELS, LABOR COSTS, CREDIT, TAXES

Introduction

Once a prospective franchisee has selected the franchise she wants to purchase, she still has one major question to answer. The question that almost every prospective franchisee asks is: "Where am I going to get the money to purchase this franchise and to support it until I am profitable?" Most franchise candidates do not have enough money to foot the entire cost in getting the franchise up and running. Most people's experience with finding financing is in the purchase of an automobile or a home. There are several types of costs in the opening and operation of a franchise, which you either need to finance yourself or locate sources from which to borrow the money. However, prior to seeking financing, one must first answer two key questions: How much money will I need to cover my start-up capital and working capital? Second, where will I find the money?

How Much Money Do You Need?

You must determine how much money you will need to open your franchise and to continue its operations until you turn a profit. Also, it is important to determine how much money you will need for you and your family to live on until such time that you can pay yourself a salary. If you do not determine these needs in advance accurately, it is very possible that you will fail for lack of adequate monies. So, how do you determine exactly how much money you will need? There are several ways to do this.

The first place you should look to determine how much money you will need is the UFOC that was discussed in Chapters 3 and 4. Items 5, 6, and 7 in the UFOC set forth the fees that will be paid to the franchisor along with the financing requirements for start-up capital and three months worth of working capital. Item 5 will tell you what initial franchise fees are due to the franchisor. Item 6 will list the other fees due to the franchisor and whether these fees are due now or later. However, you should study in detail Item 7, which lists the initial investment that will be required. Item 7 discloses information that will assist you in preparing your business plan so that you know what your financial obligations will be in purchasing the franchise and in operating and opening the franchise business.

Normally, the franchisor will list low figures and high figures for the financial items it is required to disclose in Item 7. Unless you can determine otherwise, it would be prudent to add up the numbers on the high side in calculating your initial investment. You should err on the side of caution. After all, Item 7 is nothing more than the franchisor's best faith estimates of what your initial costs will be plus your initial working capital obligations during your first three months. To the number you derive from Item 7 you should add additional funds to cover several more months of working capital and monies that you estimate you will need during the first six months that your business is open to cover you and your family's personal living expenses.

Therefore, in determining your monetary requirements, you must not only add all the numbers listed in Item 7 of the UFOC, preferably the high end of the estimates for each item, but also you need to add to this figure the costs for an additional 3 to 6 months of working capital until you make a profit, and 6 to 12 months' worth of monies that you estimate you and your family will need to survive on. However, a question you must ask yourself is, how accurate are the estimates that the franchisor has provided in Item 7?

Writing Your Business Plan

Now that you have started to get a handle on how much money you need, it is time to put together a business plan. It is also referred to as a financial plan. You can rest assured that regardless of who your lenders are they will require a strong business plan that is both comprehensive and complete. In effect, your business plan is a statement to a prospective lender about what type of franchise you plan on buying, how you plan to operate it, and how you will be able to pay back the lender.

It is beyond the scope of this book to go into all the details of what should be contained in a business plan. However, the key parts of what should be in your business plan will be covered. Your business plan should begin with an executive summary that not only lists

Ask Other Franchisees

It is imperative that you contact current franchisees from the list provided in the UFOC to determine what their actual initial investment was. You need to select those franchisees who opened their franchise businesses within the last year or two, since their numbers will more accurately reflect what your initial investment will be. You need to contact those franchisees whose variables such as location of the business, size of the unit, and other variables most closely matches your location and size

After contacting several franchisees and obtaining their numbers, you will be able to determine how accurate the franchisor's figures are and if you need to increase those numbers so that your initial investment costs are more accurate. What you are trying to avoid is underestimating your initial investment. There is nothing worse than having sufficient funds to purchase a franchise and open it, but not have enough money to keep it open and to take care of your family's personal financial needs.

Help for Your Business Plan

Even though it might appear to be overwhelming to write your business plan, you can easily obtain information from various sources to help you write it. Not only can you go to various book stores and computer stores and purchase books and software packages that will greatly assist you in writing your business plan, but you can also go to the United States Small Business Administration for help. The SBA can help you with the particulars of your business plan. Also, the SBA sponsors a volunteer service called SCORE (the Service Corps of Retired Executives), which provides free counseling to anyone interested in starting a small business.

your company name, address, contact person, and so on, but also the type of franchise you will purchase, what type of industry this franchise is in, and a history of the franchisor. You will summarize how much money you need and how you will utilize these funds.

The second item in your business plan is a business description that defines the products or services you are selling and their relationship to the industry. Third will be a section on marketing, in which you define your market, your position in the market, pricing strategies, sales strategies, and potential sources of sales. The fourth section will focus on your management. Listed are your directors and officers with a short bio on each of them. Also, you will name your key employees, your organizational structure, your management strategies, risk factors, and so forth.

Fifth, you will provide a competitive analysis in which you will discuss your competition and how you can compete. Sixth, you will discuss your design and development plans, in which you cover items such as product development, procedures, and budgets. The seventh section will be on accounting, finance, and taxes. In this section you will list start-up costs, equity and credit references, proposed financing, collateral, projected income statements, projected balance sheets, and projected cash flow statements for the first year. Also, this section will include the amount of working capital you estimate is required along with a break-even analysis on your franchise.

The eighth section will set forth the legal aspects of your business such as your franchise agreement, any licenses for the franchise, and other legal documents with the franchisor or with others. Also covered is the type of business structure you will use: corporation, limited liability company, limited partnership, etc.; what types of insurance you will purchase and their costs; and any other financial matters important to your business. After these items are covered, you will probably have an appendix that contains items such as franchisor-produced product literature, brochures, and articles.

This is just a general outline of what you can expect to include in a comprehensive and detailed business plan. However, for your particular franchise, it is quite possible you might include more information. A good accountant or business consultant can advise you of this.

Five Cs of Borrowing Money

It is important that you understand the five Cs of borrowing money. Your prospective lender will be examining these five Cs. The five Cs of credit are as follows:

1. *Capacity*–your ability to repay the loan
2. *Capital*–your personal financial strength
3. Character–what are your personal attributes; are you honest, do you have integrity, etc.
4. *Collateral*–assets you have, both personal and business, that you can pledge against the loan amount
5. *Conditions*–the general economic conditions at the time you make application for the loan (Is there a recession or is the economy strong and growing?)

A common question of a prospective franchisee is how much money does a franchisee normally borrow in getting their franchise up and running? In 1999, *Franchise Times* performed a study in which they did a random sampling of 15,000 franchisees to determine the size of their debt financing. The amount of money borrowed broke down as follows:

- Under $50,000–31% (31% of the franchisees borrowed less than $50,000)
- $50,000 to $99,999–23% (23% of the franchisees borrowed at least $50,000 but less than $99,999, and so on)
- $100,000 to $249,999–26%
- $250,000 to $499,999–12%
- $500,000 to $1,000,000–2%
- $1,000,000 or more–7%

As seen from these figures, the vast majority of people borrowed half a million or less. In fact, 91% of the franchisees surveyed borrowed less than half a million to purchase and open their franchise. But an incredible 54% of the franchisees borrowed under $100,000.

A common question of a prospective franchisee is how much money does a franchisee normally borrow in getting their franchise up and running?

Where Do You Get the Money?

Before you embark on obtaining financing from outside sources, you need to first determine how much money you personally have available to use. First, review how much cash you have in your savings accounts, investment accounts, mutual funds, and money market accounts. Second, determine what the current value is of stocks and bonds you own and the cash value of life insurance you own. Third, determine what monies you have available to you that are contained in 401(k) plans, IRAs, and other retirement plans. Fourth, determine the amount of equity you have in your home that you could borrow against. Fifth, determine the value of personal property you own and any other assets that you own that you could borrow against. Additionally, if you have just been let go from your employer, you may have a substantial severance package.

After you determine how much money you can bring to the table, you may still be short of the amount needed to purchase, open, and operate the franchise. Therefore, you will need to determine what outside sources of financing are available to you. However, you must be dedicated in your pursuit of financing since it will require you to be persistent and to show a lot of determination. Often it is not easy to convince people to loan you money.

The available sources of financing for your franchise are only limited by your creativity. However, the following are the most commonly utilized sources of financing.

Personal Savings

Most people must tap into their own funds in order to start a business. Most startups get at least some of their capital from their owners' pockets. In determining what personal funds you have available, you need to develop a net worth statement. You must determine how much cash you have available in savings, the value of your stocks and bonds, the equity in your real estate you could borrow against, and retirement funds that are available to you, such as 401(k)s, and IRAs.

Some people consider as part of their personal savings the amount of credit they have available on their credit cards. Even

> After you determine how much money you can bring to the table, you may still be short of the amount needed to purchase, open, and operate the franchise.

though this is a source of funds for your franchise, interest rates are high in the use of such funds. Other sources of personal funds were mentioned earlier in this chapter. First and foremost, you must determine your net worth and what funds you can provide to start up your business. Just like a bank will normally not lend you 100% of the purchase price of your home, a lender does not like to lend money to someone who does not sink some of her own funds in the business. Most lenders are looking for anywhere from 10 to 30% of the total start-up costs and operating costs to come from your personal funds. After all, the lenders know that the more money you have at risk, the harder you will work to make it a success.

Family, Friends, and/or Private Investors

Once you determine what you have available in personal resources, the next place to look is family and friends. It has been estimated that over 80% of all first-time business owners acquire some or all of their financing from their family and friends. It is quite common to ask your parents, relatives, your spouse's parents and relatives, and your close friends for money to invest in your franchise. Also, your siblings can be an important source of financing. There might even be an inheritance coming to you that your parents might free up and give to you now.

After all, your family, relatives, and friends want you to be a success and will be more than willing to invest in you and your opportunity as opposed to other impersonal investments. However, when you obtain financing from family, relatives, and friends, it is important to have a clear understanding with them as to whether the monies given to you are in the form of a loan or in the form of equity. With equity they have an ownership interest in your business and, therefore, do not expect to be paid back until such time as you sell your franchise. You do not want any misunderstandings or hard feelings to occur due to failure to address the circumstances of how the money will be paid back.

Another available route is to find private investors. Private investors will be looking to invest in your business in exchange for an ownership interest. Therefore, a private investor will not be looking

> It has been estimated that over 80% of all first-time business owners acquire some or all of their financing from their family and friends.

A Closer Look at the SBA

The SBA has approved nearly 12,000 loans to franchisees in the past five years. In 1996, SBA lenders approved franchise loans valued at more than $978 million. Also, the SBA has what is referred to as a low-doc loan program, which features reduced paperwork and turnaround time for loans of $100,000 or less. The SBA has been working with franchisors, franchisees, and lenders for the last several years to streamline the SBA's franchise loan review process.

for a payback on a loan. They are looking for a payback over a period of time due to the appreciation in value of the investment they made in your business. When people start out with their first business they shy away from selling ownership interests to private investors. However, this method of financing should not be overlooked. Selling ownership interests may be a feasible way to start your business.

Government Programs

There are several government programs available to prospective franchisees in obtaining financing for your business. The most common government program is run by the United States Small Business Administration (SBA). This program remains one of the greatest sources of financing available to prospective franchisees. SBA loans provide rates competitive with commercial banks but with generally longer terms for payback than other financing sources. Typically, SBA loans are made by a private bank or other private lending institution with a portion of the loan guaranteed by the SBA. The SBA guarantees up to 90% of the value of the loan.

The SBA guaranteed loan program works as follows. You apply for a commercial bank loan. If the bank rejects your loan application on the basis of your financial profile, you then become eligible to apply for a SBA guaranteed loan. If the bank you originally filed your application with is a part of the SBA backed loan program, you will be able to reapply through this program with the bank. Otherwise, if your application was with a bank that is not in the SBA loan program, then you can contact the SBA and obtain from them a list of approved participating lenders. As a rule of thumb, the SBA will loan you up to $4 for every dollar that you put into the franchise yourself.

The SBA has several programs available. One of the most common is the 7(A) guaranteed business loan program. In this program the SBA guarantees 75% of the loan up to a maximum of $750,000. The SBA oversees 16 small-business lending companies that operate under the 7(A) guaranteed loan program. These 16 companies are among the top volume leaders of SBA loans and some even have divisions that deal specifically with franchises.

Another program provided by the SBA is referred to as a certified development company. This is a private nonprofit organization licensed by the SBA as a source for providing 504 loans for small and medium sized businesses. Loans under the SBA 504 program are available to finance industrial or commercial buildings or for purchasing equipment or machinery. With this type of loan you can make as low as a 10% down payment. Then the primary lender provides up to 50% of the mortgage amount with the certified development company making a fully guaranteed second position loan of up to 40% of the mortgage. Additionally, the SBA has developed a program with small business investment companies. These companies are SBA licensed and provide equity capital and long-term debt financing. Small business investment companies tend to specialize in certain industries.

The SBA has revised its franchise eligibility guidelines and operating procedures. It has implemented a streamlined review process. This has culminated in what is called the Franchise Registry. The Franchise Registry is a source that helps the SBA and its participating lenders make consistent eligibility decisions. It also speeds access to SBA financial assistance, streamlines processing, and helps lenders recognize industry specific factors during the loan review process.

As a result, this allows the lender to verify a franchise system's lending eligibility through the Internet, reducing red tape and time involved with getting approved. Participation in the Franchise Registry is voluntary. If a franchisor chooses not to participate in this streamlined review process, loan applications by its franchisees will still be reviewed individually by the SBA or its lenders. Currently, there are over 200 franchise systems that have been approved and are listed on the Franchise Registry. Also, there are over 225 franchises in the application process to be approved for inclusion in the Franchise Registry.

Other government programs for financing are as follows:

1. **The United States Department of Agriculture's Farmers Home Administration.** Under this program business owners that live in cities or areas with a population of 50,000 or less, outside major metropolitan areas, may receive financing. These are guaranteed long-term loans backed

Look for Other Resources

The programs listed are only some of the government programs available from which you might find financing for your franchise. You should search the Web and other sources for additional programs from which you can obtain financing. Special programs also exist for those prospective franchisees who are minorities, women, handicapped, or suffer from other disadvantages.

90% by the Farmers Home Administration. The funds can be used for start-up or working capital, new equipment purchases, refinancing, expansion costs, and/or the purchase of real estate.

2. **The Economic Development Administration of the Department of Commerce.** This program makes loans and loan guarantees to new and existing businesses in depressed areas (regions with higher than average unemployment and low to average income levels). Loans can be awarded to cover working capital or to purchase fixed assets.

3. **State Business and Industrial Development Corporations (SBIDC).** Corporations in these programs are capitalized by state governments and provide long-term loans, up to twenty years, for either the expansion of an existing small business or for the purchase of capital equipment.

4. **Local Development Companies (LDCs).** These companies are capitalized through local investment groups and differ from community to community in their priorities and interests. They supply money to local businesses for the construction or expansion of the business' facilities.

> There are several government programs that are specifically targeted to women, minorities, or disadvantaged people.

There are several government programs that are specifically targeted to women, minorities, or disadvantaged people. Some of these programs include the following:

1. **The Minority Business Development Agency of the United States Department of Commerce.** This agency offers a wide variety of programs for potential franchisees who are minorities or women.

2. **The Minority Enterprise Small Business Investment Company (MESBIC).** This is an offshoot of the Small Business Administration's licensed SBICs.

3. **The Veterans Transition Franchise Initiative (VETFRAN).** This was established in 1991 to provide veterans with assistance in purchasing franchises and is sponsored by the International Franchise Association (the IFA is not a government agency).

Commercial Banks

Many commercial banks make business loans to the small business person. But many are reluctant to provide financing to small businesses, particularly in today's highly regulated banking environment. However, one cannot overlook commercial banks for financing. There are several variables involved in whether a commercial bank will grant a loan to you. Several items that the bank will look at include the following:

1. Whether the franchisor has a proven track record and is well established, or if the franchisor is new and has an unproven track record
2. How much collateral you can offer
3. Your credit worthiness
4. Current economic conditions

Commercial banks reject loans for franchises for a variety of reasons, such as:

1. Lack of collateral from the franchisee
2. Lack of credit or poor credit
3. Lack of experience by the prospective franchisee in the chosen business
4. The franchisor is small with little or no track record

Finally, a commercial lender will look at the franchise agreement to determine if there are any provisions that could impact your ability to be successful.

> A commercial lender will look at the franchise agreement to determine if there are any provisions that could impact your ability to be successful.

Nonconventional Lenders

In addition to commercial banks, savings and loans, and credit unions, there are several types of nonconventional lenders that can be considered for financing. There are finance companies, leasing firms, and property management businesses that arrange for partial funding of a franchisee's investment. For example, ITT Small Business Finance Corporation and Allied Capital

Corporation extend start-up loans to franchisees. Companies that are credit companies, such as General Electric Credit Corporation or Westinghouse Credit Corporation, provide financing for inventory, equipment, or fixtures. Additionally, there are other companies that purchase the equipment or real estate and lease it back to you.

Franchisor Financing Arrangements

Approximately one-third of all franchisors provide either direct or third party financial assistance to its franchisees. These franchisors provide the financing or assist you in your search for financing. There are a variety of programs that franchisors offer, which you need to review before you consider any other form of financing. For example, some franchisors will provide direct financing to its prospective franchisees of up to 60% of their total initial investment. However, most franchisors help you find a bank or other lender. These franchisors have developed a list of banks or other lenders through which either they themselves, or their franchisees, or both, have obtained financing. These sources are great because they are already familiar with your franchisor and its system and, therefore, are comfortable lending because they know the success rate of the franchisor.

Venture Capital Companies

Venture capital firms receive a lot of business press. However, they finance very few businesses. In the franchise industry, venture capital funds are usually only available for franchisees in the hotel, restaurant, or automobile industries or for those with multiunit franchises. Problems with obtaining venture capital funds are often that such firms demand part ownership in your franchise, and full payment over a short payout period of only five years or less, and will want a high rate of return, sometimes as high as 200 to 300% during the course of the loan. Very few franchisees obtain their financing from venture capital firms, for good reasons. However, it is still a good alternative to review.

> Some franchisors will provide direct financing to its prospective franchisees of up to 60% of their total initial investment. However, most franchisors help you find a bank or other lender.

Owner Financing

If you purchase an existing franchise, there will be a possibility that the selling franchisee does not want a lump sum payment. Most people, when they sell their business, only want some of the money up front with the rest being paid over a period of several years. A selling business owner does this for several reasons. One reason is that this stretches the payment of taxes due on the sale over a longer period of time, thereby cushioning the impact of paying such taxes. Also, many business owners want to have a steady income over a period of several years for retirement reasons. Therefore, a viable financing option is to determine if the selling franchisee is willing to take back an installment note for part or all of the purchase price of the existing franchise.

Leasing

Frequently, after a franchisee has exhausted all other sources of financing, it will turn to leasing arrangements. Leasing arrangements can be very attractive because they eliminate the need of coming up with the full purchase price to purchase the items. Instead, you will pay a monthly leasing fee to lease the items covered by your leasing arrangement. You can lease many things such as equipment, machinery, fixtures, vehicles, real estate, and so on.

Leasing is often part of the package of the franchisor's financing. In some franchise systems, the franchisor will purchase the land, building, equipment, and signage necessary for the franchise location, and lease it back to the franchisee. Leasing is a viable financing option, but it is one that must be carefully reviewed, since you will pay more money for items you are leasing than if you had purchased them outright.

There are many options to pursue when obtaining financing for your franchise. There are books that can be purchased through the International Franchise Association that provide a very detailed and comprehensive overview of possible financing sources.

In 1999 the magazine *Franchise Times* performed a study to determine how new franchisees financed the purchase of their franchises. They used a random sampling from a list of 15,000

> Leasing arrangements can be very attractive because they eliminate the need of coming up with the full purchase price to purchase the items.

franchisees. The sources of financing are as follows (in descending order of percentage used):

1. Financing from personal savings
2. Standard bank loans
3. SBA loans
4. Money borrowed from family and friends
5. Franchisor provided financing
6. Loans from sources other than banks
7. Financing from previous owners
8. Cash from continuing businesses
9. Financing from venture capital firms

By far, the most common sources of funds for new franchisees in 1999 were from personal savings, family and friends, standard bank loans, SBA loans, and franchisor-provided financing. The vast majority of new franchisees obtained their start-up capital and working capital from more than one source. The most common formula was a combination of personal savings and home equity for seed money and an SBA loan for the balance.

Conclusion

Putting together a financial package is a challenging task, but not an impossible one. One of the most common reasons a person who wants to purchase a franchise does not is because they are unable to come up with the necessary financing. Therefore, one must be persistent, determined, and never give up. It is imperative in looking for financing that you only use this chapter as a starting point. Next, you should read the book, *No Money Down Financing for Franchising*, by Roger Roll, published in 1999. This book is sold through the International Franchise Association. Also, one must extensively search the World Wide Web for additional sources of financing. One should not have to forego the opportunity to purchase a franchise due to the inability to find adequate financing with all the resources available.

> By far, the most common sources of funds for new franchisees in 1999 were from personal savings, family and friends, standard bank loans, SBA loans, and franchisor-provided financing.

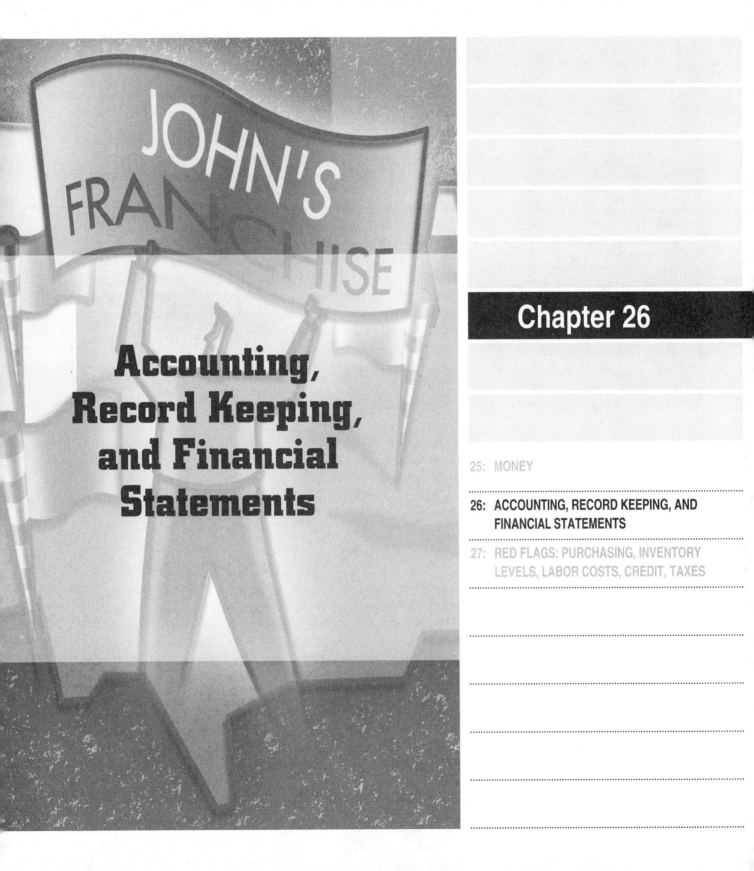

Accounting, Record Keeping, and Financial Statements

Chapter 26

25: MONEY

26: **ACCOUNTING, RECORD KEEPING, AND FINANCIAL STATEMENTS**

27: RED FLAGS: PURCHASING, INVENTORY LEVELS, LABOR COSTS, CREDIT, TAXES

Accounting is actually score keeping. The accounting records keep the score for each business. Keeping score for the franchisee is vital to your success and profits. Accounting helps manage your business finances—from balancing your checkbook to understanding your own financial statements.

Poor financial management is one of the leading causes for business failure. In many cases, failure could have been avoided if the owner had used sound financial principles in their dealings and decisions. Financial management is not something that you want to leave to your banker, financial planner, or accountant—you need to understand and use the basic principles yourself, even if you plan to leave the more formal reports to hired professionals.

Cash Registers

A cash register provides a tremendous amount of information. It will give you the total sales for the day, as well as an account of all cash receipts. You can even divide the sales down into different categories. For example, if you are in a sub sandwich shop, you may keep track of total sales, each kind of sandwich sold, the amount and kind of drinks sold, and even the french fries or potato chips sold. Many cash registers will also allow you to record the time when your staff members come to work as well as the time when they leave.

Record Keeping

The record keeping system is simply the accounting records. The system should be simple to use, easy to understand, reliable, accurate and should also provide information wanted by the franchisee on a timely basis. The financial statements that you keep reflect your financial status for a specific time period. Your financial statements help you make the proper financial decisions for the growth and development of your business. There are basically three financial statements which you should maintain. These include:

1. Cash flow statement (cash budget and sales statements)
2. Income statement (the operating statement)
3. Balance sheet (statement of financial position)

Cash Flow or Sales Budget Statement

The cash flow statement is generally the most useful financial statement and possibly the most important financial tool available to you as a franchisee. A problem that many franchisees face is that they know nothing about the value of the cash flow statement. Even though your business may be earning profits, this does not mean that you are financially okay. You may be having soaring revenues but are unable to pay your loans or other expenses.

You should be aware of the cash available in your business. Many franchise businesses that are housed in large shopping malls will receive 60% of their revenues during the Christmas shopping period of November and December. Other business, such as landscaping and lawn care, may have 80 to 100% of their business during the extended summer period. However, even though you receive a large portion of your income during just a few months, you may need to use that money for salaries and expenses throughout the entire year.

The cash flow statement projects your business's cash inflows and outflows over a year. This statement predicts the ability of your business to develop the cash necessary for support or even possible expansion. It projects your business's cash inflows and outflows and predicts your cash flow gaps. Cash flow statements are also used to prepare a budget for banks and lenders to help assure the bank, or lender, that you will have the cash available to pay back the loan.

Most businesses have some seasonality, and because of this it is wise to always maintain a cash flow statement to see what actual cash you have available and when you may be in debt.

Income Statement

An income statement (a statement of earnings or profit and loss statement) is simply a record of revenues minus expenses for a specific period of time, i.e., day, week, month, quarter, or year. You've probably seen a formal income statement for other businesses. The

7-Eleven

7-Eleven, Inc. prepares monthly financial and marketing records for the franchisee's store. Included among these records are profit and loss statements and balance sheets, financial activity summaries (e.g., daily sales receipts, purchases, cash expenditures) as reported by the franchisee, and inventory movement analysis by product category. Under this system, the franchisee has current, professionally prepared information regarding the store's financial and operating condition and current updates of all activity in the store's open account. As part of an extensive system of checks and balances to ensure the accuracy of all accounting, reports are sent to the franchisee for his or her verification.

income statement tells you the income the business has earned during the accounting period, the costs or expenses that were incurred by the business during the period, and the difference between the costs and incomes for the period, or net profit (or loss). The income statement is used for reporting federal and state taxes. You should recognize, however, that these expenses also include such noncash items as depreciation and amortization schedules.

The income statement then basically helps you to determine simple profits and losses that you have for the business and shows you if the business if profitable.

Balance Sheet

The balance sheet is a picture that illustrates the value of your business concerning your assets, liabilities, and owner's net worth at a specific time. The balance sheet follows the accounting equation or two counter-balancing sections: assets (what the business owns) = liabilities (what the business owes + your equity—your invested capital). The accounting equation looks like this:

Assets = Liabilities + Owner's Investment

According to generally accepted accounting principles, these two counter-balancing sections are generally divided into a two-column "T" account format, with the assets on the left equaling the liabilities and owner's equity on the right.

Assets

Assets (what you own) are divided into two major categories: (1) current assets and (2) fixed assets. Your assets represent those properties of the business that are used for the actual sales and revenue generating functions of the business.

Royalty Rebates

Some companies, such as Signal Graphics, offer a franchise rebate based upon the sales of the franchisees. Those stores who meet the following criteria are able to earn a royalty rebate on sales on more than $90,000 per month:

1. Pay royalty fees on time
2. Submit yearly financial statements on time
3. Submit sales reports on time

Additionally, sales of over $6.1 million per year are exempt from royalties if the criteria are met. This royalty rebate program rewards the franchisees who comply with the franchise agreement, plus it rewards them for running a successful business.

Current assets

Current assets are easily divided into three main items:

1. Cash—money in hand
2. Inventory—materials on hand
3. Accounts receivable—money due from customers through credit or credit card usage

In addition, there may be other current assets such as short-term or temporary investments, time deposit savings, or even prepaid expenses such as office space, insurance protection, taxes, and certain office supplies.

Fixed assets

Fixed assets are simply the "plant and equipment," or the properties that you own or use in running the business. Fixed assets are generally divided into:

1. Land—that you are buying or have bought
2. Building—that you are buying or have bought
3. Fixtures and equipment
4. Accumulated depreciation

Equity

Equity is the owner's net worth of the business. According to the accounting equation, this is what you own after you have paid your debts or liabilities. It is your claim on the assets of the business.

Obtaining Bank Financing

A banker will usually want to see your financial statements, including a cash flow budget income statement and a balance sheet, for the most current and prior years, as well as any projected statements you might have showing possible results of the requested loan. The banker will also want to see some of your documents to verify whether you run your business in a proper and professional manner.

As a rule of thumb: the bankers final decision to loan you money is based 50% upon your character and 50% upon your business plan—highlighted by your financial statements.

Budgeting

All businesses should develop and use a budget for planning purposes. A budget helps keep your business on track by forecasting your cash needs and helping you understand and control expenditures. In addition, if you are seeking bank financing, a banker or prospective investor will probably want to see your budget as evidence that your business is rooted and well planned. You will need accurate financial information to prepare a useful budget.

Cost Reduction Programs

Reducing costs is one of the most efficient and effective means of increasing profits. The franchisee needs to work with the franchisor to develop procurement programs that allow the franchisee to get equipment, products, materials and services for reduced costs.

The franchisee should continually look for ways to reduce costs in the following areas:

1. Equipment costs
2. Material (FOOD) costs
3. Labor costs
4. Alternative suppliers
5. Portion size
6. Product offerings
7. Hours of operation
8. Energy usage
9. Insurance
10. Professional services
11. Delivery procedures
12. Paper, packaging costs

For you to effectively reduce costs you need to receive, review, and understand your profit and loss information as well as the cash flow budget that you should have previously prepared. You need to take time out on a regular schedule to review your costs and to see if there is any way that these costs may be reduced.

Rebate Programs

The International Dairy Queen, based in Minneapolis, provides a voluntary rebate program for those franchisees who upgrade their facilities. Dairy Queen pays a rebate based on the sales increases for the 12 months following the remodeling. They reimburse the franchisee all royalties paid on any additional sales over the year prior to the remodeling.

You should ask your franchisor or other franchisees how they contain their costs and in which areas they have been able to reduce costs.

Financial Records

Income Statement	Balance Sheet	Cash Flow Statement
• Source of revenues versus expenses	• Is your business properly financed?	• What are the seasonal highs and lows of the business?
• Shows profitability of the business	• What are the asset needs of the business?	• Is there sufficient cash in the business?
• Provides tax information for the government	• What debt do you currently have?	• What are the cash needs to meet sales projections?
	• What is your business worth to you?	

Conclusion

Accounting records are invaluable. They allow you to make the correct financial decisions for your business. You need to look at obtaining the proper records for your business, including income statement, balance sheet, and cash flow statement. Your financial records are the heartbeat of your business. They will help you make the best managerial and financial decisions possible.

For more information on this topic, visit our Web site at www.businesstown.com

Red Flags:
Purchasing,
Inventory Levels,
Labor Costs,
Credit, Taxes

Chapter 27

25: MONEY

26: ACCOUNTING, RECORD KEEPING, AND
FINANCIAL STATEMENTS

27: **RED FLAGS: PURCHASING, INVENTORY
LEVELS, LABOR COSTS, CREDIT, TAXES**

Introduction

Unlike the movies where the detective always finds the answers, wins the case, and always comes up smelling like a rose, or gets the rewards, real detective work is often tedious and time consuming. As a franchisee though, there are certain aspects of running a business that you should be aware of. There are certain activities within the business that should send up red flags, cause sirens to scream, or bells to whistle. You need to be able to recognize the crises that occur in your business.

Almost all of the business media have been guilty of romanticizing the positive side of owning a franchise. Unfortunately, many negative aspects are sometimes either over looked or simply ignored. The end result is that many people enter business with blinders on . . . and therefore, are well on their way to failure before they've even begun.

A franchise business, when properly managed, provides tremendous success and profits for those running the business, but the good franchisee needs to know where the good information is, how to get it, and what to do when you have it.

Following is a list of major red flags that most successful franchisees recognize and use.

> A franchise business, when properly managed, provides tremendous success and profits for those running the business, but the good franchisee needs to know where the good information is, how to get it, and what to do when you have it.

Cost of Goods Sold

Most pizza restaurants have a cost of goods sold of somewhere around 30 to 32%. These are standard guidelines and if you are in the pizza business you should realize that if you exceed this by 2% the red flag goes up, warning lights are flashing, the bells ring. You need to take immediate action because you are losing profits.

Most fast-food hamburger places have a cost of goods sold around 30%. Casual dining establishments have costs of good sold of somewhere around 24 to 32%. One very large casual dining business has a total cost of goods sold and labor cost of 37%. This casual dining establishment has a red flag that goes up automatically if the food and labor costs go up to 39%, or below 35%. The franchisee needs to know why labor and food costs have exceeded the standard previously established.

Labor Costs

Probably the second major red flag is the cost of labor. Most fast-food hamburger places have a labor cost of around 27%. This may vary from 25 to 27% depending upon location and costs of labor in the region. Additionally, many pizza have lower labor costs of somewhere around 17 to 24%.

As you start your franchise business, you need to ask other franchisees in similar locations what are their costs of good sold and labor costs. You need to establish the red flags for your particular business. You need to recognize that for each percentage increase in either labor costs or food costs there is a corresponding percentage decrease in profits.

Rent

While some franchisees purchase their land and building, most rent the store location. In the fast-food field this rent often is 12 to 15%. Again this is dependent upon the area in which you live. It is very important that you determine your rent costs before you open for business.

Several businesses that do not need premium locations will have rent costs in the 5 to 8% range. This allows for greater bottom-line profits. But the location may be very important to obtaining customers, so you need to recognize the value of rent in opening your store.

> You need to recognize that for each percentage increase in either labor costs or food costs there is a corresponding percentage decrease in profits.

Purchasing

One of the advantages that a franchise system provides is reduced costs through purchasing power. However, be sure you are getting a fair deal.

The important part of the purchasing process it that your franchisor should be able to provide you the various equipment, products, services, and materials that you need at a "fair wholesale price." The fair wholesale price assures you that the franchisor or "approved suppliers" are not cheating or gouging you. They are offering you a competitive price and allowing you to do your business in a professional manner.

Training

Don't disregard franchise training! This will ensure that you have all the information you need to start on your own.

The training of the franchisor is centered around operations management. The franchisor wants you to learn how to manage and operate your new business. Just about everything you need to know, from opening the store to closing the store, is included. The areas of insurance, hours of operation, accounting systems, and even how to fry french fries is included in your basic training.

There is additional training provided for newly signed franchisees available from Louisiana State University. This program, through their International Franchise Forum, is aimed at training the new franchisee in basic business principles and knowledge. You will receive training to develop your own financial statements, your own profit projections, your own marketing program, your own management program, and how to bring all these business practices together in a successful business plan. This is not operations training but rather a week-long seminar in business training and human resource development training.

Operations Systems

Are your working at the maximum effectiveness? Look at the operating systems of the prototype store or other successful franchisees. Check to see how many customers can be successfully served in an hour or day. The operating systems should be effective and efficient. They should be able to help you to manage every aspect of the business that you are opening.

Existing Stores

Are they neat? Are they clean? Do they have a good ambience? How many stores does the franchisor own and operate?

Getting Repeat Customers

Remember the rule: advertising brings the customer in once—store operations bring the customer in the second time. You need to perform in your store so that the customer will come back.

The store that you are about to open is going to be very similar to the existing stores that you see. Don't think that your store is going to be any better or worse than what you experience at other locations. If the stores look dirty, shabby, and rundown, then you should realize that your store may be very similar.

Site Selection and Services

Be sure to get all the help you can get to select your business location. You should be able to get some counsel and advice from the franchisor about how to select a site or sites for your new business. A franchisor should provide expertise in helping select sites with strong market potential. You should be able to work with the franchisor to determine if you are going to open sequential sites or if you are going to have a global pattern of four or five stores in a specific market location. This will greatly influence your final site selection.

The store that you are about to open is going to be very similar to the existing stores that you see. Don't think that your store is going to be any better or worse than what you experience at other locations.

Advertising and Marketing Programs

Does the franchisor have a strong advertising and/or marketing program? Does the franchisor provide you with initial public relation announcements for the opening and grand opening of your store?

You should realize that one of the great advantages of franchising is that the franchisor provides continuous value to you through creative and exciting advertising programs. The brand recognition that McDonald's, Coca-Cola, and Wendy's have attained is primarily through their tremendous advertising programs.

Procurement Programs

The franchisor can help you get cost reduction programs for equipment, food, products, materials, and services. You should recognize that procurement programs provide you the opportunity to reduce costs, which is a very efficient way to increase profits. Most franchisors have developed procurement programs for their franchisees to ensure cost reductions and optimize profits.

Investigate to make sure that you are getting a good price reduction on all the products, services and equipment that you order for your business. This should be a strong advantage of the franchising procedure.

Franchisor "Culture"

You should send up a red flag if the franchisor's culture and philosophy towards you as a franchisee is either ruled by law (contract, dictatorial style), or controlled by the franchisor or their field staff. How does the franchisor run the business and relate to you as the franchisee? You need to find a franchisor who very much wants you to be successful. These franchisors almost always have an attitude of helpfulness and friendliness in supporting you in whatever possible. They strive to develop mutual trust through strong communication and the ability to listen to your wants, needs, and desires. Ask other franchisees and their managers what they think the franchisor's culture is really like.

Growth

Are you going to be allowed to grow in the territory around you? You may originally only want one unit but find out after you have been open for two or three years that you want to expand and create a second, third, or even fourth unit. Is there territory available for you close to your original store? Does the franchisor allow for franchisees to expand and become multi-unit owners?

Does the franchisor have area development agreements? How do you qualify for those agreements? Do your sales have to be in the top 50%? Do your store evaluations have to place you in the top third of all stores in the region? What do you have to do to become a multiunit operator?

Communication with the Franchisor

Does the franchisor want continuous feedback concerning the products, services, marketing, and advertising that you use? Does the franchisor want information about your sales, labor costs, and profits? Does the franchisor take constructive criticism?

> You should send up a red flag if the franchisor's culture and philosophy towards you as a franchisee is either ruled by law (contract, dictatorial style), or controlled by the franchisor or their field staff.

Successful franchisors involve their franchisees in most aspects of the business. What does the franchisor want of you? How will the franchisor use you as you build out your business? How easy is it for you to communicate with the franchisor? Do you enjoy communicating with the franchisor and their staff?

Dispute Resolution

How are you going to resolve differences with the franchisor? How do other franchisees resolve differences with the franchisor? How are differences solved—in a friendly amicable or destructive fashion? Before the dispute gets out of hand, you need to be able to solve it. Once the dispute goes to mediation, arbitration, or the courts, the damage is done. You need to know before opening your business how you are going to work with and resolve any differences between you and the franchisor.

Conclusion

Identify your red flags. Develop your control system. Develop those standards by which you will operate your franchise business. Set up a system so that you can communicate and work with the franchisor, which will allow you to be the most successful and profitable person you may become.

You hold the key to success. Investigate your possibilities. Become the best that you can be.

You, the Investigator

Investigating the franchise is going to require some good detective work. You are going to need to be a good listener and you are going to need to be relentless in your pursuit of information about your case.

Yes, there is glamour in what you are doing. Yes, there is a tremendous opportunity for success. Yes, franchising is exciting. But, you need to take the time to investigate and get the information on what is happening in your franchise system.

For more information on this topic, visit our Web site at www.businesstown.com

Working with the Franchisor—Blessing or Curse?

In this section, you'll learn:

- The four phases of a franchisor/franchisee relationship
- Different types of franchise organizations and councils
- What to do when your contract expires
- How to handle a disagreement with your franchisor

CHAPTER 28 THE FRANCHISOR/FRANCHISEE RELATIONSHIP **CHAPTER 29** RENEWAL, TERMINATION, OR TRANSFER
CHAPTER 30 RESOLVING DISPUTES

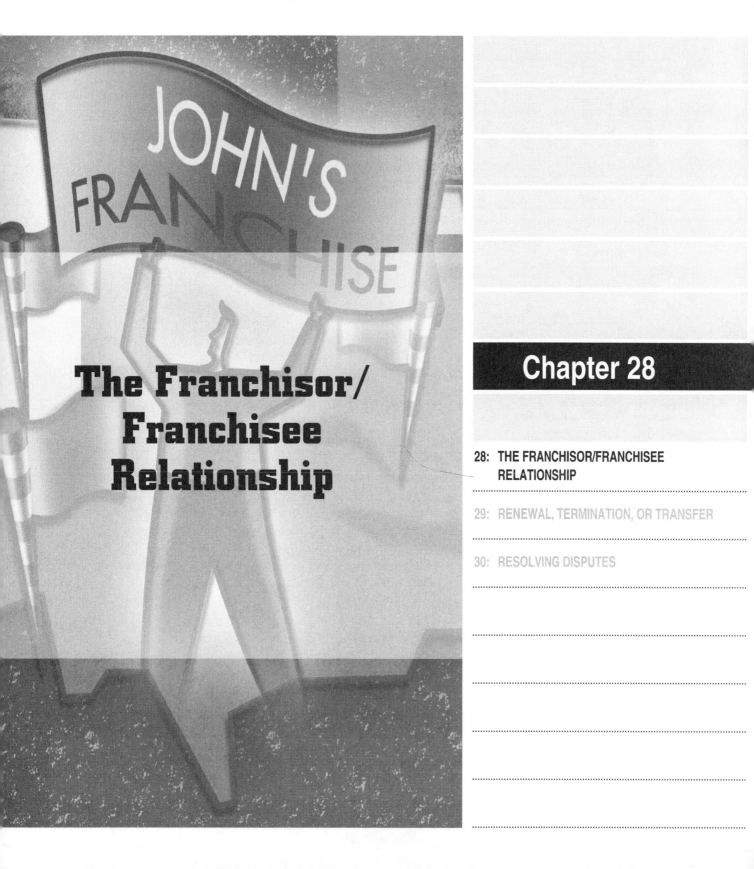

The Franchisor/
Franchisee
Relationship

Chapter 28

**28: THE FRANCHISOR/FRANCHISEE
RELATIONSHIP**

29: RENEWAL, TERMINATION, OR TRANSFER

30: RESOLVING DISPUTES

Introduction

Franchising has at its core a relationship between franchisors and franchisees of mutual interdependence and reliance. In order for this mutual interdependence and reliance to thrive, there must exist a cooperative relationship. Franchisors and franchisees have different personalities and different motivations. However, in order to be a success, they must be bound together by their common goals and mutual interests. With a sound, productive relationship the franchise system will not only survive in a highly competitive economy, but also thrive and gain market share at other franchise system's expense.

In the very beginning, the franchisor must communicate to the prospective franchisee what the mission, goals, and vision of the franchise system are and the route the franchise system must take to achieve them. If the prospective franchisee purchases a franchise without this knowledge, then the relationship is off to a rocky start. Without comprehensive and effective communication between the franchisor and all of its franchisees, there cannot be a sound, productive relationship.

Whereas communication is the main ingredient in a successful franchisor/franchisee relationship, the key is active participation by the franchisees in the direction the franchise system takes. A good franchisor knows that the best ideas come from his best franchisees because they are active in the day-to-day operation of their franchised business and are constantly on the front line. This chapter will discuss the attributes a franchise system should have in order to have a sound, productive relationship with its franchisees.

> In the very beginning, the franchisor must communicate to the prospective franchisee what the mission, goals, and vision of the franchise system are and the route the franchise system must take to achieve them.

Required Disclosures

Both the Federal Trade Commission Rule and the UFOC require that the franchisor disclose under Item 17 any provisions of the franchise and other agreements that deal with the franchise relationship. You should carefully review those provisions in Item 17 that deal with the franchise relationship. Remember, the disclosures under Item 17 refer to provisions that are included in the franchise and related agreements that you must sign. Once you sign the agreements you are bound by their terms and conditions. Make sure these provisions are fair and reasonable. Make sure you can live with them. If the provisions are not acceptable to you, look elsewhere to purchase a franchise.

The Four Phases/Stages of a Franchise Relationship

Just like the four phases a new product or service that hits the marketplace goes through, so goes the franchise relationship. The franchisor/franchisee relationship goes through four phases, which are as follows:

First Phase—the Beginning

The franchise relationship begins when the prospective franchisee is first recruited. During the recruitment process, the franchisor's and franchisee's expectations of each other are established. Both parties will put on their best faces, trying to impress each other. During this phase there will be a lot of contact. Each party is trying to show the other party why they need each other. Each party will develop trust of the other along with a shared desire for success and profitability. At this phase everything comes up roses.

Through all of this contact both parties will develop rapport, trust, and confidence in each other, leading to the signing of a franchise agreement. At this point, the franchisor and franchisee are very positive about each other and look forward to a very bright future together.

Phase Two—Growth

From the signing of the franchise agreement through the opening of your franchise and until the end of your first three years of operation, your need of the franchisor's support services is at its greatest. The growth stage of the franchise relationship begins once you sign the franchise agreement. At this point, everything is new to the franchisee and she is on a steep learning curve. The franchisee will go through an extensive training pro-

> The franchise relationship begins when the prospective franchisee is first recruited. During the recruitment process, the franchisor's and franchisee's expectations of each other are established.

gram that should build a strong, close relationship between the franchisor and the franchisee. After the comprehensive initial training program and the grand opening, the support services provided are just as important. The franchisor will also provide ongoing training. Additionally, the franchise relationship may be cultivated through newsletters, product updates, marketing suggestions, new advertising ideas, birthday cards, personal telephone calls, and visits from the franchisor's representatives to see how you are doing. During this phase there will be a lot of contact between you and the franchisor.

If things have been going as planned, you will have learned a lot that has led to a successful opening and operation of your franchised business. You will also have stayed in regular contact with the franchisor. On the other hand, this phase can also display negative traits. For example, maybe the training was not as comprehensive as you expected. Maybe you have not received support materials, accounting aids, marketing suggestions, promotional and advertising support, and so on, as regularly as you expected. You might begin to feel that you have signed on with a second-rate franchisor. During this phase any number of things can happen that lower your expectations of the relationship.

Phase Three—Maturity

The third phase of the franchisor/franchisee relationship is referred to as the maturity stage. During this phase the franchisor and franchisee know what to expect from each other. In other words, things are predictable. If all has gone according to plan, the franchisor and the franchisee have developed a mutual understanding and friendship. The franchisee has come to expect and rely on the franchisor to provide comprehensive and ongoing training, effective marketing aids and advertisements, new products, and other support services to further enhance the relationship. In return, the franchisor has come to expect an ever-increasing sales volume with the corresponding royalty increases along with the franchisee following closely the terms and conditions of the franchise agreement and operations manual.

If things have been going as planned, you will have learned a lot that has led to a successful opening and operation of your franchised business.

The danger of the maturity stage is that the franchisee may feel that he is no longer receiving continuing value from the franchisor. This goes back to the old question: What have you done for me lately? During the first two phases of the franchise relationship, the franchisee has a tremendous amount to learn. Now that the franchisee has been operating for several years, he may feel that he is no longer receiving his money's worth from the franchisor.

Phase Four—the End or a New Beginning

The final phase of the franchisor/franchisee relationship will go in one of two directions. On the one hand, the franchisee may be disenchanted with the franchisor and the franchisee's business may even be declining. At this point the franchisee may seek to terminate her franchisee agreement. The franchisee may have already decided that she will not renew her franchise because she feels there is a lack of support from the franchisor. Additionally, the franchisee's business could be falling off. As a result of the franchisor not maintaining the growth of its infrastructure, the franchisee may find that her business is falling further and further behind the competition. As a result, the franchisee becomes less and less concerned with adhering to its franchise agreement and operations manual. At this point the relationship's decline could begin to quicken.

On the other hand, the franchisee may have decided to renew her franchise agreement and continue on with the relationship. The franchisee's relationship with the franchisor could be stronger than ever. The reason for this is that the franchisor has not only continued to give plenty of support to the franchisee, but has also continually updated its support services to meet and exceed any competitive challenges. As a result the franchisee has been provided with, on a regular basis, new products and services, marketing and advertising strategies, and current research and development concepts. Consequently, the franchisee's business has continued to thrive and grow. Therefore, the franchisee is very happy with its relationship with the franchisor and wants to continue with it. In other words, the situation has truly been win-win.

> As a result of the franchisor not maintaining the growth of its infrastructure, the franchisee may find that her business is falling further and further behind the competition.

Traits of a Good Franchisor/ Franchisee Relationship

You should look for certain traits when inspecting a franchise system. When deciding on a franchise purchase, you need to determine how many of these positive traits you find in your investigation of a franchisor. The more of these traits, the better your chances for success, if you choose that franchisor.

When you speak with current franchisees see how many of these perceptions they have of their franchisor. Again, the more the better. After determining what perceptions the franchisees have, you then need to investigate the franchisor. In your investigation you will want to find that the franchisor:

- Has a comprehensive and ongoing training program
- Holds national and regional meetings
- Develops a franchisee advisory council whose input is seriously considered in decision-making
- Supports and maintains an advertising committee that has a lot of input in decision-making concerning the types of advertising and promotional activities.
- Develops newsletters, memos, e-mails, and other means of information exchange
- Develops a 24-hour toll free hotline
- Develops incentive programs for performance in sales
- Develops an award structure for achievers
- Develops effective promotional advertising packages and flyers
- Provides financial and managerial reports that can be used to improve the franchised business

These ten traits are important. If a franchisor possesses these traits then you have one who is very successful.

Determine the Degree of Communication

Communication is the main ingredient in the successful franchisor/franchisee relationship. Therefore, it is important to determine the effectiveness of the franchisor's communication with its franchisees. You should view a franchisor's commitment to effective communication by asking it the following questions:

1. Does the franchisor define and clarify its ideas prior to communicating with the franchisee? In other words, does the franchisor comprehend the concepts and ideas it is trying to convey to its franchisees prior to communicating?
2. Does the franchisor shout orders or commands or does it analyze a franchisee's situation?
3. Does the franchisor say what needs to be said clearly, concisely, and quickly?
4. Does the franchisor listen to the franchisees as well as speak to them? Does the franchisor listen to a franchisee's questions and prepare to answer such questions to facilitate understanding?
5. Does the franchisor just talk or does it seek feedback from the franchisees as well? Does the franchisor provide a means for franchisees to respond to its message?
6. Does the franchisor make negative statements? For example, does the franchisor say:

   - "We have tried that before and it didn't work."
   - "It costs too much."
   - "We don't have time to consider your idea."

   Statements like these will stifle communications between the parties. Or, does the franchisor make statements that indicate they think the idea sounds good and deserves a closer look?

7. Does the franchisor express to its franchisees just how important communication is?
8. Does the franchisor recognize franchisees for good ideas or other advice?

> Communication is the main ingredient in the successful franchisor/franchisee relationship.

Franchisee Recognition

Last but not least, effective communication requires that, when appropriate, franchisees are recognized. A successful franchisor will make its franchisees feel appreciated and will acknowledge their accomplishments. The franchisor will give awards for surpassing sales goals. If a franchisee obtains excellence in customer service they likewise will receive acknowledgment. Recognition can be something as simple as a birthday card acknowledging the franchisee's birthday and the promising year ahead.

9. Does the franchisor contact the franchisees and ask for their input if they are facing problems?

If the answers you receive to these questions are positive, then you know that the franchisor has good communications with its franchisees, which cannot be underestimated.

In addition to these questions, you need to determine what sources the franchisor uses to communicate. The successful franchisor uses several methods to communicate. Different types of communications include: newsletters, memos, e-mails, phone calls, and personal visits by representatives of the franchisor.

It is also important to determine the attitude with which the franchisor views the franchise relationship. You want a franchisor that has the attitude that it is in a business partnership with you, the franchisee. With this type of attitude, both the franchisor and the franchisee will continuously work together to develop new ways to benefit from the relationship. Both parties will look for ways to help each other improve the operation of the franchise system. You want a franchisor that feels strongly about the franchisor/franchisee partnership. This way you are sure that you are in a win-win situation since both sides will look out for each other and their best interests.

Additionally, a good franchisor involves franchisees in the decision-making process. After all, the franchisees are in the best position to give feedback as to what works and what doesn't work. Also, a successful, progressive franchisor is big on franchisee recognition, believes in strong personal rapport with each franchisee, and continually provides expertise to its franchisees not only in the nuts and bolts of the operation of the franchise, but also in the areas of finance, management, personal growth, marketing, and technology.

Franchisee Advisory Councils

One of the ways to communicate that you should look for is a franchisee advisory council. A franchisee advisory council is an organization of franchisees set up by the franchisor to promote communications and creativity with its franchisees. The franchisee members of the advisory council are normally elected by the franchisees themselves as opposed to being appointed by the franchisor. The franchisee advisory council typically meets with the franchisor either quarterly or semiannually to discuss matters affecting the franchise system. Normally, the advisory council acts strictly in an advisory capacity. However, it is rare for a franchisor to ignore the recommendations of its franchisee advisory council. Topics discussed by the franchisor with the franchisee advisory councils vary considerably and cover matters from advertising, training, and operations to new goods and services. Franchisee advisory councils are an effective way to have an interactive and two-way communication system with the franchisor. The major goal in developing a franchisee advisory council is to promote and improve communications between the franchisor and the franchisee.

Advantages

Franchisors and franchisees have found several advantages of a franchisee advisory council. First, the franchisee advisory council provides a way by which franchisees can be heard by the franchisor. Through the council, franchisees have input in matters that are important to them and the franchise system as a whole. Additionally, the franchisees are able to provide the creativity the franchisor needs in bringing fresh ideas and innovations to the system more quickly. Second, the franchisor is able to more effectively communicate the need to implement changes to adjust to competitive circumstances through the council. By having discussions with franchisees about these types of issues, the franchisor is more easily able to receive the backing of its franchisees to implement these changes. Third, franchisors are assisted by the advisory council in promoting the expansion of the franchise system. By promoting positive relations with franchisees through the council it enhances the franchisor's reputation in the marketplace as a progressive franchisor. Fourth, through the use of the advisory council, franchisees are able to communicate those matters that concern franchisees as a whole, and not just peripheral matters. Even though any issue that concerns any one or more franchisees is important, the franchisor must first concentrate its efforts on those concerns that affect the most franchisees. A fifth

Does the Franchisor *Use* the Council?

How the franchisor responds to the franchisee advisory council's advice will determine its effectiveness. A progressive and successful franchisor will use the advisory council to solicit ideas, solve problems, encourage franchisee recommendations, and listen to criticism of the system. The successful and progressive franchisor realizes that the franchisee is on the front lines and knows how to do his or her job best. When you investigate your franchisor you need to determine if it has a franchisee advisory council. If it does, you need to speak with its franchisee members to determine whether the franchisor takes its input seriously or if it ignores it. If you find that the franchisor ignores the advisory council then you know that the franchisor has a serious attitude problem toward its franchisees.

benefit of the franchisee advisory council is that the franchisor is able to be more closely in tune to what is going on with the franchisees. The franchisor and its representatives are able to be better aware as to what is going on in the marketplace, what are the most important issues, and how they will affect their franchisees.

Disadvantages

The major disadvantage of the franchisee advisory council is that it is formed by the franchisor. This can be viewed as serving only the needs of the franchisor and not the franchisees. It is not uncommon to find a franchisor who has set up a franchisee advisory council strictly for its own benefit and to prevent the organization of an independent franchisee association. Fortunately most franchisors are progressive and therefore set up franchisee advisory councils with the success of its franchisees uppermost in its mind.

> The major disadvantage of the franchisee advisory council is that it is formed by the franchisor.

Qualities of Councils

Franchisee advisory councils differ widely from one franchise system to another. However, most advisory councils share in common many of the following characteristics:

1. Franchisee advisory councils are most often formed by the franchisor either to improve communications with its franchisees or to address a system-threatening concern that requires franchisee input and consensus.
2. All or some portion of the activities of the advisory council are funded by the franchisor.
3. The franchisor dictates the frequency, location, and agenda of the meetings.
4. Advisory councils usually do not have authority to make unilateral decisions that bind the franchisor. They serve in an advisory capacity only providing the franchisor with nonbinding recommendations.
5. Advisory councils involve the joint participation of franchisees and franchisor representatives.

6. Advisory council officers may be elected by the franchisees or appointed by the franchisor or by using some combination of the two.
7. Franchisee advisory councils rely on the franchisor's advisers, consultants, and management.
8. The membership of a franchisee advisory council is usually composed of all system franchisees who are then in good standing under their respective franchise agreements. As a result, there is no payment of dues or other requirements.

Council Structures

Just as the structure and specific concerns of advisory councils can vary, so does the activities that the franchisor delegates to them. Some of the more normal items delegated to a franchisee advisory council including the following:

1. The franchisee advisory council will operate a cooperative purchasing program and will assist the franchisor in screening approved suppliers. By taking on this function, the council will promote the purchasing power of the franchisees as a whole.
2. The council will oversee regional and national advertising programs. They will assist the franchisor in the development of advertising programs and the selection of agencies.
3. The council will select a group provider of insurance furnishing coverage required by the franchise agreement.
4. The council will assist the franchisor in new product development, evaluation, test marketing, and introduction of new products and services into the marketplace.
5. The franchisee advisory council will review the training that franchisees undergo to maintain its effectiveness.

The fact that the franchisor you are investigating has in place a franchisee advisory council should be construed as a positive step. However, you must ascertain its effectiveness through interviewing key members of the council. If you find that the franchisor seeks out its

> The membership of a franchisee advisory council is usually composed of all system franchisees who are then in good standing under their respective franchise agreements. As a result, there is no payment of dues or other requirements.

> The franchisee advisory council is set up by the franchisor; the independent franchisee association is set up by the franchisees of the franchise system.

advice and its input in decision-making matters, then you know you have a progressive franchisor. If, however, your investigation reveals that the franchisor rarely gives the council anything of importance to work on, you know it is nothing more than window dressing. If such is the case, your search for the right franchise to purchase is not yet over.

Independent Franchisee Associations

An independent franchisee association, just like franchisee advisory councils, is comprised of franchisees. However, they have a key difference. The franchisee advisory council is set up by the franchisor; the independent franchisee association is set up by the franchisees of the franchise system. As a result, the franchisees have the confidence to speak up without fear of reprisal. This allows for a more interactive and balanced discussion with the franchisor on those issues important to the franchisees and their operation. Franchisors who have taken a positive attitude toward independent franchisee associations have found themselves with considerably fewer disputes. Also these franchisors recognize the importance of the association's input on new products, services, advertising, and marketing ideas.

Since independent franchisee associations are set up independent of the franchisor they are generally more powerful. For example, independent franchisee associations have set forth their opinions on such issues as:

1. Opposing the revised franchise agreement of the franchisor

In this instance, the new franchise agreement would have resulted in more stringent renewal terms, more remodeling requirements, and would have reduced territorial protections. The independent franchisee association opposed this new franchise agreement vigorously.

2. Negotiated with the franchisor a new and revised franchise agreement to be executed by the franchisees

3. Recommended to its members to reject franchise amendments and modified renewal terms they determined were not in the best interest of the franchisee members
4. Tried to stop the merger of their franchisor with a competitive franchise system
5. Opposed highly leveraged acquisition of their franchisor on the grounds that the resulting debt service would harm the franchisor's ability to fulfill its side of the bargain with its franchisees

Generally speaking, a franchisor-created franchisee advisory council does not wield this kind of power. However, an independent franchisee association does since it is set up independent of the franchisor. Independent franchisee associations share the following characteristics:

- The association is formed strictly by franchisees of the franchise system.
- The sole and financial support of the independent franchisee association comes from its member franchisees.
- The association sets its own meetings, the frequency of the meetings, the location of the meetings, and the agenda to be discussed.
- The association does more than just serve in an advisory capacity. They have key input into decisions made by the franchisor due to the fact that they are the voice of the system's franchisees.
- The franchisor does not have any participation in the association meetings and its decisions.
- Franchisors have no say in naming the officers of the association.
- Independent franchisee associations retain their own legal counsel and outside consultants.

The common thread of the previously listed characteristics is the lack of the participation of the franchisor in the formation and operation of the association.

> Generally speaking, a franchisor-created franchisee advisory council does not wield this kind of power.

Independent franchisee associations are created by the franchisees of that particular franchise system. The association is intended to serve the interests of the franchisee members. Overall the association's purpose is to work cooperatively with the franchisor to enhance the competitive position and profitability of the franchise system. Occasionally, franchisees will create an independent franchisee association if they are experiencing tensions and lack of communications with their franchisor.

Main Functions of Independent Franchisee Associations

A productive independent franchisee association will have four primary functions.

First, the association will enhance and improve communications between the franchisees and their franchisor. As a result, this will increase their ability to influence decisions of the franchisor. The association allows franchisees improved channels for communicating their views and concerns to the franchisor.

Second, the association is able to enhance the competitive position of their franchisee members. This is done by offering a host of competitive services to include, but not limited to, purchasing, advertising, insurance, legal, accounting, and other types of professional services. The association can achieve economies of scale resulting in reduced costs to its members. Individual franchisees cannot achieve such economies of scale. Thus the association is able to improve the profitability of its individual franchisee members.

Third, the franchisee association provides a fantastic opportunity for franchisees to work together to develop and expand the franchise system. Such an association can provide training, education, published information, and promote other activities that increase knowledge of their franchised business. Done correctly, this will stimulate growth and improve profits of the franchise system as a whole.

Fourth, and probably the most important, is that the association can play a comprehensive role in negotiations with the franchisor. On those issues and concerns of the franchisee, the franchisee association can negotiate with the franchisor. These issues are limited only by the imagination of the franchisees. Some franchisee associations have even negotiated the terms and conditions of their system's revised franchise agreement.

Sources of Tension/Causes of Conflict

In every relationship there are conflicts and sources of tension. The relationship between the franchisor and the franchisee is no different. The uniqueness of the franchisor/franchisee relationship results in its own causes of conflict.

There are many sources of tension that cause conflicts between the franchisor and franchisee. These areas of conflict are experienced by the individual franchisee in the system. In investigating a franchise opportunity, you should speak with current franchisees to see how many causes of conflict they have experienced. Some of the more common causes of conflict are as follows:

- Inappropriate or poor site selection
- Inadequate equipment package
- Poor initial training
- Incomplete operations manuals
- Insufficient follow-up training and information
- Inadequate availability of the franchisor for advice
- Inadequate marketing research
- Poor advertising and promotional materials
- Lack of proper disclosure of operational information
- Underestimation of expenses and income
- Lack of diversification of products and services
- Lack of exclusive territories and the use by the franchisor of alternate methods by which products and services bypass the franchisee on the way to the marketplace
- Ineffective advertising strategies
- One-sided rights of the franchisor to modify the franchise system at the franchisee's expense
- Excessive use of coupons and promotions for goods and services leading to lower profitability yet higher royalties

> In every relationship there are conflicts and sources of tension. The uniqueness of the franchisor/franchisee relationship results in its own causes of conflict.

> Running company-owned stores in competition with franchisee-owned stores can cause problems.

- Adjustment of fees allowed for in the franchise agreement
- Franchisor rights to buy back your franchise at a sum less than its value
- Excessive minimum performance requirements.
- Payment for support services thought to be included in your royalty payments
- Excessive penalties for violation of franchise agreement and related agreements
- Excessive restrictions on products, services, or prices imposed on the franchisee
- Limits on the franchisee's ability to enter into a competitive business
- Diversion of advertising funds
- Running company-owned stores in competition with franchisee-owned stores
- Franchisor taking rebates and kickbacks from suppliers.
- Excessive lease payments for leasing equipment, signs, etc., from the franchisor
- Lack of ongoing support
- Lack of financial support
- Excessive control by the franchisor concerning quality control issues
- Excessive quality control clauses resulting in the franchisee being forced to buy supplies, equipment, signs, secret ingredients, etc., from the franchisor and no one else. You want a franchisor who has a strong quality control program. However, you do not want it to be excessive resulting in reduced profitability.
- Lack of research and development
- Lack of interactive two-way communication

It goes without saying that every franchisee will experience some tension and conflict with its franchisor. The fact that both parties are alive will result in some tension and conflict. However, in your investigation of a franchise system, you need to determine that the amount of conflict between franchisor and franchisee is not excessive. Even though a certain amount of conflict and tension is healthy for the growth of the relationship and the franchise system, too much conflict and tension has the reverse effect and will negatively impact the entire system.

Conclusion

The franchisor/franchisee relationship must be a win-win situation. The business relationship must be one of a partnership (not a legal partnership) where franchisees have input on those matters that are of concern to them. A partnership relationship dictates that franchisee input be carefully considered by the franchisor in its decision-making process. However, the franchisee must always understand that there can be only one final decision-maker in the franchise system. Most decisions in a successful well-managed franchise system are frequently the product of consensus. Even though the franchisor must give serious consideration to recommendations and input of its franchisees, the franchisor is the one solely responsible for making the final decisions.

> The franchisor/franchisee relationship must be a win-win situation.

For more information on this topic, visit our Web site at www.businesstown.com

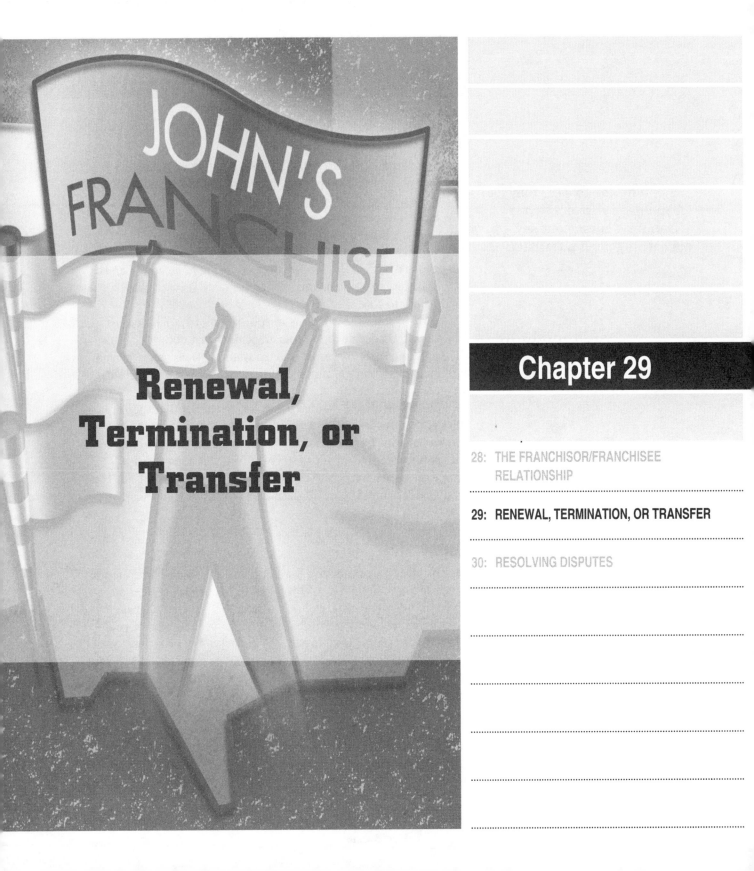

Renewal, Termination, or Transfer

Chapter 29

28: THE FRANCHISOR/FRANCHISEE
RELATIONSHIP

29: **RENEWAL, TERMINATION, OR TRANSFER**

30: RESOLVING DISPUTES

If you decide to sell your franchise, what does your franchise agreement say concerning such a transfer?

Introduction

Once you become a franchisee, it is important to know what your franchise agreement says concerning renewal, termination, or transfer of your franchise. Sooner or later the initial term of your franchise agreement will come to an end. At that point it will be time to renew your contract. What does your franchise agreement say?

You may be in default under the terms of your franchise agreement. What are the consequences of being in default? Can the franchisor terminate your franchise agreement? Do you have the opportunity to cure the default?

Perhaps someone will come to you wanting to purchase your franchise. If you decide to sell your franchise, what does your franchise agreement say concerning such a transfer? Does your franchise agreement allow you to transfer your unit to another person? Under what conditions can you transfer your franchise to another?

Every franchisee at some point during the term of their franchise agreement will address these issues. Therefore, you need to know what your franchise agreement says concerning renewal, termination, or transfer of your franchise. You will need to know what your rights are, what you can do, and what you can't do. This chapter will address these concerns.

Renewal

All franchise agreements give the franchisee the right to operate the franchise for an initial term. This initial term normally ranges anywhere from 5 to 15 years. But the real question is what happens after the initial term has expired? Is there an opportunity for you to renew the franchise? Do you have the opportunity to continue operating the franchise? Most franchise agreements provide you with an option to renew for a set period of time. Sometimes the option to renew is based upon you not being in violation of any of the terms or conditions of the franchise agreement. Other times the option to renew will require you to sign a new franchise agreement. If this is the case, you will be required to sign a new franchise agreement that contains the most current terms and conditions for owning the franchise. This new agreement could contain different conditions and stipulations such as a requirement to renovate your unit. Also, it may include a clause that increases the fees you are paying to the franchisor. In other cases, the franchise agreement will automatically renew as long as the franchisee is not in violation of any of the conditions or provisions of the franchise agreement. It is also common to pay a renewal fee when you renew your franchise agreement. Finally, most franchise agreements contain a provision that requires you to give anywhere from three to six months written notification to the franchisor prior to the end of your initial term that you plan to renew. Generally speaking, most all franchise agreements have provisions for renewal. After all, it is much cheaper to keep open existing units with the same franchisees than it is to find new ones. However, the renewal terms and their lengths can vary widely from one franchise system to another.

Federal and State Laws Concerning Renewals

Under the Federal Trade Commission Rule, a franchisor is required to disclose provisions of the franchise agreement and other agreements that deal with renewal. The franchisor is required to disclose this information under Item 17 of the UFOC (see Chapter 4). Under Item 17 the franchisor is required to disclose the following:

1. The length of the initial term of the franchise
2. Any provisions allowing for renewal or extension of the initial term (For example, the franchise agreement may state that if you are in good standing you can renew for an additional term of 10 years.)
3. Requirements of the franchisee to renew or extend (Here the franchisor lists what requirements are necessary for you to follow in order to renew. For example, you might be required to sign a new franchise agreement, pay a renewal fee, remodel your unit, or sign a general release.)
4. Your obligations if your franchise is not renewed (Listed here are your obligations if your franchise agreement is not renewed. For example, you might have to pay all remaining amounts due and de-identify your franchise.)

State Relationship Status

Several states have passed laws that are referred to as state relationship laws. These state relationship statutes restrict a franchisor's discretion in refusing to renew a franchise. Many of the states that have such a law require the franchisor to show good cause as a requirement for nonrenewal. The states that have such laws are: Arkansas, California, Connecticut, Delaware, Hawaii, Illinois, Indiana, Iowa, Michigan, Minnesota, Mississippi, Missouri, Nebraska, New Jersey, Washington, and Wisconsin. Also, such laws can be found in the District of Columbia, Puerto Rico, and the Virgin Islands. Additionally, South Dakota and Virginia have statutes that provide the franchisee with some protection in this area.

Under the Federal Trade Commission Rule, all the franchisor is required to do is disclose any and all provisions that concern renewals. However, there is no federal law that dictates when or if a franchisor can decide not to renew your franchise agreement. There is no federal law dealing with or providing the franchisee with any rights as concerns the renewal of the franchise agreement.

> There are many types of renewal provisions found in franchise agreements.

Typical Renewal Terms Found in the Franchise Agreement

There are many types of renewal provisions found in franchise agreements. Renewal provisions are only subject to the lack of creativity on the part of the franchisor. However, there are certain types of renewal provisions that are common to practically all franchise agreements. The following are some of these:

1. Prior to renewal, the franchisee shall have paid all monetary obligations owed by it to the franchisor and its subsidiaries and affiliates.
2. The franchisee cannot be in default of any provision of the franchise agreement or any other agreement between it and the franchisor or its subsidiaries and affiliates.
3. Upon renewal the franchisee will sign the then current form of the franchise agreement, which will supercede in all respects the prior franchise agreement.
4. The franchisee must give the franchisor three to six months, prior to the end of the initial term, its intent, in writing, to renew the franchise.
5. That the franchisee has completed all required renovations, modifications, updates, and implemented any new methods and programs required by the franchisor prior to the renewal.
6. If applicable, the franchisee submits the appropriate evidence that it has the right to remain in possession of the premises where the franchise is located for at least the term of the renewal.
7. The franchisee, along with its shareholders, directors, and officers, will execute a general release, releasing any and all

claims it might have against the franchisor, its subsidiaries, affiliates, and their respective officers, directors, agents, and employees. This general release shall exempt the franchisor and others from any and all claims up to and through the end of the initial term of the franchise agreement.

Points to Cover and Questions to Ask

In negotiating your franchise agreement there are certain renewal provisions you will want. For example, almost all franchise agreements require you to be in full compliance of all terms and conditions of the franchise agreement including royalties and other fee payments. However, you will want to be allowed to be in arrears for the current month's royalty payments when it comes time to renew. Also, you will want to include a provision that any royalties or fees that are in dispute will not affect your chances of renewal. Finally, most franchise agreements require notification of your intent to renew six months prior to the termination of the initial term. It would probably be better for you to get renewal terms that require only 60 to 90 days notice prior to the end of your initial term.

What rights you have concerning renewal are contained in your franchise agreement and other agreements you are required to sign. Prior to entering into such a relationship you need to determine what rights you have to renew. Therefore, there are many questions you should ask. These questions are as follows:

1. Is there a right to renew the franchise agreement?
2. For how long and how many times can you renew the franchise agreement?
3. Will you be required to renew under the terms of the prevailing franchise agreement?
4. If you must sign the then current franchise agreement, will you be required to pay higher royalties, higher advertising fees, and other higher fees?
5. Will you be required to renovate or modify your unit upon renewal?
6. Under what terms and conditions can the franchisor not renew your franchise agreement?

> In negotiating your franchise agreement there are certain renewal provisions you will want.

7. What are the other requirements that you must abide by in order to have the right to renew?
8. If you want to renew, what modifications to your existing franchise agreement will the franchisor be allowed to make?
9. Must the franchisor disclose any modifications ahead of time to the franchisee?
10. Can the franchisor refuse renewal on economic grounds? (For example, your location is in a depressed neighborhood.)
11. Will you be allowed to renew if you fail to give written notice per the terms and conditions of the franchise agreement?
12. If the franchisor misses its deadline to give you notice of its intent not to renew is your franchise agreement automatically extended?
13. Can the franchisor refuse to renew your franchise agreement if you are dealing in competitive products?
14. What happens if you lose the right to extend your lease agreement for the building and land on which your franchise is located?
15. What rights does the franchisor have not to renew you if he wants your location for a company-owned store?
16. Are you required to sign a general release in order to be allowed to renew?

Transfer

There may come a time when you are ready to get out of the business. Often franchisees become frustrated, burned out, become ill, or just want to retire. As a result they want to sell their franchise to someone else. The franchisee wants to get out but wants to be compensated for its time, effort, and good will it has generated in its franchise. At this juncture the provisions in your franchise agreement concerning the transfer of your franchise to another become very, very important. Your franchise agreement will state the terms and conditions under which you are allowed to sell and transfer your franchise to a third party.

> Will you be allowed to renew if you fail to give written notice per the terms and conditions of the franchise agreement?

Therefore, you must determine what the franchise agreement says about your right to transfer or sell your franchise to someone else. Almost always the franchisor will have the first right of refusal. This means that if you decide to sell your business, the franchisor will have the right to match the terms offered by a bona fide third party. In this scenario the franchisor, if he exercises this option, will buy back the franchise. However, if the franchisor does not exercise his right of first refusal, then you and the franchisor must begin your due diligence concerning the proposed buyer. After all, both you and your franchisor want to make sure for your own reasons that the buyer is not only financially sound and has adequate financial resources but also has the ability to operate the franchise at a profit.

Federal and State Law Pertaining to Transfers

Under the Federal Trade Commission Rule, franchisors are required to disclose in their disclosure document any provisions contained in the franchise agreement and other agreements that deal with transfers. More specifically, the franchisor must disclose the following:

> If the franchisor does not exercise his right of first refusal, then you and the franchisor must begin your due diligence concerning the proposed buyer.

1. The definition of what constitutes a transfer by the franchisee—Normally, this means that a transfer is defined as the transfer of your franchise agreement to a third party or as a change in the ownership of your franchise.
2. Whether the franchisor must approve the transfer by the franchisee—Almost always the franchisor reserves the right to approve all transfers. However, most franchise agreements dictate that the franchisor will not unreasonably withhold such approval.
3. What conditions, if any, the franchisor places on whether or not they will approve the transfer—Almost always, the franchise agreement dictates that the transferee (new franchisee) must qualify as if she is purchasing the franchise from the franchisor. Also, most franchisors reserve the right to approve the purchase agreement between its franchisee and the buyer and have the buyer pay a transfer fee and attend training. Finally, most franchisors will require

the current franchisee to sign a general release giving up its rights to pursue any and all claims against the franchisor.

4. Whether the franchisor has a right of first refusal to acquire your business—Most franchise agreements contain a clause allowing the franchisor to match any offer for your business. Therefore, most franchisors have the first right of refusal in purchasing your franchise.

5. Whether the franchisor has an option to purchase the franchisee's business

Other than the disclosure requirements under the Federal Trade Commission Rule, there are no federal laws dealing with transfers. Further, there are very few states that have any laws that give the franchisee any additional rights when they transfer their franchise. However, as with renewals and terminations, almost all states and the federal government have franchise relationship laws that deal with certain industries. For example, some industries, such as the motor vehicle industry, the petroleum industry, the farm equipment industry, and the alcoholic beverage industry, have their own specific federal and state laws that set forth rights of renewal, termination, and transfer for those franchisees. However, there are no general federal laws dealing with transfers in most industries, nor are there but a handful of state laws.

Other than the disclosure requirements under the Federal Trade Commission Rule, there are no federal laws dealing with transfers.

Typical Transfer Terms
Found in a Franchise Agreement

There are many different types of terms and conditions required in the transfer of a franchise. One must carefully study their franchise agreement along with the UFOC to determine what the parameters are concerning transfers. There are certain provisions that are common to the vast majority of franchise agreements. These include the following:

1. Either the current franchisee or the transferee must pay a modest transfer fee to the franchisor. This fee is normally a specific dollar amount. This fee is to reflect the cost incurred by the franchisor in determining whether the transferee is qualified and, if so, its preparation and execution of all legal

documents, etc. Also sometimes included in the transfer fee is the cost of training for the new franchisee.

2. The current franchisee must be in full compliance under the franchise agreement and any other agreements. This means that the franchisee is not in default under the franchise agreement and is current in the payment of all royalties and other fees.

3. The transferee must satisfy the same requirements that a new franchisee must satisfy. The transferee must meet the franchisor's then current educational, managerial, financial, and business criteria. Finally, the transferee must be of good moral character and have a solid credit rating. In other words, a transferee must meet all the requirements of a new franchisee, both financial and otherwise, before the franchisor will approve him.

4. The transferee is required to sign the then current franchise agreement and other agreements of the franchisor. Therefore, the terms and conditions of the transferee could be quite different, including a higher royalty fee and other higher fees.

5. The franchisee, along with each of its directors, shareholders, and officers, is required to execute a general release. When they execute the general release, in effect, they are giving up their rights to pursue any and all claims against the franchisor that existed prior to the signing of the general release.

6. The transferee may be required to renovate the unit to meet the then current specifications. The transferee could be responsible for all costs incurred in the modification and upgrading of the franchise.

7. The transferee and its manager and employees will have to complete the standard training programs given by the franchisor at the expense of the transferee.

8. The transferee shall receive the current UFOC and must sign an acknowledgment of receipt verifying such.

9. The current franchisee will still remain liable for any and all debts and obligations as concerns the franchise business.

> The transferee must meet the franchisor's then current educational, managerial, financial, and business criteria.

The current franchisee will be liable for such even though the transferee will assume all the obligations and debts.

These are the most common provisions found in a franchise agreement concerning transfers. However, the type of transfer provisions found in your franchise agreement are only limited by the franchisor's creativity.

Points to Cover and Questions to Ask

You must be able to live with the transfer provisions found in your franchise agreement. After all, there is a high degree of likelihood that at some point in the future you will want to sell your franchise. Therefore, you must make sure that the transfer provisions are not unnecessarily restrictive.

First, you will want to make sure that you do have the right to transfer your franchise business. Second, you will want to make sure that the franchisor cannot unreasonably withhold its approval. Third, you want to place the burden of future compliance on the transferee. Therefore, you will try to make sure that once the transferee signs on the dotted line you are no longer responsible in any form or fashion for her lack of compliance or her failure. In other words, you want to walk away and not be on the hook for her failure. Finally, if you do not understand a transfer provision, you need to get a clear explanation from the franchisor. It is up to you to make sure that the transfer provisions in the franchise agreement are fair and equitable to both you and your franchisor.

Termination

Termination. The word itself conjures up many images. One of the images it conjures up is that of finality. In the franchise context, termination means just that—the end. Assuming you are in full compliance with your franchise agreement, you will never experience the stressful feelings that you might be terminated. Most franchises make termination an easy and relatively inexpensive action for the franchisor to

> You must be able to live with the transfer provisions found in your franchise agreement. After all, there is a high degree of likelihood that at some point in the future you will want to sell your franchise.

take against the franchisee. Most franchise agreements contain numerous reasons for which you can be terminated. Some of these causes for termination will allow you to cure your default before you can be terminated. However, there will be listed several causes for termination for which you have no right to cure, and therefore, under which you have no possibility of keeping your franchise. Accordingly, termination provisions in a franchise agreement must be reviewed with great concentration, with an eye for detail, to make sure you can live with such provisions.

Federal and State Law

As stated earlier, except in specific industries such as motor vehicle and petroleum, there are no federal laws that deal with termination issues. The only federal law dealing with this issue is the requirement for disclosure of termination terms and conditions under the Federal Trade Commission Rule. A franchisor must disclose under Item 17 of the UFOC (see Chapter 4) any provisions contained in the franchise agreement and other agreements that deal with termination. The franchisor must disclose the following:

1. If it is possible for you, the franchisee, to terminate the franchise agreement
2. Under what conditions the franchisor can terminate your franchise without cause
3. Under what conditions the franchisor can terminate you with cause
4. The word "cause" must be defined as it concerns those defaults that can be cured, and the defaults that can be cured must be listed
5. The word "cause" must be defined as it concerns noncurable defaults with a list of defaults that cannot be cured, causing the franchise to be automatically terminated
6. What your obligations are upon termination of the franchise agreement
7. Any other terms, conditions, or provisions that deal with termination

> Termination provisions in a franchise agreement must be reviewed with great concentration, with an eye for detail, to make sure you can live with such provisions.

There are several state laws that deal with termination. Most states have statutes dealing with terminations in specific industries, such as motor vehicle, petroleum, farm equipment, and alcoholic beverages. In addition to industry specific statutes, there are termination laws found in 16 states plus the District of Columbia, Puerto Rico, and the Virgin Islands. These 16 states are Arkansas, California, Connecticut, Delaware, Hawaii, Illinois, Indiana, Iowa, Michigan, Minnesota, Mississippi, Missouri, Nebraska, New Jersey, Washington, and Wisconsin. Most of these termination statutes require good cause. In other words, without good cause a franchisor cannot terminate your franchise agreement. Termination for good cause is defined under state law to include the following:

1. The franchisee's failure to make timely payments of monies owed to the franchisor
2. Failure of the franchisee to meet sales quotas
3. Failure of the franchisee to adhere to the franchisor's quality standards
4. Failure of the franchisee to comply with the required hours of operation
5. Failure of the franchisee to properly use the franchisor's trademarks
6. The franchisee's failure to make required improvements and changes

These are only a sampling of the ways a franchisee can be terminated for good cause. You will need to look specifically at the statute that applies in the state that you will be located in to determine what good cause is under that specific statute.

Typical Termination Provisions Found in a Franchise Agreement

Most franchise agreements contain termination provisions. However, where the termination language differs is that some of the defaults the franchisee can cure and others he cannot. This means that under certain circumstances your franchise agreement can be

Is It in Writing?

Most of the state statutes require that prior written notice be delivered to a franchisee stating the reason for termination. However, prior written notice may not be required if the termination is due to an emergency or for a reason that is not curable such as the commission of a crime, fraudulent conduct, or the franchisee's bankruptcy.

automatically terminated without any possibility of you being able to cure your default. Under the rest of the termination provisions you are given a certain period of time, measured in days, in which to cure your default so that you will not be terminated.

The most common reasons that a franchisee is automatically terminated without the right to cure are as follows:

1. The franchisee is insolvent or makes a general assignment of assets for the benefit of creditors.
2. The franchisee has filed a bankruptcy petition or such a petition is filed against it and consented to by the franchisee.
3. The franchisee is adjudicated, bankrupt, or insolvent.
4. A bill in equity or other proceeding for the appointment of a receiver of the franchisee's business or assets is filed and consented to by the franchisee.
5. A receiver or other custodian of the franchisee's assets or property is appointed by a court.
6. Proceedings for a composition with creditors under any state or federal law are instituted by or against the franchisee.
7. A final judgment remains unsatisfied or of record for 30 days or longer.
8. An execution is levied against the franchisee's business or property.
9. A lawsuit to foreclose any lien or mortgage against the premises or equipment is instituted against the franchisee and is not dismissed within 30 days.
10. Real or personal property of the franchisee is to be sold after levy thereupon by any sheriff, marshal, or constable.
11. The franchisee fails to obtain a site for the business.
12. The franchisee loses its lease, sublease, or its right to occupy the premises. Or ceases to operate or otherwise abandons the franchised business.
13. The franchisee is convicted, or enters a plea of guilty, involving a felony or a crime involving moral turpitude or any other crime or offense that is reasonably likely to adversely affect the franchisor.

> Under the rest of the termination provisions you are given a certain period of time, measured in days, in which to cure your default so that you will not be terminated.

14. A partner or shareholder of the franchisee transfers her rights or obligations under the franchise agreement or any other interests in the franchise to a third party without the franchisor's prior written consent.
15. The franchisee misuses or makes an unauthorized use of the franchisor's proprietary marks or otherwise materially impairs the good will associated with the franchisor's marks.
16. The franchisee intentionally discloses the contents of the operations manuals to an unauthorized person or discloses the trade secrets and/or confidential information.
17. An approved transfer is not effected within a reasonable time following the death or mental incapacity of the franchisee or the person with the controlling interest in the franchise.
18. The franchisee knowingly maintains false books or false records or submits false reports to the franchisor.

Depending upon the industry or franchise system there will be other automatic termination provisions that are specific to that industry. There are franchise systems in over 70 industries so there could be several unique provisions in this regard.

Except for those reasons listed that lead to automatic termination, the franchisee will have a right to cure any other defaults. Usually the franchisee will have a period of time, numbered in days, in which to cure defaults under the franchise agreement or any other related agreements. Only if the franchisee does not cure these defaults during the cure period will the franchise agreement be terminated. Examples of defaults where the franchisee has a right to cure include the following:

1. Failure of the franchisee to make timely payments of money due to the franchisor or its subsidiaries or affiliates
2. Failure of the franchisee to maintain the quality control standards or procedures described by the franchisor
3. Failure of the franchisee to obtain the franchisor's prior written approval and consent where required

> Usually the franchisee will have a period of time, numbered in days, in which to cure defaults under the franchise agreement or any other related agreements.

4. Franchisee conducts business operation or markets services or products under a name that, in franchisor's opinion, is confusingly similar to the franchisor's proprietary marks
5. Failure of the franchisee, whether by act or omission, to adhere to the rules or regulations of any government agency or any federal, state or local laws and statutes

Under the previously listed circumstances the franchisee will have a period of time ranging from 3 to 30 days to cure such defaults. Often the franchise agreement will allow additional periods of time to cure a default if the franchisee is making solid progress towards curing that default.

Points to Cover and Questions to Ask

You must carefully review all termination provisions in your franchise agreement to make sure that you can live with them. If you cannot live with the termination provisions, you should not buy the franchise. In determining whether or not to buy the franchise, there are certain questions you need to ask:

1. What are the defaults for which there may be a termination?
2. What are the defaults for which there will be an automatic termination with no right to cure?
3. What are the defaults for which you have a right to cure prior to termination?
4. What period of time do you have to cure those defaults? Is this period of time reasonable in terms of the default?
5. Can the franchisor cancel the franchise agreement for other than good cause?
6. As the franchisee, do you have any conditions under which you can terminate the franchise agreement?
7. Upon termination is the franchisor required to buy back any of your equipment, inventory, supplies, and other assets?
8. If there is an obligation who determines the purchase price?
9. Does the franchisor have the collateral right to take over any of your lease agreements thereby not only terminating

> Often the franchise agreement will allow additional periods of time to cure a default if the franchisee is making solid progress towards curing that default.

your franchise but removing you completely from your place of business?

Goals in Negotiation

When negotiating with the franchisor, you must keep things reasonable and even handed. Due to the importance of renewal, transfer, and termination provisions, it is important that you negotiate firmly with the franchisor. All provisions negotiated should be fair and equitable to both parties.

You should have certain goals in negotiating your franchise agreement. You should try to negotiate for the following provisions:

1. A long initial term with automatic renewals
2. Termination only upon proof of good cause
3. Nonrenewal only upon proof of good cause (if unable to get automatic renewals)
4. Fair and equitable performance standards
5. Fair and equitable sales and marketing quotas
6. Written and comprehensive statements of all alleged discrepancies or deficiencies provided you by the franchisor
7. The right to require the franchisor to prove all matters of discrepancy or deficiency
8. The right to transfer the franchise to your family and heirs
9. The right to transfer and sell your franchise subject only to fair and reasonable restrictions
10. If terminated for good cause, the right to at least 90 days notice with adequate compensation for your franchise, goodwill, equity, equipment, inventory, supplies, and other materials, with the right to appeal to an internal appeals board such determination.

Conclusion

A long initial term in the franchise agreement is useful in developing goodwill between the franchisor and the franchisee. Since both parties know they will be working together for an extended period of time, they will try their best to accommodate each other to ensure each other's success. Further, a renewal clause in the franchise agreement also helps to further this constructive relationship and to promote positive attitudes between the parties.

It is unnecessary for the franchisor to have one-sided authority to terminate a franchisee because most franchisees are quick to encourage their fellow franchisees to improve their performance and to maintain the quality standards of the franchise system. After all, one bad franchisee can have a negative impact on the goodwill of other franchisees in the system. Therefore, those franchisees in compliance with their franchise agreements will seek to have those franchisees not in compliance comply.

Finally, if a franchisee is not renewed or is terminated the franchisor should have provisions under which it will compensate the franchisee for inventory, fixtures, signs, furnishings, goodwill, and equity in the franchised business. After all, you as a franchisee have put your blood, sweat, and tears into the development of this franchise and you should be compensated for such. If you are terminated or not renewed and are not adequately compensated this will be viewed adversely by the other franchisees in the system. After all, both sides need to feel that they are in a win-win situation and are being dealt with equitably.

> One bad franchisee can have a negative impact on the goodwill of other franchisees in the system.

For more information on this topic, visit our Web site at www.businesstown.com

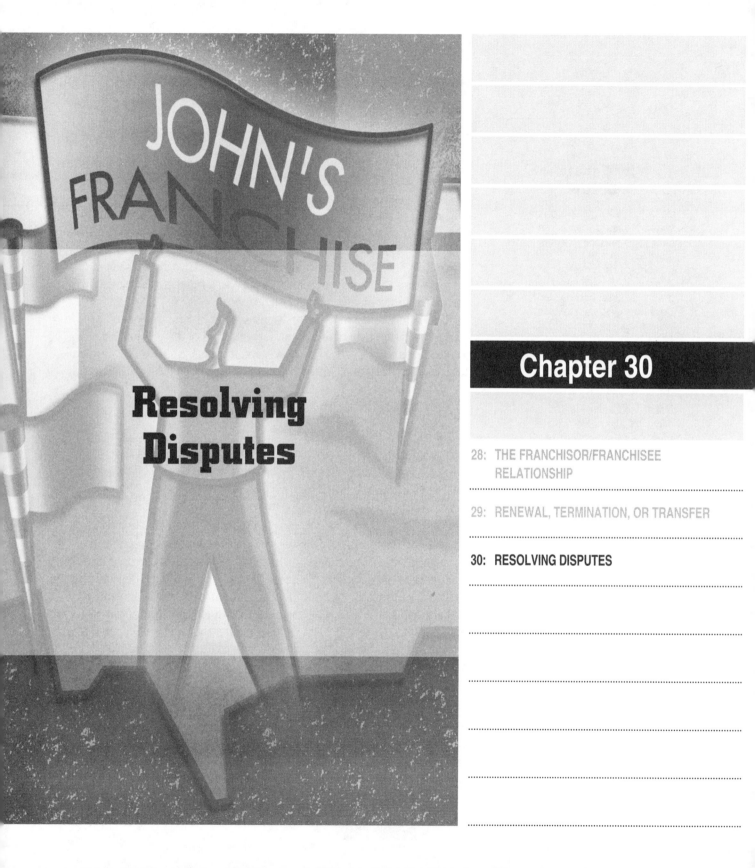

Resolving Disputes

Chapter 30

28: THE FRANCHISOR/FRANCHISEE RELATIONSHIP

29: RENEWAL, TERMINATION, OR TRANSFER

30: RESOLVING DISPUTES

Introduction

Disputes between the franchisor and the franchisee are bound to happen sooner or later. Resolving disputes between the franchisor and the franchisee can be expensive and time consuming. If there are too many disputes, the growth of the franchise system will be impeded. If there are too many disputes, the franchisor will be distracted from his mission, goals, objectives, and vision. Of course, no franchisor wants its UFOC's disclosure of lawsuits under Item 3 to read like a law firm's resume. Excessive disputes not only are expensive and time consuming, but are also a significant detriment to the franchise system and to franchise relations.

The most common cause of disputes between a franchisor and a franchisee is that they have different expectations of the relationship. Therefore, as a prospective franchisee, you must make sure that your expectations are realistic and that they coincide with those of the franchisor.

The relationship between the franchisor and franchisee is governed by three things. These are:

1. The franchise agreement signed by both parties
2. Federal and state statutes and regulations that pertain to franchising
3. Common law duties and responsibilities as defined by the law of business torts

The vast majority of disputes will involve an alleged breach of the franchise agreement or operations manual or of a federal or state franchise statute or regulation. Therefore, a prospective franchisee would be well advised to research thoroughly the proposed franchise agreement and any applicable federal and state statutes and regulations prior to entering into the relationship. Only through a thorough understanding of these can the prospective franchisee minimize future disputes that will arise with the franchisor.

Required Disclosures

Under the Federal Trade Commission Rule and the UFOC guidelines, certain disclosures are required under Item 17. It is required that under Item 17 the franchisor disclose those provisions of the franchise and other

---

Why Tensions Occur

There will always be a certain level of tension in the franchisor-franchisee relationship. On the one hand, the franchisor has invested a great deal of time, effort, and money in establishing the franchise system. The franchisor has spent this time, effort, and money to develop the operations manuals, quality control guidelines, and policy and procedures to follow in the operation of your franchised business. On the other hand, the franchisee often has a strong entrepreneurial desire not only to be her own boss, but also to only follow those policies and procedures she feels are necessary. Because of this tension, there will be disputes.

agreements dealing with dispute resolution and other important aspects of the franchise relationship. Specifically, there are three items that must be disclosed under Item 17 dealing with dispute resolution.

First, the franchisor is required to disclose under what circumstances and for what claims disputes must be arbitrated or mediated. Under this Item it must be stated when a claim or dispute must be arbitrated or mediated. Some franchisors will state that all claims, no matter the severity, will be settled through arbitration or even through mediation. However, most franchisors, will dictate that certain disputes cannot be resolved through arbitration or mediation, but only through litigation in a court of law.

Second, the franchisor must state the venue (location) for litigation and arbitration disputes. Finally, the franchisor must disclose any choice of law provisions. In the previous scenario, the franchisor will dictate, for example, that Georgia law applies. This is only natural since the State of Georgia is where the franchisor is located and henceforth the law it is most familiar with. Some franchisors make no disclosures as to choice of law or choice of forum because it is not of enough importance to them to do so. However, the vast majority of franchisors do state where any and all disputes must be brought, whether in a court of law or in arbitration, and what state law will apply. Once you review the required disclosures as found under Item 17, you should also review any state laws that might apply. Sometimes a state law will dictate that any dispute or claim concerning a franchisee within its boundaries must be heard in that state, using that state's law.

When You Can't Agree

It is in the best interest of both the franchisor and its franchisees to minimize to the greatest extent possible any potential conflict or disputes. However, in those situations where there is a dispute, it is to the benefit of both parties to resolve it as quickly as possible. However, there will be some disputes that cannot easily be settled. In those situations, it is possible that expensive and time-consuming litigation can occur, which is not only detrimental to the particular franchisee involved, but quite possibly to the entire franchise system.

Covenants not to Compete and Other Post-Term Obligations

There is a strong likelihood that you will be disallowed from competing with your franchisor during the term of your franchise agreement and for a period after its expiration or termination. Additionally, upon expiration or termination of your franchise agreement, you will be required to adhere to certain post-term obligations. The first place to look for this information is in the franchisor's disclosure document. Under the Federal Trade Commission Rule and the UFOC, the franchisor is required to disclose such matters under Item 17.

First, the franchisor is required to disclose any franchisee obligations upon termination or nonrenewal of his franchise agreement. Second, the franchisor must spell out any noncompetition covenants that will exist during the term of the franchise agreement. Third, the franchisor must disclose any noncompetition covenants that you will be required to follow after the franchise agreement is either terminated or has expired. Almost all franchisors will require post-term obligations and noncompete covenants that exist both during and after the term of the franchise agreement. Therefore, you must carefully study these disclosures to see if they are reasonable and that you can abide by them. If you should sign a franchise agreement and not abide by such covenants, you are guaranteed to be sued quickly by the franchisor to enforce them.

The franchisor is required to disclose any franchisee obligations upon termination or nonrenewal of his franchise agreement.

Covenants not to Compete

Simply put, a covenant not to compete places restrictions upon your ability to compete against the franchisor under certain terms and conditions. Almost all franchisors place restrictions against competition by their franchisees. These restrictions disallow the franchisee from competing against the franchisor in the franchisor's line of business. Also, these restrictions will be for a certain period of time and will normally cover a specific geographic area. Such covenants not to compete are generally deemed lawful under federal law, but face greater uncertainty under state law. For example, the State of California renders illegal covenants not to compete that disallow you from competing in the franchisor's business after the termination or expiration of your franchise agreement.

Nevertheless, in the vast majority of states, restrictions against competition are generally valid and enforceable under state law if the restrictions are reasonable. Of course, what is considered reasonable will vary from state to state, with the facts of each situation, and the nature of the claim asserted. A franchisor seeking to enforce a covenant not to compete must prove that it has a legitimate business interest and that the restrictions are appropriately limited with respect to the scope of the business interest and activities prohibited, duration of the restriction, and the geographical area of the restriction.

As a franchisee, you will be confronted with having to abide by two types of covenants not to compete. First, you will be required to abide by what is referred to as an in-term covenant not to compete. This means that during the term of your franchise agreement you will not be allowed to compete against the franchisor in his line of business.

The second type of covenant not to compete is referred to as post-term. This means that upon termination or expiration of your franchise agreement you will be disallowed from competing against the franchisor in its line of business for a certain period of time within a certain geographical area. You can be all but guaranteed that you will be required to sign a franchise agreement that contains both in-term and post-term covenants.

As a franchisee, you will be confronted with having to abide by two types of covenants not to compete.

The Three Parts of a Covenant

Now, let's look at the three components that comprise a covenant not to compete. Most in-term covenants not to compete contain no restrictions on the territory it covers. After all, the courts conclude that the franchisee is working with the franchisor and, therefore, should not be in competition with the franchisor. However, when it comes to post-term covenants not to compete, a court will not enforce one that is too broad in geographical scope.

In other words, a post-term covenant not to compete must be restricted to a geographical area no larger than what is required to protect the franchisor's interest. For example, if you operated a restaurant at Location A then the post-term covenant not to compete would disallow you from opening a like restaurant within a 10-mile radius. If the franchisor placed a larger geographical restriction on you, then that greatly increases the likelihood that a court would find it overly broad and disallow it. However, because in-term covenants have other purposes such as protecting the franchisor's confidential information and to prevent a franchisee from using the benefits of the franchise in operating a competing business for which the franchisor receives no pay, a court will allow for an unlimited geographical area.

The second component of a covenant not to compete is its duration. By definition, an in-term covenant not to compete exists during the entire term of the franchise agreement. However, a post-term covenant not to compete will likely not be enforced if it is to last for a period longer than two to three years.

The third component of a covenant not to compete is the scope of the prohibited activity. The franchisor normally states in his covenant that you cannot compete during the duration of the covenant in a business that is similar to or substantially like the business the franchisor is in. If a franchisor is overly broad in the activities it attempts to restrict, a court will likely disallow the covenant. For example, if you operate a fast-food hamburger restaurant, your covenant will restrict you from operating another fast-food hamburger restaurant during the duration of the covenant not to compete. A court would enforce the covenant. However, if a franchisor were to restrict you from opening any type of restaurant, then a court would strike that down as being overly broad, since the franchisor does not have a legitimate interest that broad to protect.

How Disputes Are Settled

There will be disputes. This is a given in any type of relationship, including the franchisor/franchisee relationship. Therefore, the real question is: How does a particular franchisor settle disputes? Most franchisors do not like to settle disputes through litigation. Most franchisors will try to resolve a dispute prior to a lawsuit being filed. There are important reasons for this from the prospective franchisee's viewpoint. Under Item 3 of the UFOC, a franchisor is required to disclose any material lawsuits that have been resolved or are pending against it or its principals alleging a violation of any franchise law, fraud, embezzlement, fraudulent conversion, restraint of trade, unfair or deceptive practices, misappropriation of property, or comparable allegations. Every time there is a lawsuit between a franchisor and a franchisee it must be listed and disclosed under Item 3. The more lawsuits disclosed under Item 3, the more difficult it becomes for a franchisor to find new franchisees.

Phase One: Informal Dispute Resolution

Typically, a proactive franchisor who views the franchise relationship as a business partnership will have several informal ways to settle

---

Other Post-Term Obligations

Normally, when a franchisee leaves a franchise system, the franchisor will require compliance with a variety of post-termination or expiration obligations. Most franchise agreements require a franchisee to:

1. Not disclose, reveal, or use any confidential information, trade secrets, or other proprietary information of the franchisor gained during their relationship
2. De-identify the franchise premises and stop holding yourself out as a franchisee
3. Return the operations manual and materials containing confidential information and trade secrets to the franchisor
4. Pay all monies owing to the franchisor and, if applicable, the payment of liquidated damages if you were terminated prior to the end of your franchise agreement

disputes. The first such method is by avoidance. A proactive franchisor practices avoidance through its training of the franchisee. During this type of training, the franchisor will go over in great detail all of the terms, conditions, and obligations required of the franchisee as found in the franchise agreement and other agreements that both parties have signed. Therefore, at the beginning of the franchise relationship the franchisor has made sure that the franchisee is completely aware of all of his responsibilities and obligations. This training feature alone will eliminate, or at least alleviate, numerous potential problems.

The second stage of informal dispute resolution is performed by the franchisor's field personnel who handle most of the necessary correspondence. The field personnel are those who typically first find out and become aware of any problems. Since the field personnel are the first line of resolution in a franchise system, they will meet face to face with the franchisee to discuss the problem and attempt to effect a practical solution. A great number of disputes are resolved through this one-on-one meeting at the lowest level.

However, there are occasions that dictate that the field personnel are not the appropriate people to resolve the dispute. In such a situation, there will be correspondence between the home office personnel of the franchisor and the franchisee in the form of telephone contacts, letters, and face-to-face meetings. These face-to-face meetings can occur either at the franchisor's headquarters or at the franchisee's location. Many disputes are resolved at this level.

Often, the franchisee who is in noncompliance will require franchisor assistance. In such a situation more is required to solve the dispute than face-to-face meetings with field personnel or headquarters' personnel. In these situations, the franchisor will have a program in place to help franchisees comply with their responsibilities and obligations under the franchise agreement. For example, this approach is appropriate if the franchisee is having difficulty paying royalties and other fees due to competitive market conditions, a poor location, and/or a general economic recession.

In the event these methods fail to resolve the dispute, the next stage is that of mediation. The mediation process entails a nonbinding informal presentation by both the franchisor and the franchisee of the dispute to an independent mediator. The independent mediator attempts to determine the underlying causes of the dispute and

Settling Out of Court

In this day and age, most franchisors try to settle disputes through various types of prelitigation negotiation. In the researching of a prospective franchisor, you need to determine what process they normally follow in the settling of disputes. The process a potential franchisor uses will tell you a lot about how it views its relationship with its franchisees.

have the parties agree on a mutually beneficial and satisfactory resolution. Mediation is nonbinding but does allow for an outside party to hear both sides. As a result of the use of an independent third party, often both sides will successfully resolve the dispute.

Occasionally there will arise disputes between the franchisor and a large number of its franchisees. To settle such disputes informally, the franchisor will utilize services of its franchisee advisory council or, if there is one, an independent franchisee association. However, the only time such an organization would be used is when disputes needing to be resolved involve the franchise system as a whole. Such an organization would not be used to settle disputes between individual franchisees and the franchisor.

Phase Two: Arbitration

Occasionally, the informal methods to resolve disputes mentioned will fail. At this point, arbitration usually enters the picture. Most franchisors have included mandatory arbitration in their franchise agreements. Arbitration is usually referred to as a method of alternative dispute resolution. This means that a dispute is resolved outside the judicial system or outside the courtroom. Arbitration involves the resolution of the dispute between the franchisor and the franchisee by submitting the dispute to one or more impartial persons who serve as arbitrators. These arbitrators will hear both sides present their positions, then render a final and binding decision in the matter.

When a franchisor dictates that disputes will be arbitrated, it will most likely state that the arbitrator's decision is final and binding on the parties involved. With all other methods of alternative dispute resolution such as mediation, the decision by the impartial third party is nonbinding. However, arbitration is still a process by which to submit a dispute with its arguments and evidence in an informal and nonpublic fashion to a third party who will decide the matter. The evidentiary and procedural rules are not nearly as formal as in litigation. There tends to be greater flexibility in the timing of the arbitration proceedings and in the selection of the impartial third party arbitrators.

If you are required to arbitrate, it will be set forth in your franchise agreement. As a result, the franchisor is free to structure the

> Occasionally, the informal methods to resolve disputes mentioned will fail. At this point, arbitration usually enters the picture.

scope and procedures of the arbitration. Most arbitration clauses found in franchise agreements will specify the following:

1. The place at which the arbitration will take place
2. The method by which arbitrators will be selected
3. Limitations, if any, on the award that may be rendered by the arbitrator
4. Whether both parties or the losing party will be responsible for the cost of the proceedings
5. That the arbitrator's decision is final and binding and can be enforced in a court of law
6. Any special procedural rules that will govern the arbitration
7. Which disputes must be arbitrated and which must be litigated

If arbitration is required, the clause will usually state that the commercial arbitration rules of the American Arbitration Association will be followed. The American Arbitration Association is headquartered in New York City with offices throughout the United States. If the rules of the American Arbitration Association are followed and there is a dispute to be submitted to arbitration, you will be presented with a list of approved arbitrators. At this point, you will receive resumes of the arbitrators so that you can select an individual experienced in the area of the dispute. Some franchise agreements allow for the selection of only one arbitrator to be decided upon by both the franchisor and the franchisee. Other franchise agreements allow for a panel of three arbitrators. In such a situation, each party picks one of the arbitrators independently and then both of them agree on the third arbitrator.

The pros and cons

Depending upon which side of the fence you sit, there are advantages and disadvantages to arbitration. From the franchisor's prospective there are advantages and disadvantages. The advantages to the franchisor are as follows:

1. The franchisor can control the structure of the arbitration through the writing of the arbitration language in the franchise agreement.

A Closer Look at Arbitration

Arbitration is valid in all 50 states. It is enforced through the Federal Arbitration Act also known as the United States Arbitration Act. This Act creates a federal policy favoring the enforcement of arbitration agreements. As a result, the United States Supreme Court has interpreted the United States Arbitration Act to require the enforcement of contractual arbitration provisions between franchisors and franchisees. Also, the United States Supreme Court has struck down state efforts at limiting agreements for the arbitration of disputes.

2. Disputes are resolved more quickly and with a greater degree of finality. Discovery is much more limited, which speeds up the process.

3. The franchisor avoids the possibility of establishing an adverse judicial precedent with respect to the interpretation of a provision in the franchise agreement. This can be a real benefit to the franchisor that is concerned about the ultimate interpretation of various clauses found in the franchise agreement and other agreements.

4. The franchisor has the ability to select a convenient venue as the location of the arbitration.

5. The arbitrator's decision is final and binding and can be appealed only on limited grounds. Therefore, the delay and uncertainty that often exists in a judicial setting is largely eliminated.

6. Arbitration allows the franchisor to resolve the dispute with a franchisee without breaking the continuity of the relationship. A lawsuit polarizes both parties and is very costly while arbitration results in much less polarization.

7. Quite simply, arbitration is usually less expensive than litigation.

8. Through the United States Arbitration Act, federal law has pre-empted state laws dealing with arbitration. Therefore, all arbitration agreements are enforceable and are unaffected by any state laws.

However, just like with anything else, there are certain disadvantages to the franchisor. These disadvantages are as follows:

1. Sometimes the franchisor will find it in its own best interest to delay the ultimate resolution of a dispute. Litigation will do this. However, arbitration will resolve a dispute a lot quicker and therefore can be a disadvantage in such instances.

2. Sometimes arbitrators will not follow the law and as a result their decision will be inferior to one the franchisor could have obtained in a judicial proceeding.

3. Since discovery is greatly limited in arbitration it can make it more difficult for the franchisor to prepare its case.

> Sometimes arbitrators will not follow the law and as a result their decision will be inferior to one the franchisor could have obtained in a judicial proceeding.

4. Often, an arbitrator will render a decision finding common ground that gives each side a partial victory. This is quite different from a court decision in which one side usually wins, to the detriment of the other side.

5. A franchisor who is well established might find it beneficial to be able to sustain a long drawn out legal battle. If a franchisor has greater financial staying power it can be to its benefit to outlast a franchisee who is less able financially to pursue a protracted court battle.

6. With arbitration there are very limited grounds for appeal of adverse decisions. This could work to the disadvantage of the franchisor. If an adverse decision is rendered judicially, the franchisor can appeal the decision, which could persuade the franchisee who initially won to accept a settlement.

7. Due to the relaxed procedural and evidentiary rules found in arbitration, the franchisee may be more successful in making an emotional appeal or in presenting other franchisees as witnesses to testify against the franchisor. Such strategies would not work in a courtroom.

Arbitration has become a very common method by which franchisors ultimately try to settle disputes. Arbitration tends to be less expensive, consumes fewer resources on the part of both the franchisor and the franchisee, and allows for the franchisor to have one less dispute to list under Item 3 where it must list all litigation. However, there will be situations in which even arbitration is not workable. In these situations litigation is the only alternative.

Phase Three: Litigation

Normally, the franchisor will avoid litigation. Litigation is the last resort in trying to solve a dispute. There are many reasons for this. Not only is litigation time consuming and expensive for both parties, but the franchisor may be portrayed in a very unflattering manner. The franchisor may be portrayed as Goliath in the struggle between David and Goliath. Also, the franchisor may be portrayed as a huge, dispassionate corporate entity with no feelings for the small and defenseless franchisee. Some franchisors are portrayed as vindictive and as being

> Arbitration has become a very common method by which franchisors ultimately try to settle disputes.

motivated only by greed and money. Sometimes a franchisor is portrayed as incompetent, leading to the financial ruin of its own franchisees. No party to a lawsuit likes to be portrayed in such a manner.

Almost all franchisors reserve certain disputes strictly for litigation. In most of these situations the franchisor has determined that these disputes are too important and too detrimental to the franchise system as a whole to allow for arbitration or other type of alternative dispute resolution. Usually these actions allow the franchisor to pursue injunctive relief. When a franchisor goes to court and requests injunctive relief, it is telling the judge that its interest is so profound and so important to its survival that since it will likely prevail on the merits of the case it needs the judge to award it a preliminary injunction. The preliminary injunction forces the franchisee to cease and desist all such actions under the threat of contempt of court. Actions for injunctive relief by the franchisor are appropriate in the following circumstances:

1. A franchisee has been terminated but continues to use the franchisor's trademarks, service marks, patents, etc.
2. A terminated franchisee continues to hold himself out as a franchisee or authorized dealer or distributor of the franchisor's trademarked or patented products.
3. A terminated franchisee competes with the franchisor in violation of a covenant not to compete contained in its franchise agreement.
4. A terminated franchisee has failed or refused to comply with other post-termination obligations as specified in the franchise agreement.

For matters such as these, it is critical for the franchisor to get immediate relief through the judicial system. Therefore, the franchisor will file for a preliminary injunction, which, at a later date, will become a permanent injunction.

The Franchisee Defense Manual

How can a franchisee defend itself against a franchisor? What should a franchisee be doing to protect itself? These are very important questions. Sooner or later a dispute will arise between the franchisor and the franchisee. The best way for a franchisee to protect itself is to keep comprehensive records of everything.

The franchisee should keep a comprehensive file of all correspondence between it and the franchisor. To successfully defend itself when a dispute arises, the franchisee should have at its fingertips the following materials:

1. An original of the franchise agreement and all other agreements signed by the franchisor and franchisee—These legal agreements sets forth your obligations, rights, and responsibilities. Therefore, you must maintain the original of your franchise agreement and related agreements in a safe place. You would be surprised at the large number of franchisees who cannot locate originals or even copies of the agreements they signed.
2. A complete copy of the confidential operations manuals— Not only should you have a complete copy of the current operations manuals, but you should also save those policies and procedures that have been updated or replaced.
3. You should have on file all documents, information, and records dealing with:
   a. the accounting requirements and system
   b. pricing policies
   c. quotas and/or allocation requirements
   d. purchasing requirements for all products, supplies, or other materials
   e. advertising fee requirements
   f. any threats, coercions, or pressure tactics employed against you by the franchisor
   g. sales policies
   h. customer policies
   i. list of favored franchisees
   j. any other information concerning the franchise that is in your possession
4. Copies of all correspondence sent to and received from the franchisor
5. Complete transcripts of all conversations and face-to-face meetings with a representative of the franchisor—Such a

How to Protect Yourself

There are three main points to keep in mind when protecting yourself. These are:

- First, keep a complete and comprehensive written record of all transactions with the franchisor.
- Second, make sure that in all face-to-face meetings with the franchisor two or more officers of your franchise are present.
- Third, always consult an attorney expert in franchise law, and/or an accountant if a dispute arises during the franchise relationship.

record should include names and titles of those people you spoke with or met with

6. Evidence and records of inconsistent enforcement of the obligations and responsibilities with other franchisees

7. Written records of all promises made by the franchisor

8. Records of franchisee group meetings and trade association meetings

9. Records of your refusal to sign documents concerning unfair quotas, regulations, or other deficiencies

You must keep a comprehensive and complete record of any and all contact with the franchisor. This includes keeping complete records of all conversations, telephone message slips, and memorandums reflecting understandings reached at face-to-face meetings, all correspondence between you and the franchisor, and copies or originals of all documents provided to you by the franchisor. Additionally, you should maintain copies of all inspection reports and notices. In other words, you are keeping a complete and comprehensive record of the entire relationship from the very beginning. These records should be stored in a safe place, probably off the franchise premises. You need to maintain control of the records and not allow them to be accessed by either the franchisor or any of your employees.

> The franchisor/franchisee relationship has often been described as a partnership similar to a marriage.

Conclusion

The franchisor/franchisee relationship has often been described as a partnership similar to a marriage. At the outset both parties enter the partnership expecting it to be long-term and mutually beneficial. Both parties expect to find satisfaction in the relationship. However, as the relationship continues, tensions and disputes often arise. Usually, the franchisor and franchisee are able to informally identify the underlying causes of the dispute and then resolve it in a mutually satisfactory manner. However, occasionally the franchisor and franchisee cannot settle the dispute through alternative dispute resolution. In these situations, the dispute will be settled in a court of law through litigation. If and when this occurs, if you have maintained a complete written record of the relationship, you will be in a better position to defend yourself and come out on top.

Multiunit Franchising, Growing (or Closing)

In this section, you'll learn:

- **The ins and outs of owning more than one store within your franchise system**

- **Hiring managers you can trust**

- **How to make an educated decision about how to end your relationship with the franchisor**

CHAPTER 31 OPENING THE NEW STORE (MULTIUNIT FRANCHISING) **CHAPTER 32** BUILDING A FRANCHISEE EMPIRE
CHAPTER 33 THE FINAL DECISION: SELL OR GO OUT OF BUSINESS?

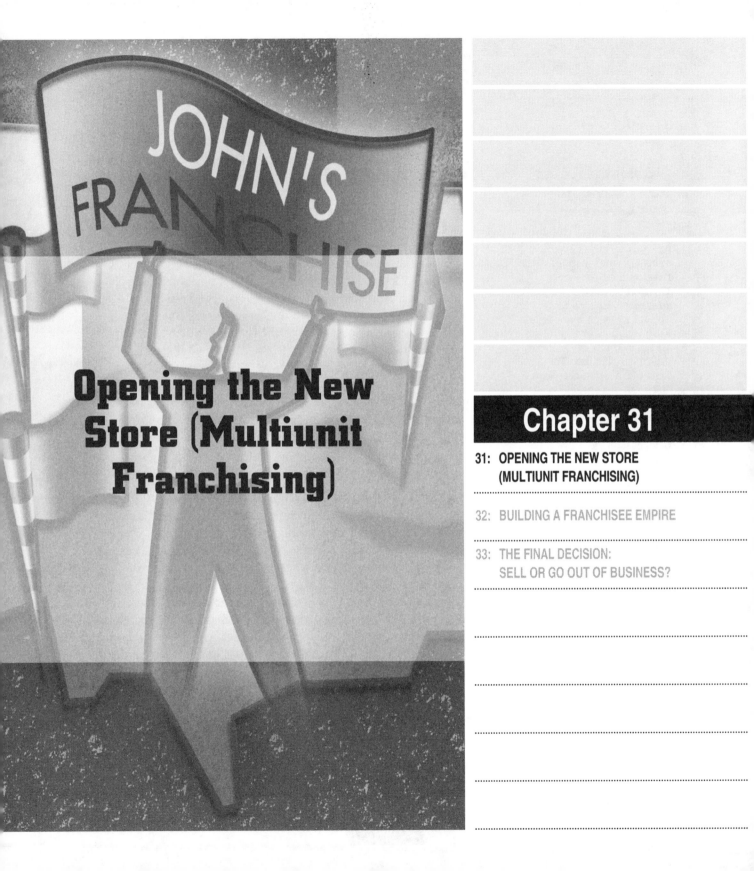

Opening the New Store (Multiunit Franchising)

Chapter 31

31: OPENING THE NEW STORE (MULTIUNIT FRANCHISING)

32: BUILDING A FRANCHISEE EMPIRE

33: THE FINAL DECISION: SELL OR GO OUT OF BUSINESS?

Smoothie King Area Development Agreement

Development Fee: You will pay a lump sum development fee when you sign the Development Agreement. The development fee is calculated at the rate of $5,000 for each Smoothie King Business that you are authorized to develop after the first franchise. For example, if you enter into a development agreement to establish five Smoothie King businesses, your development fee will be $20,000. Development fees are separate and do not apply to the franchise fees for each business opened under your development agreement. The development fee is not refundable under any circumstances. Under the development agreement, the initial franchise fee for the first franchise is $20,000. The initial franchise fee for the second, third, and fourth franchises is $17,000; and the initial franchise fee for the fifth and each other franchise is $15,000.

One of the greatest opportunities in franchising is simply to be a multiunit franchisee. One of the things that you can always look forward to is opening your second and possibly even third or fourth stores.

It is presumed in America that all franchises are individually owned and operated. The more realistic understanding of franchising throughout the world is that a franchise system, while composed of single-unit franchisees, also has many multiunit franchisee owners. On the average, McDonald's franchisees own about three franchised units.

One research report by Robicheaux, Dant, and Kaufmann reported in 1994 that "multi-unit franchising is very common and, based on our findings, seems to be the rule rather than the exception in fast food franchising in the U.S." They found that while results varied from one franchisor to another, on average 33% of franchisees owned more than a single unit. They also reported that only 13.2% of the franchisors stated that they had no franchisees in their systems with more than one unit. That leaves approximately 86% of franchised systems with multiunit owners.

Ways of Becoming a Multiunit Owner

There are two basic ways in which franchisees become multiunit owners. The most common case is when the franchisee wants to own a second store. In this case, the franchisee will be assessed the current franchise fee and royalty rate for each additional unit acquired. Simply stated, the franchisee pays the same fees that other franchisees have paid when they purchase their second store. There are certain systems where franchisees, when purchasing additional units, will pay a lower franchise fee for these units. The main reason for a lower franchise fee for a second, third, fourth, or even fifth store is because of the reduction in training and overhead costs.

A second method of becoming a multiunit owner is to acquire an area development agreement, or a contract with the franchisor that allows you to obtain an exclusive territory for a specific period of time (generally three to five years) in which to build a specific number of units. It is estimated that 75% of most restaurant franchisors as well as many franchisors use these agreements.

A common practice in developing an area development agreement for the franchisee is to assess a fixed fee for the right to develop the franchisee's territory. The franchisee then pays the current franchisee fee (often minus the previously paid assessed fee) plus the normal royalty rates for each unit. In some cases, the franchisee fee is reduced. However, it is seldom that the royalty rates are reduced for additional units.

The area development agreement enables you to have a certain time period in which to develop additional stores in the franchisee's area. The area under question is generally a target market area such as a city, county, or multicounty area. It is rare today that an entire state would be granted an area development agreement.

A typical area development agreement may be for the greater Kansas City area and require the addition of five units at $7,000 per unit for a total cost of $35,000. This $35,000 is the application fee for the area development agreement and becomes the monies of the franchisor. If the contract is not met, these monies remain with the franchisor.

Generally, with the $35,000 area development fee, when a new unit is contracted, the then-current franchise agreement would be signed, but if the franchise fee was normally $20,000, it may be reduced to $13,000 because of the $7,000 per store area development agreement fee. Generally the royalty rates would remain the same.

Multiunit Development Game

If you are still thinking about developing a second unit, then you need to learn how to play the game. Coming to the right decision is as important as buying the first franchise. This may not be easy, but at least you will have a good understanding of what it takes to evaluate the second and subsequent franchises. But following the rules of the game, you will have a greater chance of success in what you do.

> Our goal is to understand the customer better than they understand themselves. This is to appreciate the customer's needs and knowing something about their lifestyles and the extent to which they would use your current product and/or service.

Make no mistake: being a multiunit franchisee is not easy, but it may be one of the most rewarding experiences of your life. If you have also purchased a home, then you are familiar with the disciplines that are often involved in purchasing additional franchise units. Here, then, are the house rules that the game is usually lived by:

House Rule Number 1: Know Your Territory

Do you still remember the top three factors that you looked for when you were out selecting your home? Location, location, and location. This old business rule brings home a lesson that is just as important in selecting your additional franchising sites. The territory and environment will help determine which businesses will succeed and which will fail. You need to know the territory.

House Rule Number 2: Know Your Market

Our goal is to understand the customer better than they understand themselves. This is to appreciate the customer's needs and knowing something about their lifestyles and the extent to which they would use your current product and/or service.

One activity that may be helpful is to go out to talk to your customers. Talk to the people who use your product. Ask them what they are looking for in your product or service. Observe what they do with your product and how they customize or use it. People generally love to talk about where they shop, what they like, and what they don't like. It is fun to gather market information. You need it.

House Rule Number 3: Know Your Needs and Resources

Before you do anything about multiunit franchising, you need to evaluate your strengths, weaknesses, opportunities, and threats (SWOT), as well as your financial position. You need to determine if you have the financial strength to start a second, third, or fourth store. You need to realize that the profits from the first store are not going to be sufficient generally to immediately start a second or third store. However, a successful first store may provide you the means wherewith you may talk to bankers or other investors and obtain funding for your additional units. How much money do you currently have to invest? What are your financial resources? Do your family members agree with your expansion ideas? Does your current staff believe that they could help open a second or additional store?

House Rule Number 4:
Know How to Line Up Your Financing

It is never too soon to develop financial resources. The franchisor generally will not take care of this for you. One of the main reasons that franchising works so well is because usually the individual franchisees are the ones who invest their own capital resources in the business.

Start by getting your own information and financial data organized. Prepare a personal financial income statement, which you can obtain from the local bank, stationery store, or off the Internet. Talk to your franchisor about additional financial resources that they might know of, including national investors who finance specifically franchising stores. Determine if your friends or relatives may also be interested in helping finance your position. It is also smart to find out what the SBA lenders are currently doing and ask them about possible franchise financing. You may contact the local SBA office or check their Web site at *www.sba.gov*.

House Rule Number 5: Know the Game Rules

You need to check with the franchisor to find out what the rules are for obtaining an additional store and/or for obtaining an additional unit. You may also contact the franchisor about a possible area development agreement, which would provide you with a specific exclusive territory for a short period of time.

The franchisor may be willing to approve a second or additional store and reduce the initial franchise fee if you do your own training. They also may be able to help you to find used equipment or other fixtures at a reduced rate. You need to check with the franchisor to see what they provide when you build a second unit.

> Talk to your franchisor about additional financial resources that they might know of, including national investors who finance specifically franchising stores.

Normally, the royalty fees, advertising fees, and other fees (except for the franchise fee) will remain the same in a second or additional unit.

Make sure that you check with the franchisor about the then-current franchise agreement. This may be different than the one you originally signed. You should know that, when you develop your second or additional stores, you will generally be required to sign the "then-current" franchise agreement.

House Rule Number 6: Know the Property

You need to walk around the property. You need to investigate several different possible site locations that you are thinking of. You also need to make a decision about whether you are going to open up just one additional store or possibly three or four additional stores.

The addition of several stores will dramatically affect your site selection process. It is easy to pick one or two sites for stores in a city. However, if you are going to build four or five within the city, then you need to pick the locations at the start so that your sites, as you build out, do not overlap or encroach upon previously selected sites. You need to recognize that the absolute best site location may be a location where two major markets would purchase from the same location, such as a major intersection between two cities.

House Rule Number 7: Know How to Get Franchisor Approval

One of the main stumbling blocks that occurs periodically in multiunit purchases is the inability to obtain the franchisor's approval. This lack of approval may occur because of the following:

1. Low evaluation scores on your existing store
2. Poor financial structure
3. Poor site location
4. Inability to finance the second store
5. Inability to manage a second store

> If you are going to build four or five within the city, then you need to pick the locations at the start so that your sites, as you build out, do not overlap or encroach upon previously selected sites.

Franchisors are generally quite excited about offering multiunit ownership to "good" franchisees. This includes all franchisees whose stores are in the top 50% of sales throughout the system. Franchisors are not only willing but usually encourage their good franchisees to develop multiunits.

House Rule Number 8: Know Your Personnel

It is important that you know if you have the personnel who are capable of opening and running a second store. If you are currently managing the first store, you are going to need to find a manager for the second store. It is very difficult for one individual to properly manage two stores at the same time. It is possible, but very, very difficult.

As you expand, you will find that, in most cases, when you have either your third or fourth store, you will not only need individual managers per store but you will also need to have a supervisor of managers. You will generally need one district manager for each three or four stores you are operating.

Are there sufficient potential employees in the new area who could also be hired that would be qualified to help operate your store? Can you meet the payroll for the additional store?

House Rule Number 9: Know How to Develop Your Time Schedule

You need to be able to sit down and develop a time schedule for when you wish to expand into an additional unit. You need to be able to answer the question who is going to be doing what, when, where, how and why?

You need to be have a business plan for not just a second store but also now for yourself as an owner/manager of multiunits. You need to realize that you are now going to create an additional business and that is "owning" two stores.

House Rule Number 10: Know How to Run the Play

Now is the time. You have now planned your work, now work your plan.

> You will generally need one district manager for each three or four stores you are operating.

As a new multiunit franchisee, you need to follow the time schedule and the plan you have created. You need to properly implement the decisions you have made about multiunit and/or area development. You need to bring your financial and personnel resources to the forefront. You need to work with your franchisor as you select your properties and develop your additional stores.

Conclusion

The "Big Money" in franchising generally ends up with the original franchisor and multiunit franchisees. The multiunit franchisee owns two or more business units or store. Approximately 86% of all franchised systems have multiunit owners. Learn the 10 basic house rules of the Multiunit Development Game. Enjoy the work and rewards of multiunit franchising.

> The "Big Money" in franchising generally ends up with the original franchisor and multiunit franchisees.

For more information on this topic, visit our Web site at www.businesstown.com

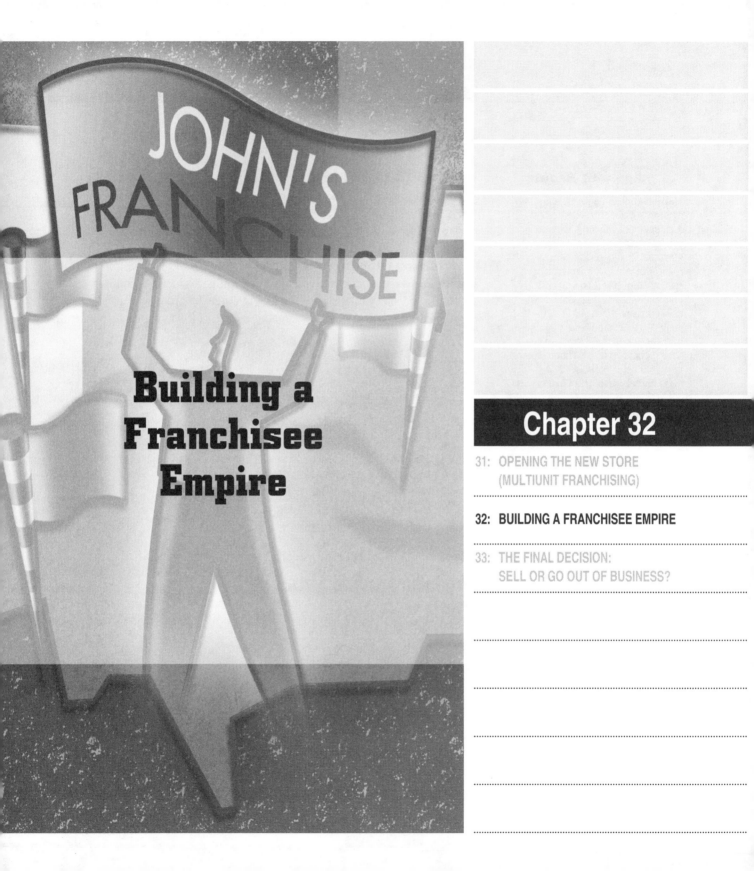

Building a Franchisee Empire

Chapter 32

31: OPENING THE NEW STORE
    (MULTIUNIT FRANCHISING)

32: BUILDING A FRANCHISEE EMPIRE

33: THE FINAL DECISION:
    SELL OR GO OUT OF BUSINESS?

To Build or not to Build?— That Is the Question

If your decision is to grow and expand, which is a great choice, then you need to recognize that you are entering a new and different world. In a way it is somewhat similar to realizing that, instead of just coaching one football team, now all of a sudden you are also coaching a team on the other side of the field. As you build, you begin to recognize that you are developing not just a second or third unit, but you are also developing a new business to run your existing stores. It is like becoming a coach for each team in the league.

If you are going to build, you need to recognize the cornerstones that would be the foundation for your building. These cornerstones generally include the following six areas:

1. Organization and structure
2. Financial
3. Marketing
4. Information systems
5. Managing external relationships
6. Managing improvements and change
7. Benchmark Performance

Organization and Structure

Two to Three Stores

There probably will not be a great change in your organization as you expand into the second or third store. Most franchisees, as they do this, will add an office manager/comptroller (controller) to help handle the administrative functions of the business. Many of the human resource activities are expanding and there is a need to handle these operations efficiently and effectively. The addition of an office manager/comptroller will help handle the payroll, keep the records, and administer to the operations of the business. As you expand into the second and third store, you will realize the need to hire managers for each of the independent stores. These managers should be responsible for the profit, growth, and development of each one of their own stores.

Four to Six Stores

At this point in time, an area or district manager needs to be promoted, hired, or developed to supervise the operations of the stores. Generally speaking, somewhere around the third or fourth store a supervisor needs to be hired to take care of the several different stores. It is no longer possible for the franchisee to adequately supervise and manage all the stores himself.

Seven to Nine Stores

At this time you need to hire a second area or district manager to supervise the different stores. Generally it is assumed that one supervisor can handle three to five stores. In addition, at this time there is a second individual that probably needs to be hired and that is the manager of training/marketing. It is important now for you to realize that you are going to have to spend time in training your supervisors as well as managers, assistant managers, and staff personnel. In addition to the training function, this individual can also work with the marketing and advertising programs that you will be utilizing in your several stores.

Some franchisors also provide cooperative advertising once you pass the five or six store level. They will pay up to half of the advertising expenses if you are going to provide regional advertising for the several stores.

KFC

KFC is part of Tricon Global Restaurants, Inc., which is the world's largest restaurant system with nearly 30,000 KFC, Taco Bell, and Pizza Hut restaurants in more than 100 countries and territories. KFC continues reaching out to customers with home delivery in more than 300 restaurants in the United States and several other countries. And in quite a few U.S. cities, KFC is teaming up with sister restaurants Taco Bell and Pizza Hut, selling products from the popular chains in one convenient location.

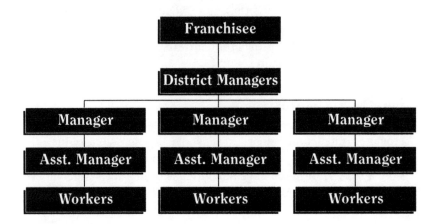

Ten to Twenty-One Stores

At this level you realize that you need to hire an operations chief or a chief operations officer. This person will oversee the supervision and management of all the stores that you have. This individual will work closely with the manager of training/marketing as well as the office manager/comptroller. The office manager/comptroller will also need to hire additional staff including a secretary/receptionist as well as a payroll manager to handle the different stores and staff needs.

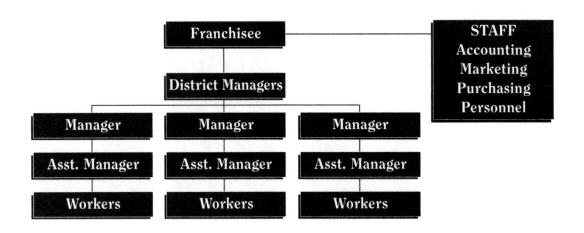

Franchisees have found it very successful to develop committees with their store managers. The two most common committees include operations and advertising/marketing. These committees created by volunteers from the managers can often look at how to best improve the operations of the several stores including training and policy procedures. In addition, they may also look at the advertising and marketing function the franchisee is using and provide possible suggestions for improvements.

More than Twenty-One Stores

At this level you are becoming a mini-franchisor. You now need to probably separate your manager of training/marketing into two separate managers. The new manager of marketing will oversee and supervise all the advertising and marketing that is done in the several stores and throughout the communities in which you operate your businesses. In addition, the trainer will now be responsible for training the district supervisors as well as the assistant managers and staff personnel. The vice president of operations or the chief operations officer will be responsible for all the operations and work directly with any committees or groups of managers. The office manager/comptroller will now probably need to hire district administrators to administer the information systems as well as financial and payroll of the different stores.

Managing the operation for growth is a very tricky business. You need to recognize as the coach of the team that you need specialists to handle various operations of your business. It is no longer possible for you to do everything. You need to be able to delegate both the responsibility, authority and accountability to your staff to help run the several units that you have operating.

Financial

One of the most important aspects of building a franchising empire is to develop a proper financial package. The financing is often a scorecard by which the game is scored. The proper financial packages need to be in place.

Dunkin' Donuts And Baskin-Robbins

One project you may wish to undertake is similar to a Dunkin' Donuts and Baskin-Robbins franchise. In certain cases they combine together because 70% of Dunkin' Donuts business occurs before noontime while 70% of Baskin-Robbins business occurs after 3:00 P.M. This allows your franchise system to work at its full potential for the day. You now have a strong flow of traffic throughout the entire day.

Combined now with Dunkin' Donuts and Baskin-Robbins is Togo's Great Sandwiches, which now provide the complete package for franchisees. Togo's Great Sandwiches provides a restaurant based upon a specific and distinctive family of specialty sandwiches and related food items. They currently have over 250 units in the United States.

Expand Your Marketing Programs

Sales and Marketing Strategy—You need to be able to identify the market segments in each store unit that you build. Each store location has its unique market segmentation. You need to understand that difference so that you can work with each store in reaching their target market. You also need to develop a pricing strategy. There may be a need for pricing variation between their stores. Generally this is not true, but if you are working in a mall your expenses may be higher and your prices may correspondingly be higher.

Develop Advertising Programs—Create your own advertising calendar. This is generally done a year in advance with the help of the franchisor. You will need to allocate out the resources from the several stores to a common advertising program.

Sell Products and Services—You need to continuously remember that you are involved in a sales game. You need to remind your employees of the importance of customer service and how it

(Continued on next page.)

Managing Financial Resources

We need to seek to develop your proper resources, including developing your sales budget, expense budget, personnel budget, marketing/advertising budget, and the overall cash flow budget for both the expanding "franchisee" business as well as the individual stores and units.

You need to identify the financial risk of investing in a second, third, fourth, and even fifth store. As you build out to the fifteenth or twentieth store, the financial backing often becomes easier and more people are willing to view your success and loan you money for added expansion.

Managing the Tax Function

You need to ensure that you have federal tax compliance. You need to work with your accountant to make sure that you have a compliance package established for tax reporting for each of your units as well as for "franchisee" business.

You also need to insure that you have state and local tax compliance and that you are involved in reporting all proper taxes on time. You need to investigate the sales tax, use tax, social security taxes, unemployment compensation taxes, and other fringe benefit taxes.

You also need to be able to work with and manage any tax controversies. However, if you have established your proper federal, state, and local tax compliance programs, then you should not run into any tax controversies.

Managing Customer Orders

Many businesses need to recognize the importance of handling all customer orders whether you are operating a restaurant or providing a bookkeeping service or rendering a plumbing service. You need to keep track of your customers and be able to fill their orders promptly and correctly. If at all possible, it is wise to collect customer information—names, addresses, and phone numbers—so that they can be contacted to see if they need further help or support.

Information Systems

Our business know-how is rapidly expanding. You need to be able to establish and manage information systems for your business. As you expand and build a large multiunit franchising program, you will recognize the importance for information systems. You will need to keep track of the sales and expenses of each individual store and be able to compare them to recognize the strengths and weaknesses of each store. You will also need to keep track of all of your employees and keep track of your expanding payroll commitments.

Managing Information Technology

You also need to be aware of managing the security of your information technology. Records you keep are private and confidential. You need to maintain that confidentiality.

Managing Information Resources

Once the equipment or hardware is in place, you need to be able to manage your records and documents. You need to be able to store your records and data warehouses and be able to retrieve your information in a timely and efficient manner. You need to be able to run comparisons between the different stores as well as sum up the total activity of all of your units. You need to be able to share certain data with each of your district managers and your headquarters' staff. You need to show your managers their strengths and weaknesses through managing your information resources.

Managing External Relationships

As you build your franchising empire, you need to recognize that the relationships you have with your franchisor as well as with your community will change. Your franchisor will see you as a greater resource and asset in building its business. Your community will look for you to have a greater part in community activity and in taking leadership roles.

Expand Your Marketing Programs, *(continued)*

impacts upon your sales. Customers return not just for the product but also for the friendly service. You need to sell to your customers through your cleanliness, your store displays, your customer service, posters, and even special store advertisements.

Add-ons— Smoothie King

Another new development is the add-on of a franchise business to an existing business. The Houston area World Gym Family Fitness Center owned by Dan and Sherry Granader established their Smoothie King franchises near two of their fitness centers and even one inside their gym. Sherry says that Smoothie King is a simple operation to add on to their existing business. Interestingly, it is not a hard sell. You finish your fitness workout and there is an inviting juice bar just across the gym. You watch as other customers down their thirst-quenching fruit smoothie. You know it is nutritious and you know it is also good for you. It is a good meal and fitness people know it. It is also a good situation because the people coming in for Smoothies can also glance into the glass-enclosed gym, which can result in a New World Gym membership for Dan and Sherry.

Communication with Headquarters

As you get bigger and bigger in your franchising program, you become of greater value to your franchisor. Your franchisor will often ask us to sit on franchising committees and help make suggestions to them for new products and services. You need to recognize that you have a commitment to your franchisor to support them and also to improve not just your own stores but also to help improve the entire system.

Communication with Employees

You need to recognize the importance of communicating with each one of your employees and making them feel that they are an integral part of your franchising family. You will need to spend time with each one of your managers on a monthly basis to ensure that they understand the visions, mission, and goals of their store as well as of the entire system. You need to work with them to help them overcome their weaknesses and further develop their strengths.

You also need to go out and work with your employees in each of the several different stores. If possible, you need to visit and work with each store at least once a month and, if not possible, at least once every two months. This does not have to be for a long period of time, but it does have to be during a time when you can show your interest and excitement in the store and work with customers as well as the employees. The employees will catch your enthusiasm and your desire for excellence.

Communication with Customers

Certain chief executives of major U.S. corporations have a rule to spend at least 20 to 30% of their time just in talking to customers. They want to know how their products or services can best serve the customer. One of the few ways that you will ever be able to find out about any problems with your product or service is by asking your customers. Customers will sense your honest concern and provide you with positive and constructive criticisms. You need to look at everything they say and try to implement positive suggestions that will improve your business.

Managing Improvements and Change

You are growing. You need to realize that as you grow you are going to run into a need for change as well as improvement. We live in a constant state of change. We all need to recognize that.

Measure organizational performance. You need to create measuring systems that will allow you to measure the performance of your stores, managers, and individual staff members. You need to further develop measuring devices to measure your product and service quality. You need to be able to measure your costs as well as the costs of your productivity. These measurement devices will help you to envision your business and manage for improvement.

Benchmark Performance

One of the things that happens as you expand is that you develop benchmark performances. You assume that a new store will reach or exceed the sales level of a previous store. You assume that a store manager will reach or exceed the performance of an existing store manager. You need to create benchmarking capabilities for your stores, managers, and staff members. Many of these benchmarking measurements will come from the evaluation form of the franchisor for your store. These may be envisioned as benchmark situations. However you need to expand them so that you can measure the strength of your businesses and be able to compare them one against another.

Develop "best practices." You need to create a commitment for improvement. As you do this, you need to develop best practices for each task in your store. This may be a best practice for cleaning the parking area or a best practice for greeting the customer. You need to establish best practices throughout your stores and your "franchisee" business.

Mobil's Speedpass

Mobil Corporation has introduced a speedpass, which introduces technology to their stores. They use a radio frequency based technology where a miniature electronic transponder is attached to the customer's key chain or the vehicle's rear window. This transponder transmits a unique secure ID number and allows the customer quick access to gas and food charges, which previously required money, check, or credit card. The speedpass service is offered free to the customers and Mobil has received over two million customers in the first year and a half of operation.

Yogen Frez Cobranding Opportunity

Yogen Frez started franchising in 1987 and today ranks as the largest franchise business of frozen desserts, yogurt, and ice cream with over 4,800 stores scattered throughout the world. They have recently acquired the Canadian franchise Paradise Juice Bar, the American I Can't Believe It's Yogurt (ICBY), and Bresler's Ice Cream and Frozen Yogurt to develop a tremendously strong international frozen fare market. This gives each of their franchisees exclusive rights to several well-known frozen dessert brands including Tropicana, Betty Crocker, and Yoplait. Their goal is to make their franchisees successful. They also believe that because of their complementary products, the compact space required for their programs can easily be inserted into convenience stores, hospitals, universities, gas stations, and other retail outlets, resulting in positive sales for many different franchising organizations. They are seeking co-branding opportunities.

Conclusion

To build or not to build is the question. You need to look at your own personal desire and make a decision if you wish to expand your current business opportunities. You need to be able to determine who is going to be doing what, when, where, how, and why. To do this, it is best if you establish the organizational principles that will allow you to expand smoothly and efficiently; the financial knowledge that will allow you to expand properly and within reason; the marketing strategy that will allow you to improve your markets and reach greater customer share; the information systems that will allow you to collect data and store it for proper use and comparisons; manage the external relationships including headquarters, staff and customers; and finally, managing for improvements and change including looking at benchmarking, measurement performance systems, and developing best practices for your business operations.

To build or not to build. Now you know how, and you can decide.

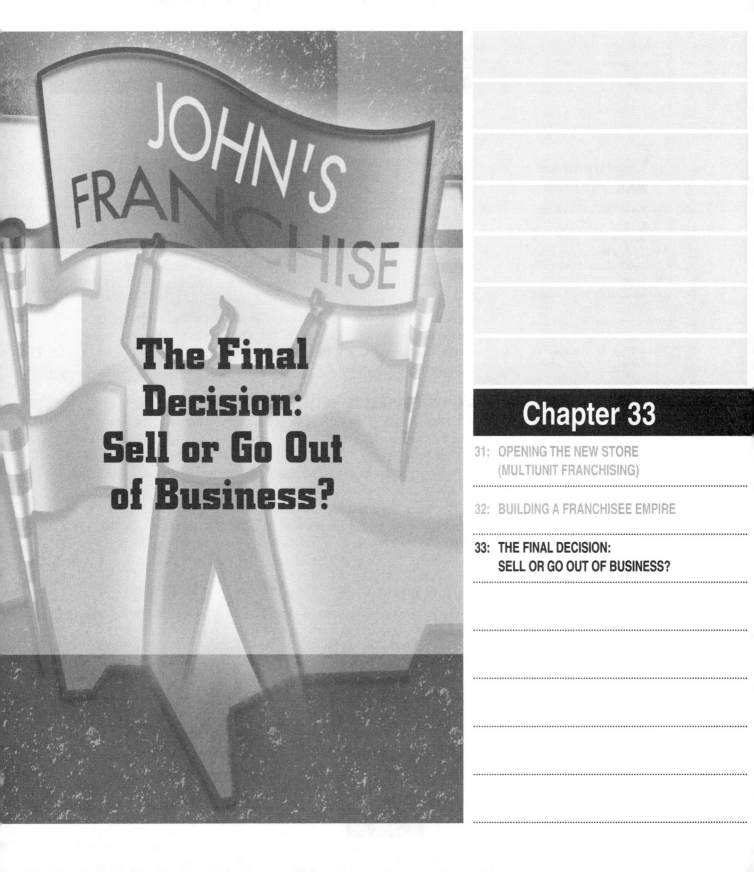

The Final Decision: Sell or Go Out of Business?

Chapter 33

31: OPENING THE NEW STORE
(MULTIUNIT FRANCHISING)

32: BUILDING A FRANCHISEE EMPIRE

**33: THE FINAL DECISION:
SELL OR GO OUT OF BUSINESS?**

Introduction

There will come a time when you will think about selling your franchised business. There are many reasons for this. You might decide to sell due to your advancing age, health reasons, or you want to retire and travel. Other reasons you might want to sell include that you are bored, tired, no longer excited about the business, or you want to do something different. Still other reasons you might want to sell have nothing to do with you personally. These reasons could include: that you are having problems with the franchisor, that you are dissatisfied with the franchisor, that competition is too stiff, or that the industry is in decline. Finally, you might want to sell due to financial considerations. If you are not making enough money to support you and your family, then it is time to move on.

Should you Hire a Business Broker?

First things first. How will you go about selling your franchise? Will you sell the franchise yourself or will you hire someone to help you sell your franchise?

If you decide to sell your franchised business by yourself, it will require a lot of work on your part. Also, it will require you to have knowledge in several areas such as taxation and legal issues, in which you may have very limited knowledge. If possible, it would be to your benefit to hire a professional to sell your franchise. Such a professional is known as a business broker.

Advantages

There are several benefits to hiring a business broker. First, the broker can say things to a prospective buyer that you cannot. For example, the broker can point out all the wonderful features of your franchise and why the prospective buyer should buy it. However, if you make the same comments to the prospective buyer, he will probably not believe you. After all, this is your business and all business owners will point out the positive features and extol the virtues of their business. Therefore, when a third party makes certain statements about your business, he or she is much more believable.

Second, the business broker, since he does not own your company, will be able to emotionally detach himself from the sell. The vast majority of business owners are personally and emotionally involved in their business. Therefore, the sale of their business is a very personal and emotional event. But the business broker will not allow personal emotions and emotional attachments to cloud his thinking. The broker will be better able to answer those questions that you would find difficult to answer, or even insulting.

Third, the business broker can do a full and comprehensive investigation of the prospective buyer. The business broker will know what to look for in qualifying the prospective buyer. You, however, do not have that experience and would be prone to accepting an unqualified buyer. The business broker effectively screens prospective buyers, and, after qualifying them, irons out all the details. A good business broker works with a qualified attorney and CPA in order to structure the sale so that it is of maximum benefit to you. Further, the broker will be able to make sure that all legal documents have been properly drawn up and, at closing, executed.

In reality, a good broker will more than make up for the commission you pay her. She will be able to get a higher sales price for your franchise and promote a smooth process in the sale of your business. Also, she will make sure that all the t's are crossed and the i's are dotted.

As a final note, you need to make sure that you get an agreement in writing with your broker. All of the terms and conditions that you and the broker have discussed must be set forth clearly in a written agreement that you both sign. You must make certain of what it is that you are expecting the broker to do. You do not want to have any misunderstandings or ambiguities with your broker. This will only negatively effect the relationship between you and your broker and the sale of your business.

Finding a Good Business Broker

There are many places to look for business brokers. The most common places are in your local newspaper under the advertisement section and in the yellow pages of your telephone book. No matter whom you select for a business broker, you must make sure that he specializes in the buying and selling of franchises. You must make sure that he understands those items that are unique to the franchise industry. Therefore, when you interview a prospective broker you must delve deeply into the types of transactions he handles. You need to determine if he has handled a significant number of franchise transactions. If a broker does not have significant experience in the handling of the buying and selling of franchises, you need to move on.

Pricing your Business

Usually the single most important aspect of the sale of your business is the selling price. A buyer will be interested in what your profitability has been to date and what the potential profitability could be. If you have retained the services of a business broker, your broker should be the one to perform a comprehensive evaluation as part of her fee. The business broker has substantial experience in determining the value of a business and hence the selling price of that business. However, if you have not hired a business broker, you should hire a CPA that specializes in business valuations and appraisals. It could be a mistake for you to name your own selling price. Why? On the one hand, the sales price you arrive at could be too low. As a result, you may not benefit fully from your hard labor, blood, sweat, and tears. On the other hand, if you price your business too high then you run the risk of turning potentially qualified buyers away. Therefore, it is very, very important to have an expert, whether a business broker or CPA, to do your business valuation and set an appropriate sales price.

Valuation Methods

There are several valuation methods that can be used in determining your selling price. A commonly used valuation method is referred to as the going concern value. A purchase price is derived from the historical earnings of the business and the return on investment that the buyer can expect to receive. There are three ways to calculate the going concern value. One way is to value your franchise based upon comparable transactions. This information is often found by asking the franchisor. A second way to calculate going concern value is through the comparable market approach. This approach is based upon financial ratios as an indicator of the market value of companies that are publicly traded in your line of business. Finally, a third way to calculate under this method is referred to as the discounted earnings approach. Under this approach, the professional will look to the present value of your franchise and anticipate earnings in the future, adjusting for risks that are associated with your franchise.

A second valuation method is referred to as the liquidation value. This valuation method determines the sales price of a franchise based upon what the value of the franchise would be if it were to be dissolved and its assets sold. Obviously, this type of valuation method

> It is very, very important to have an expert, whether a business broker or CPA, to do your business valuation and set an appropriate sales price.

is not suitable for most franchises since they are in service sectors. Franchises in service industries have a lower dollar value of assets than a business such as a manufacturer. Also, since many franchises are business format franchises, this method would greatly underestimate the value of your franchise.

A third way to price your business is referred to as price building. This method first establishes a dollar value for your tangible assets. These tangible assets include such items as real estate, leasehold improvements, equipment, furnishings, fixtures, inventory, and supplies. Then a value is determined for the intangible assets of your franchise such as goodwill, trade names, lease values, patent rights, and so on. Then these two numbers are added to come up with a selling price for your franchise.

A fourth valuation method is referred to as return on investment, or ROI for short. With this method you would first determine the net profit of the business. The net profit is the number you end up with after all expenses have been deducted from income including debt discharge and owner's salaries. Then you divide the asking sales price of the business into the net profit. The resulting number will be a percentage that will tell you what the ROI will be for your business. To strengthen your ROI, you can determine the business net profit by projecting what it will be in the future as opposed to using only current figures. All businesses expect increases in the future in their net profit. A qualified professional has the expertise to determine ROI and thereby highlight the strengths of your franchise.

> A fourth valuation method is referred to as return on investment, or ROI for short.

There are many ways to value a business. There is no correct or wrong way. However, a qualified professional, such as a business broker or CPA, can determine which method is best to value your business to give it the highest possible selling price. After all, these professionals do business valuations for a living

Financial Considerations

There are several financial considerations that must be examined in structuring the transaction. The first consideration is if the sale is strictly an asset sale or a stock sale. An asset sale means that all the buyer is purchasing is your assets, such as goodwill. If it is a stock sale, then the buyer is purchasing all of your stock in the legal entity you set up to run, own, and operate your franchise. There are specific tax consequences of each type of sale that must be addressed by your CPA or tax attorney. Further, you need a qualified professional to allocate the purchase price among the various components of the sale to minimize the amount of taxes you will pay. After all, it is not what your selling price is, but how much of that selling price you get to keep. Therefore, tax considerations are of paramount importance in negotiating the sale of your franchise.

How the Purchase Price Is Paid

Most sellers want to receive the entire sales price when they transfer their franchise to the buyer. If your entire purchase price is paid at the closing of the transaction be sure to allocate the purchase price so as to minimize your tax consequences. However, most sales of businesses are not paid for in cash. Often, the seller is asked to take back owner financing. In some situations, the selling franchisee will prefer to take back owner financing so that he can spread over a period of time the money he will receive. However, when the issue of owner financing comes up there are several issues that must be addressed.

First and foremost, the financial condition of the buyer must be explored in detail. You will want to take back collateral to guarantee that you will receive the money due you. When you accept carryback financing you will want to make absolutely certain that the risk you assume is collateralized. It is common to allow the financing to be for a period of from three to five years. It is preferable not to allow the buyer to pay you back for a period longer than five years. Even though your franchise was a success when you owned it there is no guarantee that your franchise will continue to be a success once it changes hands. The fact that the buyer wants you to take back owner financing subjects the franchise to higher expenses (due to the interest expense) and therefore increases the risk of failure.

If you do take back owner financing, you will want to make sure that you receive a cash down payment that is at least equal to the cost

> Most sellers want to receive the entire sales price when they transfer their franchise to the buyer.

of your inventory and supplies. Then you will have the buyer sign a note that you will file at the local courthouse to act as a lien against the assets of the buyer to ensure that you are paid. However, your franchise agreement may impose substantial limitations on your ability to take a lien or security interest in the assets of the franchise. If the buyer has no other assets that you can take a lien against, then your risk will be multiplied manyfold. All lenders want collateral. All lenders want to be able to have a security interest in sufficient assets to guarantee payment of the amount loaned in one form or another.

Therefore, if the buyer is unable to meet the monthly payments as required by your agreement, then at least you can fall back on her assets you took a security interest in for payment. If you do this you will be allowed to sell those assets so that you will be paid in full. You must determine whether your franchisor will allow you to take a security interest in the franchise assets either as a first-in-line position or at least a second-in-position with only the franchisor having first rights to the assets.

Employment Agreements

Often, the sale price of your franchise will be affected by employment agreements. Employment agreements are those agreements you have in which you agree to give an employee a specific term of employment with specific remuneration. Most franchises do not have any employees laboring under employment agreements. However, if you do have employment agreements with any employees, this issue must be discussed with the prospective buyer. Normally, the prospective buyer will be required to assume the employment agreements and honor their terms. Depending upon the terms of the employment agreements, it may affect the final sales price of your franchise.

Lease Agreements

With most franchises you will have lease agreements whose terms and conditions you have personally guaranteed. It is possible for you to have lease agreements covering land, buildings, equipment, and signage. The buyer must be able to take over these lease agreements. Further, he will need a satisfactory long-term lease

> You must determine whether your franchisor will allow you to take a security interest in the franchise assets either as a first-in-line position or at least a second-in-position with only the franchisor having first rights to the assets.

agreement to make the purchase of your franchise worthwhile. You and the buyer must scrutinize all of your lease agreements to determine if he can assume them. Next, you will need to determine the remaining lease term plus renewals of each lease agreement. The closer the remaining lease terms are with the remaining term of the franchise agreement the better.

Finally, you will want to determine if you can be released from the terms and conditions of each lease agreement once the buyer takes over. You want to be able to walk away after the sale and no longer be on the hook to the landlord. In other words, you want to be able to eliminate all of your liability, financial and otherwise, under the lease agreements.

> You will want to determine if you can be released from the terms and conditions of each lease agreement once the buyer takes over.

Your Obligations as the Selling Franchisee

As the seller, you have certain obligations. Since you are selling a franchise some of these obligations will be unique.

Qualifying the Buyer

Before you can seriously entertain the offer of a buyer you must determine if the buyer has the necessary qualifications to purchase your business. For example, does the buyer have sufficient managerial expertise and experience in operating such a business to make it a success? Additionally, does the buyer have sufficient financial resources to buy the business? Does the buyer have sufficient working capital to operate the business?.

However, since you are selling a franchise, the franchisor must also determine if the buyer is qualified. Most franchisors will not allow you to sell your franchise if the buyer is not qualified. The franchisor will require the prospective buyer to meet their then-current requirements for a new franchisee. For example, the franchisor will determine if the buyer has sufficient financial resources in order to operate the franchised business. Also, the franchisor will determine if the buyer has sufficient skills, qualifications, and the necessary managerial and educational experience. Additionally, the franchisor will require the buyer to successfully complete its training programs.

As a rule, the buyer will be required to sign a new franchise agreement. By signing the then-current franchise agreement the terms and conditions of the franchise could be different from what the seller has to abide by. There are occasions when the buyer will only have to assume, in writing, the franchise agreement and other agreements under which the seller is operating. However, most franchisors would require the buyer to sign their then-current form of franchise agreement and other agreements. Additionally, the buyer will more than likely be expected to pay a transfer fee to the franchisor to cover the franchisor's cost incurred in qualifying the buyer and preparing the necessary paperwork.

Governmental Matters

As the seller, you should be prepared to furnish copies of all filings, correspondence, reports, and so on, relating to any federal, state, or local regulatory agencies. These agencies could include, but are not limited to, the Environmental Protection Agency, Department of Labor, and the Equal Employment Opportunity Commission. Additionally you should be able to supply copies of your business license and all other licenses and permits required of you to be open for business.

Entity Documents

If you operate your business as a sole proprietorship then you will have no entity or corporate documents to provide to the buyer. The same holds true if you own the franchise with your spouse and operate as a general partnership. However, the overwhelming majority of franchisees operate their franchise as a corporation, limited partnership, or limited liability company.

If you operate your business as a corporation, limited partnership, or limited liability company, you need to be able to provide the buyer with your complete set of corporate records. The buyer will need these records to determine if all relevant business organization information is there. There are instances when a business owner will

Make Sure All Obligations Are Met

At the time of the transfer, the seller will be expected to be in full compliance with his franchise agreement and related agreements. The potential sale could be held up if the seller is not in full compliance. Further, many franchise agreements provide that the selling franchisee is liable to the franchisor in the event of a breach by the buyer of the terms of the franchise agreement that he signs. Therefore, you could be on the hook in case of a breach by the buyer for a long period of time after the buyer has purchased your franchise.

set up a corporation but fail to do all of the required legal paper-work. As a result, the business owner is operating as a sole propri-etor and not as a corporation. Since the corporation has not been properly set up, the corporation does not exist. As a result the corpo-ration has nothing to sell and any agreement with the corporation could very well be invalid. Therefore, the seller must be able to prove to the buyer's satisfaction that her corporation, limited liability com-pany, or limited partnership has been properly and completely set up and operating. Only then can the buyer determine if he or she is dealing with the proper individual or entity.

For example, if you operate as a corporation, you will need to present the buyer with your articles of incorporation, bylaws, min-utes of shareholders' and board of directors' meetings, stock ledgers, and any other corporate documents. Also, you will be required to obtain proof from the Secretary of State's office that your corpora-tion is in good standing. For a limited liability company and limited partnership you will supply the buyer with equivalent type docu-ments. Last, but not least, the buyer will want proof that the appro-priate shareholder and director actions have been taken approving the sell of the franchise.

Once the true owner of the franchise business has been deter-mined, the buyer will want to enter into a purchase and sell agree-ment. This agreement will set forth the sales price and the other details of the transaction between the seller and the buyer. Also, this agreement will need to be supplied to the franchisor for his review. The franchisor has a vested interest in the selling price of your fran-chise. If you sell your franchise for far more money than it is worth, causing the buyer to take on too much debt, then the likelihood the buyer will fail increases dramatically. Therefore, the franchisor will want to determine the fairness of the purchase and sell agreement between the parties.

Financial Statements

The seller will be required to provide to the buyer financial statements showing the profitability of his business. Regardless of what type of business entity you operate under, you will need to pro-vide the buyer with the following: income statements, balance sheets,

> The seller must be able to prove to the buyer's satisfaction that her corporation, limited liability company, or limited partnership has been properly and completely set up and operating.

cash flow statements, the previous three years business tax returns, and so on. The buyer requires these documents in order to do a comprehensive financial analysis of your business. As a result, you need to have your financial statements current and in order. You need to make sure that your financial statements do not reflect any personal items or expenses that do not pertain to the business.

Lease Agreements

You will be required to supply to the buyer all leases that you are a party to. You will provide any real estate leases, equipment leases, signage leases, and so forth. The importance of these leases to the buyer cannot be underestimated. The buyer will need to determine if she can live with the terms and conditions of the lease agreements you have signed. Further, she will need to determine whether she can assume the leases. Finally, she will need to determine if the leases are for a long enough period to make the purchasing of your business profitable.

Personnel Matters

The buyer will want to review your employee handbook and personnel files. The buyer will want to get a complete picture of the terms and conditions of each employee's employment. The buyer will want to know if you have entered into any employee agreements with any employee. And, if so, what the terms and conditions are of these employee agreements. The buyer will want to see what is contained in your employee handbook if you have one. The buyer will want to see what information you have set forth in your employee handbook and how it has been enforced. Last, but not least, the buyer will want to determine if you are currently in compliance with state and federal employment laws.

Obligations to Disclose Under Federal and State Law

It is unclear when the franchisee sells his franchise if the franchisor is required to give the buyer a current UFOC. If the franchisee sells the franchise without any assistance whatsoever from the franchisor, then chances are the franchisor is not subject to the disclosure requirements of the Federal Trade Commission Rule or State

> The importance of these leases to the buyer cannot be underestimated. The buyer will need to determine if she can live with the terms and conditions of the lease agreements you have signed.

Other Considerations

Often, your franchise agreement will require you to sign a general release upon the sale of your franchise that releases the franchisor from any and all claims, liability, or obligations to you that arose prior to the sale. Therefore, when you sign a general release, you are no longer able to sue the franchisor for any causes of action.

Your agreement may also give the franchisor a right of first refusal. This right of first refusal allows the franchisor to purchase your franchise rather than consent to your selling it to a third party. Most franchise agreements provide that if the franchisor elects to buy, it must offer you the same terms that your buyer is offering.

Additionally, both the franchisor and your buyer will more than likely have you sign a covenant not to compete. A covenant not to compete dictates that you or your spouse will not be able to open a similar business or the same business in or around the location where your current franchise is located for a certain period of time.

Laws. However, if the sale occurs by or through the efforts of the franchisor, then the buyer is required to receive the current UFOC. The definition of "by or through the franchisor" is not clear. It is possible that something as simple as having the buyer sign the franchisor's current franchise agreement could subject the franchisor to all federal and state disclosure requirements. Therefore, the seller should make sure that the franchisor provides the buyer with a current UFOC. It always pays to err on the side of caution.

In addition to receiving the current UFOC, the buyer will probably want to review the one you received at the time of your franchise purchase. Hopefully, you have kept your copy of the UFOC so that you can offer it to the buyer. The buyer can glean important information by comparing the franchisor's condition at the time you purchased the franchise to the current condition of the franchisor. If the franchise system has declined or has been adversely impacted then this will affect your selling price.

Conclusion

The decision to sell has been made. Now, subject to restrictions found in your franchise agreement, the sell is up to you. The franchisor will probably take an active role since the sale is in its best interest as well. The franchisor might even run ads and assist you in finding a buyer. The franchisor has a strong interest in finding a qualified buyer to maintain the integrity of your franchised business. When you find a buyer you must qualify her. Not only will the buyer investigate you and the franchise thoroughly, you will want to do likewise with the buyer.

Appendix A:
Investigating Franchise Opportunities

How Do I Get Good Information?

Your investigation should begin with the industry in which you want to buy a franchise. To investigate the industry, you should first check out the following organizations or publications:

- US Department of Commerce
- Bureau of Census
- Standard & Poor's reports
- Frost and Sullivan's Predicast Indexes
- *Wall Street Journal*
- *Business Week*
- *Forbes*

While reviewing this information you will be able to determine whether the future of the industry is bright or dim. There are several questions you should ask yourself when doing your research. Such questions include the following: Has the industry filled its current market? Is the need for products or services more than amply filled by current companies? Are the companies in the industry experiencing growth or losses? Has there been any company failures within the industry recently? Are business analysts predicting that the industry is in a slump? Has there been reports of abuses in the industry causing federal and state governments to investigate?

Next, your research should take you to general sources of information. Now that you have investigated the industry you want to buy a franchise in, you need to review information concerning the franchise industry in general. There are several sources of information available such as trade organizations, publications, magazines, and newspapers. These sources are as follows:

1. **The International Franchise Association.** The IFA serves as a resource to both franchisors and franchisees as well as to the government and the media. The IFA publishes a lot of material on buying and operating franchises. (202) 628-8000.

2. **IFA Expos.** The International Franchise Association sponsors a number of Expos throughout the United States every year. The Expos bring franchisors and their representatives from around the country face-to-face with prospective franchisees. The Expos are an excellent way to gather information and talk to people active in the industry.

3. **The American Association of Franchisees and Dealers.** This nonprofit trade association was founded in 1992. It represents the interests of franchisees and independent dealers throughout the United States. It has also developed a network from which you can obtain legal advice, financial management assistance, and general advice. (800) 733-9858.

4. **The American Franchisee Association.** This nonprofit trade association offers publications and consultations on the franchise industry. (800) 334-4232.

5. **The Franchise Handbook.** This is a magazine-format publication published quarterly. It contains articles on industry-related topics with profiles of successful franchises and franchisees. (414) 272-9977.

6. **FRANDATA.** This for-profit organization is a research and consulting group that maintains files of the UFOCs of most franchise companies. (202) 659-8640.

7. **Newspapers and magazines.** The following newspapers and magazines contain articles, on a regular basis, that provide valuable information on franchising: *National Business Employment Weekly, The Wall Street Journal, USA Today, The New York Times, Black Enterprise, Entrepreneur, INC., Nation's Business, Success, Working Woman,* and *Successful Franchising.*

8. **The Franchise Opportunities Guide.** This publication contains an extensive listing of franchisors operating in the United States with capsule descriptions of the franchised business, required initial investments, related fees, etc. (800) 543-1038.

9. **Franchise Update Publications.** This publisher publishes a variety of franchise guides. (408) 997-7796.

10. **Bond's Franchise Guide.** This annual publication is published by Robert Bond. There are detailed profiles of franchisors. (800) 841-0873.

11. **The Franchise Annual.** This annual provides brief descriptions of each franchisor including investment and fee information. (716) 754-4669.
12. *Franchise Times.* This magazine is devoted exclusively to franchising. (651) 631-4995.
13. **S.E.C. filings.** For those franchise companies that are publicly traded, you can obtain their quarterly and annual reports from the Securities Exchange Commission.

The Uniform Franchise Offering Circular (UFOC)

You begin your research by thoroughly reviewing the UFOC for that particular franchise. The UFOC is covered more extensively in Chapters 3 and 4. Once you have completed your review of the UFOC your next step will be to contact franchisees listed in Item 20 of the UFOC.

In Item 20, the franchisor is required to list, with addresses and phone numbers, people who are current franchisees and those who are no longer a franchisee. This listing will contain the names of those who left the system over the previous twelve months. These ex-franchisees could have been terminated or their franchise agreements not renewed or their franchise agreement expired or they transferred their franchise to a new franchisee.

A large number of terminated, canceled, or nonrenewed franchisees may indicate problems. You should develop a representative survey of current and former franchisees to contact. The following are some of the questions you should ask:

1. What are the advantages and disadvantages of owning this franchise?
2. What were your actual financial needs for start-up costs and working capital?
3. Were there any hidden or unexpected costs?
4. Would you buy this franchise again if you had it to do over?
5. Has the franchisor met his obligations and responsibilities to your satisfaction? If not, why not?
6. Why did you leave the system?

7. What are your plans for purchasing the rights to open additional units?
8. Are you making a profit? Is it what you expected?
9. How long did it take you to become profitable?
10. Would you recommend to another to buy a franchise in this system?
11. Overall, are you satisfied or dissatisfied?

You determine which franchisees to contact. Do not allow the franchisor to tell you which franchisees to contact.

After reviewing the UFOC and contacting current and former franchisees, it is now time to contact franchisee associations. Most franchise systems have either a franchise advisory council or an independent franchisee association. Some franchise systems have both. You can gather important information concerning franchisee relations and current issues of concern by talking with representatives of these associations.

If possible, you should obtain a copy of the franchisor's operations manuals and training manuals. The manuals will reveal the comprehensiveness of the franchisor's treatment of operational issues and of the training program.

You should also review the franchisor's promotional materials to glean additional information.

Finally, there are trade associations from which you can gather information. There are trade associations on the local, state, and national level that lobby for the common interests in legislative and regulatory matters for specific industries and business segments. By speaking with representatives of trade associations, you can ascertain those areas of concern to the industry in which the franchise is in that you are investigating.

Web Sites

A final source of information is specific Web sites. See Appendix B, "Top 50 Web Sites for Franchising Information," for a listing.

Questions To Ask Other Franchisees
Questions Concerning the Industry

1. Is the industry growing? If so, by how much each year? If the industry is not growing, is it in decline or is it stagnant?
2. How common is franchising in the industry?
3. Who does better in this industry–independent businesses or franchises?
4. What are the keys to success in this industry?
5. How competitive is the industry?
6. What market forces affect the health of the industry?

Questions Directed to the Franchisor

1. How many franchises were sold in the past 12 months? In the past 24 months? How many franchises do you plan to sell over the next 12 months?
2. Do you have a plan for your expansion or do you randomly sell franchises?
3. Over the last 12 months how many franchises have failed?
4. How many franchises have failed over the last three years?
5. Why did they fail? Where were they located? Urban areas? Rural areas? Big cities? Little towns?
6. Do you have a marketing plan? If so, is it local, regional, or national?
7. Can the marketing plan be changed quickly to respond to emerging trends?
8. How many new products and services do you plan to offer in the next 12 months? In the next 24 months? What are they?
9. Why are you coming out with new products and services? Is it due to stiff competition? Has the market changed? Are sales of your system down?
10. What are your long-term business goals?

Questions for Current Franchisees

1. Has the franchisor ever made promises he did not keep? Why?
2. How quickly does the franchisor respond to your needs and requests for assistance?
3. How stable is the franchisor's management?
4. What did you do for employment prior to purchasing your franchise?
5. Are you making as much money as you did in your previous employment?
6. When was the last time you took a vacation that lasted more than three days?
7. How long did it take for your franchise to break even?
8. What are your likes and dislikes about the franchisor?
9. How much capital did you set aside for living expenses until you were able to pay yourself from the franchise? Was it enough?
10. Are your profits high enough to support you and your family and to continue operating your franchise? Are you able to put back money for your retirement? Are you able to put back money for a rainy day?
11. Is the franchisor confident?
12. What other franchisees do you recommend I talk to?

These questions are only a sample of what you might decide to ask. You cannot gather too much information. After all, you are about to make the largest investment of your life.

How to Find a Qualified Attorney and Accountant

Now is not the time to go without legal assistance. UFOCs and franchise agreements are lengthy and complex documents. There is much legalese contained within these documents. It is extremely important that you hire an experienced franchise attorney to work with you from this point on. There are several areas where the franchise attorney can be indispensable.

How do you go about finding a qualified franchise attorney? You need to ask how long he or she has been in the practice of law. Then, you need to ask if he or she has practiced in the area of franchise law. If the answer is no, you need to move on. If the answer is yes, there are several other questions you need to ask. You need to determine how many franchisees or franchisors he or she has worked with and how many years he or she has been practicing franchise law. You need to ask what types of specialized courses and seminars he or she has attended over the last five years in the area of franchise law. Also, you need to determine if he or she is a member of the American Bar Association's Forum on Franchising. If the person is a member, find out what level of participation he or she has had with the organization.

Whatever you do, do not forego legal assistance. With the amount of money you will have at stake, this would be foolish.

Next, you will need to select an accountant. Your accountant will assist you in the preparation of budgets, cash flow statements, business projections, balance sheets, and profit and loss statements. The accountant will help you determine start-up costs, inventory control procedures, and which business structure is best for your operation. Whereas the attorney takes care of the legal side of your business, your accountant will take care of the financial side of your business.

When you choose your accountant you should choose a Certified Public Accountant. If your accountant is a Certified Public Accountant he has earned this title by undergoing extensive training and passing rigorous exams. Therefore, CPAs have much more in the way of qualifications to do your work. Also, it would be wise to find a CPA who is working with other franchisees. Certain items in the accounting arena are treated differently for a franchise business as opposed to an independent business.

You should not proceed without a qualified franchise attorney and accountant. Both of these people should be valuable members of your team. They can provide invaluable input into the decisions you make that will have a profound impact on your future.

The Seven Steps for Franchise Protection

Buying a franchise presents a risk. Some franchises will present a greater risk than others. If you leave a good job to purchase and operate a franchise, you will have a lot to loose. After all, there is always a chance that the franchise will not succeed. Therefore, you should follow the following seven steps for franchise protection:

1. Protect yourself by self-evaluation.
2. Protect yourself by investigating the franchise.
3. Protect yourself by studying the disclosure documents.
4. Protect yourself by checking out the disclosure.
5. Protect yourself by questioning earnings claims.
6. Protect yourself by obtaining professional advice.
7. Protect yourself by knowing your legal rights.

Source: U.S. Department of Commerce, *Franchise Opportunities Handbook*, 1984, pp. xxxii.

Appendix B:
Top 50 Web Sites for Franchising Information

1. *www.franchise.org*
The International Franchise Association is a membership organization of franchisors, franchisees, and suppliers. It is a one-stop shopping experience for franchise information.

2. *www.entrepreneurmag.com/franchise*
Entrepreneur Magazine's Franchise Channel: Comprehensive databases on franchises are available here.

3. *www.franchisetimes.com*
Franchise Times Magazine on the Web. A wealth of information about franchising and links to many franchise issues.

4. *www.Toolkit.cch.com*
This site offers tips on starting and planning your own business, financing, marketing, and managing your business finances. It also provides advice on dealing with the people who work for you, controlling your taxes, and building your personal wealth. Great templates for starting your business.

5. *www.microsoft.com/smallbiz*
This Web site provides many small business and franchise opportunities through their franchise development center.

6. *www.betheboss.com*
This site is focused on the opportunities available to someone interested in franchising. It will also assist you in navigating through showcases of franchisers, directories of worldwide opportunities, getting started and searching for the right franchise.

7. *www.bison1.com*
This Web site provides a place for franchisors and franchisees to buy, sell, and research potential businesses. This site also contains one of the largest databases of franchise information.

8. *www.Worldfranchising.com*
This site features a comprehensive franchise directory listing over 1,150 franchises, with profiles for each. It's an interactive online guide to franchising opportunities and resources.

9. *www.startup.wsj.com*
This is brought to you by the *Wall Street Journal*. It features links to franchisors' Web sites, franchisors

of the week, entrepreneurial help, and franchise guidance.

10. *www.franchise-update.com*
Franchise UPDATE On-Line is recognized worldwide for its coverage of franchise trade, management, and investment activity.

11. *www.ffca.com*
Franchise Financing Corporation is in the business of financing a new franchisee's business. The Web site also has information and research in the different franchise industries.

12. *www.franchise1.com*
A guide to starting and running a franchise. This site has a directory of franchise opportunities and provides you with the latest news about the franchise industry. You also have the ability to communicate with others via the message board and you can also find information on how to advertise.

13. *www.Franchiselinks.com*
This site contains hundreds of links to franchises that you can start. They are broken down into categories, and some of them are ranked by their rate of growth.

14. *www.franchiseconnections.com*
Topics include how to form a franchise system, buy a franchise, find franchise opportunities, comply with franchise laws, and find franchise resources. Links to lists of names, addresses, and telephone numbers of major franchise systems and sources of additional franchise information and assistance.

15. *www.sba.gov*
This Web site is the Small Business Administration's Web site and contains a large amount of information about small businesses, franchising, and government support.

16. *www.franchise.com*
This Web site provides franchising opportunities services and can match a franchise to an individual's budget.

17. *www.franchiseshowcase.com*
The entrepreneur's directory for franchise business opportunities. It profiles several franchises and allows you to request information from the

franchisors. This site includes a franchise profile, service suppliers, factsheet, and you can list your franchise on the FSO. Basically, you are advertising that your business has franchise capabilities

18. *www.frannet.com*
Information on purchasing franchises and of how to develop franchise ideas.

19. *www.inreach.com/sbdc/book/franchising.html*
"How to Start a Business: Franchising" is an excellent source for answering any questions related to franchising. It provides an alphabetical index that lists all topics for easy accessibility; it also provides a comprehensive list of all franchises up for sale or expansion and how to get in touch with them.

20. *www.bplans.com*
This Web site provides information about creating business plans. It also contains 20 sample business plans. The site also features useful hints and tips about starting your own small business.

21. *www.bbb.org/library/busfranc.html*
This Web site is sponsored by the Better Business Bureau to inform the potential franchisor or franchisee by outlining some of the legal requirements of franchising and also to protect the consumer from fraud and schemes.

22. *www.vfinance.com*
This Web site provides a wealth of information about potential sources of capital for starting your own small business.

23. *www.ftc.gov*
Government rules, regulations, and tips for opening a business.

24. *www.nasaa.org*
This is the home to the North American Securities Administrators Association. They also list the guidelines for the UFOC.

25. *www.topfranchises.com*
Entrepreneur's Source gives useful information in order to help you start your own business; it takes you through a process to help match you with your franchise. It also offers encouragement to you as an entrepreneur through question and answer sections, as well as, success story literature.

26. *www.franchisedirect.com*
This link features top stories as the home page, and it also features links to a variety of other topics. Some of the helpful links it has are a directory to franchisors, a guide to franchising, and a bookshop.

27. *www.smallbusiness.yahoo.com*
Contains hundreds of links to business centers, small business associations, and relevant articles.

28. *www.Businessfinance.com*
This site offers assistance from the Small Business Administration as well as several key resources that can help every aspect of your business. It also answers frequently asked questions, and helps you to determine what you need in order to start your own business.

29. *www.bizplanet.com*
This Web site gives a great deal of information about preparing business plans for new small businesses.

30. *www.franinfo.com*
The purpose of Franinfo is to provide as much information regarding all aspects of franchising within certain limits that constrain all commercial endeavors. Also, if you have an idea, or an existing business that you think has franchise potential, there is relevant information here to help you move in that direction.

31. *www.abanet.org*
American Bar Association. The most helpful thing about this site is its franchise law journal. You can also join this organization if you want to receive more law information.

32. *www.smallbizsearch.com*
This site is a search engine for small business information on the World Wide Web.

33. *www.franchisehelp.com*
Offers a world of franchise information. It specializes in franchise system ratings and research reports for the financial community and for potential investors.

34. *www.franchise411.com*
This site has a little of everything. Is has stories about fellow franchisees and franchisors, new software information to keep your franchise up to

date, and also information on seminars on all kinds of franchising.

35. *www.franchiseremedies.com*
This site talks about licensing, technology transfers, and franchise solutions. Services include restructuring your franchise relationship functionally and contractually. It also can provide review and analysis of all franchise agreements.

36. *www.businessfinance.com*
Business Funding Directory–This site offers assistance from the Small Business Administration as well as several key resources that can help every aspect of your business.

37. *www.franchiseintl.com*
The *International Herald Tribune* offers a wide range of franchising information from providing lists of franchises, to providing link sites for consultation, to providing current listings of franchising articles.

38. *www.lawlead.com*
This is a franchise and dealership law Web site giving franchisors information about the franchise details of the franchise agreement. It helps find attorneys in business law by name, location, practice area, or firm.

39. *www.moneyhunter.com*
The Money Hunter site is operated by a group of consultants whose sole business is aiding new and current franchisors or franchisees by offering a business plan template, a mentor, and even a television show on public broadcasting.

40. *www.franchisedoc.com*
Franchise.org offers free electronic newsletters, free franchise fit entrepreneurial surveys, educational articles linked to the homepage and franchise reviews.

41. *www.aafd.com*
The Web site of the American Association of Franchisees and Dealers contains many links and business tools, but some of the stuff is for members only.

42. *www.franchise-chat.com*
You can look through online magazines and franchise associations all around the world. You can

also find out what is going on with local businesses in the franchise news.

43. *www.franchisesolution.com*
The site will provide great information for both franchise and business opportunity. It provides services for business owners and services for franchise owners.

44. *www.edge.lowe.org/index.htm*
Good source of information for the marketing, management, and finance sections of the business plan.

45. *www.lycos.com/business*
This one has some small business information relevant to franchise owners, franchising do's and don'ts, and sales and marketing information.

46. *www.franchiselawteam.com*
This site just deals with the laws and regulations of franchising. It also has info on UFOCs and other things to watch out for.

47. *www.score.org*
The SCORE Cyber-Chapter is pleased to provide you with business advice via E-mail. Establish a confidential E-mail dialogue with an experienced business counselor selected by you to match your business needs.

48. *www.franinfo.com/history.html*
This site gives franchising history, but the most valuable parts are the self-tests which ask straightforward pertinent questions.

49. *www.sbfocus.com*
This Web site provides links to numerous other Web sites, and provides information on starting-up a business, business plans, franchising agreements and buying, bookkeeping, taxes, human resources, management, marketing, sales, internet, insurance, international import, export, and trade, and more.

50. *www.morebusiness.com*
This site offers different templates that can be used as an outline for your business plan.

Appendix C:
Top 200 Franchises

7-Eleven Convenience Stores *www.7-eleven.com*

A & W Restaurants Inc. . . *www.franchise1.coml/comp/awl.html*

AAMCO Transmissions Inc. . . . . *www.aamco.com*

Aaron's Rental Purchase . . . . *www.aaronsfranchise.com*

Ace America's Cash Express . . . . . . *www.acecashexpress.com*

AlphaGraphics Printshops
 Of The Future . . . . *www.alphagraphics.com*

Altracolor Systems . . . . *www.altracolor.com*

American Leak Detection . . . . *www.leakbusters.com*

American Poolplayers Association . . . . *www.poolplayers.com*

American Speedy Printing Centers . . *www.americanspeedy.com*

America's Maid Service-The Maids . . . . *www.maids.com*

AmeriSpec Home
 Inspection Services . . . . *www.amerispecfranchise.com*

Arby's Inc. . . . . *www.arby.com*

Athlete's Foot . . . . *www.theathletesfoot.com*

Atlanta Bread Co. . . . . *www.atlantabread.com*

Auntie Anne's Inc. . . . . *www.auntieannes.com*

Baskin-Robbins USA Co. . . . . . *www.dunkin-baskin-togos.com*

Bathcrest Inc. *www.bathcrest.com*

Batteries Plus . . . . *www.batteriesplus.com*

Bennigan's Grill & Tavern . . . . *www.mrg.com*

Big O Tires Inc. *www.bigotires.com*

Blimpie Int'l. Inc. *www.blimpie.com*

Blockbuster Video . . . . *www.blockbuster.com*

BrickKicker Home Inspection . . . . *www.brickkicker.com*

Buck's Pizza . . . . *www.buckspizza.com*

Budget Rent A Car . . . . *www.budget.com*

Burger King . . . . *www.burgerking.com*

Candy Bouquet . . . . *www.candybouquet.com*

Car Phone Store . . . . *www.thecarphonestore.com*

Carlson Wagonlit Travel . . . . *www.carlsontravel.com*

Car-X Muffler & Brake . . . . *www.carx.com*

Cash Converters Int'l.
 Franchise Group . . . . *www.cashconverters.com*

Cash Plus Inc. . . . . *www.cashplusinc.com*

CD Warehouse Inc. . . . . *www.cdwarehouse.com*

Century Small Business Solutions . . *www.centurysmallbiz.com*

Chem-Dry Carpet Drapery
 & Upholstery Cleaning . . . . *www.chemdry.com*

Children's Orchard . . . . *www.childorch.com*

Church's Chicken . . . . *www.churchs.com*

Cinnabon . . . . *www.cinnabon.com*

CleanNet USA Inc. . . . . *www.cleannetusa.com*

Coldwell Banker Real Estate Corp. . . *www.coldwellbanker.com*

Color-Glo Int'l. Inc. . . . . *www.colorglo.com*

ColorTyme . . . . *www.colortyme.com*

Comet 1 Hr. Cleaners . . . . *www.comet-cleaners.com*

Computer Renaissance *www.cr1.com*

Cookies By
 Design/Cookie Bouquet . . . . *www.cookiesbydesign.com*

Cost Cutters Family Hair Care . . . . *www.costcutters.com*

Cottman Transmission Systems Inc. . . . . . . *www.cottman.com*

Cousins Subs . . . . *www.cousinssubs.com*

Coustic-Glo Int'l. Inc. . . . . *www.cousticglo.com*

Coverall Cleaning Concepts . . . . *www.coverall.com*

Craters & Freighters . . . . *www.cratersandfreighters.com*

Crown Trophy Inc. . . . . *www.crownfranchise.com*

CruiseOne Inc. *www.cruiseone.com*

Culligan Water Conditioning . . . . *www.culligan.com*

Culver Franchising System Inc. . . . . *www.culvers.com*

Curves for Women . . . . *www.curvesforwomen.com*

Dairy Queen . . . . *www.dairyqueen.com*

Del Taco Inc. . . . . *www.deltaco.com*

Denny's Inc. . . . . *www.dennys.com*

Dollar Discount Stores . . . . *www.dollardiscount.com*

Domino's Pizza Inc. . . . . *www.dominos.com*

Dr. Vinyl & Associates Ltd. . . . . *www.drvinyl.com*

Dunkin' Donuts . . . . *www.dunkin-baskin-togos-com*

East of Chicago Pizza Company . . . . . *www.eastofchicago.com*

Express Services Inc. . . . . *www.expresspersonnel.com*

Fantastic Sams . . . . *www.fantasticsams.com*

Fastframe USA Inc. . . . . *www.fastframe.com*

Fastsigns . . . . *www.fastsigns.com*

Figaro's Italian Kitchen . . . . *www.figaros.com*

First Choice Haircutters . . . . *www.firstchoice.com*

Foot Solutions . . . . *www.footsolutions.com*

Furniture Medic . . . . *www.furnituremedic.com*

Gateway Cigar Store/Newstands *www.gatewaynewstands.com*

Glass Doctor . . . . *www.dwyergroup.com*

GNC Franchising Inc. . . . . *www.gncfranchising.com*

Golden Corral Franchising
 Systems Inc. . . . . *www.goldencorralrest.com*

Great Clips Inc. . . . . *www.greatclipsfranchise.com*

Great Earth Vitamins . . . . *www.greatearth.com*

Great Harvest Franchising . . . . *www.greatharvest.com*

Great Steak & Potato Co. . . . . *www.thegreatsteak.com*

Gymboree . . . . *www.gymboree.com*

Haagen-Dazs Shoppe Co. Inc. .... www.haagendazs.com

Handyman Connection ..... www.handymanconnection.com

Hawkins Pro-Cuts Inc. .... www.pro-cuts.com

Heavenly Ham .... www.heavenlyham.com

Heaven's Best Carpet
& Uphol. Cleaning .... www.heavensbest.com

Heel Quik! .... www.heelquik.com

Help U-Sell Real Estate .... www.helpusell.com

Home Instead Senior Care .... www.homeinstead.com

HomeTeam Inspection Service .... www.hmteam.com

House Doctors .... www.housedoctors.com

HouseMaster .... www.housemaster.com

Huddle House .... www.huddlehouse.com

Hungry Howie's Pizza & Subs .... www.hungryhowies.com

Huntington Learning
Centers Inc. .... www.huntingtonlearning.com

Interface Financial Group ...... www.interfacefinancial.com

Interim Services Inc. .... www.interim.com

International House of Pancakes .... www.ihop.com

Jackson Hewitt Tax Service .... www.jacksonhewitt.com

Jani-King .... www.janiking.com

Jan-Pro Franchising Int'l. Inc. .... www.jan-pro.com

Jason's Deli .... www.jasonsdeli.com

Jazzercise Inc. .... www.jazzercise.com

Jersey Mike's Submarines & Salads ... www.jerseymikes.com

Jiffy Lube Int'l. Inc. .... www.jiffylube.com

Jimmy John's Gourmet
Sandwich Shops .... www.jimmyjohns.com

KFC Corp. .... www.kfc.com

Kitchen Tune-Up .... www.kitchentuneup.com

Kumon Math & Reading Centers .... www.kumon.com

Kwik-Kopy Corp. .... www.kwikkopy.com

Lawn Doctor Inc. .... www.lawndoctor.com

Learning Express .... www.learningexpress.com

Liberty Tax Service .... www.libertytax.com

Maaco Auto Painting & Bodyworks .... www.maaco.com

Mad Science Group .... www.madscience.com

Maid Brigade USA/Minimaid Canada .. www.maidbrigade.com

Maid To Perfection .... www.maidtoperfection.org

Mail Boxes Etc. .... www.mbe.com

Management Recruiters/Sales .... www.mrinet.com

Manchu Wok .... www.manchuwok.com

Matco Tools .... www.matcotools.com

Mazzio's Pizza .... www.mazzios.com

McDonald's .... www.mcdonalds.com

Medicine Shoppe .... www.medicineshoppe.com

Meineke Discount Mufflers .... www.meineke.com

Merle Norman Cosmetics .... www.merlenorman.com

Merry Maids .... www.merrymaids.com

Minuteman Press Int'l. Inc. ..... www.minuteman-press.com

Mister Money-USA Inc. .... www.mistermoney.com

Molly Maid .... www.mollymaid.com

Moto Photo Inc. .... www.motophoto.com

Mr. Electric .... www.dwyergroup.com

Mrs. Fields' Original Cookies Inc. .... www.mrsfields.com

Music-Go-Round .... www.musicgoround.com

New Horizons Computer
Learning Centers Inc. .... www.newhorizons.com

Norwalk – The Furniture Idea ... www.norwalkfurniture.com

Novus Windshield Repair .... www.novuswsr.com

Nursefinders .... www.nursefinders.com

O.P.E.N. Cleaning Systems .... www.opencs.com

Once Upon A Child .... www.ouac.com

One Hour Martinizing Dry Cleaning ... www.martinizing.com

Orion Food Systems Inc. .... www.orionfoodsys.com

Pak Mail .... www.pakmail.com

Papa Murphy's .... www.papamurphys.com

Philly Connection .... www.phillyconnection.com

Pillar To Post .... www.pillartopost.com

Pizza Hut Inc. .... www.pizzahut.com

Pizza Inn Inc. .... www.pizzainn.com

Play It Again Sports .... www.playitagainsports.com

Ponderosa Steakhouse ..... www.metromediarestaurants.com

Popeye's Chicken & Biscuits .... www.popeyes.com

PostNet .... www.postnet.net

Precision Tune Auto Care .... www.precisionac.com

Pretzelmaker Inc. .... www.mrsfields.com

ProForma .... www.proforma.com

Quizno's Corp. .... www.quiznos.com

RadioShack .... www.radioshack.com

Re/Max Int'l. Inc. .... www.remax.com

Realty Executives Int'l Inc. .... www.realtyexecutives.com

RemedyTemp Inc. .... www.remedystaff.com

Rent-A-Wreck .... www.rent-a-wreck.com

Rita's Water Ice .... www.ritasice.com

Rocky Mountain Chocolate Factory .... www.rmfc.com

Sbarro The Italian Eatery .... www.sbarro.com

Schlotzsky's Deli .... www.schlotskys.com

Second Cup Ltd. *www.secondcup.com*
ServiceMaster . . . . *www.svm.com*
Servpro . . . . *www.servpro.com*
Sign-A-Rama Inc. . . . . *www.sign-a-rama.com*
Signs By Tomorrow . . . . *www.signsbytomorrow.com*
Signs Now Corp. . . . . *www.signsnow.com*
Sir Speedy Inc. *www.sirspeedy.com*
Smoothie King . . . . *www.smoothieking.com*
Snap-on Tools . . . . *www.snapon.com*
Sonic Drive In Restaurants . . . . *www.sonicdrivein.com*
Stanley Steemer Carpet Cleaner . . . *www.stanley-steemer.com*
Stork News of America Inc. . . . . *www.storknewsusa.com*
Subway . . . . *www.subway.com*
Sunbelt Business Brokers Network . . *www.sunbeltnetwork.com*
Supercuts . . . . *www.supercuts.com*
SuperGlass Windshield Repair . . . . *www.sgwr.com*
Sylvan Learning Centers . . . . *www.educate.com*
Taco Bell Corp. . . . . *www.tacobell.com*
Taco John's Int'l. Inc. . . . . *www.tacojohns.com*
TacoTime . . . . *www.tacotime.com*
TCBY Treats . . . . *www.tcby.com*

Terminix Termite & Pest Control . . . . *www.terminix.com*
T.G.I.Friday's . . . . *www.tgifridays.com*
Thrifty Rent-A-Car System Inc. . . . . *www.thrifty.com*
Tim Hortons . . . . *www.timhortons.com*
Togo's Eatery . . . . *www.dunkin-baskin-togos.com*
Total Car Franchising Corp. . . . . . . *www.colorsfranchise.com*
Tower Cleaning Systems . . . . *www.toweronline.com*
Travel Network . . . . *www.travelnetwork.com*
Tuffy Associates Corp. . . . . *www.tuffy.com*
U-Save Auto Rental of America Inc. . . . . *www.usave.net*
U.S. Franchise Systems . . . . *www.usfsi.com*
Valvoline Instant Oil Change . . . . *www.vioc.com*
Wienerschnitzel . . . . *www.wienerschnitzel.com*
Wild Birds Unlimited . . . . *www.wbu.com*
Worldwide Express . . . . *www.wwex.com*
Yogen Frez Worldwide . . . . *www.yogunfruz.com*
Ziebart . . . . *www.ziebart.com*

Glossary

achievement oriented leader–establishes goals and expectations at a fairly high level, then helps the staff reach those goals and expectations.

attitude–simply a predisposition to behave.

balance sheet–a document that outlines a company's assets, liabilities, and equity of the owner(s) at a particular point in time.

behavior–an action or a performance by an individual.

breach of contract–violation of a contract. To break a legal obligation that one owes to another.

business plan–a document that outlines a company's goals, defines its product and market, provides financial data and resumes of key personnel, and serves as an operating tool to manage the business and obtain financing.

CPA–Certified Public Accountant. A CPA is an accountant who has passed rigorous testing in accounting principals, taxation & business law.

chapter 7–a form of bankruptcy in which a company sells its assets in order to pay its debts.

chapter 11–a form of bankruptcy that allows a company to reorganize in order to meet its financial obligations and then resume operations.

closing–move toward allowing the customer to buy–not manipulating–it is rather an opportunity to allow the person to make a positive decision.

continuous training–where training is offered throughout the term of the franchise relationship.

copyright–the franchisor's ownership rights over the manuals and other published materials that are used in the system. The exclusive right of authors to publish, print, or sell an intellectual production for a statutory period of time.

covenant not to compete–A contractual promise to refrain from competing with another party for a certain period of time (not excessive in duration) and within a reasonable geographic area.

cure your default–Most franchise agreements contain numerous reasons for which you can be terminated. Some of these causes for termination will allow you to cure your default before you can be terminated. This means you are allowed to correct your violation of the agreement and therefore keep it in force.

demographics–the characteristics of a population that marketers can use to determine which consumers would be most interested in their merchandise.

direct marketing–a strategy that consists of targeting a group of consumers who have a need for the products or services of a business, and mailing promotional materials to them.

directive leader–one who is developing the structure and the tasks which must be accomplished.

disclosure document–also known as the UFOC, or the Uniform Franchise Offering Circular. In the disclosure document, you will find information about the franchisor, including the obligations of the franchisor and the franchise, fees, start-up costs, and other required information about the franchise system as set forth by federal and state law.

earnings–a company's income during the period.

encroachment–a situation where your franchisor places another franchise so close to you that your sales go down as a result of the new franchise. Often referred to as competing against oneself.

Federal Trade Commission (FTC)–the agency of the U.S. Government that regulates franchising.

franchise–generally speaking, this is defined as the right or license granted to an individual or group to market a company's goods or services in a particular territory. More specifically, a franchise is a special type of license that usually has three elements: (1) the franchisee uses the franchisor's name and marks; (2) the franchisor provides the franchisee with assistance or has some control over how the franchisee operates the business; and (3) the franchisee pays the franchisor $500 or more during a six-month period.

franchise agreement–the written contract between the franchisor and franchisee. The franchise agreement tells each party what it is supposed to do and not supposed to do. It lists both parties' obligations and responsibilities.

franchise attorney–a lawyer who specializes in franchise law.

franchise consultant–a business advisor with significant knowledge of the design, development, and operation of franchising and the underlying franchise relationship.

franchisee–the person or company that receives the right (license) from the franchisor to do business under the franchisor's trademark and trade name.

franchising–a method of distribution; in other words, a method of growing a business. A marketing channel of distribution whereby a company distributes its goods and services from itself to the ultimate consumer.

franchisor–the company that grants the franchisee the right (license) to do business under their trade name, trademarks, or service marks.

fraud–any misrepresentation, either by misstatement or omission of a material fact, knowingly made with the intention of deceiving another and on which a reasonable person would and does rely to his or her detriment.

FTC Franchise Rule–a rule set out by the FTC that requires franchisors to disclose certain types of information to a prospective franchisee so that the prospective franchisee has enough information upon which to base its decision on whether to purchase the franchise or not. Also referred to as a disclosure law.

income statement– a document that outlines expenses, revenues, and net income of a business. Also known as a profit and loss (P&L) statement.

initial public offering (IPO)–the first time a stock is offered for sale to the public.

intangible assets–assets that are incapable of being touched or seen. Such as patents, copyrights, trademarks, and other intellectual property.

injunction–a writ granted by a court whereby one is required to do or to refrain from doing a specified act.

investor– someone who provides money in exchange for partial ownership of a company.

joint venture–business structure that consists of two or more groups of people.

knowledge–information or experience that one has acquired about a subject, an object or a person.

limited liability company (LLC)–business structure that is taxed like a partnership and provides limited liability for its members (owners).

limited partnership–business structure that consists of general partner responsible for daily management decisions and who assumes liability for the debts, and investors who have little involvement and whose liability is limited to the amount of their investment. Investors are known as limited partners.

litigation–the process of resolving a dispute through the court system.

mission–defines your business, a statement of your unique purpose, the scope of your operations in both product and marketing terms–looking 10 years into the future.

motives–functions which help an individual activate, direct and channel behavior toward specific goals.

niche–a narrow segment of a market.

nonprofit organization–business structure whose chief advantage is its exemption from paying taxes. The main disadvantage is that it is subject to a strict set of regulations. Designed generally for religious organizations, educational institutions, and social welfare organizations.

operations manual–the manual is the place to look for instructions on how the franchisor wants the franchise to operate and for other policies concerning the system. It is an A through Z manual on how to operate the franchise.

organization costs–cost incurred in the creation of a corporation, limited partnership or limited liability company, including legal fees, registration fees, and fees to underwriters.

participative leader–a leader that encourages input from fellow workers and tries to use as many of their suggestions as is efficient and feasible.

partnership–business owned by two or more people who are jointly liable for the debts and assets of the company. Oftentimes referred to as a general partnership.

patent–a legal protection for a new product that prevents it from being copied for 17 years after its introduction.

"Ps" of benefits [five]–(1) pride, (2) power, (3) pleasure, (4) prestige, and (5) profit

point-of-purchase promotion– marketing materials (brochures, posters, and the like) that are placed directly in a retail establishment.

positioning–a marketing strategy that defines a company or a product.

press release–a brief written message sent to reporters, editors, producers, and other members of the media that describes something newsworthy about a company or individual, the objective of which is to gain media exposure.

private placement–sale of stock directly to specific investors rather than through a public offering.

probing– the act of asking simple questions of the individual to know their desires and wants.

professional corporation–business structure designed primarily for doctors, lawyers, and other professionals.

promotion– marketing strategies that use ads, newsletters, brochures, sweepstakes, and similar tools to transmit a message to prospective customers.

public relations–a form of marketing designed to increase a company's exposure in the media or community.

right of first refusal–the right to purchase personal or real property, including a business, before the property is offered to others.

ROI–return on investment.

sales mission statement–introduces you and your business to the customer–should basically cover: your name and/or company name, business objectives and benefits of your products or services.

sales playbook–consists of written samples for the mission statement, probes, listening, supporting benefit statements and closing ideas.

sales promotions–activities where an incentive is offered to induce the customer to purchase a particular good or service. We should note that sales promotions offer products with an incentive to buy while advertising products with a reason to buy.

selling–the ability to get the customer to make a buying decision.

sole proprietorship–business structure in which one person owns and manages a company. Its advantages are that it is simple to set up and the owner maintains complete control and keeps all the profits. The disadvantages are that the owner assumes liability for all debts incurred, and the personal assets of the owner are at risk in the event of bankruptcy.

start-up–a new business.

Subchapter S corporation–a business structure of multiple owners that provides liability protection like a corporation does, but is taxed like a partnership.

suggestive selling–sales person tries to broaden the customer's purchasing decision with related items.

supporting benefit statements–explains to a person how buying the product or service will benefit them.

supportive leader–a leader who is considerate of others while trying to help the other employees better understand how they can accomplish what needs to be done.

tangible assets–assets that have physical existence, for example: a car is tangible, but a patent right is intangible.

telemarketing–a strategy that uses the telephone to sell the products or services of a business.

trademark or trade name–a symbol or a name that allows the holder to use it to name or identify a specific name or service. A legal registration system allows an indefinite number of 20-year renewals.

venture capital–money provided by a pool of investors, to be used for starting or expanding a business, in exchange for partial ownership of the business.

vision–where you want to be in 20 to 30 years–an explanation of your personal desires and what you would like to do relative to your business.

wrongful discharge–an employer's termination of an employee's employment in violation of an employment contract or laws that protect employees.

zoning ordinances–the acts of an authorized local government establishing building codes, and setting forth regulations for property land usage.

Index

A

accounting/finance
   disclosures about, 58
   fees for, 95
   for multiunits, 371-372
   for sale of franchise, 381-384,
      386-387
   systems for, 9, 27, 154, 290-295
add-ons, 374
advertising, 10, 192-193
   in franchise agreement, 66, 190
   franchisees and, 128, 188, 189
   franchisor's assistance with, 10, 126
   for multiunits, 372
   for new employees, 215-216
   questions to ask about, 72
   red flags about, 301
   see also advertising fee; publicity
advertising fee, 23, 189
   disclosures about, 47-48, 91-93
   in franchise agreement, 65
   negotiating about, 80
advisory councils, 314-318. *See also*
   independent franchisee associations
aliens, undocumented, 227
American Arbitration Association, 351
Americans with Disabilities Act, 236, 250
AmeriSpec, 192
Applebee's Neighborhood Grill & Bar,
   192-193
application fees, 95
arbitration, 350-353
area development agreement, 24,
   360-361. *See also* exclusive territory
Asia, 161
assignment of lease option agreement, 84
audits, 94, 130
Auntie Anne's pretzels, 6

B

background checks, 234-236
balance sheet, 292-293
bankruptcy, 37-38
banks, as lenders, 285, 293-294
barter, 175
Baskin-Robbins, 158, 371
benchmarking, 375
billboards, 162-163

Blimpie, 12, 163, 190
bookkeeping fees, 95
brand names, 170
broker, for sale of franchise, 378-381
budgeting, 294
build-out requirement, 82-83, 145
business
   legal structures of, 385-386
   value of experience in, 36
   see also franchises/franchising
business broker, 378-381
business plan, 10, 105-107, 277-278
buyer, qualifying of, 384-385

C

CACI Marketing Systems, 140
cash flow estimation, 107
cash flow statement, 291
cash registers, 290
celebrities, 55-56
certified development company, 283
Church's Chicken, 108
Cinnabon, 106
cobranding, 376
"cocktail napkin" disclosure, 56, 101
Comfort Inns, Suites, 193
communication
   with customers, 374-375
   with employees, 374
   with franchisor, 302-303, 313-314,
      374
compensation, of employees, 210,
   246-248
competitive edge, 173-174
computer use, 27-28, 48
condemnation and causality, 67, 74
conferences, annual, 158
confidentiality. *see* noncompete
   covenants
Consolidated Omnibus Budget
   Reconciliation Act (COBRA), 264
consultant selling, 182
contracts, 7, 58-59. *See also* franchise
   agreement
copyrights, 52-53, 125-126
cost of goods sold, 9, 298
cost reduction, 294-295
Coverall North America, 154

customers
   advertising to, 186
   communication with, 374-375
   loyalty of, 171
   profiling of, 140, 171-172
   referrals from, 214-215
customer service, 206, 372

D

Dairy Queen, 294
default
   in franchise agreement, 67
   negotiating about, 82
   questions to ask about, 74
defense manual, 354-356
demographics. *see* customers
direct-mail, 162
disclosure. *see* FTC Rule; UFOC
dispute resolution, 54-55, 303, 344-356
   methods of, 348-354
   noncompete covenants and, 345-348
drug tests, 232
due diligence. *see* business plan
Dunkin' Donuts, 155, 371

E

earnings claims, 25
   disclosure of, 56, 98-99
   evaluation with, 101-103, 105
   evaluation without, 105-107
   nondisclosure of, 99-101
employees
   communication with, 374
   compensation of, 210, 246-248
   costs of, 9, 299
   evaluation of, 250-254
   leadership of, 206-211
   legal issues and, 224-238
   loyalty and, 211-212
   management of, 155, 240-248,
      256-260, 268
   multiunits and, 365, 368-371
   recruitment/hiring of, 13, 214-222,
      227-238
   sale of franchise and, 387
   termination of, 260-265
   training of, 93-94, 157-158
   wants of, 268, 269

employment agreements, 383
entity documents, 385–386
equipment, 123
    franchisee's obligation and, 129
    specifications for, 13–14
exclusive territory, 23–24, 29
    assignment of, 136–137
disclosures about, 50–51
    fees for, 95
    in franchise agreement, 63
    negotiating about, 81
    questions to ask about, 70, 137–138

F

Fair Labor Standards Act, 226–227
Farmers Home Administration, 283–284
fast food restaurants, 8, 9. *See also*
    specific restaurants
Fastframe, 23
fees, 23, 127
    comparison of, 88, 94
    disclosures about, 38–39, 88–89
    in franchise agreement, 65
    list of, 89–96
    questions to ask about, 71
    see also initial investment
finance. *see* accounting/finance; money
financing arrangements. *see* loans
first refusal, 81–82, 388
forecasting methods, 9
franchise agreements, 62–76
    common elements of, 62–69
    negotiating about, 78–83
    questions to ask about, 69–76
    sample, 112, 113
    supplements to, 83–84
franchisee(s)
    obligations of, 41–42, 66–68, 73, 75,
        127–130
    obligations of, at sale of franchise,
        384–388
    rules of game for, 18–20
    steps to becoming, 14–16
    talking with other, 105, 156, 312
franchisee advisory councils, 314–318.
    See also independent franchisee
    associations
Franchise Registry, of SBA, 283

franchises/franchising
    beginnings of, 32
    benefits of, 4–14
    as business, 7
    multiunit, 360–366, 368–376
    sale of, 378–388
    see also business
franchisor
    communication with, 302–303,
        313–314, 374
    culture of, 302
    financing arrangements of, 42, 286
    obligations of, 120–127
    questions to ask of, 19–20, 35–39, 46
    relationships with, 309–311
    rules of game for, 25–29
    tensions/conflicts with, 321–323, 344
    traits of good, 312–314
    UFOC disclosures about, 34–43
    UFOC responsibilities of, 46–60
FTC Rule, 32–34

G

general release agreement, 84
Gingiss Formalwear, 153
going concern value, 380
government loan programs, 282–284
Granadar, Dan and Sherry, 374
grand opening, 160–161
    in Asia, 161
    assistance with, 124–125
    checklist for, 165–166
    fees for, 95
    publicizing of, 161–165
    training for, 156–157, 166
guarantee fees, 95

H

handbooks, for employees, 243–246
Heel Quik!, 104
home-based business, 132–133
Home Instead Senior Care, 208
honesty, 183
House, Robert, 210

I

I-9 Employment Eligibility Verification,
    233–234

improvement, 71
income statement, 291–292
independent franchisee associations,
    318–321. *See also* franchisee advisory
    councils
industrial development corporations,
    284
information systems, 373
initial franchise fee, 89–90
initial investment, 13, 20, 276, 277
    disclosures about, 39
    negotiating about, 80
    see also fees
inspection, 129
insurance
    franchisee's obligation and,
        128–129
    questions to ask about, 73
    required in franchise agreement, 66
intellectual property protection
    in franchise agreement, 68
    questions to ask about, 75
    see also noncompete covenants
International Franchise Forum, 300
Internet, 26–27
interviews, of applicant, 232–233
inventory, 123–125, 129
investors, 281–282

J

job applications, 229–230
job descriptions, 228

K

KFC, 198, 369
Kwik Kopy Corporation, 27, 153

L

labor. *see* employees
leadership, 206–212, 271
    kinds of, 210–211
    see also management
leases, 287–288, 299
    negotiating of, 142–143
    provisions of, 144–146
    sale of franchise and, 383–384, 387
    terminology of, 143–144
leasing fees, 94

legal issues, 14
  of dispute resolution, 348–354
  of employee evaluation, 250
  of franchise sale, 384–388
  franchisor's disclosures about, 36–37
  of hiring, 224–238
  liability limitations, 82
  personnel policies and, 241–248
  of renewal, 326–330, 340
  of termination, 260–265, 334–340
  of transfer, 330–334
liquidation value, 380–381
litigation, 354–356
loans
  disclosures about, 42
  for multiunits, 363
  sources of, 282–286, 293–294
location. see exclusive territory; site
  selection
Los Angeles Times, 189
lottery, 164
Louisiana State University, 300

M

Mail Boxes Etc., 10, 11, 19, 157
management, 198–199, 269–271
  functions of, 199–200
  planning and, 202–204
  skills of, 200–202
  see also leadership
management assistance fees, 95
managers, for multiunits, 368–371
Manchu Wok, 165
Manhattan Bagel Company, 368
market development, 172–175
marketing
  contrasted to sales, 174
  defined, 171
  for multiunits, 372, 373
  plan for, 161
  red flags about, 301
  training in, 155
  see also advertising; publicity
market research, on products/services,
  10, 114–118
McDonald's, 10, 156, 183
medical examinations, 236–237
Merry Maids, 191

minority business development, 284
Mobil Corporation, 375
money
  borrowing of, 279, 282–288
  determining amount needed, 276–278
  sources of, 280–282
  see also accounting/finance; fees;
    initial investment
motivation, 208–210, 268
multiunit franchises, 360–366
  organization of, 368–376

N

negative disclosure, 99–101
negotiation, 78–83, 340
newspaper advertising
  for new employees, 215
  to promote business, 161–162
No Money Down Financing for
  Franchising (Roll), 288
noncompete covenants, 84, 128
  dispute resolution and, 345–348
  for employees, 226
  in franchise agreement, 68
  in lease, 145
  negotiating about, 81
  questions to ask about, 75
nonconventional lenders, 285–286
North American Securities
  Administrators Association, 32
Novak, David, 198

O

opening. see grand opening
operation, of business
  assistance with, 124–125
  manuals for, 28, 126
  training in, 154
outlets, list of franchise's other, 57
owner financing, 287

P

participation, required of owner, 53, 82
partnering, 162
part-time employees, 220
patents, 52–53
performance evaluation, 250–254
performance quotas, 83

personal guaranty agreement, 83–84
personnel policies, 240–248
point-of-sale systems, 9
Popeye's Chickens & Biscuits, 103
positive attitude, 183–184
PostalAnnex+, 26
post-term obligations, 345–348
Precision Tune Auto Care, 22
pre-employment testing, 230–232
premium offers, 165
price building, 381
pricing strategies, 12, 26
priorities, managing, 198
procurement. see purchasing
products, 7–8
  disclosures about, 40–41, 54, 110–112
  flexibility in selling, 181–182
  negotiating about, 81
  requirements for purchasing, 113–118
  research/development and, 11
promotions, 178. See also advertising;
  marketing
proprietary information, 52–53, 125–126
public figures, 55–56
publicity, 190–191
  for grand opening, 161–165
  see also advertising
purchasing, 299–302

Q

quality control, 11
  in franchise agreement, 66
  questions to ask about, 72–73
quick service restaurants, 8, 9. See also
  specific restaurants

R

radio advertising, 162
real estate broker, 137
real estate criteria, 12–13. See also site
  selection
rebate programs, 294
receipt of UFOC, 59
recitals, in franchise agreement, 62–63
record keeping, 290
recruitment, of employees
  problems with, 221–222
  tips for, 214–220

Red Roof Inns, 293
registration states, 26
relationship of the parties, 68–69, 76
renewal rights, 29
    disclosures about, 54–55
    fees for, 96
    in franchise agreement, 63
    legal issues of, 326–330, 340
    negotiating about, 80
    questions to ask about, 70
rent. *see* leases
reporting requirements, 65, 72, 129
resale. *see* sale, of franchise
research and development, 126–127
retail business, 133
return on investment, 381
Roll, Roger, 288
royalty fee, 23, 65, 90–91
    negotiating about, 80
rebates of, 292
    sales per unit and, 106–107

S

sale, of franchise, 128
    broker for, 378–381
    financial considerations of, 381–384,
        386–387
    legal issues of, 384–388
    questions to ask about, 378
    valuation and, 380–381
sales, of products/services
    contrasted to marketing, 174
    playbook for, 181
    process of, 179–184
    promotions and, 178
sales per unit, 106–107
savings, personal, 280–281
scholarships, 207
7-Eleven, Inc, 291
security deposit, 94
services, 8
    disclosures about, 40–41, 54, 110–112
    in franchise agreement, 64
    negotiating about, 81
    purchasing requirements for, 113–118
    questions to ask about, 71
shopping malls/areas, 138–139
Signal Graphics, 292

signs, 163–164, 187–188
    about moving, 165
    help wanted, 215
Singer Sewing Machine Company, 32
site selection, 25, 28
    assistance with, 94, 122–123,
        134–135, 136, 137
    development and, 123, 146–147
    disclosures about, 49, 133–134
    in franchise agreement, 64
    negotiating about, 82
    questions to ask about, 70, 135–136
    red flags about, 301
    tips for, 139–142
    types of sites, 132–133, 138–139
    see also exclusive territory
skill contests, 164
Small Business Administration (SBA),
    282–283
Smoothie King, 14–16, 20, 22, 164, 172,
    290, 360, 374
special events, 164–165
staff. *see* employees
start-up capital. *see* initial investment
strategic planning. *see* business plan
supplemental agreements, 83–84
supplies, 123–125, 129
sweepstakes, 164, 166

T

tax compliance, 372
teenagers, 269
television advertising, 162
termination, of employee, 225, 246,
    260–265
termination, of franchise agreement, 67,
    68
    disclosures about, 54–55
    involuntary, 28
    legal issues of, 334–340
    negotiating about, 82
    questions to ask about, 74
    voluntary, 25
territory. *see* exclusive territory
testing, of job applicants, 230–232
Texaco, 368
Togo's Great Sandwiches, 371
trademarks, 51–52, 125–126

trade secrets, 263, 264
training, 11–12, 22–23, 27, 300
    disclosures about, 49
    fees for, 93
    franchisee's obligation and, 128
    franchisor's obligation and, 124
    negotiating about, 82
    typical program, 152–156
transfer, of franchise
    disclosures about, 54–55
    in franchise agreement, 67
    franchisee's obligation and, 128
    legal issues of, 330–334
    negotiating about, 81
    questions to ask about, 74
Tricon Global Restaurants, Inc., 369

U

UFOC (Uniform Franchise Offering
    Circular)
    creation of, 32
    disclosures of franchisor in, 34–43
    FTC Rule versus, 32–34
    responsibilities of franchisor in,
        46–60, 120–122
    table of contents of, 21
unemployment compensation, 264

V

valuation, of franchise, 380–381
venture capital, 286
veterans franchise initiatives, 284

W

Wendy's, 186
wrongful discharge, 260, 261, 262

Y

Yogen Frez, 376

About the Authors

Robert T. Justis is a professor in the Management Department and the Entrepreneurship Institute, E. J. Ourso College of Business Administration, Louisiana State University. He formerly held the Marshall Chair of Franchising at the University of Nebraska. Dr. Justis received his B.S. and M.B.A. from Brigham Young University, and his Doctor of Business Administration degree from Indiana University. His present teaching and research areas are franchising, entrepreneurship, international businesses, and strategic business practices. He has helped develop over $25 million for the E. J. Ourso College of Business Administration at LSU.

While working on his doctoral degree, Dr. Justis established a small business with two other students in Indiana and Florida that grossed over two million dollars a year. He has also been the owner of an insecticide business, and had an affiliation with an ice cream parlor/restaurant. He has consulted for more than 250 franchises, including Burger King, Borg Warner Corporation, Texas Instruments, Wendy's, McDonald's, Pizza Hut, Popeye's, Selection Research, Inc., and National Research Corporations. In addition, Dr. Justis has developed and presented management programs internationally.

The Freedom Foundation at Valley Forge has conferred upon Dr. Justis the Leavey Award for Excellence in Private Enterprise Education. He has also received distinguished teaching awards from every university where he has taught, including: Indiana University, Texas Tech University, University of Nebraska, and Louisiana State University. He is often called "the father of small business" and more recently he has become known as "the father of franchising."

Professor Justis has published over 100 articles in publications including the *Academy of Management Journal, Academy of Management Executive,* and *The Journal of Small Business.* He has served on the National Steering Committee of the Small Business Administration for five years and was a founder of the Society of Franchising and the Small Business Institute Directors' Association (SBIDA). He is the author of *Managing Your Small Business, Dynamics of American Business, Strategic Management and Policy,* and *Basics of Franchising.* His most recent textbook, *Franchising* (co-authored with Richard Judd) is the bestselling textbook in the field.

William Slater Vincent Sr., J.D., M.B.A, B.A, joined the faculty of Kennesaw State University as an assistant professor of business law in 1993. Previously he was a guest lecturer and research associate for the Goizueta School of Business at Emory University and an adjunct professor at Georgia State University. William Vincent received his B.A. from Furman University in 1977, his M.B.A. from Emory University in 1982, and his J.D. from Emory University in 1982. His primary areas of interest are entrepreneurship, franchise management, franchise law, business law, and trust and estate planning. He is on the Editorial Board for the *Journal of Marketing Channels.*

William has an active law practice in trust and estate planning, business law, and franchise law. Also, he has an active consulting practice in franchising assisting both franchisees and franchisors on numerous managerial and legal issues. He developed and teaches courses in franchise management and in franchise law and, along with Dr. Tim Mescon, organized the Franchise Institute at the University. He has made numerous presentations to local, regional, national, and international audiences and has published many articles in both trade and academic newspapers, magazines, and journals in the fields of franchising and estate planning. He is the co-author of *The Network Expansion Conflict Handbook—Developing a Successful Solution* published by the International Franchise Association. William is a licensed attorney and a member of the State Bar of Georgia, American Bar Association, Voting Member of the National Academy of Television Arts and Sciences, International Society of Franchising, and the International Franchise Association, where he serves on the franchise relations and the minorities in franchising committees. William is married (Sandra) and has three children (Natalie, Amanda, and Billy).

William can be reached by phone: (770) 977-6067 or (770) 423-6717 or (770) 565-1730; fax: (770) 579-0152; mail: 1810 Wicksley Way, Marietta, GA, 30062; or e-mail: *vincent.all@worldnet.att.net.*

FIND MORE ON THIS TOPIC BY VISITING
BusinessTown.com
The Web's big site for growing businesses!

- ☑ **Separate channels on all aspects of starting and running a business**
- ☑ **Lots of info on how to do business online**
- ☑ **1,000+ pages of savvy business advice**
- ☑ **Complete web guide to thousands of useful business sites**
- ☑ **Free e-mail newsletter**
- ☑ **Question and answer forums, and more!**

Also available from Adams Media

STREETWISE® BOOKS

Small Business Start-Up
$17.95, ISBN 1-55850-581-4

When you start a small business, you soon discover that things just don't happen in the real world the way they tell you in business textbooks: invoices don't get paid by their due dates, ads don't consistently bring in customers, sales don't continually rise, and profits aren't always there. In this book, small business maverick Bob Adams shows you how things really get done and acts as your mentor by providing instant access to Streetwise® advice on every small business topic.

Also available in this series:

Maximize Web Site Traffic
$19.95
ISBN 1-55850-369-7

Marketing Plan
$17.95
ISBN 1-58062-268-2

Do-It-Yourself Advertising
$17.95
ISBN 1-55850-727-2

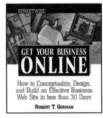

Get Your Business Online
$19.95
ISBN 1-58062-368-9

Relationship Marketing on the Internet
$17.95
ISBN 1-58062-255-0

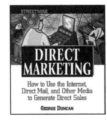

Direct Marketing
$19.95
ISBN 1-58062-439-1

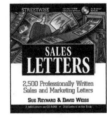

Sales Letters w/CD-ROM
$24.95
ISBN 1-58062-440-5

Available wherever books are sold.

For more information, or to order, call 800-872-5627
or visit www.adamsmedia.com

Adams Media Corporation, 260 Center Street, Holbrook, MA 02343